HM TREASURY

Meeting the aspirations of the British people

2007 Pre-Budget Report and
Comprehensive Spending Review
October 2007

Presented to Parliament by
the Chancellor of the Exchequer
by Command of Her Majesty

Cm 7227   LONDON: The Stationery Office   £45.00

HM Treasury contacts

This report can be found on the Treasury website at:
hm-treasury.gov.uk/budget2007

For general enquiries about HM Treasury and its work, contact:
Correspondence and Enquiry Unit
HM Treasury
1 Horse Guards Road
London
SW1A 2HQ
Tel: 020 7270 4558
Fax: 020 7270 4861
E-mail: public.enquiries@hm-treasury.gov.uk

This and other government documents can be found on the
Internet at:
www.official-documents.co.uk

ISBN: 978-0-10-172272-8
Printed by The Stationery Office 10/07 379627
PU395

The Economic and Fiscal Strategy Report and the Financial Statement and Budget Report contain the Government's assessment of the medium-term economic and budgetary position. They set out the Government's tax and spending plans, including those for public investment, in the context of its overall approach to social, economic and environmental objectives. This Pre-Budget Report and Comprehensive Spending Review includes, with other material, updated forecasts for the economy and projections for the public finances. Subject to the usual scrutiny and approval for the purposes of Section 5 of the European Communities (Amendment) Act 1993, these reports will form the basis of submissions to the European Commission under Article 99 (ex Article 103) and Article 104 (ex Article 104c) of the Treaty establishing the European Community.

Contents

OVERVIEW

The Government's objective is to build a strong economy and a fair society, in which there is opportunity and security for all. The 2007 Pre-Budget Report and Comprehensive Spending Review, *Meeting the aspirations of the British people*, presents updated assessments and forecasts of the economy and public finances, describes reforms that the Government is making and sets out the Government's priorities and spending plans for the years 2008-09, 2009-10 and 2010-11, including:

- **maintaining macroeconomic stability**, with the economy continuing to grow strongly and with the Government meeting its strict fiscal rules over the forecast period;

- **investing in the future**, with total public spending rising from £589 billion in 2007-08 to £678 billion in 2010-11, an average increase of 2.1 per cent per year in real terms, including an addition of £2 billion to the plans set at Budget 2007 in order to take forward vital capital investment in public services;

- **continuing the sustained investment in the NHS**, with resources increasing from around £90 billion in 2007-08 to £110 billion by 2010-11 – an average real increase of 4 per cent a year – which alongside value for money savings of at least £8.2 billion will fund the conclusions of the Darzi Review to build a health service fit for the 21st century;

- **further sustained increases in resources** for education, science, transport, housing, child poverty, security and international poverty reduction as well as fully funding the 2012 Olympic Games and Paralympic Games;

- **building on the SR04 efficiency programme** with at least 3 per cent value for money savings per year over the CSR07 period across central and local government, totalling £30 billion of annual savings by 2010-11;

- **simplifying the tax system** to make it fairer, simpler and more efficient with the announcement of three simplification reviews and a package of simplification measures;

- **continuing to modernise the tax system through announcing major reforms to inheritance tax and capital gains tax**; and

- **taking steps to protect the environment**, including by reforms and increases to the tax regime for aviation and a new Environmental Transformation Fund worth £1.2 billion over the CSR07 period, to support the demonstration and deployment of new energy and efficiency technologies in the UK and to advance poverty reduction through environmental protection in developing countries.

1.1   The Government's objective is to build a strong economy and a fair society, in which there is opportunity and security for all. A decade ago the Government laid the foundations for achieving this through a series of fundamental reforms to the macroeconomic framework, the public spending framework and the tax and benefit system. These have underpinned a decade of investment and reform, which has helped to achieve a sustained period of economic expansion, low unemployment and significant improvements in public services.

LONG-TERM CHALLENGES AND OPPORTUNITIES

I.2 A decade on, the 2007 Comprehensive Spending Review has provided the opportunity to undertake an extensive programme of analysis and public engagement in order to inform the Government's response to the new challenges and opportunities facing the UK, including:

- demographic and socio-economic change, with rapid increases in the old age dependency ratio and rising consumer expectations of public services;

- increasing pressures on natural resources and the global climate, requiring action by governments, businesses and individuals to maintain prosperity and improve environmental care;

- the intensification of cross-border economic competition, with new opportunities for growth, as the balance of international economic activity shifts towards emerging markets such as China and India;

- the rapid pace of innovation and technological diffusion, which will continue to transform the way people live and open up new ways of delivering public services; and

- continued global uncertainty with ongoing threats from international terrorism and conflict and the continued imperative to tackle global poverty.

I.3 These developments will have complex and far-reaching implications for government, citizens, businesses and the third sector that demand a shared sense of purpose and coordinated interventions across tax, spending and regulatory levers. The 2007 Pre-Budget Report and Comprehensive Spending Review sets out how the Government plans to respond to these challenges and opportunities in order to make further progress against its goals of:

- **sustainable growth and prosperity,** in order to continue to improve people's standard of living;

- **fairness and opportunity for all,** so that everyone can make the most of their talents and share in rising national prosperity;

- **stronger communities and a better quality of life,** enabling people to lead healthy, safe and fulfilling lives; and

- **a more secure, fair and environmentally sustainable world,** with the UK playing a leading global role.

I.4 To contribute to the achievement of these overarching goals, **the Government has agreed 30 Public Service Agreements (PSAs),** that articulate the Government's highest priority outcomes for the forthcoming period, setting out a shared vision, spanning departmental boundaries and leading collaboration at all levels of the delivery system.

MAINTAINING MACROECONOMIC STABILITY

I.5 The Government is committed to maintaining macroeconomic stability as the essential foundation for achieving its priorities, as it underpins its ability to raise the productivity of the economy, reduce poverty, expand opportunity and sustain increased investment in public services.

1.6   The Government's macroeconomic framework and promotion of flexible and open labour, product and capital markets continue to deliver sustained economic growth with low inflation. The economy has grown for 60 consecutive quarters and inflation is close to target. This macroeconomic stability puts the UK in a strong position to respond to global economic challenges, and to take advantage of the opportunities of the coming decade. The 2007 Pre-Budget Report and Comprehensive Spending Review provide for further investment in public services to help equip the country for change while entrenching the macroeconomic stability needed to enable the UK to prosper in the increasingly competitive global economy.

1.7   In 2007, the UK economy has continued to perform strongly, with GDP growth in the first half of the year reaching 3¼ per cent on a year earlier, towards the upper end of the Budget 2007 forecast range. Reflecting the combination of momentum in the economy, but higher interest rates than markets expected at the time of Budget 2007 and the assumed impact of financial market disruption, the 2007 Pre-Budget Report economic forecast is for GDP growth of 3 per cent in 2007, slowing to 2 to 2½ per cent in 2008, before strengthening to trend at 2½ to 3 per cent in 2009 and 2010.

1.8   The 2007 Pre-Budget Report projections for the public finances show that the Government is meeting its strict fiscal rules:

- the current budget shows an average surplus as a percentage of GDP over the current economic cycle, ensuring the Government is meeting the golden rule. Beyond the current cycle, the current budget moves clearly into surplus; and

- public sector net debt is projected to remain low and stable over the forecast period, stabilising below 39 per cent of GDP and so meeting the sustainable investment rule.

Table 1.1: Meeting the fiscal rules

	Per cent of GDP						
	Outturn	Estimate	Projections				
	2006-07	2007-08	2008-09	2009-10	2010-11	2011-12	2012-13
Golden Rule							
Surplus on current budget	-0.4	-0.6	-0.3	0.2	0.6	0.8	1.1
Average surplus since 1997-1998	0.1	0.1	0.0	0.1	0.1	0.1	0.2
Cyclically-adjusted surplus on current budget	-0.2	-0.7	-0.2	0.3	0.6	0.8	1.1
Sustainable investment rule							
Public sector net debt[1]	36.7	37.6	38.4	38.8	38.9	38.8	38.6

[1] Debt at end March; GDP centred on end March.

TRANSFORMING PUBLIC SERVICES

1.9   Delivering better outcomes in the Government's 30 priority areas will require world-class public services that respond to people's rising aspirations and equip the UK for global change. The Government's approach to improving outcomes from public services comprises: investing for the long term; driving better value for money from public spending; and taking forward the next stage in public service reform by empowering users and frontline professionals to shape services.

I.10   Budget 2007 set the overall spending envelope for the CSR07 period, locking in the historic increases in investment of the past decade while allowing public spending to increase by an average of 2 per cent a year in real terms. The strength of the UK's public finances enables the Government to announce an addition of £2 billion to public sector net investment in 2010-11, to take forward vital investment in public services. With this addition, total public spending over the CSR07 period will rise by an average of 2.1 per cent a year in real terms with:

- current spending increasing by an average of 1.9 per cent per year in real terms; and

- net investment rising to $2\frac{1}{4}$ per cent of GDP.

I.11   These increases in spending will enable the Government to sustain the pace of improvement in frontline public services seen in previous spending rounds and focus additional investment on its key long-term priorities, including:

- meeting the challenge of globalisation by investing in the human and physical capital that will keep the UK economy competitive over the long-term, with additional spending by 2010-11 of £14.5 billion on education, £900 million on science and £3.6 billion on transport;

- making the UK a better place to live by continuing to improve the NHS with further investment of £19 billion by 2010-11 and progressing towards its objective of decent and affordable housing for all, with total spending on new housing of at least £8 billion over the next three years;

- protecting the nation from external and internal threats, with total spending on counter-terrorism and intelligence rising from £2$\frac{1}{2}$ billion in 2007-08 to £3$\frac{1}{2}$ billion in 2010-11 and continuing the longest period of sustained real increases in defence expenditure in over 20 years; and

- ensuring a lasting cultural and sporting legacy for the nation by investing £3.6 billion in the construction costs of the Olympics over the CSR07 period, with further funding to be announced in the next spending review.

I.12   The Government is committed to driving better value for money from this increased public spending over the CSR07 years by:

- delivering at least 3 per cent net, cash-releasing value for money savings per year across central and local government, a total annual saving of £30 billion thereby maximising the resources available to improve front line services and fund new priorities;

- reducing administration budgets by 5 per cent a year in real terms across departments, bringing the proportion of public spending spent on administration to a new record low; and

- the release of £30 billion from fixed asset disposals between 2004-05 and 2010-11 as well as further funds from the sale of financial assets for reinvestment in new infrastructure.

I.13   In addition, the Government will continue to make reforms to public services to improve both outcomes and people's experience of those services, including through:

- a new performance management framework for central and local government that supports a sharper focus on key priorities, a more collaborative approach to achieving outcomes, and a reduction in burdens on frontline services; and

- putting users at the heart of services, including through a programme of service transformation that will build service delivery around the needs of citizens and businesses;

SUSTAINABLE GROWTH AND PROSPERITY

1.14 The pace of change in the global economy is intensifying, with growing movement of people, investment and goods. Rapid technological change and the emergence of newly industrialised economies are driving shifts in the competitive environment, with knowledge and other intangible assets growing in importance, creating new opportunities for individuals and businesses. In order to equip the UK to respond to these changes and support *sustainable growth and prosperity* the Government's priorities set out in PSAs will be to:

- raise the productivity of the UK economy, sustaining high rates of economic growth and improving the standard of living;

- improve the skills of the population, on the way to ensuring a world class skills base by 2020, setting stretching national targets to support working age people to acquire the skills they need to succeed at all levels;

- ensure controlled, fair migration that protects the public and contributes to economic growth, including developing a strong identity management system, reducing the processing time for asylum applications, removing those that cause the most harm to society first and managing migration to reduce skills shortages;

- promote world class science and innovation in the UK, with world-class research in UK centres of excellence, increasing business investment in R&D, and using the education system to deliver a strong base of future scientists, engineers and technologists;

- deliver reliable and efficient transport networks that support economic growth, tackling congestion and increasing the capacity of the rail network;

- deliver the conditions for business success in the UK, providing a world-class competition and corporate governance regime, a flexible labour market and better regulation; and

- improve the economic performance of all English regions and reduce the gap in economic growth rates between regions.

I.15 The 2007 Pre-Budget Report and Comprehensive Spending Review sets out a number of steps that the Government will take towards delivering on these priorities, including:

- increasing spending by the Department for Innovation, Universities and Skills on higher education and skills from £14.2 billion in 2007-08 to £16.4 billion by 2010-11 to implement the recommendations of the Leitch Review, developing a strong partnership with employers and individuals to deliver higher skills;

- increasing public investment in the science base from £5.4 billion in 2007-08 to £6.3 billion by 2010-11 to implement the recommendations of the Sainsbury Review. Total public support for business innovation through the Technology Strategy amounting to over £1 billion will ensure the UK's continued success in generating new ideas and using them in wealth creation;

- confirming a 2¼ per cent annual real increase in the Department for Transport's programme budget, consistent with the Long Term Funding Guideline which is extended to 2018-19. This will continue renewal of the UK's transport infrastructure including the funding package for Crossrail;

- simplifying the tax system to make it fairer and more efficient with the announcement of new principles, three reviews and a package of measures;

- simplifying business support to reduce confusion and the time businesses spend understanding what support is available and accessing it, and to improve the quality, effectiveness and efficiency of schemes;

- supporting the private equity industry's moves to increase transparency and a number of measures to ensure that tax arrangements are sustainable and appropriate; and

- allowing local authorities to invest in economic development through levying a local business rate supplement and focusing the strategic role for the Regional Development Agencies on economic growth as announced in the *Review of sub-national economic development and regeneration*.

FAIRNESS AND OPPORTUNITY FOR ALL

I.16 A decade ago, the Government set itself the twin aims of employment opportunity for all and a fair society in which everyone shares in rising national prosperity. These objectives are mutually reinforcing: work is the surest route out of poverty, while the tax and benefit system must work with public services to make sure that everyone is supported and given a chance to achieve their potential. The Government is also committed to a modern and fair tax system that ensures that everyone pays their fair share of tax. In order to promote *fairness and opportunity for all*, the Government's priorities as set out in PSAs will be to:

- maximise employment opportunity for all, raising the overall employment rate and narrowing the gap between the employment rates of disadvantaged groups and the overall rate;

- halve the number of children in poverty by 2010-11, on the way to eradicating child poverty by 2020, with a national target to reduce the number of children in relative low income households, supplemented by indicators to track progress on reduction in the number of children in absolute low income poverty and the number in relative low income and material deprevation;

- raise the educational achievement of all children and young people, raising standards at all levels of learning and development with stretching national targets;

- narrow the gap in educational achievement between children from low income and disadvantaged backgrounds and their peers, with national targets focused on pupil level progression and improving outcomes for the most vulnerable;

- improve the health and well-being of children and young people, turning round long term trends on childhood obesity and improving the experience of parents of disabled children with the services they receive;

- increase the number of children and young people on the path to success, reducing the number not in education, employment and training, reducing teenage pregnancy and reducing drug and alcohol use by teenagers;

- improve children and young people's safety, reducing bullying, reducing unintentional and deliberate injuries to children and reducing the number of preventable deaths;

- address the disadvantage that individuals experience because of their gender, race, disability, age, sexual orientation, religion or belief, reducing discrimination in employment, increasing participation in public life and narrowing the persistent gap between men and women's wage rates;

- increase the proportion of socially excluded adults in settled accommodation and employment, education or training, especially for care leavers, offenders under probation supervision, adults with secondary mental health problems and adults with moderate to severe learning disabilities; and

- tackle poverty and promote greater independence and well-being in later life, improving employment opportunities, improving health outcomes, and ensuring older people share in the rising prosperity of the UK.

1.17 The 2007 Pre-Budget Report and Comprehensive Spending Review sets out a number of steps that the Government will take towards delivering on these priorities, including:

- ensuring that all married couples and civil partners can benefit from double the inheritance tax allowance - £600,000 immediately, rising to £700,000 by 2010-11 in addition to the entitlement to full inheritance tax spouse relief;

- a major reform of capital gains tax, introducing a single rate of 18 per cent from April 2008, ensuring a more sustainable system that is straight forward for taxpayers, and internationally competitive;

- announcing that, in addition to the £150 increase announced at Budget 2007, the child element of Child Tax Credit will increase by £25 per year above indexation from April 2008, and by a further £25 above indexation, from April 2010 and that the child maintenance disregard in the main income related benefits will increase to £20 by the end of 2008, with a further increase to £40 from April 2010, together lifting an estimated 100,000 children out of poverty;

- education spending in England will rise an average by 2.8 per cent a year in real terms between 2007-08 and 2010-11, meaning that UK education spending as a proportion of GDP is projected to increase from 4.7 per cent in 1996-97 to 5.6 per cent in 2010-11;

- increasing the Jobseekers Allowance and Income Support rates for 16-17 year olds from April 2008 to align with the 18-24 rates, to help to simplify the system and ensure a higher minimum level of income for this group;

- the national roll-out from April 2008 of the In-Work Credit for lone parents at a rate of £40, retaining a rate of £60 in London, ensuring a substantial financial gain from moving into work;

- announcing the continuation of the Financial Inclusion Fund at £130 million over the the CSR07 period and an £11.5 million package of support for schools to teach children financial skills; and

- further reforms to modernise the tax system and protect tax revenues, including work to tackle avoidance.

STRONGER COMMUNITIES AND A BETTER QUALITY OF LIFE

1.18   Stable growth with high employment and low inflation provide the platform for rising living standards, while world class standard of education and modern tax and benefit system help to expand opportunity, ensure fairness and delivery security for the most vulnerable. However, public services also play a crucial role in building the foundations of communities and enabling individuals to lead healthy and fulfilling lives. To support *stronger communities and a better quality of life* the Government's priorities as set out in PSAs will be to:

- promote better health and well-being for all, with national targets to narrow the gap in life expectancy between the poorest areas and the national average, reducing smoking rates and improving access to psychological therapies;

- ensure better care for all, with no one waiting more than 18 weeks from GP to referral to hospital appointment, increased focus on patient experience and reducing hospital acquired infections;

- improve long-term housing supply and affordability, increasing housing supply, increasing the number of affordable homes, and improving the energy performance of new homes;

- deliver a successful Olympic Games and Paralympic Games with a sustainable legacy and get more children and young people taking part in high quality PE and sport;

- build more cohesive, empowered and active communities, enhancing the shared sense of purpose and belonging, as well as increasing participation in volunteering, sporting and cultural activities;

- make communities safer, reducing levels of serious violent crimes and serious acquisitive crimes, increasing confidence in local crime reduction agencies, and reducing reoffending;

- deliver a more effective, transparent and responsive Criminal Justice System for victims and the public, increasing public confidence in the fairness of the system and delivering better standards of service for victims and witnesses;

- reduce the harm caused by alcohol and drugs, improving the level of effective treatment for drug users therby reducing the harm to communities as a result of associated crime, disorder and anti-social behaviour, and for the first time extending this to focus on alcohol abuse; and

- reduce the risks to the UK and its interests overseas from international terrorism, stopping attacks, mitigating their impacts and tackling violent extremism.

I.19 The 2007 Pre-Budget Report and Comprehensive Spending Review sets out the steps that the Government will take towards delivering on these priorities, including:

- increasing spending on the NHS by an average of 4 per cent a year in real terms, taking its budget from £90 billion in 2007-08 to £110 billion by 2010-11, and delivering the vision set out by the Darzi Review for a health service which is fair, personalised, effective, safe and locally accountable;

- funding the delivery of more personalised adult social care that will give people greater choice and control, and announcing plans to consult on reform of the adult care and support systems;

- delivering the target of 2 million new homes by 2016, by increasing spending on housing from £8.8 billion in 2007-08 to £10 billion by 2010-11, reforming the tax and planning systems, and laying the ground for new planning charges to support essential investment in infrastructure;

- strengthening the role of local authorities to reshape local services around the individuals, families and communities that use them – underpinned by resource growth of 1 per cent a year in real terms over the CSR07 period, which the Government expects will enable the overall council tax increase to stay well below five per cent in each of the next three years;

- maintaining funding in real terms for the arts, museums and galleries, and ensuring a lasting cultural and sporting legacy for the nation by contributing £3.6 billion to the first phase of the construction costs of the Olympics over the next three years;

- increasing resources for the Home Office by 1.1 per cent a year in real terms over the CSR07 period, with an addition of over £220 million by 2010-11 to lead the fight against terrorism, alongside wider steps to roll out neighbourhood policing and deliver a more effective criminal justice system; and

- protecting the UK's security by increasing spending on counter-terrorism, intelligence and resilience from £2½ billion in 2007-08 to £3½ billion in 2010-11, within a new single security and intelligence budget for counter-terrorism.

A MORE SECURE, FAIR AND ENVIRONMENTALLY SUSTAINABLE WORLD

I.20 Advances in transport and communications technology mean the links between nations are now closer and more immediate than ever before. This brings new opportunities but also significant challenges, with economic, environmental and security risks no longer easily contained within one country. To help build *a more secure, fair and environmentally sustainable world*, the Government's priorities as set out in PSAs will be to:

- lead the global effort to avoid dangerous climate change, which sets out the UK's ambitions to secure robust global commitments for the period after 2012, adopt and promote cost effective policies which reduce net greenhouse gas emissions, and adapt to unavoidable climate change;

- secure a healthy natural environment for today and the future, monitoring water quality, biodiversity and air quality and protecting and enhancing the natural environment;

- reduce poverty in poorer countries through quicker progress towards the Millennium Development Goals, building global partnerships and focusing action on where it is most needed in Africa and South Asia; and

- reduce the impact of conflict through enhanced UK and international efforts to prevent, manage and resolve it, creating the conditions for effective state-building and economic development and strengthening international institutions.

1.21   The 2007 Pre-Budget Report and Comprehensive Spending Review sets out the next stage in the Government's strategy to meet these challenges, including:

- increasing the Department for Environment, Food and Rural Affairs' budget by an average of 1.4 per cent a year in real terms, from £3,508 million in 2007-08 to £3,960 million in 2010-11. This includes increasing funding for flood and coastal erosion risk management from £600 million in 2007-08 to £800 million in 2010-11;

- creating an Environmental Transformation Fund of £1.2 billion over the CSR07 period, to support the demonstration and deployment of new energy and efficiency technologies in the UK and to advance poverty reduction through environmental protection in developing countries;

- publishing the interim report of the King Review on vehicle and fuel technologies which over the next 25 years could help 'decarbonise' road transport;

- replacing air passenger duty with a duty payable per plane rather than per passenger, from 1 November 2009;

- increases to the Department for International Development's (DfID) budget by 11 per cent a year in real terms over the CSR07 period from £5.4 billion in 2007-08 to £7.9 billion in 2010-11;

- an overall CSR07 settlement, that puts the UK on track to spend 0.56 per cent of Gross National Income (GNI) on Official Development Assistance (ODA) by 2010-11, meeting the EU's collective commitment, and on course to reach 0.7 per cent of GNI by 2013;

- a new Stabilisation Aid Fund jointly managed by DfID, the Foreign and Commonwealth Office (FCO) and the Ministry of Defence (MoD) worth over £260 million during the CSR07 period, for conflict stabilisation activity in volatile or hostile areas;

- an increase for the MoD budget of 1.5 per cent a year in real terms over the CSR07 period, enhancing capability including funding for two new aircraft carriers, new protected vehicles for the Army, further Air Transport capability while providing the resources necessary to sustain the UK's nuclear deterrent; and

- **a CSR07 settlement for the FCO**, which enhances security across the overseas diplomatic network, funds a new embassy in Kabul, and provides an additional £21 million by 2010-11 for a Farsi TV service and for a 24/7 Arabic TV service.

PRE-BUDGET REPORT AND COMPREHENSIVE SPENDING REVIEW POLICY DECISIONS

1.22 Consistent with the requirements of the *Code for fiscal stability*, the updated public finance projections in the Pre-Budget Report take into account the fiscal effects of all firm decisions announced in the Pre-Budget Report or since Budget 2007. The fiscal impact of these measures is set out in Table 1.2. Full details are provided in Annex B.

Table 1.2: Estimated costs for Pre-Budget Report policy decisions and others announced since Budget 2007[1]

	£ million			
	2007-08	**2008-09**	**2009-10**	**2010-11**
Sustainable growth and prosperity				
Tax simplification: increase income tax self assessment payment on account threshold	0	0	-90	0
Fairness and opportunity for all				
Increase in housing benefit disregard[2]	-5	-	-	-
Implementing state second pension White Paper reforms	0	0	+290	+440
Modernisation of residence and domicile taxation	0	0	+800	+500
Increase child element of CTC by £25 in April 2008 and a further £25 in April 2010[3]	0	-30	-30	-60
Transferable inheritance tax allowances for married couples and civil partners	-100	-1,000	-1,200	-1,400
Capital gains tax reform: 18% single rate	0	+350	+750	+900
Protecting revenues				
Removal of national insurance contributions exemption	+100	+200	+200	+200
Tackling income shifting	0	+25	+260	+200
Life insurance companies avoidance	0	+35	+45	+45
Countering interest relief exploitation by individuals	+25	+10	0	0
Vehicle excise duty enforcement	0	+10	+20	+25
Protecting the environment				
Aviation duty[4]	0	-55	+100	+520
Non-car vehicle excise duty rates for 2008-09	0	-5	-5	-10
Fuel benefit charge: revalorisation since 2003	0	+65	+40	+25
Extending the exemption for oils used in electricity generation	-5	-5	-5	-5
Enhanced capital allowances for biofuel plants	0	+30	+20	+35
Other policy decisions				
Addition to the special reserve	-400	0	0	0
TOTAL POLICY DECISIONS	-385	-370	+1,195	+1,415
Additional investment in public services	0	0	0	-2,000

[1] Costings shown relative to an indexed base.

[2] From 2008-09 onwards, included within the Comprehensive Spending Review settlement.

[3] Negative tax costs. AME spending consequences are included within the Comprehensive Spending Review settlement.

[4] Intention to replace air passenger duty by per plane duty from November 2009.

Departmental Expenditure Limits (DEL)

1.23 Table 1.3 shows total allocations made to each department in the 2007 Comprehensive Spending Review. Details of each department's settlement are given in Annex D, and Annex B shows public expenditure plans for 2008-09 to 2010-11.

Table 1.3: Comprehensive Spending Review total DEL settlements

	£ billion				Per cent
	Baseline[1]	Plans			Average annual real growth[2]
	2007-08	2008-09	2009-10	2010-11	
Resource and net capital DEL					
Children, Schools and Families	50.1	52.9	55.6	59.5	3.1
Health	91.8	97.9	104.4	111.4	3.9
of which: NHS England	90.4	96.4	102.9	109.8	4.0
Transport	12.6	13.4	13.8	14.5	2.1
Innovation, Universities and Skills	18.0	18.7	19.7	20.8	2.2
CLG Communities	10.3	11.3	11.8	12.1	2.9
CLG Local Government[3]	23.9	24.8	25.7	26.5	0.9
Home Office	9.2	9.8	9.9	10.3	1.1
Justice	9.5	9.6	9.7	9.7	-1.7
Law Officers' Departments	0.7	0.7	0.7	0.7	-3.2
Defence	32.6	34.1	35.4	36.9	1.5
Foreign and Commonwealth Office	1.6	1.7	1.7	1.7	-0.1
International Development	5.4	5.8	6.8	7.9	11.0
Business, Enterprise and Regulatory Reform	3.4	3.4	3.4	3.4	-2.6
Environment, Food and Rural Affairs	3.5	3.7	3.8	4.0	1.4
Culture, Media and Sport	1.7	2.6	2.0	2.2	6.6
Work and Pensions	7.7	7.5	7.3	7.0	-5.6
Scotland	26.1	27.2	28.4	29.8	1.8
Wales	13.6	14.3	15.0	15.8	2.4
Northern Ireland Executive	8.4	8.8	9.2	9.6	1.7
Northern Ireland Office	1.2	1.2	1.2	1.2	-1.9
Chancellor's Departments	4.9	4.8	4.7	4.6	-4.9
Cabinet Office	1.9	2.2	2.4	2.5	7.2
Independent Bodies[4]	0.8	0.8	0.9	1.0	4.9
Modernisation Funding	-	0.5	0.4	0.1	
Reserve	2.5	3.2	3.5	3.8	-
Total DEL	**344.6**	**361.1**	**377.5**	**396.9**	**2.1**

[1] Baselines exclude one-off and time limited expenditure

[2] Average annual real growth rates are calculated off a 2007-08 baseline

[3] Resource growth for local Government is 1.0%

[4] Independent bodies within Departmental Expenditure Limits that are not settled as part of the Comprehensive Spending Review. Includes the Statistics board, House of Commons, House of Lords, National Audit Office and the Office of the Parliamentary Commissioner.

GOVERNMENT SPENDING AND REVENUE

1.24 Chart 1.1 presents public spending by main function. Total Managed Expenditure (TME) is expected to be around £589 billion in the current financial year, 2007-08. TME is divided into Departmental Expenditure Limits (DEL), shown in Table B13, and Annually Managed Expenditure (AME) shown in B11.

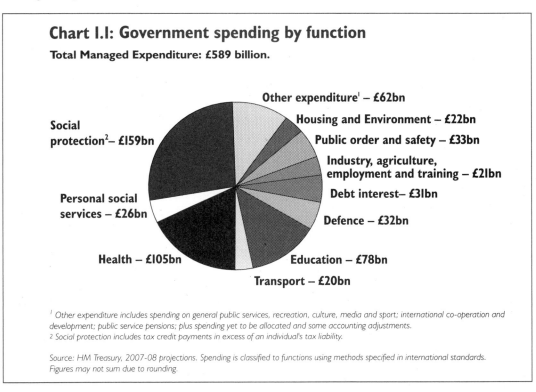

Chart 1.1: Government spending by function

Total Managed Expenditure: £589 billion.

- Other expenditure[1] – £62bn
- Housing and Environment – £22bn
- Public order and safety – £33bn
- Industry, agriculture, employment and training – £21bn
- Debt interest– £31bn
- Defence – £32bn
- Education – £78bn
- Transport – £20bn
- Health – £105bn
- Personal social services – £26bn
- Social protection[2]– £159bn

[1] Other expenditure includes spending on general public services, recreation, culture, media and sport; international co-operation and development; public service pensions; plus spending yet to be allocated and some accounting adjustments.
[2] Social protection includes tax credit payments in excess of an individual's tax liability.

Source: HM Treasury, 2007-08 projections. Spending is classified to functions using methods specified in international standards. Figures may not sum due to rounding.

1.25 Chart 1.2 shows the different sources of government revenues. Public sector current receipts are expected to be around £551 billion in 2007-08. Table B8 provides a more detailed breakdown of receipts consistent with this chart.

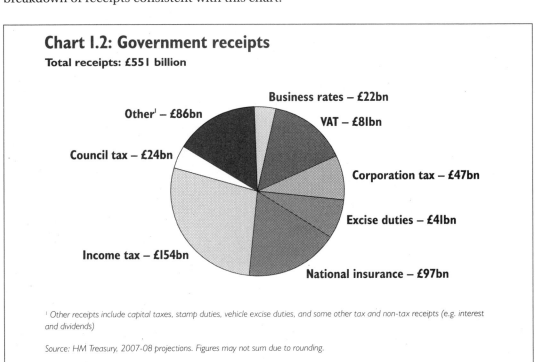

Chart 1.2: Government receipts

Total receipts: £551 billion

- Business rates – £22bn
- VAT – £81bn
- Corporation tax – £47bn
- Excise duties – £41bn
- National insurance – £97bn
- Income tax – £154bn
- Council tax – £24bn
- Other[1] – £86bn

[1] Other receipts include capital taxes, stamp duties, vehicle excise duties, and some other tax and non-tax receipts (e.g. interest and dividends)

Source: HM Treasury, 2007-08 projections. Figures may not sum due to rounding.

2 MAINTAINING MACROECONOMIC STABILITY

> The Government's macroeconomic framework and promotion of flexible and open labour, product and capital markets continues to deliver sustained economic growth with low inflation. The economy has grown for 60 consecutive quarters and inflation is close to target. This macroeconomic stability puts the UK in a strong position to respond to global economic challenges, and to take advantage of the opportunities of the coming decade. The 2007 Pre-Budget Report and Comprehensive Spending Review provides for further investment in public services to help equip the country for change while entrenching the macroeconomic stability needed to enable the UK to prosper in the increasingly competitive global economy.
>
> In 2007, the UK economy has continued to perform strongly, with GDP growth in the first half of the year reaching $3\frac{1}{4}$ per cent on a year earlier, towards the upper end of the Budget 2007 forecast range. Reflecting the combination of momentum in the economy, but higher interest rates than markets expected at the time of Budget 2007, the 2007 Pre-Budget Report economic forecast is for GDP growth of 3 per cent in 2007, slowing to 2 to $2\frac{1}{2}$ per cent in 2008, before strengthening to trend at $2\frac{1}{2}$ to 3 per cent in 2009 and 2010.
>
> The 2007 Pre-Budget Report projections for the public finances show that the Government is meeting its strict fiscal rules:
>
> * the current budget shows an average surplus as a percentage of GDP over the current economic cycle, ensuring the Government is meeting the golden rule. Beyond the current cycle, the current budget moves clearly into surplus; and
> * public sector net debt is projected to remain low and stable over the forecast period, stabilising below 39 per cent of GDP and so meeting the sustainable investment rule.

THE MACROECONOMIC FRAMEWORK

2.1   The Government's macroeconomic framework is designed to maintain long-term economic stability. Stability allows business, individuals and the Government to plan more effectively for the long term, improving the quality and quantity of investment in physical and human capital and helping to raise productivity. Economic stability provides the essential backdrop for addressing the priorities identified as part of the 2007 Pre-Budget Report and Comprehensive Spending Review (2007 PBR and CSR), enabling the Government to address the key social, economic and environmental challenges of the next decade.

2.2   The macroeconomic framework is based on the principles of transparency, responsibility and accountability.[1] The monetary policy framework seeks to ensure low and stable inflation, while fiscal policy is underpinned by clear objectives and two strict rules that ensure sound public finances over the medium term while allowing fiscal policy to support monetary policy over the economic cycle. The fiscal rules are the foundation of the Government's public spending framework, which facilitates long-term planning and provides departments with the flexibility and incentives they need to increase the quality of public services and deliver specified outcomes. These policies work together in a coherent and integrated way, and continue to deliver unprecedented growth and stability. As the OECD recently noted, the UK economy's "strong performance is not only due to the willingness to embrace the opportunities offered by globalisation, but also to sound institutional arrangements for setting monetary and fiscal policy".[2]

---

[1] Further details can be found in *Reforming Britain's economic and financial policy*, Balls and O'Donnell (eds.), 2002.
[2] *OECD Economic Surveys: United Kingdom*, OECD, September 2007.

Monetary policy framework

2.3 The monetary policy framework introduced in 1997 is based on four key principles:

- clear and precise objectives. The primary objective of monetary policy is to deliver price stability. The adoption of a single, symmetrical inflation target ensures that outcomes below target are treated as seriously as those above, so that monetary policy also supports the Government's objective of high and stable levels of growth and employment;

- full operational independence for the Monetary Policy Committee (MPC) in setting interest rates to meet the Government's target of 2 per cent for the 12-month increase in the Consumer Prices Index (CPI), which applies at all times;

- openness, transparency and accountability, which are enhanced through the publication of MPC members' voting records, prompt publication of the minutes of monthly MPC meetings, and publication of the Bank of England's quarterly Inflation Report; and

- credibility and flexibility. The MPC has discretion to decide how and when to react to events, within the constraints of the inflation target and the open letter system.

2.4 These arrangements have removed the risk that short-term political factors can influence monetary policy and ensured that interest rates are set in a forward-looking manner to meet the Government's symmetrical inflation target.

Performance of the monetary policy framework

2.5 The monetary policy framework has improved the credibility of policy making and continues to deliver clear benefits. Since the new framework was introduced:

- the annual increase in inflation up to December 2003, when RPIX was used as the inflation target measure, remained close to the target value of $2^1/_2$ per cent, the longest period of sustained low inflation for the past 30 years; and

- inflation expectations have remained close to target following the switch to a 2 per cent CPI target. CPI inflation has averaged 2 per cent since 2003 and has moved away from its target by more than 1 percentage point on only one occasion;

- on average the UK has had the lowest inflation in the G7 so far this decade, with the exception of Japan, which has been through a protracted period of deflation. By contrast, in the 1980s and 1990s, the UK had one of the highest inflation rates among the major economies; and

- long-term interest rates have averaged 5 per cent compared with an average of just over 9 per cent in the previous economic cycle. Alongside the UK's macroeconomic stability in recent years, the effective exchange rate has also been relatively stable. The sterling effective exchange rate remains close to levels at Budget 2004.

2.6 Responding to reduced spare capacity and above-trend growth, and with inflation above target, the MPC raised interest rates on five occasions between August 2006 and July 2007, to reach their present level of $5^3/_4$ per cent. Inflation has come down swiftly since peaking in March, at 3.1 per cent, and is expected to remain close to target over the forecast horizon.

2.7 In April 2007, the Governor of the Bank of England wrote the first open letter since the inception of the MPC. The open letter system is an integral part of the macroeconomic framework. It requires the Governor to explain to the Chancellor the reasons for any deviation in inflation of more than one percentage point above or below target, plus the action the MPC proposes to take, the expected duration of the deviation and how the proposed action meets the remit of the MPC. The MPC's forward-looking approach has been a cornerstone of economic policy since 1997. The Chancellor, in his response, underlined that the Government will continue to support the MPC in the forward-looking decisions it takes in the future.

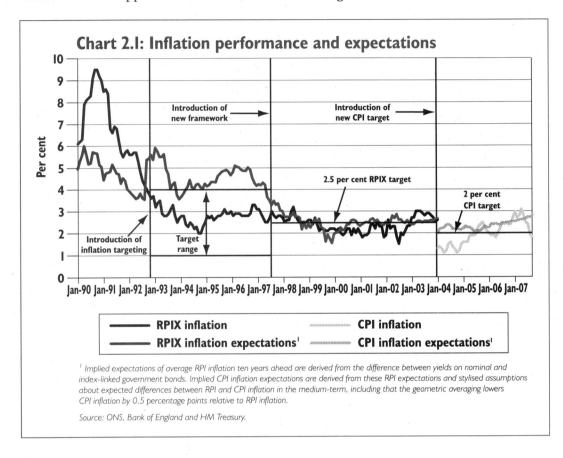

Chart 2.1: Inflation performance and expectations

	RPIX inflation	CPI inflation
	RPIX inflation expectations[1]	CPI inflation expectations[1]

[1] *Implied expectations of average RPI inflation ten years ahead are derived from the difference between yields on nominal and index-linked government bonds. Implied CPI inflation expectations are derived from these RPI expectations and stylised assumptions about expected differences between RPI and CPI inflation in the medium-term, including that the geometric averaging lowers CPI inflation by 0.5 percentage points relative to RPI inflation.*

Source: ONS, Bank of England and HM Treasury.

Box 2.1: UK macroeconomic stability

The Government's frameworks for monetary and fiscal policy have helped to deliver an unprecedented decade of growth and stability for the UK economy. Since 1997, GDP growth has averaged 2.9 per cent while inflation has averaged 1.6 per cent, compared with average growth of 2.3 per cent in the previous decade and average inflation of 4.1 per cent.

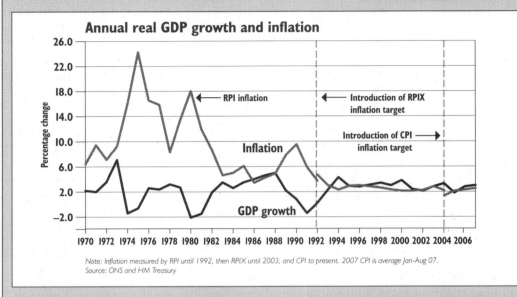

Annual real GDP growth and inflation

Note: Inflation measured by RPI until 1992, then RPIX until 2003, and CPI to present. 2007 CPI is average Jan-Aug 07.
Source: ONS and HM Treasury

Both the monetary and fiscal frameworks are underpinned by flexibility:

- the monetary framework gives the independent MPC the flexibility to respond to events in a forward-looking manner. For example, the open letter system, outlined above, creates a transparent approach to significant deviations of inflation from its target level, giving the MPC an opportunity to respond sensibly to particular economic shocks; and

- the fiscal rules are set over the economic cycle, allowing the automatic stabilisers to operate fully to help dampen economic cycles. This flexibility in fiscal policy, along with a context of low and stable borrowing and debt, has enabled fiscal policy to contribute to macroeconomic stability. The IMF noted the "shallowness of the UK growth slowdown during the last global downturn",[a] which they attributed in part to fiscal responsiveness.

Policy reforms that have increased the responsiveness of the economy also contribute to resilience. The OECD recently noted that the "United Kingdom's open and flexible approach to economic policy is reflected in support for free trade, openness to foreign direct investment (FDI), a willingness to open its labour markets to citizens from new EU countries that joined in May 2004, and the adoption of regulatory policies that promote efficiency and economic resilience."[b] The 2007 PBR and CSR reports on progress made on enhancing flexibility.

The flexibility introduced by macroeconomic policy and microeconomic reforms since 1997 has allowed the UK economy to withstand a number of global challenges, with policymakers responding proactively in the face of significant risks. During the Asian, Russian and Long Term Credit Management (LTCM) crises of 1997 and 1998, UK GDP growth remained robust; following the bursting of the dotcom bubble after 2000 and in the aftermath of the terrorist attacks of 11 September 2001, the UK economy continued to expand while many other major economies experienced recession. The UK economy is the only G7 economy to have avoided any quarters of negative output growth this decade.

[a] *Concluding statement to the 2007 Article IV mission to the UK*, IMF, March 2007.
[b] *OECD Economic Surveys: United Kingdom*, OECD, September 2007.

Performance of **2.8** It is important that the macroeconomic policy framework continues to evolve to
the monetary maintain its status at the forefront of international best practice. In line with the principles of
policy framework transparency and accountability, which underpin the monetary policy framework, the
Chancellor announced to the Treasury Select Committee (TSC) on 14 June 2007 three
important changes to the process by which external appointments are made to the MPC:

- the timetable for appointing a new external member will now be pre-
  announced well before an existing member's term is due to come to an end,
  providing greater clarity and certainty about the appointments process;

- there will be an invitation of 'expressions of interest' from potential
  candidates, enhancing openness in the process without limiting the field of
  candidates to individuals that come forward in response to the invitation; and

- in inviting expressions of interest, additional criteria on the kind of candidate
  the Chancellor is seeking will be published, providing greater transparency on
  the Chancellor's thinking on the skills required in a specific appointment.

2.9 In addition, to reinforce transparency and increase parliamentary scrutiny, new
appointees to the MPC will now be subject to a TSC confirmation hearing before they take up
a post on the Committee. This will apply to all appointees to the MPC, including for the
Governor and Deputy Governors of the Bank of England.

Reforms to the **2.10** Statistics make a crucial contribution to the operation of the macroeconomic
statistical system framework. Following the commitment made by the Chancellor in November 2005, and a full
public consultation, legislation for the reform of the UK statistical system has been
successfully delivered. The Statistics and Registration Service Act 2007[3], which gained Royal
Assent in July, establishes an independent Statistics Board, reporting directly to Parliament,
responsible for promoting and safeguarding the quality and comprehensiveness of all official
statistics that serve the public good, wherever produced in government. The Board will have
a statutory duty to set professional standards in a Code of Practice, and to assess
independently statistics against this Code. The Board will also replace Ministers as the top
layer of governance for the Office for National Statistics. The Government intends that the
new system will be up and running in Spring 2008.

Fiscal policy **2.11** The Government's fiscal policy framework is based on the five key principles set out
framework in the *Code for fiscal stability*[4] – transparency, stability, responsibility, fairness and efficiency.
The Code requires the Government to state both its objectives and the rules through which
fiscal policy will be operated. The Government's fiscal policy objectives are:

- over the medium term, to ensure sound public finances and that spending
  and taxation impact fairly within and between generations; and

- over the short term, to support monetary policy and, in particular, to allow the
  automatic stabilisers to help smooth the path of the economy.

2.12 These objectives are implemented through two strict fiscal rules, against which the
performance of fiscal policy can be judged. The fiscal rules are:

- the golden rule: over the economic cycle, the Government will borrow only to
  invest and not to fund current spending; and

---

[3] Further details, including the Act and associated documentation, can be found on the HM Treasury website at
http://www.hm-treasury.gov.uk.
[4] *Code for fiscal stability*, HM Treasury, 1998.

- the sustainable investment rule: public sector net debt as a proportion of GDP will be held over the economic cycle at a stable and prudent level. Other things being equal, net debt will be maintained below 40 per cent of GDP over the economic cycle.

2.13   The fiscal rules ensure sound public finances in the medium term while allowing flexibility in two key respects:

- the rules are set over the economic cycle. This allows the fiscal balances to vary between years in line with the cyclical position of the economy, permitting the automatic stabilisers to operate freely to help smooth the path of the economy in the face of variations in demand; and

- the rules work together to promote capital investment while ensuring sustainable public finances in the long term. The golden rule requires the current budget to be in balance or surplus over the cycle, allowing the Government to borrow only to fund capital spending. The sustainable investment rule ensures that borrowing is maintained at a prudent level. To meet the sustainable investment rule with confidence, net debt will be maintained below 40 per cent of GDP in each and every year of the current economic cycle.

Performance of **2.14**   Since 1997, fiscal policy has resulted in low and stable borrowing, in contrast to
the fiscal policy previous UK experience. In the 1986-87 to 1997-98 economic cycle, net borrowing reached
framework nearly 8 per cent of GDP, and averaged 3.1 per cent of GDP. During the current economic cycle, net borrowing has averaged 1.0 per cent of GDP and at its peak reached just 3.3 per cent of GDP. The fiscal framework has successfully supported economic stability by allowing the automatic stabilisers to operate, as set out in more detail in Chart 2.4. The fiscal framework has also protected an historically unprecedented increase in public sector net investment, while net debt has been maintained at a low and sustainable level.

Public spending **2.15**   The fiscal rules underpin the Government's public spending framework. The golden
framework rule states that, over the economic cycle, the Government will only borrow to invest. Departments are therefore given separate resource and capital allocations, which ensures that public investment is not crowded out by short-term current spending pressures. The sustainable investment rule sets the context for the Government's public investment targets and ensures that borrowing for investment is conducted in a responsible way. Chapter 3 sets out the next stage of development in the public spending and performance management framework for the 2007 Comprehensive Spending Review period to drive increased value for money and the delivery of key outcomes.

Financial stability **2.16**   The framework for co-operation on financial stability between the Bank of England,
framework the Financial Services Authority (FSA) and HM Treasury is set out in the 2006 *Memorandum of Understanding*.[5] The Memorandum of Understanding between the three authorities defines the roles and responsibilities of each in maintaining financial stability, in responding to operational disruptions to the financial sector, and for financial crisis management.

2.17   The Standing Committee on Financial Stability, comprising the Chancellor, the Governor of the Bank of England and the Chairman of the FSA, meets monthly (at Deputies level) to discuss individual cases and developments relevant to financial stability, focusing on risks to the financial system. The Committee regularly reviews the key systemic risks to the UK's financial intermediaries and infrastructure and coordinates the three authorities' response and contingency plans. As set out in more detail in Chapter 4, the authorities have

---

[5] The full text of the 2006 Memorandum is available at www.hm-treasury.gov.uk

worked together as appropriate, in line with their responsibilities, during the period of disruption in global financial markets.

RECENT ECONOMIC DEVELOPMENTS AND PROSPECTS

2.18   The UK's macroeconomic performance continues to be strong and stable. GDP in the UK has now expanded for 60 consecutive quarters, the longest expansion since quarterly National Accounts began in the mid-1950s.

The economic **2.19**   Since Budget 2007, upward revisions to estimates of non-oil GVA growth in 2006, **cycle** combined with estimates of 0.8 per cent growth in each of the first two quarters of 2007, show the UK economy to have been growing at slightly above-trend rates for seven consecutive quarters through to mid-2007. Evidence from the broad range of cyclical indicators monitored by the Treasury, the latest National Accounts data and the Treasury's trend output assumptions imply output passed through trend towards the end of 2006 and that a small positive output gap, of around a $1/4$ per cent, has opened up. However, it is too soon to assess whether or not the economic cycle has ended.

Economic **2.20**   As reported in Budget 2007, the UK economy grew by $2^3/4$ per cent in 2006. GDP **prospects** growth in the first half of 2007 was towards the upper end of the Budget 2007 forecast range for the year as a whole, at $3^1/4$ per cent on a year earlier. Private sector business surveys suggest the economy carried significant momentum into the second half of 2007. In light of such evidence, the 2007 Pre-Budget Report forecast is for GDP growth of 3 per cent in the year as a whole, in line with the Budget 2007 forecast. The world economy is expected to remain robust in 2007, growing by 5 per cent, with emerging markets continuing to expand rapidly. Growth in the G7 economies in 2007 is expected to slow to 2 per cent, due in particular to the ongoing slowdown in the US.

2.21   The MPC has raised Bank Rate by more than financial markets expected at Budget time, which can be expected to impact on growth in 2008. In addition, disruption in financial markets has meant economic prospects have become more uncertain, and events need to unfold further before the impact on the economy can be rigorously quantified. For the purposes of the economic forecast, it has been assumed that there will be some feed-through to tighter credit conditions and to household and company spending in the short term. Growth in the G7 economies is expected to remain moderate, at 2 per cent, in 2008.

2.22   Against this backdrop, GDP growth in 2008 is forecast to slow to 2 to $2^1/2$ per cent, below its trend rate. The economy is forecast to strengthen, returning to trend in 2009, with growth forecast to be in the range of $2^1/2$ to 3 per cent from then onwards.

Table 2.1: Summary of UK forecast[1]

	Outturn		Forecasts		
	2006	**2007**	**2008**	**2009**	**2010**
GDP growth (per cent)	$2^3/4$	3	2 to $2^1/2$	$2^1/2$ to 3	$2^1/2$ to 3
CPI inflation (per cent, Q4)	$2^3/4$	2	2	2	2

[1] See footnote to Table A9 for explanation of forecast ranges.

2.23   CPI inflation is forecast to remain close to the 2 per cent inflation target throughout the forecast horizon reflecting the offsetting effects of a number of factors. These include upward cost pressures from food and oil prices, and downward pressures from the ongoing effect of monetary policy tightening over the past year and below-trend growth in 2008.

Risks **2.24** The disruption in global financial markets has meant economic prospects have become more uncertain. It presents clear risks to the economic forecast, though these are judged to be broadly balanced. Considerable uncertainty surrounds the timing and extent to which the disruption might affect the wider economy, and the longer it persists, the greater the risk of it detracting from growth. However, the UK economy has proved resilient to a number of shocks over the past decade, demonstrating the success of the Government's macroeconomic framework and the promotion of open and flexible labour, product and capital markets. As such, growth could also slow by less than expected.

Box 2.2: Inflation and pay

The UK economy is experiencing both an unprecedented period of growth and its longest period of sustained low and stable inflation since the 1960s. Low inflation has provided the platform for record employment levels, higher investment, productivity and economic growth.

Over the recent past, inflation has been boosted by temporary, unforeseen shocks: increases in energy prices, driven by developments in the oil market and, in particular, a tight wholesale gas market during late 2005 and early 2006. On top of this, food price inflation was pushed higher by the effects of the unusually hot UK summer in 2006 and, more recently, global supply and demand pressures.

Seasonal food and energy price inflation rates tend to be more volatile than headline inflation. Stripping out these short-term influences, underlying 'core' inflation (excluding energy and seasonal food) has remained low and generally under 2 per cent.

In contrast to periods of higher inflation in previous decades, the credibility of the UK's monetary policy framework has kept inflation expectations anchored and earnings growth has remained subdued. The Government has demonstrated its commitment to this by delivering overall headline awards for Pay Review Body groups in 2007-08 that average 1.9 per cent. Headline inflation has fallen back from its peak earlier in the year and currently stands at 1.8 per cent. The Treasury's forecast is for inflation to remain around its 2 per cent target, in line with the view of external forecasters.

There remains a risk of second-round effects of higher inflation feeding into inflation expectations and higher average earnings growth. It is therefore important that public sector pay settlements continue to be consistent with the achievement of the Government's inflation target of 2 per cent, as set out in Chapter 3.

Box 2.3: The impact of the financial sector on the economy and public finances

As outlined in more detail in Annex A, financial market disruption has had an impact on UK and global financial markets. Such events have the potential to impact on the wider economy through the price and availability of credit for companies and individuals, which could dampen private consumption and investment growth. It is not yet clear what the extent or duration of any impact might be. For the purposes of the Pre-Budget Report economic forecast, it has been assumed that there will be some feed-through to tighter credit conditions and to household and company spending in the short term.

The performance of the financial sector also impacts on the public finances, most directly through financial company corporation tax and income tax and NICs on bonuses, where receipts from the sector are significant. While the effect on the public finances of current global financial market disruption is uncertain, the projections for the public finances in this Pre-Budget Report allow for an impact on receipts from corporation tax and income tax and NICs, along with other factors.

The financial sector is not only important in terms of its impact on the wider economy, but also as a successful industry, one in which Britain is a global leader. Financial companies' share of UK GDP and of overall corporate profits has been on an upward trend for over two decades. The sector has successfully weathered major financial disruption in the past, such as the Russian debt default and Long Term Credit Management (LTCM) related disruption of 1998 and the global stock market falls in 2001.

The innovation and responsiveness of the City, against the backdrop of a stable UK economy, puts it in a strong position to adapt to global changes. The UK not only has a comparative advantage in financial services, but also in the wider business services sectors, including areas such as computer and information services and other business services.[a] Chapter 4 provides further detail on the financial sector's strength and global competitiveness.

---

[a] *Productivity in the UK 6: Evidence and Progress*, HM Treasury, 2003.

RECENT FISCAL TRENDS AND OUTLOOK

2.25 Under the *Code for fiscal stability*, the Government is committed to publishing a Pre-Budget Report at least three months prior to the Budget. As described previously, one of the roles of the Pre-Budget Report is to increase transparency, including by presenting an interim forecast update on the outlook for the economy and public finances ahead of the next Budget. The projections for the public finances presented below take into account the fiscal effects of all decisions announced in this Pre-Budget Report or since Budget 2007 including the overall fiscal impact of the final Comprehensive Spending Review settlement, in accordance with the *Code for fiscal stability*.

Outturn for 2006-07
2.26 The deficit on the current balance in 2006-07 is £4.7 billion lower than expected at the Budget, as shown in Table 2.2. This is lower in 2006-07 due to continued success in tackling MTIC fraud and growth in consumer expenditure feeding through to higher-than-expected VAT payments. The deficit is also reduced by lower government expenditure than expected at the Budget, in particular spending by local authorities. The 2006-07 outturn for net borrowing is £3.9 billion lower than the Budget 2007 estimate.

2.27   From 2005-06 to 2006-07 the deficit on the current balance fell by £9.3 billion, or 0.8 per cent of GDP. Net borrowing in 2006-07 fell by 0.7 per cent of GDP compared with 2005-06. The fall in borrowing is slightly less than the fall in the current deficit, due to the 0.1 per cent of GDP rise in net investment in 2006-07.

Table 2.2: Fiscal balances compared with Budget 2007

	Outturn[1] 2006-07	Estimate[2] 2007-08	Projections				
			2008-09	2009-10	2010-11	2011-12	2012-13
Surplus on current budget (£ billion)							
Budget 2007	−9.5	−4.3	3	6	9	13	
Effect of revisions and forecasting changes	4.7	−3.6	−6$\frac{1}{2}$	−4	−1$\frac{1}{2}$	−1	
Effect of discretionary changes	0	−0.4	−$\frac{1}{2}$	1	1$\frac{1}{2}$	1$\frac{1}{2}$	
2007 Pre-Budget Report	**−4.7**	**−8.3**	**−4**	**3**	**9**	**14**	**20**
Net borrowing (£ billion)							
Budget 2007	35.0	33.7	30	28	26	24	
Changes to current budget	−4.7	4.0	7	2$\frac{1}{2}$	0	−1	
Changes to net investment	0.8	0.4	0	0	2	2	
2007 Pre-Budget Report	**31.0**	**38.0**	**36**	**31**	**28**	**25**	**23**
Cyclically-adjusted surplus on current budget (per cent of GDP)							
Budget 2007	−0.5	−0.3	0.2	0.4	0.6	0.8	
2007 Pre-Budget Report	**−0.2**	**−0.7**	**−0.2**	**0.3**	**0.6**	**0.8**	**1.1**
Cyclically-adjusted net borrowing (per cent of GDP)							
Budget 2007	2.5	2.4	2.0	1.8	1.6	1.4	
2007 Pre-Budget Report	**2.2**	**2.8**	**2.4**	**1.9**	**1.7**	**1.5**	**1.3**
Net debt (per cent of GDP)							
Budget 2007	37.2	38.2	38.5	38.8	38.8	38.6	
2007 Pre-Budget Report	**36.7**	**37.6**	**38.4**	**38.8**	**38.9**	**38.8**	**38.6**

Note: Totals may not sum due to rounding.
[1] The 2006-07 figures were estimates in Budget 2007.
[2] The 2007-08 figures were projections in Budget 2007.

Estimates for 2007-08 and 2008-09   **2.28**   The rise in borrowing compared with Budget 2007 projections is concentrated in 2007-08 and 2008-09, driven in part by recent financial market disruption and the consequent impact on the economy, as described in Box 2.3. Other factors which reduce receipts in 2007-08 compared to the Budget are a fall in North Sea revenues, as a result of lower-than-expected gas prices, and a series of one-off corporation tax repayments. In 2008-09 receipts are also lower due to reduced oil production forecasts. Table 2.2 shows that by the end of the projection period, borrowing and the current surplus return to close to their Budget levels, as the impact of temporary factors diminishes, with spending growing in line with GDP and as discretionary measures introduce a modest tightening.

2.29   With output close to or at trend throughout the projection period, the profile of cyclically-adjusted borrowing is very similar to that of headline PSNB. The cyclically-adjusted deficit peaked at 3.2 per cent of GDP in 2004-05, declined in 2005-06 and fell sharply in 2006-07. Both the cyclically-adjusted and the main measure of net borrowing are expected to rise in 2007-08 before falling in every year of the projection period, reaching 1.3 per cent of GDP in 2012-13. The rise in 2007-08 is driven by the same short-term negative impacts on receipts from the financial sector and gas prices described above. Cyclically-adjusted borrowing is slightly higher than the main aggregate in 2007-08 because the economy appears to be slightly above trend in this year.

2.30 Cyclical adjustment cannot take account of non-cyclical temporary shocks to the public finances, nor cyclical shocks with different impacts than those experienced in the past. Therefore to the extent that cyclical adjustment is not taking account of the impact of temporary financial market disruption, structural PSNB may be lower than Pre-Budget Report projections suggest.

Table 2.3: Public sector net borrowing compared with Budget 2007

	Outturn[1]	Estimate[2]	Projections			
	2006-07	2007-08	2008-09	2009-10	2010-11	2011-12
Budget 2007 (£ billion)	35.0	33.7	30	28	26	24
Changes since Budget 2007						
Total economic and other forecasting effects	-3.9	4.0	6½	4	1½	3
Total before discretionary measures	31.0	37.6	36	32	27	27
Discretionary measures	0	0.4	½	-1	½	-1½
2007 Pre-Budget Report	31.0	38.0	36	31	28	25

Note: Figures may not sum due to rounding.
[1] The 2006-07 figures were estimates in Budget 2007.
[2] The 2007-08 figures were projections in Budget 2007.

2.31 Details of changes to the receipts forecast, the estimate for spending for 2007-08 and changes to the annual managed expenditure forecast are set out in Annex B. Later chapters provide more detail on the firm departmental spending plans for the years 2008-09, 2009-10 and 2010-11 fixed by the 2007 CSR.

Discretionary **2.32** In considering the impact of additional discretionary policy changes on the fiscal
policy changes position, the Government has taken into account the following factors:

- the importance of ensuring the strict fiscal rules are met over the cycle;

- its broader, medium-term objectives for fiscal policy, including the need to ensure sound public finances and that spending and taxation impact fairly both within and between generations; and

- the need to ensure that fiscal policy supports monetary policy.

2.33 Consistent with the requirements of the *Code for fiscal stability*, the updated projections take into account the fiscal effects of all decisions announced in this Pre-Budget Report or since Budget 2007. This includes:

- an addition of £2 billion to total public sector net investment, in 2010-11, to take forward vital capital investment in public services;

- ensuring that all married couples and civil partners automatically benefit from double the standard inheritance tax allowance;

- reforming capital gains tax by introducing a single rate of 18 per cent, ensuring a more sustainable system that is straightforward and internationally competitive; and

- action to protect tax revenues and further modernise the tax system, including a number of measures to tackle tax avoidance.

PERFORMANCE AGAINST THE FISCAL RULES

Table 2.4: Summary of public sector finances

	Per cent of GDP						
	Outturn	Estimate	Projections				
	2006-07	2007-08	2008-09	2009-10	2010-11	2011-12	2012-13
Fairness and prudence							
Surplus on current budget	−0.4	−0.6	−0.3	0.2	0.6	0.8	1.1
Average surplus since 1997-98	0.1	0.1	0.0	0.1	0.1	0.1	0.2
Cyclically-adjusted surplus on current budget	−0.2	−0.7	−0.2	0.3	0.6	0.8	1.1
Long-term sustainability							
Public sector net debt[1]	36.7	37.6	38.4	38.8	38.9	38.8	38.6
Core debt[1]	35.8	36.9	37.6	38.0	38.1	38.1	37.9
Net worth[2]	26.0	25.3	24.1	23.4	22.8	22.5	22.4
Primary balance	−0.7	−1.0	−0.9	−0.4	−0.1	0.2	0.3
Economic impact							
Net investment	2.0	2.1	2.2	2.2	2.3	2.3	2.3
Public sector net borrowing (PSNB)	2.3	2.7	2.5	2.0	1.7	1.5	1.3
Cyclically-adjusted PSNB	2.2	2.8	2.4	1.9	1.7	1.5	1.3
Financing							
Central government net cash requirement	2.8	2.7	2.6	2.4	2.0	2.0	1.6
Public sector net cash requirement	2.7	2.4	2.4	2.3	1.8	1.8	1.5
European commitments							
Treaty deficit[3]	2.6	2.9	2.8	2.4	2.1	1.8	1.6
Cyclically-adjusted Treaty deficit[3]	2.4	3.0	2.7	2.3	2.1	1.8	1.6
Treaty debt ratio[4]	43.4	43.9	44.8	45.1	45.3	45.2	44.9
Memo: Output gap	*−0.1*	*0.2*	*−0.3*	*0.0*	*0.0*	*0.0*	*0.0*

[1] *Debt at end March; GDP centred on end March.*
[2] *Estimate at end December; GDP centred on end December.*
[3] *General government net borrowing on a Maastricht basis.*
[4] *General government gross debt on a Maastricht basis.*

Golden rule **2.34** The current budget balance represents the difference between current receipts and current expenditure, including depreciation. It measures the degree to which current taxpayers meet the cost of paying for the public services they use and it is therefore an important indicator of intergenerational fairness. The golden rule is set over the economic cycle to allow fiscal policy to support monetary policy in maintaining stability through the operation of the automatic stabilisers. Progress against the rule is measured by the average annual surplus on the current budget as a percentage of GDP since the cycle began, in 1997-98.

2.35 The deficit on the current budget fell by £9.3 billion from 2005-06 to 2006-07, falling from 1.1 per cent of GDP to 0.4 per cent of GDP. The deficit on the current budget increases slightly in 2007-08 to 0.6 per cent of GDP before reaching surplus in 2009-10. From 2009-10 onwards, the surplus on the current budget strengthens, reaching 1.1 per cent in 2012-13. The average surplus on the current budget since the start of the 1997-98 cycle is positive in every year of the projection period. The economy appears to have passed through trend in the final quarter of 2006. On this basis, and based on cautious assumptions, the Government would have met the golden rule with a margin of £18 billion, higher than estimated at the Budget.

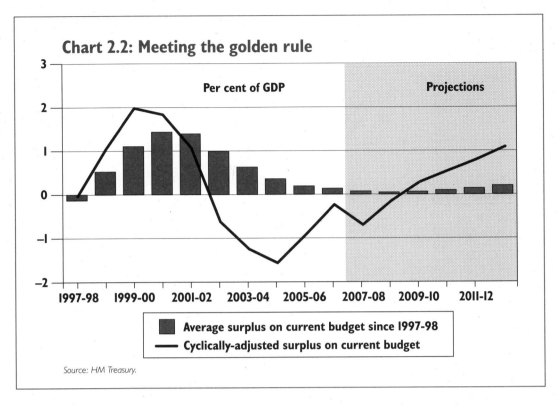

Chart 2.2: Meeting the golden rule

Per cent of GDP   Projections

Legend:
- Average surplus on current budget since 1997-98
- Cyclically-adjusted surplus on current budget

Source: HM Treasury.

2.36 With the economy appearing to have passed through trend in the final quarter of 2006, Pre-Budget Report projections show that the current budget moves into surplus in 2009-10, with the surplus rising to 1.1 per cent of GDP by 2012-13. At this early stage, and based on cautious assumptions, the Government is therefore on course to meet the golden rule in the next economic cycle.

Sustainable investment rule **2.37** The Government's primary objective for fiscal policy is to ensure sound public finances in the medium term. This means maintaining public sector net debt at a low and sustainable level. To meet the sustainable investment rule with confidence, net debt will be maintained below 40 per cent of GDP in each and every year of the current economic cycle. Chart 2.3 shows that despite output having been generally below trend since 2001, net debt remains below 39 per cent of GDP and starts to decline by the end of the projection period, reaching 38.6 per cent of GDP in 2012-13. Therefore the Government meets its sustainable investment rule while continuing to borrow to fund increased long-term capital investment in public services. Chart 2.3 also illustrates projections for core debt, which excludes the estimated impact of the economic cycle on public sector net debt.

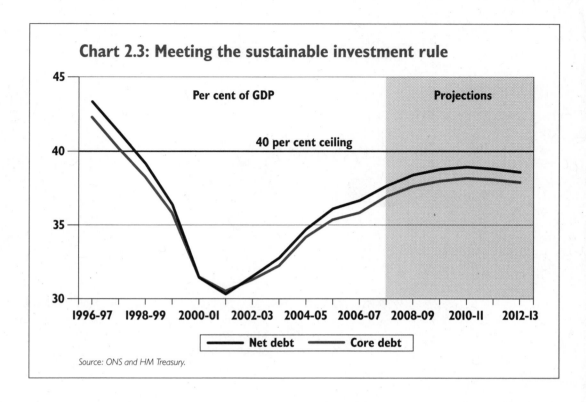

Chart 2.3: Meeting the sustainable investment rule

Per cent of GDP

Projections

40 per cent ceiling

Net debt   Core debt

Source: ONS and HM Treasury.

Economic impact 2.38 While the primary objective of fiscal policy is to ensure sound public finances, fiscal policy also affects the economy and plays a role in supporting monetary policy over the cycle. The overall impact of fiscal policy on the economy can be assessed by examining changes in public sector net borrowing. These can be broken down into changes due to the effects of the automatic stabilisers and those due to the change in the fiscal stance, as illustrated in Chart 2.4.

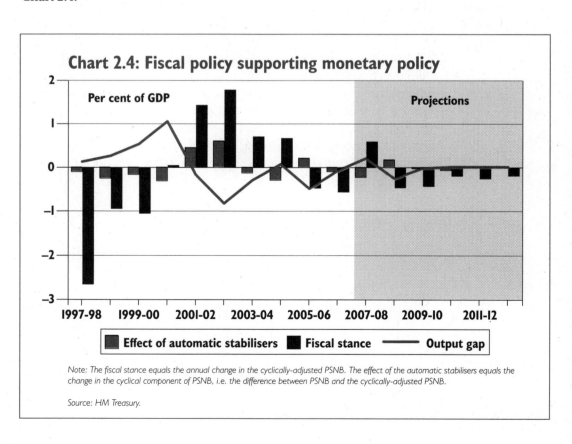

Chart 2.4: Fiscal policy supporting monetary policy

Per cent of GDP

Projections

Effect of automatic stabilisers   Fiscal stance   Output gap

Note: The fiscal stance equals the annual change in the cyclically-adjusted PSNB. The effect of the automatic stabilisers equals the change in the cyclical component of PSNB, i.e. the difference between PSNB and the cyclically-adjusted PSNB.

Source: HM Treasury.

2.39 During the late 1990s, the fiscal stance and the automatic stabilisers tightened at a time when the economy was above trend. As the economy moved below trend in 2001, the automatic stabilisers and the fiscal stance supported the economy. With the output gap closing and the economy appearing to have passed through trend in the final quarter of 2006, the fiscal stance was tighter in 2005-06 and 2006-07 and further tightening of the fiscal stance is forecast over the projection period, except in 2007-08. Pre-Budget Report projections show the public finances accommodating the impact of financial market disruption with borrowing increasing in 2007-08 and with modest discretionary fiscal loosening in 2007-08 and 2008-09 helping to smooth the path of the economy. From 2008-09 borrowing falls year on year, supported by discretionary fiscal tightening from 2009-10, the impact of which builds towards the end of the projection period.

European commitments **2.40** The Government supports a prudent interpretation of the Stability and Growth Pact as reflected in reforms to the Pact agreed in March 2005. This takes into account the economic cycle, the long-term sustainability of the public finances and the important role of public investment. The public finance projections set out in this Pre-Budget Report, which show the Government is meeting its fiscal rules over the cycle, maintaining low debt and sustainable public finances, combined with sustainable increases in public investment, are fully consistent with a prudent interpretation of the Pact.

Dealing with uncertainty **2.41** Forecasts for the public finances are subject to a considerable degree of uncertainty, in particular the fiscal balances, which represent the difference between two large aggregates. In order to create a safety margin against uncertain events, the Government bases the public finance projections on deliberately cautious assumptions, which are audited by the National Audit Office. The degree of caution in these assumptions increases over the projection period. For example, the public finances forecasts are based on an assumption that trend growth is $^1/_4$ percentage point lower than the neutral trend growth assumption used in the economy forecast. By the end of the projection period, in 2012-13, this implies that the level of GDP in the public finances forecast is $1^1/_4$ per cent below the neutral level.

2.42 The 2007 *End of year fiscal report*, published alongside this report, examines fiscal trends in recent years and forecast performance, measured in terms of accuracy and caution. Overall since 1997, the Treasury's year-ahead borrowing forecasts have been more cautious than prior to the introduction of the macroeconomic framework.

2.43 In addition to basing the public finance forecasts in the Pre-Budget Report and Budget on cautious assumptions, including one of lower trend growth, it is also sensible to test the robustness of these projections. The projections are tested against an alternative scenario in which the level of trend output is assumed to be one percentage point lower than in the central case. This addresses an important source of potential error, from misjudging the position of the economy in relation to the trend level of output. Chart 2.5 illustrates the projections for this cautious case and shows that the cyclically-adjusted balance will be in surplus at the end of the projection period.

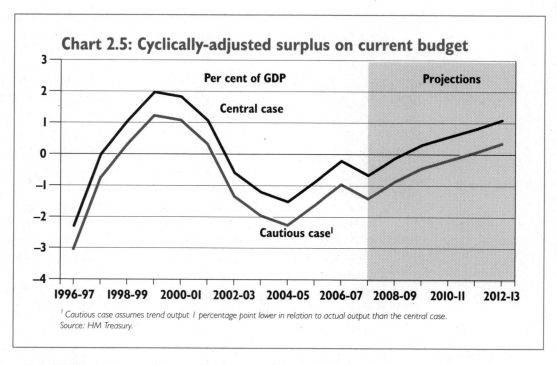

Chart 2.5: Cyclically-adjusted surplus on current budget

Per cent of GDP

Central case

Projections

Cautious case[1]

1996-97 1998-99 2000-01 2002-03 2004-05 2006-07 2008-09 2010-11 2012-13

[1] Cautious case assumes trend output 1 percentage point lower in relation to actual output than the central case.
Source: HM Treasury.

LONG-TERM FISCAL SUSTAINABILITY

2.44   While a key objective of fiscal policy is to ensure sound public finances over the short and medium term, the Government must also ensure that fiscal policy decisions are sustainable in the long term. Failure to do so would see financial burdens shifted to future generations, with detrimental effects on long-term growth. It would also be inconsistent with the principles of fiscal management set out in the *Code for fiscal stability*.

2.45   Since 2002 the Government has published the Long-term public finance report on an annual basis to provide a comprehensive analysis of long-term socio-economic and demographic developments, and their likely impact on the public finances, based on the most up to date information available. The population projections provided by the Office for National Statistics (ONS) are central to this analysis. Given that the ONS will publish its 2006-based population projections on 23 October, the next Long-term public finance report will be published at a later date.

2.46   The most recent assessment, published in the 2006 *Long-term public finance report*, shows that the UK fiscal position is sustainable over the long term. The UK is in a strong position relative to other developed countries to face the challenges of an ageing society. A further discussion of long-term fiscal sustainability is included in Annex B.

3 TRANSFORMING PUBLIC SERVICES

> Over the last ten years the Government has laid the foundations for improved public services – with sustained investment, more frontline professionals, increased efficiency and rigorous performance management raising standards and outcomes across the board. The challenge now is to continue this progress by creating world-class public services that respond to people's rising aspirations and equip the UK for global change.
>
> The 2007 Comprehensive Spending Review therefore launches a new strategy for transforming public services over the decade ahead, focused on:
>
> - **driving forward the next stage of reform**, including through a new performance management framework which defines the Government's top 30 priorities for the coming period, and empowers the public and frontline professionals to shape the services needed to deliver excellent outcomes and experiences for all;
>
> - **investing in Britain's future**, with total public spending over the CSR07 period rising from £589 billion in 2007-08 to £678 billion in 2010-11 – an average increase of 2.1 per cent a year in real terms consistent with the fiscal rules – enabling further investment in the Government's priorities of education, health, transport, the Olympics, security and housing. Within these plans the continued strength of the UK's public finances have enabled an addition of £2 billion to the plans set at Budget 2007 to take forward vital capital investment in public services;
>
> - **embedding value for money** across government – with savings of at least 3 per cent a year over the CSR07 period, releasing £30 billion by 2010-11 to reinvest in further improvements in key public services, building on the success of the SR04 efficiency programme and implementing the results of a series of zero-based reviews of spending in each department.

The Government's goals for public services

3.1   Excellent public services are at the heart of the Government's vision of a society in which economic prosperity is underpinned by social justice, providing stability, security and opportunity for all. High quality education and training, a modern health service, a fair and effective criminal justice system and a fast and reliable transport network provide the essential foundations for a flexible economy and a fair society, equipped to meet the global challenges ahead. To deliver this vision, the Government is committed to public services that deliver three mutually reinforcing goals:

- first, **excellent outcomes for all** – unlocking the talent and potential of every individual by providing first class education and skills, ensuring people are healthy and cared for, and ensuring all citizens live in safe, secure and thriving communities;

- second, **excellent personal experiences for all** – meeting rising expectations by matching the standards offered by the best of the private sector, with flexible, personalised, tailored public services that treat people with care, respect personal preferences and appreciate the value of people's time; and

- third, **value for money for the taxpayer** – ensuring that world-class public services are not just pursued through increased spending alone, but by targeting resources on the most effective policies, reforming delivery to raise productivity and increase efficiency wherever possible – thereby ensuring sustainable levels of public spending which entrench macroeconomic stability and maintain the UK's competitive position in the global economy.

Progress over the last decade

Sustained investment in public services 3.2 Ten years ago the Government began its programme of public service transformation with the launch of the first Comprehensive Spending Review (CSR) – a fundamental and in-depth examination of public spending to re-focus resources on its urgent priorities such as health and education. Building on the platform of stability provided by the new macroeconomic and fiscal frameworks described in Chapter 2, the 1998 CSR and subsequent Spending Reviews in 2000, 2002 and 2004 delivered sustained increases in spending for key public services, tackling the legacy of decades of under-investment. This year, compared with 1997-98:

- spending on the National Health Service is nearly 90 per cent higher in real terms;

- total spending on education is over 60 per cent higher in real terms, and as a proportion of GDP has risen from 4.5 to 5.5 per cent – from one of the lowest in the industrialised world to among the highest;

- public expenditure on transport is over 60 per cent higher in real terms; and

- spending on the police, criminal justice system and wider public order and safety is over 50 per cent higher in real terms.

3.3 These increases in spending have been made possible by the stable and sustainable economic growth described in the last chapter, with falling debt interest payments and low unemployment releasing resources for key priorities, as illustrated by Chart 3.1.

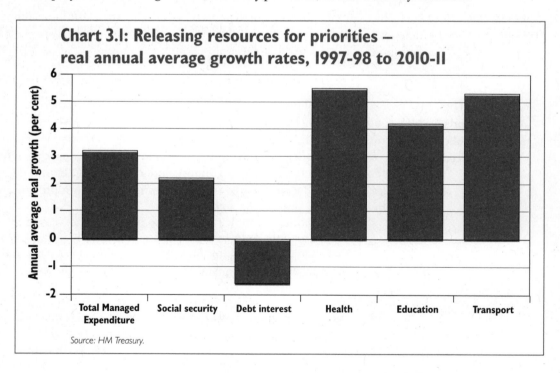

Chart 3.1: Releasing resources for priorities – real annual average growth rates, 1997-98 to 2010-11

Source: HM Treasury.

Building the 3.4 This additional investment has been matched by a series of steps to reform the public
framework for spending and performance management frameworks, driving improvements in outcomes
delivery and increasing value for money:

- the 1998 CSR set for the first time fixed, three-year budgets for all departments, separated into resource and capital spending, removing the previous bias against investment and enabling public services to plan for the long term. Departments were given full end-year flexibility to carry forward any underspends from one year to the next to help prevent wasteful end-year surges in spending. The 1998 CSR also saw the introduction of the first systematic, transparent, outcome-focused performance management system for public services, in the form of Public Service Agreements (PSAs);

- the 2000 and 2002 Spending Reviews saw the introduction of Resource Accounting and Budgeting to capture accurately the full cost of running public services and sharpen asset management incentives. They also saw further improvements to the PSA framework and targets, including the introduction of selected value for money targets within PSAs and formal monitoring of PSA delivery; and

- the 2004 Spending Review represented the first systematic attempt to drive operational efficiencies across the public sector through the review led by Sir Peter Gershon, focusing on key processes that are common across government and bringing the performance of all delivery units up to the level of the best.

Improvements in 3.5 By matching this sustained growth in spending with ambitious reforms to support the
frontline services efficiency, delivery and accountability of public services, the Government has been able to
raise standards and achieve major improvements in outcomes across key services:

- deaths from cancer have fallen by 14 per cent, and from heart disease by 31 per cent. In total, over 200,000 lives have been saved since 1996 as a result of reductions to mortality rates from cancer and circulatory diseases among people aged under 75;

- in education, over 58 per cent of 16 year olds now achieve five or more good GCSEs, up from 45 per cent in 1997, with some of the biggest improvements seen in disadvantaged areas with a history of low achievement;

- the number of offences brought to justice has increased by 40 per cent in the last five years, overall crime has fallen by around a third in the last ten years, the fear of crime has reduced and re-offending rates fell by 6.9 per cent between 1997 and 2004; and

- the transport system is improving, with over 100 road schemes completed, people travelling further by rail than in any year since the 1940s and bus use increasing year on year for the first time in decades.

The next decade

3.6 While much has been achieved in the past decade, the context in which public services operate is changing rapidly, becoming increasingly challenging and complex. The social, economic and environmental trends affecting the UK are generating new pressures on public services, and these developments together with the achievements of the past ten years are generating rising expectations from the public.

2007
Comprehensive
Spending Review

3.7 To ensure that public services are ready to respond to these challenges, over the last two years the Government has been consulting with frontline professionals, outside experts and the public to prepare for a second Comprehensive Spending Review, which a decade on from the first CSR lays the foundations for the transformation of the UK's public services over the next ten years. The departmental spending plans and priorities set by the 2007 CSR for the years 2008-09, 2009-10 and 2010-11 are described in detail in the chapters that follow. This chapter sets out the overarching strategy for the delivery of these priorities, consisting of three strands:

- **driving forward the next stage of reform,** including through a new performance management framework which defines the Government's top 30 priorities for the coming period, and empowers the public and frontline professionals to shape the services needed to deliver excellent outcomes and experiences for all;

- **investing in Britain's future,** focusing sustained additional resources on the key services that are crucial to meet long-term challenges and tackle the barriers to individual fulfilment and economic success; and

- **embedding value for money** in departmental expenditure planning, building on the SR04 efficiency programme with more ambitious reforms to release £30 billion of savings by 2010-11 to reinvest in further improvements in public services.

DRIVING FORWARD THE NEXT STAGE OF REFORM

The changing
context for
public services

3.8 Over the last decade far-reaching social, economic and technological changes have transformed the environment in which public services operate. An ageing population, changing patterns of work and family life, globalisation, technological innovations such as the internet and other developments are creating new and rising demands on a range of public services including childcare, education and training, and health and social care.

3.9 There have also been substantial changes in public attitudes and expectations. As real incomes have grown – the benefit of a strong and stable economy – so too have people's expectations of public services. Across the economy standards of service have improved enormously, the result of rising disposable incomes and intensifying competition for businesses. Opening hours fit around the needs of the customer, new methods of payment and delivery have been created, and a much greater focus is placed on high quality customer service.

3.10 People are therefore now accustomed to much greater choice and control over their lives. Higher educational levels mean they are better equipped to exercise this choice, less likely to accept advice without question and less likely to allow others to make choices on their behalf. With the advent of the internet and other new media, people now have immediate and unfettered access to information on virtually any topic that interests them. The old divides between producers and users, experts and amateurs, are being broken down and blurred. Public services need to be ready to respond to these trends.

3.11 Alongside these responsibilities for government, citizens will also need to take on a more active and responsible role themselves in order to fulfil their aspirations and meet the challenges of the decade ahead. For example, in order to tackle climate change, regulation and investment by the Government will be crucial, but not sufficient unless individuals also act with greater environmental and social responsibility in the way they use resources. Likewise, public investment in education and training will not be enough to meet the challenges of an increasingly competitive global economy unless individuals also take responsibility for upgrading their own skills and seeking out new career opportunities. Collaborative action is a key theme for the Government's policy and reform agenda over the CSR07 period.

Principles for the next stage of reform

3.12   In order to create the conditions in which better public service outcomes are forged in partnership with citizens, the Government is building a new model of public service delivery for the next decade based on three key principles:

- **setting a clear focus on ambitious priorities,** consulting with the public and professionals to define the key goals for the next ten years in order to respond to the challenges facing the UK, and ensuring the resources and policies are in place to deliver these ambitions;

- **putting users at the heart of services,** through new channels of engagement that help the publlic shape services; new mechanisms to deliver accountability, including greater use of real-time data; new opportunities for people to exercise choice in how to access and tailor their services, coupled with clear responsibilities for all; and

- **freeing up the frontline to drive public service improvements,** placing greater trust in those delivering services to respond to the priorities of individual areas, communities and citizens.

The new performance management framework

3.13   Since their introduction in the 1998 CSR, Public Service Agreements (PSAs) have played a vital role in ensuring that the sustained increases in resources have been translated into higher standards across public services and led to major improvements in outcomes. But the challenges of the next decade are different, and so following extensive consultation with the public and frontline professionals over the last two years the Government has decided to make a decisive shift in the way it sets its priorities and drives performance. **The 2007 CSR therefore announces a new performance management framework based on a stronger relationship with public sector professionals, with a streamlined set of 30 new PSAs setting the Government's priority outcomes for the CSR07 period.** Box 3.1 describes the key elements of the new framework.

> **Box 3.1: The new performance management framework**
>
> The new performance management framework consists of the following elements:
>
> * a streamlined set of 30 new Public Service Agreements (PSAs), which articulate the Government's highest priority outcomes for the CSR07 period and span departmental boundaries, setting out a shared vision and leading collaboration at all levels in the delivery system;
>
> * a single Delivery Agreement for each PSA, developed in consultation with frontline workers and the public, and published to strengthen accountability and ownership across organisational boundaries;
>
> * new Cabinet Committees announced in July which will play a key role in driving performance on cross-government PSAs by regularly monitoring progress and holding departments and programmes to account. The Government is also examining the scope for building PSAs explicitly into the performance management framework for the civil service – ensuring a relentless focus on PSA delivery in Whitehall;
>
> * a small basket of national, outcome-focused indicators to support each PSA, ensuring robust and transparent performance measurement alongside genuine rationalisation, with a significant reduction in the overall number of priority indicators attached to PSAs;
>
> * targets used where appropriate to deliver improved performance and accountability; with nationally set targets reserved for a small subset of PSA indicators that require firm central direction, and far greater space for increased local target setting;
>
> * a more comprehensive approach to performance monitoring, with each department publishing a set of Departmental Strategic Objectives (DSOs) for the CSR07 period, alongside the smaller, prioritised set of PSAs. This will for the first time bring all performance monitoring into a single framework, covering both the Government's highest priorities (PSAs) and the wider span of departmental business; and
>
> * across the whole framework, a premium on the use of high quality, timely data while freeing up the frontline by reducing low value data burdens.
>
> The full set of PSAs and their indicators are set out in Annex C.

3.14 The new framework creates the conditions for public services to work collaboratively in delivering excellent outcomes and excellent experiences for all. By prioritising a radically reduced set of PSA indicators and rationalising the use of targets attached to PSAs, the new framework will allow more space to deliver innovative and flexible services, with a greater role for local communities to focus action on their priorities. The changes represent a new balance of accountability where central co-ordination works in synergy with greater direct accountability to service users and local communities; citizens' personal experiences of services will increasingly shape design, delivery and measurement of success; and staff in the public sector will be empowered – respecting their skills and professionalism – to respond to citizens' needs.

3.15 Alongside reforms to the national framework, the Government has agreed a single, aligned framework for the performance management of outcomes delivered by local government working alone or in partnership, with a much smaller and more focused set of 198 performance indicators, down from an estimated 1,200. The new set of indicators will be published by the Secretary of State for Communities and Local Government, and includes all relevant PSA and DSO outcomes, replacing the range of current issue-specific performance indicator sets and reducing the reporting burden for local authorities. Local authorities and their partners will shortly begin negotiating new Local Area Agreements, with designated local improvement targets for up to 35[1] of the indicators from the national set. The Government will not mandate targets for any Local Area Agreement, so even where targets are set out for PSAs at national level, local areas will have the flexibility to respond to these national ambitions in the most appropriate way, in negotiation with regional Government Offices.

Reducing data burdens   **3.16**   The availability of good quality, timely data at all levels is critical to drive strong accountability and improved outcomes in public services. Alongside reforms to the performance management framework, the Government will take steps to ensure that all data it requests from the frontline is proportionate, appropriate and collected efficiently. To reduce unnecessary burdens on the frontline, the Government is announcing a commitment to reduce by 30 per cent by 2010 the total amount of data that central departments and agencies request from the frontline. With work led by the Better Regulation Executive, this commitment will be delivered through departmental simplification plans, which are already being used successfully to reduce administrative burdens on businesses.

Empowering the workforce and public to shape services

3.17   At the heart of the Government's programme of public service reform for the CSR07 period are new plans to ensure the public has a greater say in the design, delivery and governance of their services, giving them more control over and responsibility for their outcomes in health, education and other key areas. This will be accompanied by steps to give frontline professionals greater opportunities and more power to shape service delivery and respond to the needs of the public, including through the reforms to the performance management framework outlined above. Bringing the public and workforce together in this way will help contribute to greater innovation and efficiency, improved outcomes and higher levels of customer satisfaction and staff motivation. This vision will be realised by:

- **strengthening people's voice in service provision** – for example through the roll-out of Parent Councils in schools and the establishment of local involvement networks allowing clients to express their views on their needs and experiences of health and social care services; and through new participatory budgeting pilots to involve communities directly in decisions over how to prioritise local budgets on the issues that matter most to them;

- **driving forward the personalisation of services** to ensure they more effectively meet the particular needs and preferences of different individuals. Following the Gilbert Review, schools will extend the provision of personalised learning so that teachers can tailor support to each student's specific learning goals. Individualised budgets for social care will be rolled out, giving people greater ability to shape their own care packages;

- **enabling service providers and the public to work collaboratively together** to shape positive outcomes – for example by rolling out the Expert Patient Programme across the NHS that enables patients and frontline professionals to work together in improving management of chronic illnesses;

---

[1] Plus 17 statutory early years target for DCSF.

- enhancing the accountability of local services, for example, neighbourhood charters will allow local citizens and service providers to agree on expected levels of service and provide mechanisms for users to hold service providers to account;

- reaching out to all of society by improving approaches that engage hard-to-reach groups, harnessing third sector expertise where appropriate. The Government will develop a more flexible approach to New Deal, with support tailored to meet the individual needs of long-term benefit claimants, lone parents, and incapacity benefit claimants. The views of local communities will be better represented in the delivery of justice, through Community Legal Advice Centres and Community Justice Centres, delivered in partnership with third sector organisations; and

- working with individuals and businesses to encourage behavioural changes that benefit them and society – for example, the Healthy Schools Programme will be rolled out, encouraging healthy eating and active lifestyles to help reduce childhood obesity. To tackle the problem of climate change, the Government will improve information about the steps individuals can take to reduce their energy consumption, introducing a web-based personal emissions calculator and providing advice on green electricity and gas tariffs.

Transforming service delivery

3.18   The investment and reforms of the last decade have raised standards of delivery across individual public services. The challenge now is for more radical cross-government reform that will be the foundation of personalised public services. This means moving away from the old model of service provision which meets the public's various needs through a number of separate government agencies, each with their own interactions with customers. This compartmentalisation of delivery means that, to date, the Government has struggled to keep pace with the expectations set by the leading edge of the new service economy that has emerged over the last decade, which, by focusing on the totality of the relationship with the customer is able to deliver more immediate and convenient services with less intrusion on their time.

3.19   The Prime Minister has appointed Sir David Varney, former Executive Chairman of HMRC and Chairman of O2, to advise the Government how to meet this challenge and put in place the vision set out in his report on Service Transformation.[2] The Government recognises that succeeding in this aim, and securing a cross-departmental commitment to build services around the needs of citizens and businesses, will be integral to the achievement of each of the PSA outcomes set in the 2007 CSR. In order to deliver this, the Government is publishing for the first time a Service Transformation Agreement, which underpins delivery of the whole of the new PSA framework. The Agreement sets out an ambitious programme of reforms which will be taken forward across government as part of the PSA framework, including:

- piloting a new 'Tell Us Once' service that enables citizens to inform public services just once about changes of circumstances, starting with bereavement;

- rationalising the plethora of government websites by closing down the

---

[2] Service Transformation: A better service for citizens and businesses, a better deal for taxpayers, December 2006, available at www.hm-treasury.gov.uk.

majority and moving their citizen and business content to the Government's two single access websites, Directgov and Businesslink.gov.uk, thereby giving customers access to the information and services they need with greater speed and ease;

- requiring all publicly funded call-centres to undergo formal published accreditation to ensure faster and better services for citizens and businesses;

- reducing avoidable or duplicated contacts with call centres and local offices;

- empowering individuals to influence their services, with greater opportunities and direct involvement to influence the way they are designed and delivered; and

- improving management of information and identity across the Government's delivery systems to reduce wasted time and inconvenience for citizens, businesses and frontline workers.

3.20   In addition, the Service Transformation Agreement commits all departments to specific plans for transforming the services they provide across all delivery channels, coordinating with other departments where relevant. Examples of the initiatives that are being developed include the Driver and Vehicle Licensing Agency (DVLA) and Department for Work and Pensions (DWP) working to merge the application processes for driving licences and National Insurance numbers; DWP, HM Revenue and Customs (HMRC) and some local councils developing a single transaction approach for working age benefits, housing benefit and tax credit; and HMRC and the Department for Environment Food and Rural Affairs (Defra) working to develop an International Trade Single Window to enable traders or their agents to submit all regulatory information required in a single message that can then be shared by the relevant government departments. Local government will also play a vital role in delivering this agenda, including on reducing avoidable contact which has been included in the new National Indicator Set.

3.21   The Minister for the Cabinet Office, who chairs the new Cabinet Committee on Public Engagement and Delivery, and the Chief Secretary to the Treasury will hold departments to account for delivery of these commitments as part of the overall performance management framework, and will continue to identify new opportunities for transforming services over the CSR07 period and beyond.

INVESTING IN BRITAIN'S FUTURE

The fiscal   **3.22**   Continued investment will be needed in key areas in order to underpin this new
framework   model of public service delivery and meet the long-term challenges facing the UK. The last decade has shown how it is possible to deliver a strong economy and sound public finances at the same time as sustained investment in public services. The Government's fiscal rules have been central to this achievement, and will continue to provide the framework for the CSR07 period, ensuring that the public finances are prudently managed over the economic cycle and that spending and taxation impact fairly between generations – removing the past discrimination against capital spending and ensuring that borrowing for investment is conducted in a sustainable way. This framework has helped protect significant increases in the level of public sector net investment from $\frac{1}{2}$ per cent of GDP in 1997-98 to 2.1 per cent of GDP this year – addressing the backlog of under-investment in public services and putting in place some of the vital infrastructure required to promote the UK's economic growth and productivity.

Spending plans for the CSR07 period

3.23   The challenges of the decade ahead require a balance to be struck between delivering further investment in public services to equip the country for change, while entrenching the macroeconomic stability that is essential in the increasingly competitive global economy. Budget 2007 set out the overall spending envelope for the CSR07 period, locking in the historic increases in investment since 1997 while allowing total public spending to increase by an average of 2 per cent per year in real terms. Having assessed the future investment needs of the country, the continued strength of the UK's public finances with net debt remaining below 39 per cent throughout the forecast period, enables **the Government to announce an addition of £2 billion to total public sector net investment in 2010-11,** to take forward vital capital investment in public infrastructure. With this addition, total public spending over the CSR07 period will rise from £589 billion in 2007-08 to £678 billion in 2010-11, an average increase of 2.1 per cent a year in real terms, with:

- current spending increasing by an average of 1.9 per cent per year in real terms; and

- net investment rising to $2\frac{1}{4}$ per cent of GDP.

Table 3.1: CSR07 spending envelopes

	£ billion			
	Estimate	Spending Plans		
	2007-08	2008-09	2009-10	20010-11
Total Managed Expenditure				
Budget 2007	586.6	615	644	674
Effect of neutral classification and depreciation changes to TME[1]	*2.1*	*2.0*	*2.2*	*2.5*
Discretionary policy additions[2]	*0.4*	*0.0*	*0.0*	*2.0*
CSR 07	589.2	617.4	646.6	678.3
of which public sector current expenditure	*541.2*	*566.0*	*592.5*	*620.3*
of which public sector net investment	*29.7*	*32.3*	*33.9*	*36.7*
of which depreciation	*18.3*	*19.1*	*20.2*	*21.2*

[1] Includes changes to take account of the inclusion by the Office of National Statistics of imputed subsidies from Local Authorities to the Housing Revenue Account within public spending and changes to depreciation that reduce TME but leave net investment and current spending unaffected.

[2] Includes additional public sector net investment in 2010-11 and addition to the Special Reserve in 2007-08.

Setting the CSR07 DEL envelope

3.24   Within these overall envelopes, the 2007 CSR sets out the forecast for Annually Managed Expenditure (AME), consistent with the economic assumptions and policy decisions included in this report, and fixes firm departmental spending plans for the years 2008-09, 2009-10 and 2010-11. Table 3.2 sets out real growth over the CSR07 period in AME and Departmental Expenditure Limits (DEL) both of which grow at 2.1% per year on average. A detailed breakdown of the AME forecast is set out in Annex B.

Table 3.2: CSR07 DEL envelope

	£ billion				Annual
	Estimate	Spending Plans			Average Real
	2007-08	2008-09	2009-10	2010-11	Growth
Departmental Expenditure Limits	344.6	361.1	377.5	396.9	2.1%
Annually Managed Expenditure	244.6	256.4	269.2	281.4	2.1%
Total Managed Expenditure	589.2	617.4	646.6	678.3	2.1%

Investing in priorities

3.25 Together with the resources released from the Government's ambitious value for money programme for the CSR07 period, described in more detail below, these increases in departmental spending will enable the Government to sustain the pace of improvement in public services and focus additional resources on its key long-term priorities, including:

- meeting the challenge of globalisation by investing in the human and physical capital that will keep the UK economy competitive over the long term, with additional spending by 2010-11 of £14.5 billion on education, £900 million on science and £3.6 billion on transport;

- making the UK a better place to live by continuing to improve the NHS with further investment of £19 billion by 2010-11 and progressing towards its objective of decent and affordable housing for all, with total spending on new housing of at least £8 billion over the next three years, a 50 per cent increase;

- protecting the nation from external and internal threats, with total spending on counter-terrorism and intelligence rising from £2.5 billion in 2007-08 to £3.5 billion in 2010-11 and continuing the longest period of sustained real increases in defence expenditure in over 25 years; and

- ensuring a lasting cultural and sporting legacy for the nation by investing £3.6 billion in the construction costs of the Olympics over the CSR07 period, with further funding to be confirmed in subsequent spending reviews.

Improving transparency and accountability

3.26 As announced in *The Governance of Britain Green Paper*,[3] the Government intends to strengthen Parliament's ability to hold Ministers to account for public spending by ensuring that it reports to Parliament in a more consistent fashion, in line with the fiscal rules, on departmental budgets set in Spending Reviews, in annual Estimates and in resource accounts. The Government will be consulting Parliament and others with an interest on how best to take forward this reform, with the aim of introducing changes before the end of the CSR07 period.

3.27 Budget 2007 announced that from 2008-09 the annual accounts of government departments and other public sector bodies would be prepared using International Financial Reporting Standards (IFRS), adapted as necessary for the public sector. The Government is developing an IFRS-based Financial Reporting Manual for the public sector and considering how best to manage the transition. Where necessary, IFRS standards may be adapted for the public sector to support the Government's wider aim of improving transparency from the fiscal rules through budgets, Estimates and accounts.

---

[3] *The Governance of Britain*, Ministry of Justice, July 2007, available at www.justice.gov.uk.

[4] *Releasing resources for the frontline: Independent Review of Public Sector Efficiency*, July 2004, available at www.hm-treasury.gov.uk.

EMBEDDING VALUE FOR MONEY

SR04 Efficiency Programme

3.28 The Government recognises that additional resources alone are not enough to secure excellent and modern public services. Increased investment must be matched by an unwavering commitment to maximise the value of every pound of taxpayers' money. Sir Peter Gershon's Independent Review of Public Sector Efficiency in 2004[4] marked a major step forward in embedding value for money into the planning and delivery of public services. In line with his recommendations, and as part of the 2004 Spending Review, the Government set an aim to achieve annual efficiency gains of £21.5 billion by 2007-08, alongside significant reductions and relocations in the civil service and public sector workforce. The programme remains on track to deliver these goals, with departments and local authorities reporting at the end of June 2007:

- annual efficiency gains of over £20 billion, meaning that the Government has achieved the high-level ambition set out by the Gershon review, and is on track to deliver the goal of £21.5 billion by the end of March 2008, as agreed by departments at the 2004 Spending Review;

- gross reductions of over 79,000 civil service and administrative and support-related military posts towards the target of 84,150, with over 13,000 of these reallocated to frontline roles; and

- continued progress against the ambitions of the Lyons Review, with 13,300 public sector posts relocated away from London and the South East to destinations like Sheffield, to which over 1,000 posts have been moved since the programme began.

3.29 As the National Audit Office noted earlier this year,[5] the programme is having a clear positive impact on the efficiency of public services, with many examples of improvements in the way public services are being delivered, including:

- the Ministry of Defence has rolled out a single personnel management system for all three armed services, improving services to staff – for example by reducing the time taken for service personnel allowances to arrive in bank accounts from six weeks to six days – and saving over £45 million a year;

- better management of patient admissions has reduced the average length of hospital stay, cutting costs by over £500 million a year and freeing up over 1 million bed days to treat more patients, more quickly; and

- the Department for Transport has achieved over £60 million of efficiency gains by switching services to online channels, such as the booking of driving tests, with the convenience of being available 24 hours a day.

---

[4] *Releasing resources for the frontline: Independent Review of Public Sector Efficiency*, July 2004, available at www.hm-treasury.gov.uk.

[5] *The Efficiency Programme: A Second Review of Progress*, NAO, February 2007, available at www.nao.org.uk.

Value for money in the 2007 CSR

3.30 Building on the achievements of the SR04 efficiency programme, the Government has developed a more ambitious and far-reaching value for money programme for the CSR07 period – releasing the resources needed to sustain the pace of public service improvement and meet the global challenges of the decade ahead. As part of this programme the Government has:

- deepened the government-wide efficiency programme in the operational areas established by the Gershon Review, harnessing the benefits of greater collaboration across organisations and engaging with frontline professionals to identify opportunities for service improvements;

- conducted a series of zero-based reviews of departments' baseline expenditure, taking a radical look at the way that government spends money on policies and programmes ten years on from the first CSR;

- provided over £1 billion in modernisation funding to help departments meet the up-front costs associated with the implementation of their value for money programme;

- integrated pay and workforce planning more closely into departments CSR07 preparations, to ensure that pay spending represents value for money for taxpayers and supports macroeconomic stability; and

- improving the management of the public sector asset base to underpin service delivery, taking forward the recommendations of the Lyons Review of Asset Management.

3.31 Each department has bought the elements together into a coherent and comprehensive strategy for improving services and driving value for money gains over the full range of their activities in the CSR07 period, enabling the Government to commit to:

- at least 3 per cent value for money savings per year over the CSR period across central and local government, all net of implementation costs, cash-releasing and totalling over £30 billion of annual savings by 2010-11, thereby maximising the resources available to improve frontline services and fund new priorities;

- 5 per cent annual real reductions in administration budgets across departments, as a successor to the SR04 workforce reduction target and thereby ensuring significant additional resources are redirected to public service delivery; and

- the release of £30 billion from fixed asset disposals between 2004-05 and 2010-11 as well as further funds from the sale of financial assets for reinvestment in new infrastructure.

Box 3.2: Examples from the CSR07 value for money programme

- Alongside increased investment, the NHS is delivering savings of at least £8.2 billion a year by 2010-11, including up to £500 million from improving community-based services so that people with long-term conditions can receive greater support in the community; £1.5 billion by reducing variations in productivity across the NHS through the use of new technologies and sharing best practice; and £1 billion from improved procurement practices.

- HM Court Service's Business Strategy aims to generate savings of around £100 million by 2010-11 through reforms aimed at placing the public at the centre of court operations, with services designed around their needs. HMCS aims to build on existing success in managing court caseloads by enabling better case progression through improved technology, introducing simpler, more proportionate procedures for the simplest cases and diverting cases that should not come to court to other methods of resolution.

- HMRC will generate total savings of £673 million by March 2011 through a programme of modernisation and reform across the department. £125 million of these savings will be achieved by investing in a modern, high capacity IT infrastructure to support higher take-up of online services, more efficient processing and communication of information and better risk-based compliance checks. In addition, the department will extend the use of lean processing techniques to make more efficient use of resources and undertake a major consolidation and transformation of HMRC's estate to release £280 million annual savings by 2010-11.

- The FCO has developed plans to save at least £22 million a year by 2010-11 by sharing services with other public bodies at home and overseas, including increased co-location with DFID.

Monitoring CSR07 savings 3.32 The SR04 efficiency programme has demonstrated the importance of public accountability as a powerful driver for improved value for money. By the end of the year, departments will publish value for money Delivery Agreements setting out how they will achieve their proposed savings, and departments will monitor and report on progress throughout the CSR07 period. Reflecting the higher level of ambition in the CSR07 programme, the new monitoring and reporting framework will put more emphasis on mainstreaming value for money into core departmental business, including through stronger integration with the PSA framework. Greater accountability will therefore be devolved to departments, with common requirements for reporting progress to the public to ensure rigour and consistency. The Government also expects that the National Audit Office will play an important role in reviewing reported savings, providing Parliament and the public with a further level of assurance.

Administration budgets 3.33 By harnessing the potential of new technologies and increasing efficiency in the running of departmental business, the Government will be able to make further progress in reducing the proportion of taxpayers' money that is spent on administrative functions within departments and the core civil service. Having frozen administration budgets in nominal terms over the 2004 Spending Review period to ensure that all additional expenditure went directly to frontline services, the Government will go further over the CSR07 period with 5 per cent annual real reductions in administration budgets across all departments, releasing over £1.2 billion by 2010-11 for investment in priority areas and reducing the running costs of central government to a record low as a percentage of public spending.

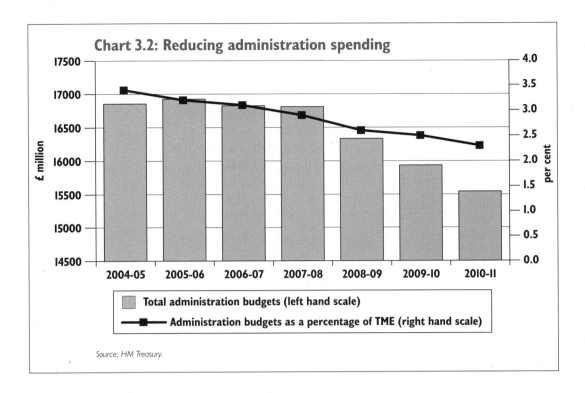

Chart 3.2: Reducing administration spending

Total administration budgets (left hand scale)

Administration budgets as a percentage of TME (right hand scale)

Source: HM Treasury.

Pay and workforce planning

3.34 The Government's commitment to high quality public services can only be realised through the skills and dedication of public sector workers. Over the last ten years the Government has therefore sought to increase the number of frontline professionals, with 36,000 more doctors than in 1997, 79,000 more nurses, 35,000 more teachers and 102,000 more teaching assistants. Training has been improved and pay increased significantly to reflect the crucial contribution of public service professionals to the country. The competitiveness of the public sector reward package, which includes valuable pension benefits, is demonstrated by healthy levels of recruitment and retention.

3.35 Over the CSR07 period, the Government is committed to continuing to support public sector professionals in their efforts to deliver the best possible public services, with departments taking forward their workforce planning for the CSR07 period consistent with the following objectives:

- maintaining macroeconomic stability in order to promote growth and employment, with public sector pay settlements consistent with the achievement of the Government's inflation target of 2 per cent, as set out in more detail in Chapter 2;

- ensuring total pay bills represent value for money and are affordable within departments' overall expenditure plans, taking into account other spending that is key to service improvements and the ability of staff to do a good job, such as equipment and new technologies; and

- maintaining the necessary levels of recruitment and retention needed to support service delivery, taking into account the wider labour market conditions relevant to the public sector.

Improving asset management

3.36   Public investment in infrastructure is crucial both to underpin the delivery of high quality public services and to help increase the flexibility and productivity of the wider economy. In order to take full advantage of the sustained investment over the past decade, the 2007 CSR will introduce a more strategic approach to the management of public assets, driving better value for money and supporting improvements in frontline services. Each department is therefore developing an asset management strategy, to be published by the end of the year, which will ensure that:

- assets are adequately maintained and efficiently utilised to deliver high performing public services;

- future investment decisions are based on a more complete assessment of the condition and performance of the existing asset base; and

- there are plans in place for the disposal of surplus assets no longer required for service delivery.

3.37   A key tool for helping to improve asset management practice is the updated National Asset Register, which was published in January 2007. The Register provides information on the assets held by over 370 different government bodies, constituting the most comprehensive list of central government assets and maintaining the UK's position at the forefront of international best practice in public sector asset management.

3.38   The Government remains ahead of schedule to deliver its ambition to dispose of £30 billion of surplus fixed assets between 2004-05 and 2010-11, having already sold £18.3 billion for reinvestment in new equipment and infrastructure by March 2007. In addition, the Government is taking forward the sale of its financial assets, such as student loans, where private ownership delivers better value for money. Planned asset sales for the forthcoming period include:

- the Ministry of Defence is in the process of selling Chelsea Barracks, the proceeds from which will be reinvested to improve Armed Forces accommodation;

- the Department for Transport plans to dispose of land and buildings held by the Highways Agency, Channel Tunnel Rail Link and the British Railways Board (Residuary) Ltd;

- the Ministry of Justice is developing plans to rationalise land and buildings held by Her Majesty's Court Service, with the proceeds recycled into its courts modernisation programme; and

- over the CSR07 period the Department of Health will release over £500 million for reinvestment in the NHS through the disposal of surplus property.

3.39   Box 3.3 sets out the Government's approach to improving procurement to support public service delivery, including through the Private Finance Initiative.

---

[6] *Transforming Government Procurement*, HMT, January 2007, available at, www.hm-treasury.gov.uk.

Private Finance Initiative

3.40   The Private Finance Initiative (PFI) plays a small but important role in the Government's investment in public services. Approximately 600 PFI projects have been signed, with a total capital value of £56.9 billion, and public authorities report a high level of user satisfaction. Over £10 billion worth of projects have been signed in the last 18 months. Full details of the PFI programme are published in the supplementary charts and tables.

3.41   PFI projects worth a total of £22.2 billion are expected to reach financial close before April 2011. The Government believes PFI should continue to form a significant part of its strategy for delivering high quality public services, alongside a broader range of traditional and alternative procurement models depending on the circumstances. For the CSR07 period the Government has allocated a total PFI Credit envelope of £10.9 billion. Consistent with this allocation, the Government will continue to pursue PFI projects where they demonstrate value for money, alongside conventional capital programmes.

4 SUSTAINABLE GROWTH AND PROSPERITY

> Over the last decade there have been significant increases in both employment and productivity, but the growing movement of people, investment and goods is increasing the pace of change in the global economy. Rapid technological change and the emergence of newly industrialised economies are also driving shifts in the competitive environment. The Government is committed to equipping the UK to respond to these changes and focusing reform on the drivers of productivity through:
>
> - **increasing spending by the Department for Innovation, Universities and Skills on higher education and skills from £14.2 billion in 2007-08 to £16.4 billion by 2010-11** to implement the recommendations of the Leitch Review, developing a strong partnership with employers and individuals to deliver higher skills;
>
> - **increasing public investment in the science base from £5.4 billion in 2007-08 to £6.3 billion by 2010-11** to implement the recommendations of the Sainsbury Review. **Total public support for business innovation through the Technology Strategy amounting to over £1 billion** will ensure the UK's continued success in generating new ideas and using them in wealth creation;
>
> - **confirming a $2\frac{1}{4}$ per cent annual real increase in the Department for Transport's programme budget,** consistent with the Long Term Funding Guideline which is **extended to 2018-19.** This will continue renewal of the UK's transport infrastructure including the **funding package for Crossrail;**
>
> - **simplifying the tax system** to make it fairer and more efficient with the announcement of new principles, three reviews and a package of measures;
>
> - **simplifying business support** to reduce confusion and the time businesses spend understanding what support is available and accessing it, and to improve the quality, effectiveness and efficiency of schemes;
>
> - **supporting the private equity industry's moves to increase transparency and a number of measures to ensure that tax arrangements are sustainable and appropriate;** and
>
> - **allowing local authorities to invest in economic development through levying a local business rate supplement and focusing the strategic role for the Regional Development Agencies on economic growth** as announced in the *Review of sub-national economic development and regeneration.*

4.1 A decade ago, the Government set itself the objectives of achieving high and stable levels of growth and employment and narrowing the productivity gap with the UK's major competitors. Economies with periods of strong employment growth often see relatively low productivity growth particularly because new workers can be less productive as they gain new skills. By contrast, as shown in Chart 4.1, in the UK since 1997 there have been significant increases in both employment and productivity:

- employment has risen by more than 2.6 million since 1997. The Government has made good progress on increasing employment among disadvantaged groups – the employment rate for lone parents has risen by over 12 percentage points; by 6.4 percentage points for working-age people aged over 50; and by 9.8 percentage points for people with a health condition or disability; and

- the Government has made significant progress in raising the long-run rate of productivity growth, narrowing the productivity gap with its main industrialised competitors over this same period on both the productivity per worker and productivity per hour worked measures.

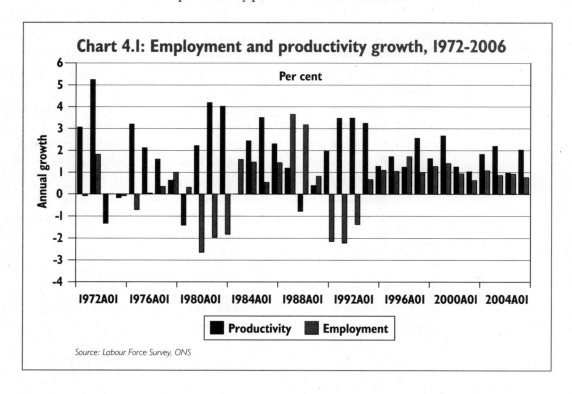

Chart 4.1: Employment and productivity growth, 1972-2006

Source: Labour Force Survey, ONS

4.2 Over the next decade, the pace of change in the global economy will intensify, with growing movement of people, investment and goods. Rapid technological change and newly industrialised economies will increase competition in the global economy, with knowledge and other intangible assets growing in importance in maintaining competitiveness. A recent HM Treasury Economic Working Paper,[1] described in Box A3, investigates the consequences for the measurement of productivity of treating spending on intangible assets as investment. It finds that traditional measurement techniques may underestimate the importance of investment in intangibles in driving productivity growth in recent years, highlighting the importance to the UK economy of science, innovation and knowledge-based industries.

4.3 Pressures on the climate and natural resources are also a key challenge facing the UK and the world. Environmental pressures have economic and social consequences, but tackling them also presents opportunities for business. *The Stern Review on the Economics of Climate Change* (October 2006) showed how the cost of tackling climate change with well-designed policies would be lower than the cost of dealing with the consequences of unchecked greenhouse gas emissions. Chapter 7 sets out the steps the Government is taking to ensure the economy is environmentally sustainable.

---

[1] *Intangible investment and Britain's productivity*, Treasury Economic Working Paper No.1, available at: www.hm-treasury.gov.uk

4.4   The Government is committed to equipping the UK to respond to these changes. Macroeconomic stability has provided the platform for investment and the UK has led the world in understanding and responding to the economic impact of climate change. World-class innovation and an attractive and competitive business environment are helping businesses take advantage of wider trade and rising living standards, while individuals are developing higher skills to take advantage of new opportunities.

Productivity **4.5**   The Government has contributed to raising UK productivity by pursuing microeconomic reforms to remove barriers preventing markets from working efficiently. These have been focused on the drivers of productivity. As part of the 2007 Comprehensive Spending Review **the Government announces a new Public Service Agreement (PSA) to raise the productivity of the UK economy** by:

- enhancing the skills of the UK workforce;

- investing in the UK science base and promoting innovation;

- modernising the UK's critical infrastructure;

- improving the business environment in the UK; and

- narrowing the productivity gap between the regions.

4.6   In June 2007 the Department for Innovation, Universities and Skills (DIUS) and the Department for Business, Enterprise and Regulatory Reform (BERR) were set up in recognition of the challenges and opportunities created by the changing global economy. DIUS brings together science, innovation, Higher Education and skills policies in recognition of the vital role that higher skills and university research play in driving innovation. BERR has responsibility for further improving the business environment and driving productivity through better regulation and competition. Details of their 2007 Comprehensive Spending Review settlements are set out later in this chapter and in Annex D.

WORKFORCE, SKILLS AND MIGRATION

4.7   The skills of the workforce are a key driver of the productivity of an economy. Improving the skills of individuals enables firms to improve products and processes, to adapt more quickly to changing competitive environments and to increase opportunities for innovation.

4.8   The UK's skills base has improved over recent years as reforms and investment have begun driving improvements. The skill level of young people joining the workforce is improving with 71.4 per cent of 19 year olds gaining at least a Level 2 qualification (achieving 5 GCSEs at grades A* to C) in 2006 compared with 66.3 per cent in 2004, and more young people than ever before participating in Higher Education. The number of young people participating in apprenticeships is at a record level with more than 250,000 now in learning – up from around 75,000 in 1997. Advances have also been made in the skill level of adults already in the workforce. Over 1.7 million adults have boosted their basic skills since 2001, and the proportion of people with no qualifications has fallen from 22 per cent in 1994 to 12.4 per cent in 2006.

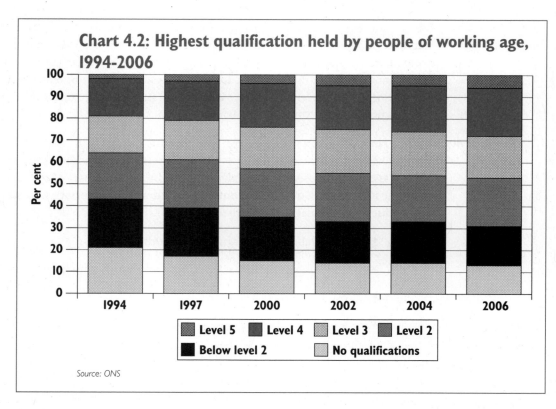

Chart 4.2: Highest qualification held by people of working age, 1994-2006

Legend: Level 5, Level 4, Level 3, Level 2, Below level 2, No qualifications

Source: ONS

A new ambition for skills

4.9   However, the UK still has a relatively large number of people with low skills compared with comparator OECD countries. In response to this challenge, the Government commissioned the Leitch Review of Skills[2] to assess the UK's long-term skills needs. In July 2007 the Government published its plans for taking forward the recommendations of the Leitch Review in *World Class Skills: Implementing the Leitch Review of Skills in England* and today the Government announces a new PSA to improve the skills of the population, on the way to ensuring a world-class skills base by 2020. The PSA sets stretching national targets to support working age individuals to acquire the skills they need to succeed at all levels, from functional literacy and numeracy to qualifications at further and higher levels and apprenticeships.

4.10   Combined with the new PSA to maximise employment opportunity for all (see Chapter 5) this PSA will provide a clearer focus on integrating the two systems to deliver the objective of sustainable employment and progression. The indicators in the skills PSA are underpinned by a new commitment to measure the employment outcomes of training to ensure the skills system delivers qualifications that are valuable to individuals and employers.

DIUS spending settlement

4.11   To provide the resources needed to make progress towards these goals, the budget for DIUS will grow by 2.2 per cent per year on average in real terms over the CSR07 period increasing total spending on Higher Education and skills from £14.2 billion in 2007-08 to £16.4 billion by 2010-11, including Higher Education spending on science. The spending settlement for the Department for Children, Schools and Families, as outlined in Chapter 5, will also see a further improvement in the number of young people continuing in education and training beyond compulsory school age.

---

[2] *Prosperity for all in the global economy – world class skills, Final Report*, Leitch Review of Skills, December 2006.

Implementing the Leitch review **4.12** The Government is building a stronger partnership with employers and individuals to deliver the higher skills ambitions recommended by the Leitch Review. Employers are being encouraged and supported to develop the skills and qualifications of their workforce by making a Skills Pledge[3] – a promise to their workforce by the leadership of an organisation to support all its eligible employees to develop their basic skills and work towards relevant qualifications to at least a first full Level 2. The public sector has played a leading role in this and all central government departments have now signed up to the Skills Pledge. In total, over 300 public and private employers, covering over 2 million employees, have made a Pledge.

4.13 The Government and employers are also investing to develop the National Skills Academy network, giving employers direct influence over the content and delivery of training in their sector. Six Academies are already operational or are in the process of becoming operational in the areas of Fashion Retail, Manufacturing, Construction, Financial Services, Food and Drink Manufacture and Nuclear. Over their first five years of operation, we expect these six Academies to have offered learning opportunities to over 150,000 people in total. The Government will continue to develop the network and by 2008 aims to have 12 Academies operational.

Train to Gain and apprenticeships **4.14** To deliver the Government's skills ambitions it is essential that funding for training is increasingly driven by the specific needs of employers and individuals. Train to Gain is an employer demand-led training service that delivers training in the workplace. It provides free training for employees who lack basic skills or a first full Level 2 qualification, as well as subsidies for a proportion of Level 3 training, and it signposts employers to other training and business support services. Since its launch last year, 36,890 employers have supported over 96,000 employees to achieve a full Level 2 qualification. Over the CSR07 period, Train to Gain will be expanded significantly. At the same time, the Government will aim to expand the number of apprenticeships to around 300,000 by 2010-11, as a step towards realising the Leitch Review ambition of 500,000 apprenticeships in the UK by 2020.

4.15 Paragraph 4.46 sets out further details of the merger of support offered through the Train to Gain skills brokerage service with the range of services provided through Business Link to simplify support for businesses of all sizes.

Commission for Employment and Skills **4.16** The UK Commission for Employment and Skills, as recommended by Leitch, will be fully operational by April 2008. Sir Michael Rake, chair of BT Group, has been appointed as chair of the Commission and is now working with the Government and Devolved Administrations to complete the set up of the new body. The Commission strengthens the collective employer voice in the skills system. It will articulate employer views on skills better; assess progress towards the UK's 2020 skills ambitions; performance manage the Sector Skills Councils, including making recommendations to the Government on re-licensing; promote employer investment in training; and advise Ministers on the policies needed to increase employment rates and skill levels.

Migration **4.17** Migration will continue to make a vital contribution to economic growth and to meeting skills gaps in the labour market. Migrants raise UK economic output through increasing employment and bring skills which complement those in the existing workforce. For these benefits to be realised it is important that migration is carefully managed.

---

[3] www.traintogain.gov.uk/skillspledge

4.18   The Government announces a new PSA to ensure controlled, fair migration that protects the public and contributes to economic growth which will be delivered by strengthening UK borders, fast tracking asylum decisions, and enforcing compliance with immigration laws. The e-Borders system will be introduced to track 95 per cent of movements across the UK's borders, enabling the Government to count people in and out of the country. Biometric visas will be rolled out to all migrants requiring a visa to improve the security of the immigration processes. The new and simpler points-based system will deliver transparent decisions based on objective criteria to facilitate economic migration to the UK.

SCIENCE AND INNOVATION

4.19   In an increasingly knowledge-based global economy, the UK's future economic success depends crucially on the ability to generate innovative ideas and to translate new knowledge into high-value products and services.

4.20   Good progress has been made towards the Government's long-term ambitions for science and innovation. The UK remains second only to the US in global scientific excellence, and knowledge transfer from the research base continues to increase. There are also encouraging signs that attainment and take-up of science, technology, engineering, and mathematics skills is beginning to improve. However, further steps are needed to increase the level of business innovation and ensure that the UK is well placed to benefit from the opportunities of globalisation.

4.21   The Government announces a new PSA to promote world-class science and innovation in the UK which commits to world-class research in UK centres of excellence, investment to enable Higher Education Institutions and Public Sector Research Establishments to develop their capacity to engage with business, increased business investment in Research and Development (R&D), and a strong supply of future scientists, engineers and technologists through the take-up of A-levels and PhDs.

4.22   The 2007 Comprehensive Spending Review confirms that total public investment in the science base will rise from £5.4 billion in 2007-8 to reach £6.3 billion by 2010-11, meeting the Government's commitment to increase investment in the public science base in line with the trend rate of growth in the economy.

Sainsbury Review **4.23**   Building on the Government's existing science and innovation policies, the Chancellor asked Lord Sainsbury in November 2006 to examine what more needs to be done to ensure the UK's continued success in wealth-creation and scientific policy making. The Sainsbury Review published its conclusions on 5 October 2007.[4] The Review found that while the UK remains well-placed to make the most of the opportunities of globalisation, further action is needed to deliver a world-class innovation system and increase the economic impact of research. The main recommendations are summarised in Box 4.1. **The Government welcomes the Sainsbury Review and accepts the recommendations.** DIUS will lead on implementing the Review's recommendations and reporting on progress.

---

[4] *The Race to the Top: A Review of Government's Science and Innovation Policies*, Lord Sainsbury of Turville, October 2007.

Box 4.1 Sainsbury Review recommendations

The Sainsbury Review argues that the UK's long-term competitive advantage in the global economy lies in high-value goods, services and industries, and that continued success in this area depends on creating the right environment to foster world-class science, innovation and skills. To this end, the Sainsbury Review proposes further action to create an effective UK innovation system, building on the *Science and Innovation Investment Framework 2004-2014* and *Next Steps.*[5] The Review:

- supports the establishment of the **Technology Strategy Board (TSB)** as an arms-length body from 1 July 2007, and recommends that it should be given a lead role in co-ordinating innovation support activities across the economy;

- recommends that performance management of the **Research Councils** focuses on knowledge transfer, including the amount of collaborative research they will conduct in partnership with the TSB;

- recommends that the next round of funding provided through the **Higher Education Innovation Fund (HEIF)** should be allocated wholly by formula, and that a greater share of funding should support knowledge transfer between universities working with regional and local firms, many of whom may not have worked with a university before;

- recommends a new package of measures to promote **science, technology, engineering and mathematics (STEM)** skills, including financial incentives to improve teacher qualifications and retention, and an overhaul of careers advice;

- recommends a new **National Science Competition**, building on existing schemes to engage young people in the exciting opportunities science provides; and

- recommends that the **Small Business Research Initiative (SBRI)** should be reformed to more closely resemble the successful scheme in the US, with a clear focus on supporting early-stage, high-technology companies.

Technology Strategy Board 4.24 In line with the recommendations of the Sainsbury Review, the Technology Strategy Board (TSB) will take a lead role in coordinating public funding for business innovation. Together with co-funding of at least £120 million committed by the Research Councils, and co-funding of £180 million committed by the Regional Development Agencies (RDAs), total public support for business innovation in support of the Technology Strategy will amount to over £1 billion over the CSR07 period.

4.25 The TSB will publish its detailed strategy in early 2008, but plans include:

- three new Innovation Platforms to find technological solutions to major societal challenges: health care for ageing populations; low environmental impact buildings; and low carbon transport;

- extending the TSB's sector coverage by creating two new Knowledge Transfer Networks in digital communications and the creative industries; and

- doubling the number of Knowledge Transfer Partnerships to get highly qualified science and technology graduates working with businesses.

---

[5] *Science & innovation investment framework 2004 – 2014*, HM Treasury, Department for Trade & Industry and Department for Education & Skills, July 2004; *Science & innovation investment framework 2004 – 2014: next steps*, HM Treasury, Department for Trade & Industry, Department for Education & Skills and Department of Health, March 2006.

Medical research **4.26**   Following the 2007 Comprehensive Spending Review settlements for science and
and development health, total investment in medical research will reach £1.7 billion by 2010-11. The budgets of
the National Institute for Health Research (NIHR) and the Medical Research Council (MRC)
will together form the single health research budget to be managed by the new Office for the
Strategic Coordination for Health Research (OSCHR), in line with the recommendations of
the Cooksey Review of UK Health Research.[6] This will support a number of priorities
highlighted in the Cooksey Review, including increased support for translational research and
clinical trials, and helping to realise the research benefits of the National Programme for IT.

INFRASTRUCTURE

4.27   Public investment makes a crucial contribution to the productivity and flexibility of
the wider economy. The 1998 Comprehensive Spending Review and subsequent spending
reviews have substantially addressed the legacy of under-investment in the UK's public
infrastructure, increasing public sector net investment from just 0.6 per cent of GDP in
1997-98 to 2.1 per cent in 2007-08. This investment will rise to $2\frac{1}{4}$ per cent of GDP over the
CSR07 period.

Box 4.2: Transforming government procurement

The Government set an ambitious new agenda with the publication of *Transforming
government procurement* (January 2007) to improve procurement for the benefit of
taxpayers, users of public services and businesses. The Government is committed to
transforming public procurement by:

- raising the calibre of procurement professionals in key departments with large
procurement budgets to achieve better value for money through innovation;

- restating that the Government will use innovation and sustainability to drive value
for money over the lifetime of the product;

- using 'forward procurement' to ask businesses to come up with the innovative
solutions the public sector needs; and

- working with the TSB to develop technology pilots before proceeding with large
high-tech procurement projects.

Transport **4.28**   The Eddington Transport Study[7] highlighted the vital role that transport plays in
supporting the continued economic success of the UK. The Study found that a
comprehensive and high performing transport system is important for sustained economic
prosperity. A 5 per cent reduction in travel time for all business and freight travel on the roads
could generate around £2.5 billion of cost savings – some 0.2 per cent of GDP.

4.29   To implement Eddington's recommendations, the Government announces a new
PSA to deliver reliable and efficient transport networks that support economic growth. This
sets out the strategy for managing urban traffic routes and the strategic road network and will
build on progress already made on the rail network through a national target to
increase capacity.

---

[6] *A review of UK health research funding*, Sir David Cooksey, December 2006.
[7] *The Eddington Transport Study*, HM Treasury, December 2006.

4.30 To achieve this, the 2007 Comprehensive Spending Review confirms a $2^1/_4$ per cent annual real increase in the Department for Transport's (DfT) programme budget, consistent with the Long Term Funding Guideline for transport announced in the 2004 Spending Review. Furthermore the Government extends its commitment to the Long Term Funding Guideline to 2018-19.

4.31 This sustained increase in funding will allow the DfT to meet the challenges set out in the Eddington Transport Study. The DfT will prioritise growing and congested urban areas, key inter-urban corridors and major international gateways. Subject to the Office of Rail Regulation's determinations, the majority of the Government's £15.3 billion support for railways over 2009-14 will be used to enhance capacity on the rail network. This will include an extensive network-wide programme of station improvements, a 19 per cent reduction in journey times between Liverpool and Leeds, the Thameslink upgrade, and the addition of 1,300 carriages to increase capacity on key routes. The DfT will also provide funding for the 2012 Olympics alongside the Department for Culture, Media and Sport, and Communities and Local Government, through the single central Government Olympics budget. Further details are set out in Annex D.

4.32 Continued stability in the public finances allows investment in major infrastructure projects and the 2007 Comprehensive Spending Review also makes provision for Crossrail. This will be taken forward by Cross London Rail Links, which will become a wholly owned subsidiary of Transport for London, subject to certain rights retained by the DfT to reflect the department's contribution to the project. A significant funding contribution has also been agreed with the private sector. See Box 4.3 for further details.

Box 4.3: Crossrail

Crossrail is a major new infrastructure project which will provide a rapid direct link between London's main economic centres of the West End, the City and Canary Wharf, linking these directly with Heathrow Airport and the Thames Gateway.

London's population and employment are projected to grow by around 900,000 by 2025. Crossrail will support this growth by increasing London's overall public transport capacity by 10 per cent, and by 40 per cent on the east-west corridor.[a] This comes on top of the planned 25 per cent increase in capacity on the Underground network and the major upgrade of Thameslink announced in July 2007. Crossrail is projected to generate transport and economic benefits that are more than double its cost, and to create up to 30,000 high-value jobs. It will open up new employment opportunities to thousands of people in some of London's most deprived areas.

The expected cost of up to £16 billion (including contingency and allowing for inflation) has represented a considerable challenge for successive governments, and agreement has only been possible because of sustainable management of the public finances. Agreement has now been reached with the Mayor of London and businesses on an equitable funding package with the Government, passengers and businesses each contributing approximately one third of the expected cost.

The Government will contribute around a third of the construction cost by means of a grant from the DfT of over £5 billion during Crossrail's construction.

Crossrail farepayers will ultimately contribute around another third of the cost, with revenue servicing debt raised during construction by Transport for London and by Network Rail in repect of works on the national rail network.

London businesses will contribute broadly another third through a variety of mechanisms:

- **Direct contributions** have been agreed with some of the project's key beneficiaries along the route. Canary Wharf Group has agreed to make a significant contribution to the project and will in addition be responsible for delivering the Isle of Dogs station on advantageous terms. The City of London Corporation will make a significant contribution from their own funds, and will assist in delivering additional voluntary contributions from the largest London businesses. The Government will offer the Corporation its support, where necessary, to deliver these additional contributions. BAA have also agreed in principle to make a financial contribution.

- The Government is separately publishing a White Paper setting out its proposal to introduce a power for local authorities to raise **supplementary business rates** to fund economic development (see paragraph 4.72). Following discussions with the Government, the Mayor has indicated that, subject to appropriate consultation, he envisages using these powers to levy a supplement of two pence per pound of rateable value across London from April 2010, with relief for businesses with a rateable value below £50,000, which will be used to service £3.5 billion of debt raised by the Mayor during construction.

- The Mayor has further indicated that he envisages securing contributions from **property developers**, particularly those who develop in the vicinity of Crossrail stations, and that subject to any appropriate obligations such as Examination in Public, he expects to bring forward London Plan alterations to this effect.

The Crossrail Hybrid Bill is proceeding through Parliament and is likely to receive Royal Assent in summer 2008. Full construction is expected to be underway during 2010, with services commencing in 2017.

[a] *Transport 2025 – Transport vision for a growing world city,* Transport for London, November 2006.

4.33 The Local Transport Bill will increase flexibility for local authorities to introduce road pricing schemes as part of packages of measures to tackle local congestion problems. The DfT continues to work with local authorities who have submitted or are considering a bid for Transport Innovation Funding to support such packages. The DfT is also inviting industry to demonstrate the feasibility of distance-based road charging where the charge varies according to time of day and place. A number of companies have expressed interest in participating in these demonstrations.

4.34 The DfT's settlement also supports local and regional investment across the UK including continued investment through the Integrated Transport Block and Regional Funding Allocations (together worth over £1.3 billion in 2008-09).

Supporting the haulage industry **4.35** The Chancellor announced on 1 October 2007 that vehicle excise duty for heavy goods vehicles (HGVs) would be frozen in 2008-09 (see Chapter 7 for further details). By April 2009 the rates will be 21 per cent lower in real terms than in 2001. Building on the additional expenditure announced in Budget 2007, the Government recently announced that a further £2 million a year will be dedicated to enforcing road safety law for hauliers to protect the competitiveness of legitimate hauliers. New measures, planned for introduction next year, will allow inspectors from the Vehicle Operator and Service Agency and the Police to collect on the spot penalties from drivers suspected of an offence without a valid British address.

4.36 The DfT has published a progress report on other ways of delivering more targeted enforcement on foreign vehicles alongside the 2007 Pre-Budget Report.[8] One option under consideration is a 'vignette' – a time-based charge for the use of UK roads designed to ensure foreign hauliers help pay for the wear and tear inflicted by their vehicles.

Airport capacity **4.37** Additional airport capacity will increase competition between airlines and ease congestion, benefiting passengers and the wider economy. The Eddington Transport Study and the Stern Review made clear that infrastructure projects should proceed where there is a net economic benefit once external costs – including environmental impacts – have been taken into account. The Government will consult shortly on whether the expansion of Heathrow, the UK's only major hub airport, can take place while meeting stringent environmental conditions.

Spectrum auction **4.38** Spectrum is a valuable part of the UK's infrastructure. The Government is undertaking digital switchover to ensure optimal use of spectrum and considers that the spectrum released by switchover should be auctioned on a neutral basis, thereby allowing different potential users to compete for it openly. The Office of Communications (Ofcom) will publish its conclusions on future use of the spectrum later this year.

Planning system **4.39** The Government remains committed to ensuring that the planning system delivers sustainable housing and economic development and will shortly bring forward legislation creating a new planning regime for major infrastructure projects. This will be based on the recommendations from the Barker Review of Planning[9] and the Eddington Transport Study, and follows consultation on the Planning White Paper, *Planning for a Sustainable Future* (May 2007). It will increase the speed and certainty with which applications are dealt, improve and extend public and community engagement, and ensure that the planning system helps deliver the UK's infrastructure needs. To make developer contributions through the planning system fairer and more certain, the Government will introduce a new statutory planning charge (see Chapter 6).

---

[8] *The Freight Data Feasibility Study Progress Report*, Department for Transport, October 2007.
[9] *Barker Review of Land Use Planning, Final Report – Recommendations*, Kate Barker, December 2006.

BUSINESS ENVIRONMENT

4.40   Globalisation will intensify competition across many sectors. It is therefore increasingly important that the Government creates conditions that attract both domestic and foreign investment, support business and encourage enterprise. **The Government announces a new PSA to deliver the conditions for business success in the UK.** This commits to provide a competition regime and corporate governance framework ranked among the best in the world, open competitive energy markets which deliver supplies at competitive prices, regulation that is appropriate and justified, and a target to reduce administrative burdens on business.

BERR spending settlement   **4.4I**   **The new Department for Business, Enterprise and Regulatory Reform (BERR) will lead the delivery of this PSA, with an annual budget of £3.2 billion fixed on average in nominal terms over the CSR07 period.**

Gibbons Review   **4.42**   The BERR settlement provides funding for the programme of measures proposed by the Government on employment law simplification. This will result in savings to business of around £500 million. Proposed measures include better guidance on all aspects of employment law and improvements to the system for resolving disputes in the workplace as recommended by Michael Gibbons' Review, *Better Dispute Resolution: a review of employment dispute resolution in Great Britain* (March 2007).

Encouraging enterprise

Business support simplification   **4.43**   To tackle the proliferation of business support schemes and simplify the current large number of uncoordinated schemes provided by different tiers of government, the Business Support Simplification Programme is working with business and all tiers of government to reduce the number of business support schemes from over 3,000 to 100 or fewer by 2010. This will reduce complexity and the time business spends understanding what support is available and accessing it, and will improve the quality, effectiveness and efficiency of schemes.

4.44   To meet this goal, the Government has identified the support it is most appropriate to provide, reflecting the existence of market failures or social equity considerations. Following extensive analysis and public consultation, **the Government is announcing the high-level portfolio of products from which business support will be provided in the future.** Details of these products are set out in Box 4.4 and on the BERR website. The schemes developed on the basis of these products will begin to be phased in from March 2008.

Box 4.4: The new business support portfolio of products

Innovation collaborations – helping businesses to work with the science and research base;

Innovation finance – helping develop and commercially exploit innovative ideas;

Growing internationally – increasing the contribution of foreign direct investment;

Preparing to go international – helping businesses enter new overseas markets;

Export credits guarantee – helping business manage non-payment risks overseas;

Getting into new overseas markets – tailored help to access specific markets;

Risk capital targeted at the equity gap – equity financing for high growth Small and Medium Sized Enterprises (SMEs);

Financial awareness and capability – providing SMEs with the skills and expertise to secure private sector funding;

Debt finance – security and loan finance for young SMEs with viable business plans;

Capital investment grants – supporting capital investment projects either by SMEs or by companies operating in the assisted areas;

Promoting resource efficiency and sustainable waste management – helping create a low carbon economy and tackle climate change;

Business creation – helping to overcome barriers to setting up a new business;

Business expertise for growth – helping get expertise for targeted SMEs to grow;

Local community business coaching – helping disadvantaged individuals start up in business;

Skills solutions for business – helping improve skills for business;

Business collaboration networks – helping businesses to work together to improve performance and exploit market opportunities; and

Shared business support environments – helping businesses share premises and facilities in which to develop and grow.

4.45   Arrangements will be put in place to subject the portfolio to regular review and robust evaluation, to ensure the products most effectively meet business needs and deliver value for money. Business will be strongly represented in this process.

4.46   Businesses also need a simple route to access the support they need to thrive and grow. The Government is therefore bringing together information, diagnosis and brokerage services, currently supplied by many providers, and integrating them with Business Link. Following the recommendation in the *Review of sub-national economic development and regeneration* (SNR),[10] BERR and DIUS are committed to the launch of a single, integrated business support brokerage service in April 2009, to include skills brokerage as a major component.

Enterprise in disadvantaged areas   **4.47**   The Government is committed to promoting enterprise and reducing worklessness in deprived areas by giving local areas the freedom and flexibility to develop approaches that respond to local needs. A new enterprise and renewal fund will foster enterprise in these areas and will place a stronger emphasis on economic development in tackling neighbourhood deprivation. Further details of the fund can be found in Chapter 6.

---

[10] *Review of sub-national economic development and regeneration*, HM Treasury, Department for Business, Enterprise and Regulatory Reform, and Communities and Local Government, July 2007.

Social enterprise   **4.48**   The Government recognises the potential of businesses that want to combine profit generation with social and environmental goals. It will therefore invest further in raising awareness of the social enterprise business model. As set out in the recent review of the third sector,[11] this will include coverage of social enterprise in business studies education, improving access to finance and advice for social entrepreneurs – consistent with the Business Support Simplification Programme – and investigating how the social enterprise business model can improve government policy delivery and outcomes.

Simplifying business tax

4.49   The Government is committed to ensuring that the UK provides a world-class environment for business. To help achieve this, Budget 2007 announced improvements which made the tax system fairer, simpler and more efficient by:

- modernising and simplifying both the personal and business tax systems;

- publishing the implementation plan[12] for the 2006 Review of HM Revenue & Customs' (HMRC) Links With Large Business; and

- delivering £300 million of administrative savings to business, helping HMRC towards achieving its administrative burden targets.[13]

4.50   Building on these and other reforms, **the Government is renewing its commitment by launching a significant programme of tax simplification** – setting out new principles, new reviews and a package of measures – to enhance UK productivity and competitiveness.

Principles of   **4.51**   **The Government commits to three principles of tax simplification,** which underpin
simplification   this new programme:

- simplification will be a priority when designing and reviewing tax policy, alongside sound public finances and fairness;

- the Government will work in partnership with business to identify further opportunities to simplify the tax system; and

- the Government will share its findings on the viability of tax simplifications with business.

Simplification   **4.52**   The Government **today publishes its findings, for discussion with business, on the**
reviews   **case for administrative alignment of the income tax and national insurance systems** (see Chapter 5 for more detail). This autumn the Government will launch **three reviews** where HM Treasury and HMRC will work in partnership with business to evaluate how a range of tax policies could be simplified. These initial reviews will cover:

- how to simplify VAT rules and administration in the UK and the EU;

- how anti-avoidance legislation can best meet the aims of simplicity and revenue protection; and

- how to simplify the Corporation Tax (CT) rules for related companies.[14]

---

[11] *The future role of the third sector in social and economic regeneration: final report*, HM Treasury and Cabinet Office, July 2007.

[12] *Making a difference: delivering the review of links with large business*, HM Revenue and Customs, March 2007.

[13] At Budget 2006, the Chancellor announced targets for HMRC to reduce the administrative burdens imposed on business by the tax system, focusing on forms and returns, and on audits and inspections. Further progress against these targets will be reported at Budget 2008.

[14] Further details of these reviews and how to participate are available at: www.hm-treasury.gov.uk/pbr_csr/pbr_csr07_index.cfm

Delivering **4.53** As part of this new approach, the Government will make immediate progress with
simplifications over 20 tax measures, set out at Box 4.6. Together, these simplifications will help businesses
across the UK economy, by:

- reducing their administrative burdens by up to £100 million;

- making improvements to income tax self-assessment, benefiting 1.6 million
  small businesses;

- benefiting up to 0.5 million employers and 3 million self-employed; and

- enhancing the City's competitiveness by simplifying and modernising the tax
  system for financial services.

Maintaining international competitiveness

Business tax **4.54** Budget 2007 announced a major package of reforms to the business tax system
reform designed to enhance the UK's international competitiveness, encourage investment,
promote innovation and ensure fairness across the tax system. The package was designed to
increase the efficiency and simplicity of the system through:

- a reduction in the main rate of CT from 30 per cent to 28 per cent;

- a new Annual Investment Allowance of £50,000 for all firms, to replace the
  existing first-year capital allowances: 95 per cent of firms will now be able to
  write off all of their capital expenditure in the year it is incurred;

- extensive reforms of the capital allowances system;

- an increase in the value of the R&D tax credits for SMEs to 175 per cent and
  large companies to 130 per cent from April 2008; and

- an increase in the small companies' rate of CT to 22 per cent by April 2009.

4.55 In July 2007 the Government launched a consultation on the details of the changes to
the capital allowances system, *Business tax reform: capital allowances changes*. Later this year,
the Government will publish draft legislation for further comment.

Taxation of **4.56** The Government released the discussion document *Taxation of the foreign profits of*
foreign profits *companies* in June 2007. The Government welcomes the very constructive dialogue to date
and continues to work with business to consider the issues raised. The Government will now
develop a more detailed, broadly revenue neutral package of proposals to improve the
competitiveness of the UK's corporate tax system in relation to foreign profits.

Private equity **4.57** The UK's internationally competitive position has contributed to the development of
a strong private equity industry in the UK. The scale of private equity buy-outs has increased
over recent years, although recent sharp moves in credit markets may alter the frequency of
large-scale deals in the short term. Large-scale buy-outs have raised concerns over reduced
transparency, most obviously when a listed company is taken private. The Government
welcomes the private equity industry's resolve to become more transparent and the
commissioning of Sir David Walker to develop a voluntary code to promote high standards of
disclosure and valuation. The Government looks forward to the outcome of this work and to
the development of a code that has strong industry buy-in; that results in meaningful
disclosure of a breadth and depth to carry credibility with wider stakeholders, especially in
relation to employee impacts; and that sets in place an effective monitoring framework with
sufficient independence to command acceptance.

4.58 In March 2007 the Government announced a review of the rules that apply to shareholder debt where it replaces part of the equity element in leveraged private equity deals. Following completion of this review the Government is satisfied that the 2005 changes to the Transfer Pricing rules have sufficiently extended the scope of the rules to include all private equity transactions. However, the Government is concerned that these rules may be less effective in the context of highly leveraged private equity transactions. The Government will therefore continue to monitor the operation of the rules where a tax deduction is being claimed for interest on shareholder debt in these types of transactions.

4.59 The reform of capital gains tax to a single rate of 18 per cent from 6 April 2008 (see Chapter 5) establishes a system that is more sustainable, straightforward for taxpayers and internationally competitive. Along with measures to address loopholes and anomalies in the residence and domicile rules (see Chapter 5) this will increase the fairness of the tax system, including for individuals in the private equity industry. The Government remains interested in wider aspects of the ways in which those involved in the private equity and other industries are rewarded, including the application of the legislation on employment related securities, in the context of the need to ensure that the tax system as a whole is fair and sustainable.

Improving competition

Enhancing competition enforcement and redress   **4.60** Undistorted competition within the UK and wider European Union (EU) markets is critical to encouraging efficiency, innovation and flexibility in the economy. The UK has a world-class competition regime, but it can be improved. By the end of the year the Government intends to consult on measures to further enhance the speed and simplicity of the UK merger regime and to reduce the barriers preventing those suffering loss as a result of anti-competitive behaviour from obtaining redress, through the courts where necessary, without encouraging ill-founded claims.

Competition in the water and sewerage industry   **4.61** The introduction of competition in the UK's utilities has delivered significant benefits. A limited competition regime came into force in the water sector in December 2005, which the Government committed to review within three years. The Government has already said that it will bring forward the review, since competition has not developed in the sector. The review will look at all the necessary elements to ensure the regime delivers benefits for consumers and the wider economy, giving specific consideration to investment in infrastructure, innovation and the environment. The Department for the Environment, Food and Rural Affairs will set out further details of the review in the Government's Water Strategy, which will be published early next year.

EU reform   **4.62** Ongoing reform of the EU is also required for the UK to realise the full benefits of globalisation. The Single Market has delivered real benefits for the UK, but the need for significant reform continues – particularly in network industries like energy. The Government will continue to oppose unnecessary bureaucracy arising from EU rules and to push for the European Commission to increase the level of competition throughout the EU. Reform in each Member State will be important. For these reasons, the Government looks forward to the Review of the Single Market and a robust update to the Lisbon Strategy for Jobs and Growth in March 2008.

A strong and competitive global financial centre

4.63 The financial sector remains a significant area of comparative advantage for the UK economy, in 2006 contributing around 9 per cent to UK GDP output, supporting 1.1 million jobs, and producing a trade surplus with the rest of the world of £25.1 billion, the largest in the world.

Global market disruption **4.64** The UK financial system, in common with other financial systems, has been affected by the recent disruption in global markets triggered by deterioration in the US sub-prime mortgage market. Although direct exposures to losses from sub-prime mortgages have been less significant in the UK than in some other countries, some financial institutions have found themselves under significantly more funding pressure due to the seizing up of the asset-backed commercial paper markets and the contraction of liquidity in the inter-bank markets. Northern Rock plc faced specific difficulties in these circumstances. Following advice from the Governor of the Bank of England and the Chairman of the Financial Services Authority (FSA), the Chancellor concluded that it was appropriate and necessary for the Bank of England to provide liquidity support to Northern Rock plc. Subsequently the Chancellor has announced that, should it be necessary, the Government, with the Bank of England, would put in place arrangements that would guarantee all the existing deposits in Northern Rock plc during the current instability in the financial markets.[15] The Government recognises the need to learn lessons from these events and will bring forward proposals for further reforms to give consumers confidence that their savings and deposits are accessible, safe and secure, and to handle banks facing difficulties.

City competitiveness **4.65** The Government will ensure that financial sector regulation remains effective, proportionate, and risk-based, protecting investors and consumers appropriately and ensuring market integrity whilst encouraging innovation and keeping pace with market developments. Supporting and promoting the sector's competitiveness, including through the High-Level Group on the City of London's international competitiveness, remains a key priority. A number of substantive proposals were announced at the second meeting of the High-level Group in May, as set out in Box 4.5, and the third meeting will take place in November. The Government also continues to facilitate the development of new areas of finance, for example encouraging growth in Islamic Finance (see Annex B) and carbon markets.

Taxation of financial services **4.66** The ongoing development of an innovative, flexible and internationally competitive financial sector also requires a tax system that reflects commercial developments. The 2007 Pre-Budget Report simplification measures on areas such as 'Schedule 19' within Stamp Duty Reserve Tax, direct tax treatment of financial derivative transactions, offshore funds and the Investment Manager Exemption (outlined in more detail on Box 4.6) will give businesses and investors greater certainty about how the tax system will operate given recent market developments, as well as reducing administrative and compliance costs. Box 4.6 also outlines simplification measures on Stamp Duty on Shares and on life insurance, and publication today of a discussion paper setting out proposals to simplify and modernise the offshore funds tax regime, with the aim of providing more certainty to UK investors and offshore funds.

---

[15] The Treasury has issued further statements on the scope of these safeguards. For further details see HM Treasury press notices 95/07 and 96/07 and RNS 2413E from the Regulatory News Service provided by the London Stock Exchange.

Box 4.5: High-Level Group on the City of London's international competitiveness

At its second meeting on 9 May 2007 the High-level Group, chaired by the Chancellor, discussed progress on a number of substantive proposals, including:

- a package of regulatory simplification measures designed to increase the global competitiveness of the UK's fund management industry by reducing costs for fund managers by up to £290 million per year;

- the launch of a prospectus setting up a new world-class International Centre for Financial Regulation (ICFR) in London. Mervyn Davies is chairing the interim executive committee, representing donor interests, that will now prepare the centre for launch;

- the work of Lord Levene and the London Insurance Market Review Group on modernisation of the wholesale insurance market, which will report to an 'Insurance Summit', which is scheduled to be held on 7 November 2007; and

- delivery of the new strategy for overseas promotion of the UK-based financial sector, with the launch of new promotional materials including a brochure and a new website, www.thecityuk.com by UK Trade & Investment, the Corporation of London, Think London and International Financial Services London.

The next meeting of the High-level Group, which will be chaired by the Chancellor, is scheduled to be held on 14 November 2007.

PROMOTING REGIONAL ECONOMIC GROWTH

4.67   The most recent data show that the economies of all English regions have grown between 2002 and 2005 and that progress is being made on narrowing the gap in growth rates between the regions. This progress has been underpinned by stronger employment performance in the North, Midlands and South West regions than in London, the South East and East of England. A narrowing in the intermediate skills gap may also have played a part. The Government will only be able to fully assess trends in regional economic activity and disparities when a full economic cycle is complete.

4.68   The Government believes that unfulfilled economic potential in every nation, region, city and locality must be released to increase the long-term growth rate of the UK. The Government therefore announces a new PSA to improve the economic performance of all English regions and reduce the gap in economic growth rates between regions by maintaining macroeconomic stability to help businesses and individuals plan for the future, implementing reforms to tackle market failures in the underlying drivers of growth, and devolving decision making to the regional and local levels to ensure that delivery is responsive to the challenges of each particular area.

Sub-national **4.69**   The Government published in July 2007 the *Review of sub-national economic*
review *development and regeneration* (SNR) which set out a comprehensive package of reform aimed at enabling more effective and efficient delivery of improved economic performance at the regional, sub-regional and local levels. This review announced an enhanced strategic role for the RDAs, supported by increased freedoms and flexibilities and a simplified sponsorship framework. The outcomes and recommendations of the SNR are set out in more detail in Annex D.

4.70 This refined role for the RDAs enables them to deliver significant efficiency and value for money savings. **The 2007 Comprehensive Spending Review provides for the RDAs' single programme budget to be £2,220 million in 2008-09, £2,191 million in 2009-10 and £2,140 million in 2010-11.** Underpinning this, the RDAs have committed to an ambitious value for money programme that will release significant savings over the CSR07 period.

4.71 The 2007 Comprehensive Spending Review has benefited from advice from each of the regions, as well as from the Northern Way, which provides a clear strategy for improving the economic performance of the North of England. Building on their role as strategic leaders of growth in each region, and increasing regional input to national decisions, the RDAs will also be asked to contribute to the development of Budget 2008 in four areas: building regional intelligence of business priorities; implementing the SNR; responding to the long-term challenge of globalization; and ensuring that all regions can benefit from the Olympics legacy.

Business rate supplements **4.72** Following the recommendations of the Lyons Inquiry [16] and SNR the Government has today published a White Paper setting out proposals to allow local authorities to invest in economic development through levying a local business rate supplement. This power will be subject to four levels of protection for business, with spending only available for a specified economic development purpose and subject to detailed statutory consultation, a maximum limit of two pence per pound of rateable value, an exemption for properties with a rateable value less than £50,000 and a requirement to ballot where the supplement supports more than a third of the cost of the project.

Business rate reliefs and exemptions **4.73** The Government accepted a Lyons Inquiry recommendation to review all reliefs and exemptions within business rates. The review has now concluded. In addition to its reform of Empty Property Relief, **the Government will now simplify a number of smaller reliefs** (see Box 4.6). There will be no other substantive changes arising from this review, or to Business Improvement Districts. However the Government will continue to consider the merits of extending business rates to include derelict and vacant previously developed land, and will keep business rates policy more generally under review.

---

[16] *Place-shaping: a shared ambition for the future of local government*, Lyons Inquiry, March 2007.

Box 4.6: Delivering tax simplification

As part of the Government's new approach to tax simplification, it will make immediate progress with over 20 tax measures:

Business

- beginning this year, doubling the three line account threshold to £30,000 and introducing shorter self-employment pages for businesses with turnovers below the VAT registration threshold, helping 1.3 million businesses submit shorter tax returns;

- doubling the payment on account threshold for income tax self assessment to £1,000 from April 2009, simplifying the payment system for 320,000 businesses;

- consulting this autumn on how best to collect tax on benefits in kind and expenses through the payroll, helping up to 500,000 employers by removing the need for a separate end of year process;

- including consultation on removing the £8,500 a year threshold at which most benefits in kind become taxable, making it simpler for employers when reporting benefits;

- consulting on how to improve the present separate systems for collecting Class 2 and 4 national insurance contributions (NICs), to make it easier for around 3 million self-employed to understand and pay their NICs;

- working closely with business to improve the guidance on tax and NICs, making it easier for all employers to understand and meet their tax obligations;

- repealing outdated legislation relating to expenditure on fire safety equipment from April 2008, making the tax code easier to understand;

- consulting on principles-based responses to avoidance involving income stripping to improve clarity and certainty; and

- consulting on principles-based responses to avoidance involving disguised interest to improve clarity and certainty.

Assets

- removing the need for 250,000 non-residential and residential Stamp Duty Land Tax (SDLT) returns by introducing a notification threshold of £40,000 for all freehold and leasehold transactions at Budget 2008. In addition, notifications will only be needed for certain high-value leases;

- simplifying the relevant legislation for companies that choose to invest in life insurance policies;

- responding to industry concerns about pensions taxation by simplifying the rules for protecting rights to pre-April 2006 lump sums and by cutting the administrative burden of a lifetime allowance anti-avoidance rule; and

- consulting on proposals to rationalise and simplify the business rate relief system while protecting those currently covered by reliefs and continuing the support offered to charities.

Financial Sector

- removing a range of smaller financial and other transactions from the charge to Stamp Duty – cutting the number of forms that need to be presented for stamping by more than 60 per cent;

- consulting on options to make 'Schedule 19' of the Stamp Duty Reserve Tax (SDRT) legislation simpler to administer and easier for investors to understand. This will benefit collective investment funds, improving the industry's international competitiveness;

- publishing HMRC guidance to clarify the direct tax treatment of financial derivative transactions, making it easier for investment funds and investors to deal with the tax system by giving more certainty on future tax treatment of investment strategies;

- publishing a discussion paper today setting out proposals which simplify the offshore funds tax regime, remove tax barriers impacting on the development of offshore funds of funds and ensure the regime continues to prevent UK investors gaining unfair tax advantages. This follows the Budget 2007 announcement that, subject to consultation, the Government intends to legislate for a modernised offshore funds tax regime in Finance Bill 2008;

- modernising the Investment Manager Exemption legislation to clarify and simplify the scope of exempt transactions and ensure a proportionate tax response if a single condition for exemption is not met, so increasing certainty for UK-based fund managers involved in a wider range of activities;

- continuing to consult with the life insurance sector on proposals for further simplification, including on the repeal of complex inherited estates legislation; and

- publishing the latest draft of regulations as part of the final step toward the simplification of rules relating to transfers of life insurance business.

Charities

- continuing to consult with charities to identify ways of making the Gift Aid system – already worth more than £800 million a year to the charitable sector – simpler and easier to use. Further detail on the consultation is available in Chapter 5.

The Environment

- reviewing the hydrocarbon oil duties legislation to simplify the duty rates structure and remove obstacles to the introduction of more environmentally friendly fuels.

Tax Appeals

- consulting on how to streamline and make more consistent across all taxes the process for reviewing decisions and handling appeals before they come before a tribunal, in the context of wider tribunal reform.

5 FAIRNESS AND OPPORTUNITY FOR ALL

A decade ago, the Government set itself the twin aims of employment opportunity for all and a fair society in which everyone shares in rising national prosperity. These objectives are mutually reinforcing: work is the surest route out of poverty, while the tax and benefit system must work with public services to make sure that everyone is supported and given the chance both to achieve their potential and to reap the rewards of the modern world. The Government is also committed to a modern and fair tax system that ensures that everyone pays their fair share of tax. The 2007 Pre-Budget Report and Comprehensive Spending Review sets out how the Government will promote fairness and opportunity for all, including by:

- **ensuring that all married couples and civil partners can benefit from double the inheritance tax allowance – £600,000 immediately, rising to £700,000 by 2010-11, in addition to the entitlement to full spouse relief;**

- **a major reform of capital gains tax, introducing a single rate of 18 per cent from April 2008, ensuring a more sustainable system that is straightforward for taxpayers and internationally competitive;**

- **announcing that, in addition to the £150 increase announced in Budget 2007, the child element of the Child Tax Credit will increase by a further £25 per year above indexation from April 2008 and by a further £25 above indexation from April 2010 and that the child maintenance disregard in the main income related benefits will increase to £20 by the end of 2008, with a further increase to £40 from April 2010, together lifting an estimated 100,000 children out of poverty;**

- **education spending in England will rise on average by 2.8 per cent a year in real terms between 2007-08 and 2010-11, meaning that UK education spending as a proportion of GDP is projected to increase from 4.7 per cent in 1996-97 to 5.6 per cent in 2010-11;**

- **increasing the Jobseeker's Allowance and Income Support rates for 16-17 year olds from April 2008 to align with the 18-24 rates,** to help to simplify the system, and ensure a higher minimum level of income for this group;

- **the national roll-out from April 2008 of the In-Work Credit for lone parents at a rate of £40, retaining a rate of £60 in London,** ensuring a more substantial financial gain from moving into work;

- **announcing the continuation of the Financial Inclusion Fund at £130 million over the CSR07 period** and an **£11.5m package of support for schools to teach children financial skills;** and

- **further reforms to modernise the tax system and protect tax revenues,** including work to tackle avoidance.

5.1 In a constantly changing world, people have far greater opportunities than ever before. As barriers to trade and investment fall, and as technology improves, there is the potential for everyone in society to benefit. There is also, however, an increased risk of skills obsolescence and insecurity for a minority. The Government must therefore put in place policies to equip people to take advantage of change and to share in rising national prosperity.

5.2   The personal tax and benefit system is central to achieving the Government's aims of opportunity and fairness. Since 1997, the Government has therefore embarked upon a series of reforms to the tax and benefit system. These reforms have both improved incentives to work and save, and provided support in line with the principle of progressive universalism. This means providing support to all, with the greatest help offered to those who need it most.

5.3   Over the past ten years, the Government has delivered sustained economic growth alongside low inflation, while simultaneously increasing employment and tackling poverty. Compared with a decade ago:

- there are now 1.9 million fewer children in absolute poverty, and some 600,000 fewer in relative poverty;

- there are 2.6 million more people in work, and the Government has introduced the first ever National Minimum Wage, which was increased to £5.52 per hour from 1 October 2007; and

- there are 2.4 million fewer pensioners in absolute poverty and over 1 million fewer in relative poverty.

5.4   This chapter sets out how the Government is building on these achievements by:

- making progress on its objective of employment opportunity for all – the modern definition of full employment – through labour market policies and reforms to make work pay;

- ensuring that every child has the best possible start in life;

- promoting a fair and inclusive society free from discrimination, and promoting well-being and independence for older people; and

- delivering a fair and modern tax system that supports opportunity and fairness, in which people pay their fair share of tax, and all taxpayers operate on a level playing-field.

EMPLOYMENT OPPORTUNITY FOR ALL

Labour Market Performance   **5.5**   The last decade has seen strong labour market performance, with 2.6 million more people now in work than in 1997. As Chart 5.1 shows, the working age employment rate is now 74.4 per cent and the International Labour Organisation (ILO) unemployment rate is 5.4 per cent. The Jobseeker's Allowance (JSA) claimant count has almost halved, falling by 800,000 to around 850,000. The UK has the fourth highest employment rate of the EU27 countries (after Denmark, the Netherlands and Sweden), and an unemployment rate below that of France, Germany, Italy or the EU as a whole.

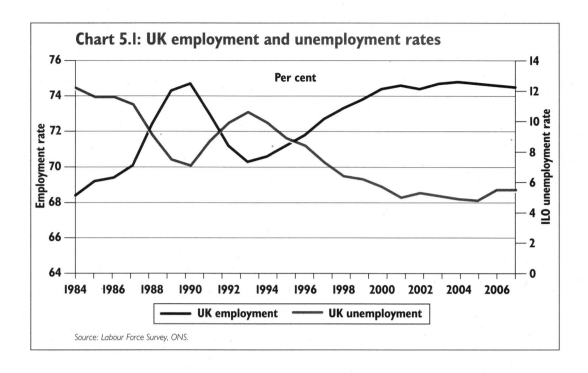

Chart 5.I: UK employment and unemployment rates

Per cent

Employment rate / ILO unemployment rate

— UK employment — UK unemployment

Source: Labour Force Survey, ONS.

5.6 Some of the most significant improvements in labour market outcomes since 1997 have been seen by previously disadvantaged groups:

- the lone parent employment rate has increased by over 12 percentage points, from 44.7 per cent to 57.2 per cent;

- the number of people on incapacity benefits has stabilised and begun to fall for the first time in a generation; and

- there are 400,000 fewer children in workless households, a major contributor to lifting 600,000 children out of relative poverty.

5.7 The strength of the labour market over the last decade reflects the Government's policy to link improved incentives to work with active help for people at a disadvantage in the labour market, including through:

- integrating benefits and employment support through the roll-out of the Jobcentre Plus network;

- introducing tailored support for disadvantaged groups, such as the New Deal for the unemployed and for voluntary participants, and Pathways to Work to help people with a health condition or disability back to work; and

- introducing City Strategies to empower local partners to deliver locally tailored support.

Building on success: Active Labour Market Policies

5.8 As Chart 5.2 illustrates, the employment rates of most disadvantaged groups have increased in the last few years. They remain, however, well below the national average, and the employment rate among the declining number of individuals with no qualifications has deteriorated. Moving towards the Government's long-term aspiration of an employment rate equivalent to 80 per cent of the working age population will require increased employment among the most socially excluded groups and those facing the greatest labour market barriers. As part of the 2007 Comprehensive Spending Review (CSR), **the Government announces a new Public Service Agreement (PSA) to maximise employment opportunity for all**, which will drive further progress on raising the overall employment rate, as well as narrowing the gap between employment rates of disadvantaged groups (such as people with a disability, or lone parents) and the overall rate. The PSA will also drive reductions in the numbers on out-of-work benefits and the time spent on these benefits.

Principles of Welfare Reform
5.9 These new challenges require a new approach; one which builds on the successes of the last decade with further steps to deliver employment opportunity for all. The Government's approach to welfare reform is based on the five core principles set out at Budget 2007:

- rights and responsibilities underpinning the welfare reform agenda;

- a personalised and responsive approach to meet individual needs;

- retention and progression, with employment support focused not just on job entry but also on helping people remain and progress in work;

- working in partnership to make best use of expertise across the public, private and third sectors; and

- devolution and local empowerment, recognising the important role regions, cities and localities should play in identifying strategic priorities and delivering solutions.

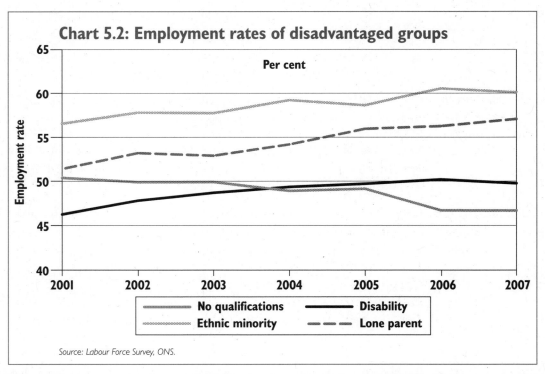

Chart 5.2: Employment rates of disadvantaged groups

Source: Labour Force Survey, ONS.

In work, better off
5.10 Consistent with these principles, the Green Paper *In work, better off: next steps to full employment*, published in July 2007, set out proposals for reforming active labour market support. The Green Paper invited views on proposals to:

- end entitlement to Income Support (IS) for lone parents with older children, with lone parents who move onto JSA receiving personalised support and advice to help them look for suitable work;

- introduce a new Flexible New Deal for all JSA claimants, offering more responsive and personally tailored support; and

- establish a more effective approach to contracting, designed to increase flexibility and cost-effectiveness, and achieve better outcomes for participants.

Support for lone parents 5.11 The Government's support for lone parents focuses on ensuring that work pays, that barriers to employment are addressed and that lone parents are made aware – in particular through Work-Focused Interviews with skilled Personal Advisers – of the employment opportunities available to them. Following the end of the consultation period, the Government will set out its plans for moving forward with the changes proposed in *In work, better off*. The Government is also introducing enhanced support for lone parents on benefits to move into employment in the interim, through new group interviews with personal advisers, guaranteed job interviews, enhanced pre-work training and an extension to Work Trials from two to six weeks.

In-Work Credit 5.12 Since April 2004, the Government has piloted the In-Work Credit (IWC), a £40 per week (£60 per week in London) payment for lone parents who have been on IS for more than 12 months, during their first 12 months back in work. The IWC further increases the financial benefit from a move into employment and is helping lone parents move away from benefit dependency. As announced in September 2007, the IWC will be rolled out nationally from April 2008 at a rate of £40, retaining a rate of £60 in London.

Support for the unemployed 5.13 A key aim of support for those who are unemployed is to prevent long-term detachment from the labour market by helping as many as possible into work in the early stages of their claim. The JSA regime has been particularly successful in achieving this, with regular interventions helping nearly 60 per cent of claimants leave the benefit within three months. **To strengthen this, the Government will, from January 2008, pilot a new rights and responsibilities seminar for those who have not found work after eight weeks on JSA.**

Support for people with a health condition or disability 5.14 Pathways to Work helps Incapacity Benefit claimants back to work by combining ongoing mandatory contact with skilled Jobcentre Plus Personal Advisers, and high quality employment, health and financial support. It will be rolled out across the country by April 2008 and will be delivered by the private and third sectors in the majority of the country. The first phase of contracts to deliver national rollout was awarded in September 2007 and the second and final phase will be awarded by the end of this year.

Employment and Support Allowance 5.15 From 2008, an integrated and simplified Employment and Support Allowance (ESA) will replace the current system of incapacity benefits for new claimants. The new ESA will have a clearer balance of rights and responsibilities, focusing on what a person can, rather than cannot, do. People with the most severe health conditions and disabilities will be supported by ESA at a higher rate and will not be required to participate in Pathways to Work, although they will still be able to choose to take up programme support, should they wish.

Support for ethnic minorities

5.16   The employment rate of ethnic minorities remains around 14 percentage points below the national rate, although, as Chart 5.2 showed, the rate has been increasing in recent years. Department for Work and Pensions (DWP) employment programmes have helped people from ethnic minority groups into 265,000 jobs, and DWP needs to ensure that its programmes continue to deliver high employment outcomes for all ethnic groups. The 2005 Pre-Budget Report announced that the National Employment Panel's Business Commission on Race Equality in the Workplace, chaired by Gordon Pell, Executive Chairman (Retail Markets), Royal Bank of Scotland, would advise the Government on measures to increase the recruitment, retention and progression of ethnic minorities in the private sector. The National Employment Panel will publish the Commission's report shortly and the Government will carefully explore its recommendations.

Personalised integrated skills and employment support

5.17   Chapter 4 set out the steps that the Government is taking to implement the recommendations of the Leitch Review. As part of this, the Government's successful welfare to work policies need to link up with skills provision to deliver more personalised support that helps low-skilled people access the training they need to stay and progress in work. Jobcentre Plus will work with the Learning and Skills Council in England and with the Devolved Administrations in Scotland and Wales, to ensure an integrated employment and skills service. This will include skills health checks, careers advice based on individual circumstances and needs, and access to training through skills accounts and Train to Gain. Through the Local Employment Partnerships announced in Budget 2007, employers will work with Jobcentre Plus and training providers to ensure that training meets employers' needs, and to provide support and employment opportunities once benefit claimants are ready for work. One example of this is the work that the West Midlands City Strategy consortium is doing with local employers to develop packages of up to eight weeks full-time training and work experience, aiming to guarantee job interviews for all those who complete training. The Government will explore the most appropriate way to allow long-term jobseekers to participate in this training while retaining their benefits.

Making work pay

The National Minimum Wage and Working Tax Credit

5.18   The Government is committed to making work pay by improving incentives to participate and progress in the labour market. Through the Working Tax Credit (WTC) and the National Minimum Wage (NMW), the Government has boosted in-work incomes, thereby improving financial incentives to work and tackling poverty among working people. From 1 October 2007, the NMW adult rate rose to £5.52. The Government is taking forward measures to toughen the NMW enforcement regime, including increased penalties for non-compliant employers and a fairer method of calculating arrears.

5.19   The Government announces the uprating of all elements of the WTC, except for the childcare element, in line with the Retail Prices Index (RPI). It also confirms the Budget 2007 measures to increase the income threshold below which WTC can be claimed in full by £1,200 to £6,420 and the increase in the withdrawal rate for tax credits by two percentage points to 39 per cent. Also from April 2008, the disregard of tax credits in Housing Benefit will increase in line with RPI, to help enhance financial incentives to work.

Tackling the unemployment trap

5.20   The unemployment trap occurs when those without work find the difference between in-work and out-of-work incomes too small to provide an incentive to enter the labour market. Table 5.1 shows that, since the introduction of the NMW in April 1999, the Government has increased the minimum income that people can expect when moving into work, thereby reducing the unemployment trap.

Table 5.1: Weekly minimum income guarantees (MIGs)

	April 1999	April 2008[2]	Percentage increase in real terms[3]
Family[1] with one child, full-time work	£182	£290	25%
Family[1] with one child, part-time work	£136	£226	30%
Single person, 25 or over, full-time work	£113	£187	29%
Couple, no children, 25 or over, full-time work	£117	£221	48%
Single disabled person in full-time work	£139	£233	31%
Single disabled person in part-time work	£109	£169	21%

Assumes the prevailing rate of NMW and that the family is eligible for Family Credit/Disability Working Allowance and Working Tax Credit/Child Tax Credit. Full-time work is assumed to be 35 hours. Part-time work is assumed to be 16 hours.
[1] Applies to lone parent families and couples with children alike.
[2] Assuming indexation in line with HM Treasury's economic forecasts.
[3] RPI growth is taken from HM Treasury's economic forecasts.

Tackling the poverty trap

5.21   The poverty trap occurs when those in work have limited incentives to move up the earnings ladder because it may leave them little better off. Marginal deduction rates (MDRs) measure the extent of the poverty trap by showing how much of each additional pound of gross earnings is lost through higher taxes and withdrawn benefits or tax credits. Table 5.2 shows the progress made in reducing the number of families facing MDRs in excess of 70 per cent since April 1997. Increased incidence of MDRs of between 60 and 70 per cent is primarily due to the extension of financial support for families through tax credits, so that far more families benefit, including low-income families without children.

Table 5.2: The effect of the Government's reforms on high marginal deduction rates

Marginal deduction rate[1]	Before Budget 1998	2008-09 system of tax and benefits
Over 100 per cent	5,000	0
Over 90 per cent	130,000	30,000
Over 80 per cent	300,000	150,000
Over 70 per cent	740,000	195,000
Over 60 per cent	760,000	1,880,000

[1] Marginal deduction rates are for working heads of families in receipt of income-related benefits or tax credits where at least one person works 16 hours or more a week, and the head of the family is not receiving disability benefits.

Note: Figures are cumulative. Before Budget 1998 figures based on 1997-98 estimates caseload and take-up rates; estimates for the 2008-09 system of tax and benefits are based on tax credits caseload in April 2007, and earlier data for housing and council tax benefits.

GIVING EVERYONE THE BEST START IN LIFE

5.22   The Government believes that every child's potential should be fulfilled. A decade ago it set out its key priorities of improving education and eradicating child poverty, and, through a sustained commitment to these goals, has made substantial progress in improving the life chances of all children. The Government is determined to build on the progress of the last decade, starting with a series of steps in the CSR07 period to improve outcomes and reduce child poverty for the current generation of children, raising their aspirations and attainment and thereby tackling the root causes of future disadvantage.

Tackling child **5.23**   Child poverty is both an unacceptable injustice in itself and a key factor leading to a
poverty wide range of other poor outcomes, both in childhood and adulthood. Some 600,000 children
have been lifted out of relative low-income poverty since 1998-99. The announcements made
in Budget 2007, including **increasing the child element of the Child Tax Credit (CTC) by £150
above earnings indexation in April 2008**, are expected to lift around 200,000 children out of
poverty. Rates of Child Benefit and the disabled child elements of the CTC will rise in line with
RPI from April 2008.

5.24   To support the ambitious goal of eradicating child poverty in a generation, the
Government confirms its **PSA to halve the number of children in poverty by 2010-11, on the
way to eradicating child poverty by 2020**, with a national target to reduce the number of
children in relative low-income households, supplemented by indicators to track progress on
reductions in the number of children in absolute low-income, and the number in relative low-
income and material deprivation. This combined indicator recognises that tackling child
poverty means improving the standard of living for children, and captures the extra costs
faced by some families, for example, those with disabled children.

5.25   In addition to the measures set out below to improve outcomes for children and
young people, which will be key to eradicating child poverty, this Pre-Budget Report and
Comprehensive Spending Review is announcing further financial support measures that will
lift around 100,000 further children out of poverty by:

- **raising the child element of the CTC by £25 a year above earnings indexation
in April 2008**, in addition to the Budget 2007 commitment to increase the
child element by £150 and **raising it again by a further £25 above indexation
in April 2010;** and

- **substantially increasing the child maintenance disregards in income-related
benefits.**

5.26   In December 2006 the Government published the White Paper *A new system of child
maintenance*, which set out proposals to establish a new and radically different organisation
– the Child Maintenance and Enforcement Commission (C-MEC) – to administer child
maintenance. To improve incentives for parents to make arrangements for the benefit of
their children, by the end of 2008, when the Government expects parents with care and
claiming benefit no longer to be required to apply for child maintenance, **the child
maintenance disregard in IS, income-based ESA and income-related JSA will rise from £10
to £20 per week, where maintenance is being paid. In April 2010 the disregard will rise
further to £40 per week.**

5.27   **The increase in the maintenance disregard in IS to £20 will be accompanied by an
increase in the maintenance disregard in Housing Benefit and Council Tax Benefit, from the
current £15 per week to a full disregard.** This will help to ensure that work pays for lone
parents receiving maintenance income.

5.28   Chart 5.3 shows the effect by income decile of the Government's reforms to financial
support for families with children. It shows the reforms have been consistent with the
principle of progressive universalism, providing support to all families, with the greatest help
offered to those with the greatest need.

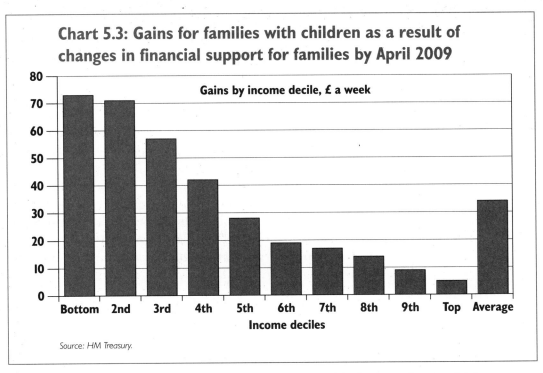

Chart 5.3: Gains for families with children as a result of changes in financial support for families by April 2009

Gains by income decile, £ a week

Income deciles

Source: HM Treasury.

Education and schools

5.29 An excellent education system is the key building block of a society in which everyone is able to make the most of their potential throughout life, and in recognition of this the Government will continue to prioritise education in the CSR07 period. Education spending in England will rise on average by 2.8 per cent a year in real terms between 2007-08 and 2010-11, meaning that UK education spending as a proportion of GDP is projected to increase from 4.7 per cent in 1996-97 to 5.6 per cent in 2010-11. On top of the education settlement announced at Budget 2007, the 2007 CSR announces:

- an additional £250 million in total over the CSR07 period to help ensure that all children at school are ready to learn and able to benefit from truly personalised services and support; and

- an additional £200 million of capital investment to accelerate the primary capital programme and newly build or entirely refurbish an additional 75 schools by 2010-11. Together with further funding of £550 million available within the existing Department for Children, Schools and Families (DCSF) CSR07 settlement, this will allow at least one school to be newly built in every authority by 2010-11.

5.30 To ensure that these increases in investment deliver real improvements in outcomes, the Government announces a new PSA to raise the educational achievement of all children and young people, focusing efforts on raising standards at all levels of learning and development, with stretching national targets from early years to age 19. Alongside this, the Government announces a new PSA to narrow the gap in educational achievement between children from low-income and disadvantaged backgrounds and their peers. Recognising that this is a persistent problem, which must be tackled to raise social mobility, the PSA sets national targets focused on individual pupil-level progression and will drive improvement for the most vulnerable, such as young people in care. Key measures that the Government will put in place to deliver these PSAs include:

- raising the quality and standards of early education and care, through the introduction of the Early Years Foundation Stage and greater graduate leadership of teaching in early years settings;

- extending one-to-one tuition in English and maths to 300,000 underachieving children a year in each subject by 2010-11;

- pilots to personalise all children's learning and help all to progress; and

- enabling every young person to achieve more by the age of 19 than ever before by providing new qualifications including, from 2008, introducing new lines of diplomas.

Work-life balance **5.31** The Government is committed to ensuring that parents have greater choice and flexibility in balancing work and family life. In April 2007 the Government increased paid maternity leave from six to nine months, and has a goal to increase it to 12 months by the end of this Parliament.

Early years **5.32** Building on the commitments set out in *Choice for parents, the best start for children: a ten year strategy for childcare*, this Comprehensive Spending Review allows the Government to deliver a nationwide network of 3,500 Sure Start Children's Centres, one in every community by 2010 (details in Chapter 8).

Improving health and well-being of children and young people **5.33** Good physical, mental and emotional health is a key aspect of well-being, and healthy children are more likely to benefit from their education. Improving children's health will also lead to better outcomes throughout life. Recognising these benefits, the Government therefore announces a new PSA to improve the health and well-being of children and young people, which commits to reverse long-term trends on childhood obesity and includes action to improve the experience of parents of disabled children with the services they receive. Key measures to achieve this PSA include:

- promoting healthy food and activity choices through early years settings, schools and in families and a £240 million subsidy of the direct costs of providing a healthy school lunch;

- providing an additional £60 million funding for targeted mental health work in schools; and

- additional provision of £280 million from the DCSF to provide 40,000 short breaks for severely disabled children, further resource to match this support for disabled children from the NHS settlement, and the development of a "Core Offer" to improve the responsiveness of local services to the needs of disabled children and young people and their families.

Improving children's and young people's safety **5.34** Staying safe is vital for children and young people's happiness, health, well-being and achievement. Harm to children can have a fundamental impact both during their childhood and lasting effects into adult life. Improving children's safety means tackling a wide range of issues – abuse and neglect, accidental injury and death, bullying, crime and anti-social behaviour, as well as ensuring a stable home environment. Therefore the Government announces a new PSA to improve children and young people's safety, which will focus on reducing bullying, reducing unintentional and deliberate injuries to children, and reducing the number of preventable deaths. Measures the government will take to improve the safety of children include:

- implementing the most robust vetting and barring system ever, to ensure a safe children's workforce;

- helping parents and children to understand and manage risks to safety;

- improving the effectiveness of Local Safeguarding Children's Boards;

- raising public awareness and understanding of safety issues; and

- providing better support for children and young people who have suffered harm.

Increasing the number of young people on the path to success 5.35 Most young people in the UK today are seizing the opportunities provided by a changing world and making a successful transition to adulthood. Participation and attainment in education are on an upward trend, and rates of teenage pregnancy are now at their lowest level for more than twenty years. However, for a minority of young people, particularly those who are disadvantaged, vulnerable and do not have support from peers and parents, challenges remain. Research clearly shows that young people who experience one poor outcome typically experience several. For instance, those who are not in education, employment or training (NEET) are disproportionately likely to misuse drugs and alcohol, become parents at a young age, and are more likely to suffer from persistent spells of disadvantage later in life.

5.36 The Government wants to ensure that every young person makes a successful transition to adulthood. To achieve this goal the Government recognises the need for a much greater alignment and integration of the various public services and programmes for young people. To deliver the necessary cross-government focus and coordination, the Government therefore announces a new PSA to increase the number of children and young people on the path to success. The PSA includes national targets to reduce the number of young people who are NEET, and to tackle teenage pregnancy, alongside a focus on reducing drug and alcohol use by teenagers, and getting more young people engaged in positive activities. Delivery of this PSA will include:

- reforming accountability and delivery – for example by merging a range of existing funding programmes – to ensure the integration of services for young people and improvements in outcomes for the most vulnerable in particular;

- supporting active participation of young people and their families in the commissioning, design and delivery of services;

- developing the capacity of the workforce at all levels, particularly through leadership and management, attracting people into the youth workforce and a common platform of skills and training; and

- encouraging more young people to stay in education, in advance of the Government's plans to introduce compulsory participation in education and training for all 16 and 17 year olds.

JSA and IS for young people 5.37 The Government also today announces an increase in the JSA and IS rates for 16-17 year olds to align with the 18-24 rates. This will help to simplify the system, and will ensure a higher minimum level of income for this group.

A FAIR AND INCLUSIVE SOCIETY

5.38 The Government is committed to building a fair, tolerant and inclusive society, based on a conviction that no group should be excluded from the benefits of increasing prosperity. Ensuring that everybody has real and substantive opportunities to fulfil their ambitions and protecting and supporting vulnerable groups are key priorities for the CSR07 period and beyond.

Empowering and protecting marginalised groups

Equality **5.39** The Government's objectives on equality are reflected throughout the new performance management framework in the key areas of health, education and employment. Alongside this wider commitment, the Government announces a new PSA to address the disadvantage that individuals experience because of their gender, race, disability, age, sexual orientation, religion or belief, by enabling people to benefit from opportunities, and participate in the economic and social success of communities, through a measurable reduction in inequalities. The PSA includes commitments to reduce discrimination in employment and increase participation in public life by under-represented groups. It also seeks to reduce the gap between men's and women's wage rates.

5.40 The new Government Equalities Office will promote the equalities agenda throughout Government, acting as a centre of knowledge and expertise on equalities. The Government will also shortly respond to the final report of the Equalities Review[1], setting the direction for a joined up approach to equalities.

5.41 The Equalities and Human Rights Commission came into being on 1 October 2007. This independent Non-Departmental Public Body will work towards reducing inequality, eliminating discrimination, strengthening good relations between people, and protecting human rights.

Support for **5.42** The Government is committed to improving life chances for the most vulnerable **vulnerable adults** groups in society. Too often, vulnerable adults fall between different service providers and are not given the support that they require. Without the firm foundations of a job and a home, individuals suffering from multiple disadvantages risk a lifetime of exclusion. To provide the opportunity for these groups to get onto the path to a more successful life, the Government announces a new PSA to increase the proportion of socially excluded adults in settled accommodation and employment, education or training. The PSA focuses on four at-risk client groups: care-leavers, offenders under probation supervision, adults with secondary mental health problems and adults with moderate to severe learning difficulties.

5.43 This PSA will be delivered in partnership across central government, with local authorities and their partners having a key responsibility in tackling exclusion. The priority actions for the Government in delivering the PSA will be:

- to help the most socially excluded adults to access and maintain settled accommodation, across both the social and private sectors;

- to improve access to employment for excluded groups and improve the availability of quality education and training;

- to ensure specialised support is delivered for at risk groups; and

- to ensure design, delivery and governance of key public services support the most excluded.

---

[1] *Fairness and Freedom: The Final Report of the Equalities Review*, The Equalities Review, 2007. www.theequalitiesreview.org.uk

Promoting saving, financial capability and inclusion

5.44   The Government seeks to support saving and asset ownership for all, from childhood, through working life and into retirement. Since 1997, the Government's savings strategy has focused on improving the environment for saving, providing adequate incentives for saving, and empowering individuals with the capability to make the right saving choices. In addition, the Government aims to promote financial capability and inclusion to ensure that people have the right skills to manage their finances, and have access to the appropriate products and services.

Child Trust Fund **5.45**   The Child Trust Fund was introduced in April 2005 to promote saving and financial education, and to ensure that in the future all young people have a financial asset at 18. Under the scheme, all newborn children receive £250 to be invested in a long-term savings or investment account, and children from lower-income families receive £500. Over 3 million children now have a Child Trust Fund account open in their names. The Government will make further payments at age seven, and additional payments for looked after children. The Child Trust Fund will also be used as a focus for financial education in schools.

Individual **5.46**   Individual Savings Accounts (ISAs) have been successful in developing and extending
Savings Accounts the saving habit and ensuring a fairer distribution of tax relief. To build on this success, Budget 2007 announced a new, simpler and more flexible regime from April 2008, making ISAs available indefinitely, introducing a new ISA structure and raising the annual investment limits. Every adult will have an annual allowance of £7,200. Up to £3,600 of this can be saved in cash with one provider. The remainder can be invested in stocks and shares with either the same or another provider. Savers will also be able to transfer money saved in cash ISAs into stocks and shares ISAs, and all Personal Equity Plans will automatically become stocks and shares ISAs.

Saving Gateway **5.47**   The Government has successfully piloted the Saving Gateway to explore the use of matching – a Government contribution for each pound saved – to encourage saving among lower-income households. Over 22,000 participants took part in the pilots, achieving a total of over £15 million in saving. The pilots confirmed the success of matching as a targeted incentive for lower-income savers. They also demonstrated clear benefits around promoting regular saving and bringing individuals into contact with financial institutions.

5.48   The Government announces that it is taking forward feasibility work into the system requirements to enable the rollout of the Saving Gateway. Subject to the results of this work, further announcements on rollout will be made in the Budget.

Financial **5.49**   Many consumers are not confident in making decisions about their money. In
capability January 2007, the Government set out its aspirations for increasing consumers' capability over the next 10-20 years[2]. This includes ensuring that:

- all adults have access to high-quality generic financial advice;

- all children and young people have access to a planned and coherent programme of personal finance education; and

- there is a range of Government programmes focused on improving financial capability, particularly to help those who are most vulnerable to the consequences of poor financial decisions.

---

[2] Financial Capability: the Government's long-term approach, HM Treasury, January 2007.

Thoresen Review 5.50   To take forward this agenda the Government established an independent review, led
of Generic by Otto Thoresen, to research and design a national approach to generic financial advice; and
Financial Advice a ministerial group, led by the Economic Secretary, to develop a cross-government approach
and next steps to financial capability. The Thoresen review has begun consumer testing of generic advice
and will publish an interim report later in the Autumn, setting out principles for a national
approach, and a final report in the New Year. The Government will respond to the review and
publish its action plan in Spring 2008.

Box 5.1: Ministerial Group on Financial Capability

The group brings together Ministers from key departments to deliver an action plan for
incorporating measures to improve financial capability into a range of Government
services, from early years to pensions.

Since the group began its work, the Government has announced a dedicated economic
well-being and financial capability programme, as part of Personal, Social, Health and
Economic education (PSHE) in secondary schools, to begin in September 2008. In addition,
the Government has announced an £11.5 million package of support for schools to teach
children financial skills over the Spending Review period. A substantial part of this money
will be used to develop Child Trust Fund branded teaching resources.

The group will continue to work, considering plans to embed financial capability within
adult skills programmes and initiatives to tackle social exclusion; use Children's Centres to
deliver appropriate information and advice; develop the evidence-based information and
communications strategy for pensions and personal accounts to support retirement
decision-making; and ensure public services can best make use of generic financial advice.

Financial 5.51   Access to financial services is a key element in ensuring that everyone can participate
inclusion in, and benefit from, the modern economy. The report of the Financial Inclusion Taskforce
last month shows that good progress continues to be made towards the goal shared by the
Government and the banks to halve the number of adults without access to a bank account,
with over 800,000 people brought into banking between 2002-03 and 2005-06.

5.52   Over 100 credit unions and community development finance institutions have now
received funding from the Government's £42 million Growth Fund and over 37,000 affordable
loans have been made to financially excluded people. Taskforce working groups have been
established to consider how to further scale up third sector lenders, and to take forward work
on access to insurance.

5.53   Good progress is also being made by the Department for Business, Enterprise and
Regulatory Reform (BERR) in delivering the £47.5 million face-to-face money advice fund,
with over 500 advisors recruited and trained, and more than 44,000 clients advised to date.

5.54   In March 2007, the Government announced a new policy framework for the spending
period 2008-2011, including the extension of the Financial Inclusion Taskforce.[3] The
Government announces the continuation of the Financial Inclusion Fund at £130 million
over the CSR period. The fund will include continuing support for financial inclusion
initiatives aimed at helping vulnerable people with problem debt, including BERR's money
advice projects, and the DWP Growth Fund. A ministerial working group on financial
inclusion will develop a detailed action plan, to be published later in the year.

---

[3] *Financial Inclusion: the way forward*, HM Treasury, March 2007.

> ## Box 5.2: Personal over-indebtedness
>
> **Personal credit is an important financial tool; an efficient, competitive and fair consumer credit market is a key component of a successful economy. The Government's macroeconomic framework has delivered stability and rising prosperity, and people are now more confident in taking on personal debt.**
>
> **As set out in Annex A, total personal debt stands at almost £1.3 trillion, a figure far outweighed by almost £4 trillion of household financial assets (over £1 trillion in cash and bank deposits). However, the Government recognises that a small minority of people do experience problems when they take on too much debt, and that targeted action is needed to help those at risk, or already in difficulty. The Government has identified five specific areas for action:**
>
> - **helping those most vulnerable to the causes and consequences of problem debt, using the £130 million Financial Inclusion Fund for 2008-11 to support the continued provision of free money advice for financially excluded people, and widen access to affordable credit;**
> - **improving consumers' financial decision-making to prevent problem debt, through the financial capability action plan to be published in the spring, including the Government's response to the Thoresen Review of Generic Financial Advice;**
> - **recognising the role of saving to increase personal financial resilience, including promoting access to savings opportunities through ISAs and the Child Trust Fund, and taking forward feasibility work into the system requirements to enable the roll-out of the Saving Gateway;**
> - **acting on evidence of specific indicators of problem debt, including mortgage repossessions and Individual Voluntary Arrangements (IVAs), building on the regulatory framework through the FSA's work reviewing mortgage regulation, and Insolvency Service work to agree a protocol for IVAs by the end of the year; and**
> - **setting out action taken across Government to tackle over-indebtedness, including a new review of current evidence on the drivers of problem debt, in the annual report of the Ministerial Group on Over-indebtedness, to be published later this year.**

Supporting people in later life

5.55 Pensioner poverty was an important issue facing the Government in 1997, with 2.8 million pensioners in relative poverty,[4] and growing inequality between rich and poor pensioners. The Government's support for pensioners is based on the principle of progressive universalism, providing support for all, with more for those who need it most.

Support for pensioners **5.56** Through measures such as increases in the basic State Pension, the introduction of Pension Credit, Winter Fuel Payments, and free television licences for the over 75s, the Government has sought to provide support for pensioners, and is spending around £11 billion a year more in real terms on pensioners now than in 1997. As a result of measures implemented since 1997, the poorest third of households will be on average £2,050 a year, or around £39 a week, better off by 2008-09. Overall, pensioner households will be on average £1,450 a year, or around £28 a week better off over the same period. Pensioners also benefit from free eye tests, free prescriptions and free bus travel. Pensioners are now less likely than the population as a whole to be in poverty: over 2 million pensioner households have been

[4] i.e. having an income below 60 per cent of median income after housing costs, as set out in the *Households Below Average Income: an analysis of the income distribution series*, Department for Work and Pensions.

lifted out of absolute poverty, and over 1 million have been lifted out of relative poverty since 1997.

5.57 In common with much of the world, the UK's population includes an increasing proportion of older people. To support older people and ensure the UK adapts to and benefits from the ageing society, **the Government announces a new PSA to tackle poverty and promote greater independence and well-being in later life.** The PSA commits to improvement in areas that older people themselves have said are important, such as employment opportunity, levels of health in later life, and continuing to ensure pensioners share in the rising prosperity of the nation. The Government will:

- continue to tackle pensioner poverty, particularly through payment of pensions and benefits in the short term, and through implementing pensions reform and improving financial capability in the long term;

- support and encourage longer working lives, and help older people to be active and healthy as they age;

- support older people to live independently, if they so choose, by allowing users to shape the social care they want; and

- work to increase older people's satisfaction with both their homes and their neighbourhood.

Uprating of Pension Credit

5.58 The Pension Credit is the foundation through which the Government provides security for the poorest pensioners and rewards those with modest savings. The Government announced in the Pensions White Paper[5] that it would uprate the Pension Credit standard minimum guarantee in line with earnings over the long term to ensure that pensioners share in rising national prosperity. The Government will increase the Pension Credit standard minimum guarantee to £124 for single pensioners and to £189 for couples in 2008-09, demonstrating the Government's continued commitment to tackling pensioner poverty.

Voluntary Class 3 National Insurance contributions

5.59 A key element of the Government's state pension reforms was to reduce the number of qualifying years required to receive a full basic State Pension to 30 from 6 April 2010. However, during debate on the Pensions Bill, concerns were raised that some individuals, particularly women and carers, may still have gaps in their national insurance contribution records (meaning that they would not be eligible for the full amount of the basic State Pension) and that the reforms would create a divide between those retiring before and after 6 April 2010. To address this, proposals were made that individuals should be able to buy voluntary contributions for a greater number of missed years than the system currently allows. The Government will continue to analyse the options in terms of fairness, affordability and simplicity, and to hold informal discussions with stakeholders.

State Second Pension (S2P)

5.60 Following the Pensions White Paper, the Pensions Act 2007 puts in place proposals to reform the State Second Pension so that it becomes a simple, flat-rate weekly top-up to the basic State Pension by around 2030, providing a clearer foundation for private saving. To ensure this timetable is met, while delivering the personal tax reforms announced at Budget 2007, the Government will introduce the **Upper Accruals Point for the State Second Pension in 2009.**[6] **Legislation will be introduced in the NICs Bill to ensure there is no delay in State Second Pension simplification.**

---

[5] *Security in retirement: towards a new pensions system*, Department for Work and Pensions, May 2006.

[6] This was originally intended for 2012, to coincide with wider pension reforms.

Financial Assistance Scheme **5.61**   The Financial Assistance Scheme was established in 2004 to assist those who lost significant amounts when their pension schemes started winding up between 1 January 1997 and 5 April 2005 as a result of the sponsoring employer becoming insolvent. Budget 2007 announced an extension of the scheme so that all members of affected pension schemes receive assistance of 80 per cent of the core pension rights accrued in their scheme. The Secretary of State for Work and Pensions also set up a review, whose interim report was published in July, to look at making best use of assets within these schemes. **The Government subsequently committed to match any increase in assistance levels that could be realised by the review, with the goal of moving towards 90 per cent of expected core pension for all recipients. The review will report by the end of the year.**

Encouraging retirement saving **5.62**   The stability of the economy over the past decade has allowed individuals to plan for retirement with greater confidence. Building on this success, the Government is committed to developing a retirement framework that empowers individuals to take personal responsibility for decisions regarding how much to save and when to retire. The Government's state pension reforms – including improving the outcomes for women and carers from 2010, linking the basic State Pension to earnings from 2012,[7] and raising State Pension Age in line with life expectancy over the longer term – will together provide a simpler and more generous state pension foundation to support private saving. Meanwhile DWP continues to make progress on reforms to the private pension system. The response to the Personal Accounts White Paper was published in June.[8]

Pensions tax relief **5.63**   Successive Governments have provided generous tax relief to encourage pension saving to produce an income in retirement. This relief, worth an estimated £17.5 billion in 2007-08, is an important part of the Government's approach to encouraging future pensioners to save for their retirement.

Pensions tax modernisation **5.64**   The Government has sought to remove obstacles to saving imposed by complexities in the pensions tax regime and in April 2006 (A-day) introduced a new, simplified regime for the taxation of pensions. Since A-day, the Government has worked with industry to identify areas of friction in the new system to simplify the task for providers to comply with the rules and to ensure practice remains in line with original intentions. A range of further simplifications are announced today, as set out in Chapter 4.

5.65   **Today the Government has issued draft legislation for anti-avoidance measures preventing the use of scheme pensions and annuities to enable inheritance of tax-relieved savings and changes to the inheritance tax (IHT) rules to ensure that UK tax-relieved pensions funds in overseas schemes continue to be protected from IHT.**

Innovation in the annuity market **5.66**   Following a commitment in the 2006 Pre-Budget Report, the Government has consulted widely with industry on tax barriers to the further development of 'hybrid' decumulation products, which combine an element of drawdown with a guaranteed income. The Government has decided not to change the tax rules as this would add complexity to the tax system and potentially benefit only a small number of consumers with large pension savings.

---

[7] As stated in the Pensions White Paper: "Our objective, subject to affordability and the fiscal position, is to do this in 2012, but in any event by the end of the next Parliament at the latest. We will make a statement on the precise date at the beginning of the next Parliament."

[8] *Personal Accounts: a new way to save – Summary of the responses to the consultation*, DWP, June 2007.

Box 5.3: Open Market Option review

Under the Open Market Option, (OMO) an individual can shop around to get the best annuity deal to provide their retirement income, rather than simply taking the annuity offered by their pensions saving provider. The Government announced at the 2006 PBR that HM Treasury and DWP would work together with a range of stakeholders to improve the operation of the OMO for consumers.[a] The review has now concluded and full details, together with all the measures agreed with industry, consumer and other stakeholder groups, are available at http://www.hm-treasury.gov.uk/pbr_csr/pbr_csr07_index.cfm These measures include:

- the Pensions Advisory Service (TPAS) setting up a web-based structured choice tool to guide people through their retirement income options;

- work by the Financial Services Authority (FSA) with firms on OMO processes – particularly in terms of delays in OMO transfers and compliance with the Treating Customers Fairly principle;

- work by DWP with stakeholders to facilitate development of better-focused information for consumers about their annuity options.

Stakeholders will continue to be involved in developing and implementing the measures, and the operation of the OMO will be monitored so improvements can be assessed.

[a] *The Annuities Market*, HM Treasury, December 2006.

Helping vulnerable households to heat their homes

5.67 The Government is committed to ensuring that the most vulnerable households – both pensioners and others – can afford to heat their homes to an adequate standard, and has made substantial progress, cutting fuel poverty in England by 50 per cent, an estimated 2.7 million households, between 1996 and 2007, despite energy price rises since 2004.

5.68 The Government's approach addresses the key determinants of fuel poverty through:

- financial support, for example Winter Fuel Payments to pensioners (support equivalent to taking an additional 500,000 out of fuel poverty);

- help for low-income households to take advantage of the benefits of a competitive energy market by switching supplier; and

- enhancing energy efficiency through continuing the Warm Front programme (which has spent over £1.6 billion since 2000, assisting 1.4 million vulnerable households) and plans to expand the Carbon Emissions Reduction Target (CERT) obligations on energy suppliers. Subject to final decisions, the combination of Warm Front and the CERT Priority Group will enable spending on energy efficiency and other measures for low-income households to rise in the CSR07 period compared to the previous spending period.

A MODERN AND FAIR TAX SYSTEM

5.69 A modern and fair tax system encourages work and saving, responds to business developments and globalisation and supports the provision of world-class public services to ensure that everyone has the opportunities they deserve in a changing world. The Government will continue to develop a modern and fair tax system that provides a level playing-field for all taxpayers.

Modernising the personal tax and benefit system

5.70   The personal tax and benefit system is at the heart of the relationship between the citizen and the Government. Personal taxation provides a significant proportion of the tax revenue used to fund the public services that are the foundations of a flexible economy and a fair society. An important innovation has been the introduction of the Child and Working Tax Credits, which as part of that system provide support to nearly six million families and ten million children. The tax and benefit system can also be used to provide incentives to work and save. The personal tax and benefit system therefore underpins many of the themes set out in this chapter.

5.71   The introduction of tax credits has greatly reduced the effective tax burden on many families, increasing incentives to work as well as reducing poverty. For example, from April 2008, a single-earner family with two children will pay no net tax until their income reaches £20,440. A couple with no children will pay no net tax until their income reaches £11,700. The comparable figures for 1997-98 were £14,400 for a single earner family with two children, and £4,210 for a couple with no children.

Budget 2007 personal tax reforms   **5.72**   Since 1997, the Government has undertaken a comprehensive programme of reforms to the tax and benefit system with the aims of simplifying the system, improving incentives to work, eradicating child poverty, supporting families and ensuring security for all in old age. Budget 2007 announced the next stage in these reforms. Once fully implemented, these reforms and the new measures announced today mean that by April 2009: [9]

- a single-earner family with two children on male mean earnings (£35,900) will be £320 a year better off, with the direct tax burden on the family falling to 20 per cent, lower than any year of the 1980s and 1990s;

- a single-earner family with two children on median earnings (£27,000), will be around £540 a year better off;

- a single-earner couple without children on half median earnings (£13,500) and receiving the WTC will be £175 a year better off;

- the numbers of children in relative poverty will be around 200,000 lower;

- around 600,000 fewer pensioners will pay income tax than would otherwise be the case, so that in total only 43 per cent of pensioners will be taxpayers. By April 2011, no pensioner aged 75 or over will pay any tax until their income reaches £10,000; and

- the tax burden on small unincorporated businesses will be reduced by £50 million in 2009-10, as the self-employed pay income tax and national insurance contributions (NICs) on their business profits.

Income tax and NICs   **5.73**   The income tax personal allowances for under 65s and NICs thresholds and limits, except the upper earnings and profit limits, will be raised in line with the RPI from April 2008. As announced at Budget 2007, age-related personal tax allowances for the over-65s will be raised by £1,180 above inflation, and the national insurance upper earnings and profit limits will increase by £75 above inflation per week in 2008-09 before they are aligned with the increased level at which higher rate tax begins to be paid in 2009-10. This alignment will ensure that people paying higher rate tax under the new thresholds will be no worse off than under the current arrangements. There will be no changes to the NICs rates for employers and employees, or to the profit-related NICs paid by the self-employed.

---

[9] Assuming indexation in line with HM Treasury's economic forecasts

ax and
.iCs review

5.74   At Budget 2006, the Government announced that it would conduct a review of the case for further aligning the administration of the income tax and NICs systems. The findings of the review are published today. The review has examined ways, within the current policy framework, of improving the administrative alignment of the two systems for employers and the impact this might have on individuals. It has particularly focused on the proposal, often put forward by employers, that NICs should operate more like tax, by being moved onto an annual basis and being collected cumulatively. The report concludes that potential savings for employers are lower than might have been expected, there would be mixed outcomes for lower-paid individuals, and alignment would come at a high exchequer cost. The Government has therefore concluded that the benefits of administrative alignment of the tax and national insurance systems do not outweigh the costs.

5.75   The review did, however, identify a number of areas where improvements to the current systems could be made, reducing administrative burdens on business. These include improving and aligning HM Revenue and Customs (HMRC) guidance on tax and NICs, collecting tax on benefits in kind through the payroll, and improving the collection of national insurance for the self-employed. HMRC will consult on how best to introduce improvements in each of these areas. Further details are in Chapter 4.

Inheritance tax   **5.76**   The inheritance tax (IHT) spouse relief rules mean that there is no IHT paid on assets passing between married couples or civil partners. Many people therefore leave all their assets to their spouse or civil partner, and do not make use of their individual tax-free allowance of £300,000. The Government will therefore make the IHT system fairer by ensuring that if a person's tax-free allowance is not used on their death, it can be transferred to their surviving spouse or civil partner, **enabling every married couple or civil partnership to benefit from double the tax-free allowance – £600,000 this year – in addition to spouse relief.**

5.77   Furthermore, to ensure that people who have lost a spouse or civil partner prior to today can also benefit, **the Government will extend this entitlement to the three million existing widows, widowers and bereaved civil partners.**

5.78   Following the announcement made at this year's Budget and the changes announced today, **the IHT allowance will rise by April 2010 to £350,000 for individuals and £700,000 for couples.** In future years the Government will consider both house prices and retail price inflation when setting the appropriate IHT allowance.

Capital gains tax
reform

5.79   The Government is committed to ensuring that the UK has an internationally competitive capital gains tax (CGT) system that promotes flexibility and competition, and responds to the changing needs of investors. Building on the Government's ongoing programme of tax reform, the Government announces a major reform of the taxation of individuals' capital gains. This will put the CGT regime on a more sustainable footing and help investors plan for the long term. **For disposals on or after 6 April 2008 there will be a single CGT rate of 18 per cent, resulting in a more straightforward system for taxpayers.** As part of this new system the annual exempt amount (currently £9,200) will remain in place, but taper relief and indexation allowance will be withdrawn. HMRC have today published further details of the reform package, and will immediately begin discussion on implementation with interested parties.

Residence and **5.80** The Government today announces the completion of the review of the residence and
domicile review domicile rules that apply to personal taxation. The Government has concluded that the
existing arrangements make an important contribution to the UK's competitiveness, by
making the UK an attractive place for skilled people to come to work and do business and
where non-domiciles contribute £4 billion of tax on UK earnings. Reforms are required to
make the current arrangement operate fairly:

- firstly, from April 2008 resident non-domiciles who have been in the UK for
  longer than seven out of the past ten years will only be able to access the
  remittance basis of taxation on payment of an annual charge of £30,000,
  unless their unremitted foreign income or gains are less than £1,000;

- secondly, people who use the remittance basis of taxation will, from April
  2008, no longer be entitled to income tax personal allowances. Again, people
  with small amounts of foreign income will be exempt;

- thirdly, the Government will introduce changes to the residence rules so that
  days of arrival in and departure from the UK will count toward establishing
  residence. This brings the UK into line with international practice; and

- finally, the Government will amend the current rules to remove flaws and
  anomalies that allow individuals using the remittance basis of taxation to
  sidestep UK tax, where it is due on foreign income and gains.

5.81 The Government will consult on a wider range of options and specifically on whether
people who have been resident in the UK for longer than ten years should make a greater
contribution, and on the detail of these proposals before the changes are introduced to ensure
non-domiciles pay their fair share of UK tax.

Modernising the business tax system

5.82 The Government believes that the tax system should ensure fairness between all
business taxpayers and support the Government's wider economic and social objectives. This
Pre-Budget Report and Comprehensive Spending Review announces changes to the tax
system to ensure that it remains modern and relevant for businesses in a changing world.

Sale of leasing **5.83** The Government has become aware of a flaw in the legislation governing the sale of
companies leasing companies, which is resulting in an unintended tax charge and could prevent genuine
commercial restructuring. **The Government will therefore bring forward legislation to
remove this unintended consequence with retrospective effect from 5 December 2005, the
date of the original legislation's introduction.**

Hedging currency **5.84** **The Government will amend regulations on the tax treatment of loans and
risk** **derivatives that hedge a company's currency risk from investment in foreign operations, to
ensure only the "hedged" position is taxed.** The changes, to have effect from 1 January 2008,
represent a short-term solution to technical problems that have been highlighted through
discussions with business. **The Government will consult on draft regulations to implement
more extensive changes, to take effect from January 2009.**

Stamp Duty **5.85** Earlier this year the Government announced that it intends to extend the changes
Reserve Tax made to stamp duty intermediary relief to shares admitted to trading on Multilateral Trading
intermediary Facilities. However, the FSA has first to consider the regulatory implications of the proposed
relief changes. The FSA is expected to report the initial findings of its consultative process shortly,
and a further update will be given following that report.

North Sea Oil   **5.86**   The latest round of discussions on the North Sea fiscal regime with the oil and gas industry ended in September 2007. The Government is considering the conclusions from these discussions and will publish a consultation document examining the options for further action in due course.

Modernising tax administration

5.87   HMRC continues to work on transforming its relationship with citizens and business. This includes a range of simplification measures which make it clearer and more straightforward for businesses to comply with their obligations. Further detail on the simplification agenda can be found in Chapter 4 of this Pre-Budget Report and Comprehensive Spending Review. The measures set out in this section are designed to make it easier for taxpayers to comply with the tax system while at the same time making certain HMRC collects the right amount of tax.

Review of Business Links   **5.88**   HMRC is on track in delivering its commitment to the 2006 Review of Links with Large Business and today publishes *Making a Difference: Clarity and Certainty*. This announces a new Advance Agreements Unit to provide certainty to business on significant inward investment and corporate reconstructions, provides clarity on how HMRC and business will develop a shared understanding of risk and how issues will be resolved more speedily and efficiently, and announces the extension of individual Relationship Managers to more large businesses.

Review of HMRC powers, deterrents and safeguards   **5.89**   HMRC's review of powers, deterrents and safeguards seeks to provide modern tools for the department, and corresponding safeguards for taxpayers. The first major changes as a result of the review – the modernisation of the law on criminal investigations by HMRC and on penalties for incorrect returns – were introduced in Finance Act 2007. Consultations on compliance assurance checks, taxpayer safeguards and on payments and repayments of tax were held in summer 2007. Publication of responses and further consultations, including on further modernisation of penalties, is planned for later this year.

Excise reviews and appeals   **5.90**   Following a consultation held over the summer, the Government will shortly be publishing draft legislation which will extend statutory rights to an independent review and appeal against a wider range of decisions made by HMRC on excise duty matters.

Electronic vehicle licensing   **5.91**   To facilitate the use of Electronic Vehicle Licensing, from 1 September 2008 the requirement to display an up-to-date tax disc at all times will be waived for the first five working days following re-licensing.

Consultation on Gift Aid   **5.92**   Budget 2007 announced that the Government would consult with the charitable sector to identify possible measures to increase giving through Gift Aid. The consultation closed on 30 September 2007 following seven regional and national events, and submissions from a wide range of local and national third sector organisations. A summary of responses to the consultation will be published on the HM Treasury website later in the autumn. Ahead of next year's Budget, the Government will explore, with charitable sector representatives, a number of areas raised during the consultation.

Protecting tax revenues

5.93   The vast majority of business and individual taxpayers in the UK comply with their tax obligations. By contrast, avoidance of tax by a minority leads to distortion in competitive markets, unfairness between individuals and pressure on the public finances. The Government will continue to support the compliant majority while responding to avoidance and fraud with timely and targeted action. The Government will also continue to defend the tax system robustly against challenges under EU law.

Tackling tax avoidance **5.94**   The disclosure regime, introduced at Budget 2004, allows the Government to respond to avoidance swiftly and in a targeted fashion. To identify and tackle more effectively those who make use of marketed avoidance schemes, the Government will consult on options to improve the operation of Scheme Reference Numbers.

5.95   The Government will continue to protect future revenues by introducing measures:

- countering the exploitation of interest relief by individuals;

- amending the disguised interest rules to prevent abuse;

- ensuring that scheme pensions and lifetime annuities are used solely to provide an income for life and not as a means of diverting tax-relieved pension savings into inheritance, in line with Government principles that the generous tax regime for pensions supports saving for an income retirement;

- tackling deferral of corporation tax through structural management of employer contributions to pensions schemes; and

- taking action to prevent the avoidance of tax through leasing plant and machinery.

Stamp Duty Land Tax **5.96**   To ensure that where there is a transfer of an interest in a property held within an investment partnership there is no charge to stamp duty land tax (SDLT), the Government will legislate to amend the stamp duty land tax anti-avoidance provisions introduced in Finance Act 2007. This follows representations made to the Government from the property investment sector. The amendment to the legislation will apply retrospectively from the date Royal Assent was given to Finance Act 2007.

5.97   Following on from action in 2006-07 on SDLT avoidance, the Government will continue to tackle SDLT avoidance, while ensuring that the competitiveness of the UK is not harmed. The Government will consult interested parties later this year on how to extend the disclosure regime to high value residential property transactions.

5.98   In addition, the Government believes that the use of special purpose vehicles to reduce stamp duty liability on high value residential property is unfair to the compliant majority who pay SDLT on the purchase of such property in the UK. The Government will also consult interested parties later this year on the issues involved in implementing a measure to address this issue.

Income shifting **5.99**   The Government believes it is unfair that some individuals arrange their affairs to gain a tax advantage by shifting part of their income, from dividends or partnership profits, to another person who is subject to a lower rate of tax.

5.100   The Government will be launching a consultation shortly on draft legislation to prevent such income shifting, with the intention that this legislation will take effect from 2008-09. The Government aims to ensure, through consultation, that only arrangements intended to reduce tax, rather than commercial arrangements, are affected by this legislation and that the administrative burdens of the legislation are minimised.

Removal of NICs exemption   **5.101**   The Government acknowledges the role that a long-standing NICs exemption for holiday pay paid via a third party has had in addressing the problems of labour mobility in the construction industry, as well as helping to form the basis for additional benefits and collective bargaining agreements for employees in this industry. However working time regulations now ensure holiday entitlement is preserved in all sectors even where individuals are employed for short periods of time, and the Government has become aware that the exemption is now being used by employers outside construction solely to reduce their and their employees' NICs liability, contrary to the original policy intention. Therefore it has been announced today that schemes in the construction industry will maintain this exemption for five years to allow time to adjust to these changes, while for all other schemes the exemption is removed from 30 October 2007.

Life insurance   **5.102**   The Government will consult on legislation, effective from today, that will prevent life insurance companies benefiting from tax relief for expenses in respect of reinsured business which have been met by the reinsurer of that business.

Tackling VED evasion   **5.103**   To assist in the fight against vehicle excise duty (VED) evasion, the Government today strengthens VED enforcement powers, to include motorists driving unlicensed vehicles and parking in certain areas where enforcement is not currently permitted. Therefore, in addition to public roads, from 1 September 2008, VED enforcement will also cover vehicles parked in public places that are not intrinsically part of a private dwelling, where a Statutory Off-Road Notification has not been made.

MTIC fraud   **5.104**   New estimates of Missing Trader Intra Community (MTIC) fraud, published today, show that the scale of attempted fraud fell by up to £1½ billion in 2006-07, to between £2¼ billion and £3¼ billion. The estimated impact on VAT receipts fell to between £1 billion and £2 billion. These reduced estimates demonstrate the success of the Government's strategy for tackling MTIC fraud. HMRC will take further steps to apply both criminal and civil sanctions to those who are found to be knowingly involved in fraudulent trading.

Alcohol and tobacco   **5.105**   Good progress has been made to reinforce the Tackling Tobacco Smuggling and Alcohol Compliance Strategies. These measures will make life harder for smugglers and other fraudsters though the Government recognises the ongoing challenges to further reducing the illicit market share as organised crime continues to target this area.

6 STRONGER COMMUNITIES AND A BETTER QUALITY OF LIFE

Public services play a crucial role in building flourishing communities and enabling individuals to lead healthy and fulfilling lives. To respond to the rising aspirations of the British people and the desire for stronger, safer, more sustainable communities, the Government is:

Delivering modern and responsive health and social care by:

- increasing spending on the NHS by 4 per cent a year in real terms, taking its budget from £90 billion in 2007-08 to £110 billion by 2010-11, and delivering the vision set out by the Darzi Review for a health service which is fair, personalised, effective, safe and locally accountable; and

- funding the delivery of more personalised adult social care that will give people greater choice and control, and announcing plans to consult on reform of the adult care and support systems.

Increasing access to decent and affordable homes by:

- delivering the target of 2 million new homes by 2016, by increasing spending on housing from £8.8 billion in 2007-08 to £10 billion by 2010-11, reforming the tax and planning systems, and laying the ground for new planning charges to support essential investment in infrastructure.

Building strong and cohesive communities by:

- strengthening the role of local authorities to reshape local services around the individuals, families and communities that use them – underpinned by resource growth of 1 per cent a year in real terms over the CSR07 period, which the Government expects will enable the overall council tax increase to stay well below five per cent in each of the next three years; and

- maintaining funding in real terms for the arts, museums and galleries, and ensuring a lasting cultural and sporting legacy for the nation by contributing £3.6 billion to the first phase of the construction costs of the Olympics over the next three years.

Building safe and secure neighbourhoods by:

- increasing resources for the Home Office by 1.1 per cent a year in real terms over the CSR07 period, with an addition of over £220 million by 2010-11 to enable it to lead the fight against terrorism, alongside wider steps to roll out neighbourhood policing and deliver a more effective criminal justice system; and

- protecting the UK's security by increasing spending on counter-terrorism, intelligence and resilience from £2$\frac{1}{2}$ billion in 2007-08 to £3$\frac{1}{2}$ billion in 2010-11, within a new single security and intelligence budget for counter-terrorism.

6.1 Stable growth with high employment and low inflation provide the platform for rising living standards, while world-class standards of education and a modern tax and benefits system help to expand opportunity, ensure fairness and deliver security for the most vulnerable. Beyond providing for these material requirements, public services also play a crucial role in building the foundations of communities and enabling individuals to lead healthy and fulfilling lives. This chapter sets out four Government priorities for the next decade to respond to the aspirations of the British people and the desire for stronger, safer, more sustainable communities:

- **delivering modern and responsive health and social care** fit for the 21st century – giving people real choices, more local care, greater control over their health, and support to remain independent wherever possible;

- **ensuring more people have access to a decent home at an affordable price,** in the place they want to live and work – meeting the rising demands of a growing population;

- **building strong and cohesive communities,** by investing in the shared public institutions and facilities that support thriving social networks, with a revitalised role for local authorities and the third sector to reshape services around the communities that use them; and

- **building safe and secure neighbourhoods,** by continuing to invest in the police and security services to lead the fight against crime and terrorism, and working with local communities to tackle the root causes of these threats.

MODERN AND RESPONSIVE HEALTH AND SOCIAL CARE

Progress over the last decade
6.2   The Wanless Review of 2002 argued that while the NHS of 1997 had the right system of funding, it lacked the investment and capacity needed to deliver the standards of healthcare achieved in other leading countries. One highly visible result of this was the 284,000 people then waiting more than six months for an operation, with some waiting as long as two years. The Government responded with a major programme of investment, with resources almost doubling in real terms since 1997 to over £90 billion this year, delivering unprecedented investment in services, equipment, buildings and staff. The introduction of more demanding clinical standards has been accompanied by reforms to ensure that people's needs and wishes are put at the heart of services, through greater choice and a drive to support people at home and in their own communities. Steps have also been taken to raise productivity growth, ensuring further advances are delivered with value for money for the taxpayer. This has delivered:

- over 79,000 more nurses and 36,000 more doctors, 90 per cent more heart and cataract operations and over twice as many knee replacements compared with 1997;

- falling waiting lists in the NHS, waits of over six months virtually eliminated as shown in Chart 6.1; and

- 14 per cent reductions in the number of deaths from cancer and 31 per cent from heart disease – in total, over 200,000 lives have been saved since 1996 as a result of reductions to mortality rates from cancer and circulatory diseases among people aged under 75.

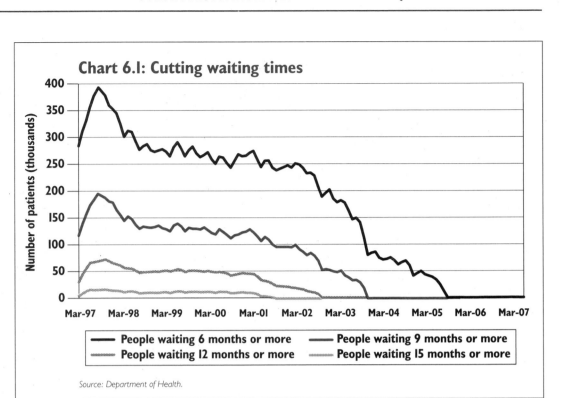

Chart 6.1: Cutting waiting times

Source: Department of Health.

Challenges for **6.3** Having addressed the capacity constraints of a decade ago, the key challenge now is
the next decade to deliver a more responsive and personalised NHS, focused not just on treating illnesses but
on achieving good health for all. However, the social and demographic context for delivering
these goals is becoming more challenging. The UK population is getting older, with the
number of people aged over 85 increasing by around a quarter over the next decade – placing
increasing demands on health and social care. Rising levels of obesity are also adding to the
pressures on the health system, and fifteen million people with long-term needs, such as
diabetes, stroke, high blood pressure or cardiovascular conditions, need better prevention
and earlier care. Despite the improvements of the past decade, there are still wide
inequalities, with the poorest areas seeing the poorest health outcomes.

6.4 Alongside these demographic and social changes, new technologies are advancing
the frontiers of medical knowledge, creating new cures and treatments that will transform the
daily lives of millions of patients. At the same time, expectations of the health service have
increased year on year, and will continue to do so. People expect real choices, more local care,
greater control over their health, and support to remain independent wherever possible.

Building a NHS **6.5** An increasingly collaborative approach between healthcare professionals and
fit for the patients will be needed to respond to these challenges and opportunities, focusing on
21st century prevention and promoting individual responsibility for health and wellbeing; and delivering
services in more local settings in a way that is genuinely flexible, integrated and responsive to
people's needs and wishes. The Government therefore asked one of the world's leading
surgeons, Lord Ara Darzi, to lead a review of how to meet the challenges of delivering health
care over the next decade. Following discussions with patients, doctors, nurses, and many
other health professionals, Lord Darzi published his interim review on 4 October, the findings
of which are outlined in Box 6.1.

Box 6.1: Interim findings of the NHS Next Stage Review – *Our NHS, Our Future*

The NHS Next Stage Review, led by Lord Ara Darzi, was launched in July 2007 to advise on how to meet the challenges of delivering health care over the next decade. Following extensive consultation, Lord Darzi published an interim report on 4 October laying out the core principles for his vision for the NHS:

- **fair** – equally available to all regardless of circumstances – and making best use of resources;

- **personalised** – to the needs and wants of each individual, especially the most vulnerable; providing access to the health services most suited to every individual at the time and place of their choice; and with clinicians and individuals working closely together in partnership to improve health as well as treat illness;

- **effective** – focused on delivering outcomes for patients that are among the best in the world – saving more lives and improving the quality of life;

- **safe** – giving patients and the public the confidence they need in the care they receive; and

- **locally accountable** – empowering staff locally to lead change and innovate, ensuring that change is based on the best clinical evidence and meets local needs, with patients and the public consulted to ensure they shape and champion their own local services.

The review will report finally to the Prime Minister, Chancellor and Secretary of State for Health before the NHS's 60th anniversary in July 2008.

6.6 To provide the platform for delivering this vision, the Government is increasing resources for the NHS by 4 per cent a year in real terms over the CSR07 period, taking total expenditure up to £110 billion by 2010-11, compared with £35 billion in 1997-98. These resources will be supported by value for money savings releasing at least £8.2 billion to the frontline by 2010-11. Together these will fund the delivery of two new PSAs to promote better health and wellbeing for all and to ensure better care for all, implementing the vision set out in the Darzi review to secure:

A fair NHS by:

- introducing a new comprehensive strategy to reduce health inequalities in life expectancy and infant mortality; and

- investing in programmes to tackle childhood obesity, to reduce the number of obese and overweight children to 2000 levels by 2020.

A more personalised NHS by:

- providing greater choice and convenience for patients by improving GP access, with £250 million for 150 new walk-in health centres open 7 days a week from 8 until 8, and over 100 new GP practices in the areas with the poorest provision;

- delivering the commitment to reduce maximum waiting times to 18 weeks from GP referral to hospital treatment by the end of next year;

- providing better support for those with long-term illnesses to live independently and control their own condition, including by moving towards a care plan for every person with a life-limiting illness; and

- providing better maternity care including more choice for women during pregnancy and birth.

An effective NHS by:

- establishing a new Health Innovation Council to increase innovation across the NHS; and

- increasing funding for the Department of Health's research and development programme to over £1 billion by 2010-11, and with investment from the science budget fully funding the Cooksey Review[1] recommendations to maximise translation of research excellence into health and economic benefit.

A safe NHS by:

- ensuring visibly cleaner hospitals, with increased powers for matrons to tackle MRSA and the introduction of screening for all elective patients next year, and for all emergency admissions as soon as practicable within the next three years.

Empowering people to live independent lives

Supporting independence 6.7 Regardless of age, every individual should be able to contribute to his or her community, treated with dignity and respect, and given choice and control in the way they lead their lives, free from the fear of poverty and neglect. Many older people need help to prolong their independence and maintain their wellbeing, whether this is in their own home or in residential or nursing care. This help may include practical support in their daily lives and financial support from the state to pay for these services or to help with the extra costs of disability. In this, there is an underlying assumption that there is a joint financial responsibility between the Government and the individual or family.

Adult social care 6.8 Adult social care plays a central role in protecting and promoting independence and wellbeing among some of the most vulnerable groups in society. Investment in local authorities, which provide adult social services, will be £2.6 billion higher in 2010-11 than in 2007-08, representing annual average growth of 1 per cent in real terms. Growth in the Department of Health's social care funding, which directly supports new policy initiatives, will increase by £190 million, taking it to £1.5 billion by 2010-11. This funding will enable local authorities to build on progress already made in developing personalised services that give people and their carers greater choice and control over the way in which their needs are met. In particular this investment will enable:

- further expansion of care tailored to the individual, including through individual budgets (which enable service users to commission their own care), subject to a thorough evaluation to be completed in 2008, enabling people to stay independent and in control of their lives;

- continued investment in prevention, enabling people to retain their independence and improve their quality of life. This includes a national roll-out of the Partnership for Older People's Projects; and

---

[1] *A Review of UK health research funding*, Sir David Cooksey, December 2006. Available at www.hm-treasury.gov.uk.

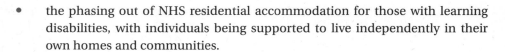

- the phasing out of NHS residential accommodation for those with learning disabilities, with individuals being supported to live independently in their own homes and communities.

Future challenges for social care

6.9   Expected demographic trends over the next 20 years and beyond will result in a substantial increase in the number of older people in need of care and support. The current system of state support, conceived and operated for the 20th century, appears unlikely to be able to target state resources most effectively or meet 21st century aspirations for the quality of life of older people. To achieve these goals requires more than incremental investment in the current social care system. A radical rethink is required of the way the state supports people to retain their independence. As set out in more detail in Box 6.2, the Government plans to produce a Green Paper on reform to the care system, with a focus on older people.

Box 6.2: Long-term sustainable funding for people in need of care and support: the opportunity for reform

As noted in the 2006 Pre-Budget Report, recent reports from Derek Wanless for the King's Fund, the Joseph Rowntree Foundation and others have made important contributions to the growing debate around the need for change to the care and support system for older people. These reports highlight the potential benefits for older people of reform to the care and support system. The Government welcomes the contribution of these assessments but also believes that the case for reform might be extended to all those adults receiving care and support. It will now undertake work to look at reform options and consult on a way forward.

The Government has three requirements for reform: it must promote independence, well-being and control for those in need; be consistent with the principles of progressive universalism; and it must be affordable.

The Government believes that there are real opportunities for reform within a system that shares the cost between the individual and the state and that provides both universal and progressive elements. Greater overall benefits for individuals may also be achieved by reviewing the state systems that people are able to access for such support. There is an opportunity to replace the current systems with a new offer focusing on service users and placing the individual at the centre of these care and support systems, giving them more personal choice and control and directing state resources to where they can have the greatest impact on wellbeing.

The Government therefore intends to develop a reform strategy, and will spend the next period in consultation with public, private and third sector organisations who have contributed to the debate thus far. Next year the Government will set out a process involving extensive public engagement and ultimately leading to a Green Paper identifying key issues and options for reform.

DELIVERING DECENT AND AFFORDABLE HOUSING FOR ALL

6.10   The Government believes that everyone should have access to a decent home at a price they can afford in communities where they want to live and work. The sustained economic growth and stability described in Chapter 2, with low inflation and low interest rates, have helped over one million people to become homeowners over the last decade. Housing supply grew by over 185,000 net additional homes last year, the highest level since the 1980s, and investment in social housing has reduced the number of households living in non-decent homes by over one million.

6.11   Despite this progress, significant challenges remain. The UK's ageing and growing population means that the supply of housing is still not keeping pace with rising demand. As Kate Barker's Review of Housing Supply[2] identified, this is contributing to declining affordability, frustrating the home ownership aspirations of many individuals and families. Failing to respond to new patterns of housing demand has the potential to increase social inequality and reduce labour mobility by forcing up living costs – damaging the flexibility and performance of the UK economy. In responding to this growing demand, the challenge of climate change makes it imperative that new homes are built in a more sustainable way, given that domestic energy consumption accounts for around a quarter of the UK's carbon emissions.

6.12   The Housing Green Paper, *Homes for the Future*,[3] published in July 2007 set out the Government's strategy for responding to these challenges, including a new target of over 240,000 net additional homes a year by 2016, delivering 2 million new homes by 2016 and 3 million by 2020. **The 2007 CSR provides the resources and co-ordination needed to deliver these ambitions, with a new PSA to increase long-term housing supply and affordability, underpinned by increases in spending on housing from £8.8 billion in 2007-08 to £10 billion in 2010-11.**

Reforming the planning system   **6.13**   The planning system plays a vital role in supporting these goals, ensuring that new developments are delivered in a strategic and sustainable way. The *Review of sub-national economic development and regeneration*[4] published in July 2007 announced proposals to move to a single integrated strategy in each region setting out housing plans alongside wider economic, social and environmental objectives; and the Housing Green Paper set out how current regional plans will be reviewed to ensure each area is on track to deliver the Government's housing growth targets. This will be supported by the recently published planning policy statement for housing (PPS3) that requires local authorities to identify enough land to deliver the homes needed in their area over the next 15 years. To provide incentives for local authorities to bring forward more housing, **the Government is announcing a new housing and planning delivery grant worth £500 million over the CSR07 period.**

Recycling homes and land   **6.14**   Alongside planning reforms, to meet its ambitious targets for new housing and tackle the problems of undersupply and declining affordability the Government will take forward wider action to promote the use of empty properties and disused land, including:

- considering further reforms to land remediation relief and the landfill tax exemption for waste from contaminated land to bring more brown-field land

---

[2] *Review of Housing Supply, Delivering Stability: Securing our Future Housing Needs*, HM Treasury, March 2004. Available at www.hm-treasury.gov.uk.

[3] *Homes for the Future*, CLG, July 2007, available at www.communities.gov.uk.

[4] *Review of sub-national economic development and regeneration*, HM Treasury, BERR and CLG, July 2007. Available at www.hm-treasury.gov.uk.

back into effective use. Following the consultation launched at Budget 2007, which indicated support for these reforms, a summary of responses will be published shortly, with further announcements at Budget 2008; and

- working with local authorities and and other interested parties to assess the effect that the discretionary power to vary the council tax discount on long-term empty properties has had since its introduction in 2004, with the aim of identifying further options for reform in this area if there is evidence that it will improve access to housing.

- to encourage more rapid alteration or renovation of empty homes, from 1 January 2008 the reduced rate of 5 per cent chargeable VAT will be extended to all homes that have been unoccupied for 2 years or longer, down from 3 years;

Infrastructure to support housing growth   **6.15**   It is essential that new housing developments are accompanied by the investment in schools, transport and other infrastructure needed to support flourishing and prosperous communities. The 2007 CSR has therefore been informed by a review into the investment needed to support the Government's housing ambitions, the conclusions of which are set out in Box 6.3. To support this strategy over the next three years the Government is providing £1.7 billion of targeted funding for infrastructure in Growth Areas, the Thames Gateway, New Growth Points and eco-towns, including £300 million to continue the Community Infrastructure Fund over the CSR.

Box 6.3: Review into support housing growth

The 2005 Pre-Budget Report announced the launch of a policy review to develop a co-ordinated, long-term approach for the delivery of infrastructure to support housing growth. At a national level the review recommended:

- appropriate prioritisation of investment to support housing growth with all major infrastructure departments signing up to the housing PSA and held accountable via the Delivery Agreement; and

- as set out in more detail in the Housing Green Paper, specific changes to the processes for allocating departmental spending to ensure timely delivery of housing related infrastructure. For example, the Department for Transport's appraisal system will be changed to better capture the value of housing.

At the local level the review recommended more coordinated infrastructure planning and delivery with mechanisms to support up-front investment, including:

- a more systematic approach to planning and delivering housing related infrastructure, involving key infrastructure providers at an early stage. Further details are set out in the Planning White Paper.[5] These proposals will be taken forwards as part of the Government's forthcoming consultation on Local Development Frameworks; and

- the development of bespoke funding vehicles to help fill the timing gaps before developer contributions come on stream, such as the South West Regional Development Agency's proposed Regional Infrastructure Fund, alongside existing mechanisms such as prudential borrowing or English Partnerships funding. The Government is keen to continue to work with stakeholders to address this 'front-funding' issue.

CLG will lead a programme of three month bilateral reviews with each infrastructure department to test the outcomes of this review in specific locations and for specific types of infrastructure.

Funding for infrastructure
6.16 Kate Barker's review of Housing Supply proposed the introduction of a Planning-gain Supplement (PGS), a new levy on development to raise additional resources to invest in the infrastructure needed to support housing growth. In its response the Government accepted that local communities should benefit more from the often significant increases in land values arising from planning permission. Following extensive consultation, the Prime Minister indicated in July 2007 that the Government would be prepared to defer legislation to introduce PGS if a better way could be found to ensure that local communities receive more of the benefits from planning gain, to invest in necessary infrastructure and transport. The Housing Green Paper sought views on PGS and possible alternatives.

6.17 Following discussions with key stakeholders, the Government will legislate in the Planning Reform Bill to empower Local Planning Authorities in England to apply new planning charges to new development, alongside negotiated contributions for site-specific matters. Charge income will be used entirely to fund the infrastructure identified through the development plan process. Charges should include contributions towards the costs of infrastructure of regional or sub-regional importance. Legislation implementing PGS will therefore not be introduced in the next Parliamentary session. Further details will be published shortly by CLG.

---

[5] *Planning for a Sustainable Future: White Paper*, CLG, May 2007, available at www.communities.gov.uk.

Supporting property investment through REITs

6.18   The UK Real Estate Investment Trusts (REITs) regime, launched in January 2007, has been a marked success. REITs aim to promote greater efficiency in the property investment market by equalising tax treatment between indirect and direct investment in property, exempting eligible property companies from corporation tax, and instead taxing their investors at marginal rates. To date 16 companies have become UK-REITs with total market capitalisation of around £30 billion. The Government has recently reviewed the viability of residential REITs and the REITs listing requirements – but has concluded that there is not at present a compelling case for change. However, the REITs regime will continue to be kept under review.

Making houses more affordable

Helping first time buyers

6.19   Alongside steps to improve long-term affordability by building more homes, the Government recognises that more support is needed to help young people and families to buy their own homes. As part of the new housing PSA it has therefore set a target for 70,000 more affordable homes a year by 2010-11. But recognising the particular difficulties faced by first time buyers, the Government doubled the starting threshold for stamp duty land tax in Budget 2005, and increased the threshold again in 2006. Last year, a survey by the European Mortgage Federation showed that average transaction costs of buying a home in the UK was 1.9 per cent of the house price – the lowest amongst major European countries. Building on these steps,the Government will now also:

- explore whether it can reform the stamp duty treatment of initiatives including the First Time Buyers Initiative, to bring it into line with other shared ownership products. The Government will be assisting at least 25,000 households a year into homeownership through its shared equity and other low cost homeownership policies by 2010-11; and

- seek to increase the affordability of longer-term fixed rate mortgages. Relative to their incomes, first time buyers generally borrow more than home movers and so have higher interest payments and are most exposed to unexpected changes in mortgage rates (see also Box 6.4).

Box 6.4 Housing Finance Review

Improving the efficiency of mortgage finance markets is key to lowering mortgage costs and delivering mortgages that are well suited to the needs of households. The Government wants to see mortgage markets in which lenders can offer a wide range of products, including affordable longer-term fixed rate mortgages of ten years or more, which can give consumers greater certainty of their regular mortgage payments.

The Housing Finance Review, launched in July of this year and reporting at Budget 2008, aims to tackle the remaining barriers to the efficient supply of mortgage finance. The Review will take account of other countries' experiences and build on work already underway, such as the Treasury's consultation[a] on legislative proposals for a covered bonds regime and the Private Members Bill on building society funding which is currently progressing through Parliament. The Review team has already held discussions with a number of mortgage lenders, investment banks, regulators, consumer groups and academics, and has identified several priority areas for investigation:

- **Debt Management Office (DMO) issuance of hedging instruments**: the Miles Review[b] proposed that the DMO consider issuing specific derivatives which may help mortgage lenders to hedge longer-term fixed rate mortgages more cost effectively, and in turn pass on the benefit to households. Together with the DMO, the Review team has begun a full investigation into the benefits and costs of this strategy within the existing DMO mandate of minimising the cost of meeting the financing needs while taking account of risk and ensuring consistency with monetary policy.

- **Wholesale funding markets**: well functioning wholesale funding markets are an essential part of a diversified and efficient mortgage finance system. Initial consultations with external stakeholders suggest greater transparency in this market would be beneficial to both mortgage lenders and investors. The Review will consider measures to improve the operations and transparency of the wholesale market, learning from the experiences of other countries.

- **Shared equity schemes**: the Shared Equity Task Force report explained how sharing the equity in a home can be an affordable and sensible way for households to access home ownership. Over the next three years the Government will be assisting 25,000 households a year into homeownership through the shared ownership and shared equity programmes and other policies, with scope for the private sector to help many more. The Review will contribute to the work that CLG are undertaking to follow up on the Task Force report and the development of the shared equity market.

Efficient mortgage markets also require that borrowers are able to make well-informed decisions. The Thoresen Review is developing options aimed at giving consumers greater access to generic financial advice. The Financial Services Authority is continuing its programme of work to improve standards and deliver fair consumer outcomes, including by undertaking reviews of the quality of advice provided to consumers, with a major review of firms' processes reporting in June 2008. A second phase of consultations is due to begin at the end of October.

[a] *Proposals for a UK Recognised Covered Bonds legislative framework*, HM Treasury, July 2007.
[b] *The UK Mortgage Market: Taking a longer-term view*, David Miles, March 2004.

Shared ownership 6.20   The Government will also continue to provide direct assistance to homebuyers through its shared equity and shared ownership programmes, which will help over 120,000 households to enter homeownership by 2010-11. Recognising the key role of charitable Registered Social Landlords (RSLs) in supporting these programmes, the Government has worked with the housing sector and others since Budget 2007 in producing shared guidance and setting up an HMRC procedure to provide the housing sector with greater tax certainty on its affordable housing activities.

Social housing and homelessness 6.21   Alongside these steps to extend private ownership the Government will continue its long-term commitment to increase the quality and availability of social housing, by investing over £6.5 billion over the next three years to deliver 45,000 new units of social housing a year by 2010-11. As set out in Chapter 5, the Government will also take further steps to prevent homelessness, aiming to reduce the number of households living in temporary accommodation by 50 per cent by 2010-11 and increasing the number of people that move into settled accommodation.

Improving the mortgage market 6.22   Alongside these measures, the Government wants to ensure that mortgage finance markets operate as efficiently as possible. In July this year the Chancellor announced the launch of a Housing Finance Review, reporting at Budget 2008, which will work closely with the industry to identify any remaining barriers to lenders supplying mortgage finance, including longer-term fixed rate mortgages. Further details are set out in Box 6.4.

Regeneration and renewal

Neighbourhood renewal 6.23   The review of sub-national economic development and regeneration set out the Government's approach to delivering economic prosperity and tackling deprivation in all regions, placing local authorities at the heart of economic development and regeneration, supported by the Regional Development Agencies and stronger cross-government coordination. Following this review, the Government is establishing a new enterprise and renewal fund as part of the £2 billion allocated over the CSR07 period for neighbourhood and local renewal. This new fund will focus more intensively on the worst deprived areas, with a stronger emphasis on tackling worklessness, promoting enterprise and improving skills, and a new reward element to strengthen incentives to improve performance. Further details will be set out later this year.

Homes and Communities Agency 6.24   Local authorities will be supported in their regeneration role by the new Homes and Communities Agency, which will combine English Partnerships, the Housing Corporation and key delivery functions from CLG. In addition to its role supporting housing growth and delivering affordable housing, the new agency will provide the powers, skills and resources to help regenerate some of the most deprived areas of the country. The new agency will bring together housing-led regeneration programmes, building on work already underway through Market Renewal Pathfinders and Decent Homes, and will continue to use the Private Finance Initiative and stock transfers to improve the quality of housing.

BUILDING STRONG AND COHESIVE COMMUNITIES

6.25   Public services have a key role to play in enabling individuals and families to realise their potential and fulfil their aspirations. However, the Government believes that the value of public services extends far beyond this. Investment in the public realm is not just about providing the services needed by individuals, but about creating shared institutions that provide the hub for thriving social networks, building a sense of community, civic pride and belonging. Public spaces – whether they are schools, local health centres, sports facilities, museums, Sure Start centres or youth clubs – bring people together and enable them to build strong communities.

Community cohesion

6.26 While socio-economic trends such as globalisation, migration and technological advances generate greater wealth and new opportunities, they also bring the risk of wider divisions between people of different social groups, together with diminishing participation in local life and the public sphere. Despite these pressures, the last Citizenship Survey in 2005 found that community cohesion was strong in most areas of Britain: for example, 80 per cent of people agreed that they lived in an area where people from different backgrounds got on well together, and 20.4 million people were regularly volunteering, an increase of 2 million compared with 2001. The Government's efforts over the last decade to tackle social exclusion, ensure equality of opportunity for all, promote volunteering, and build an understanding of citizenship both in schools and wider society have played an important role in this respect.

6.27 Recognising that it must build on this progress and respond to the growing desire across Britain for stronger communities in a rapidly changing world, the Government is setting a new PSA to build more cohesive, empowered and active communities. At the heart of this PSA is a vision of communities in which there are shared values and a sense of belonging; strong and positive relationships are developed between people of different backgrounds and circumstances within each neighbourhood; and a wide range of people in each community volunteer on a regular basis, get involved in local projects and participate in cultural and sporting events. Local government and third sector organisations will play a leading role in delivering this vision, as set out in more detail below.

Strengthening the role of local government

6.28 The 2006 Local Government White Paper, *Strong and Prosperous Communities*, set out the Government's strategy for strengthening the role of local authorities to reshape local services around the individuals, families and communities that use them, with less top down control from central government. Sir Michael Lyons advanced this vision in his final report[6] on the role and funding of local government published alongside Budget 2007, in which he set out the critical function of local authorities in 'place-shaping' – acting as the locus for citizens and communities to shape their areas according to their priorities.

6.29 The 2007 CSR increases the resource budget for local government by an average 1 per cent per year in real terms over the next three years, providing the sustained resources needed to underpin this vision. The Government expects this will enable the overall council tax increase to stay well below five per cent in each of the next three years. Building on the proposals set out in *Strong and Prosperous Communities*, the 2007 CSR marks a significant step forward in the Government's commitment of devolution to the local level, developing a new relationship with local authorities based on greater trust and flexibility with:

- a significant reduction in the level of funding provided through specific and ring-fenced grants, with over £5 billion by 2010-11 to be mainstreamed into the Revenue Support Grant or Area-Based Grant;

- a streamlined performance management framework through a single set of 198 performance indicators for local government and no mandatory targets for Local Area Agreements; and

- new powers for local authorities, working with businesses, to raise supplementary business rates and proposals to better reward authorities for economic growth in their areas.

---

[6] *The Future role of the third sector in social and economic regeneration: final report*, HM Treasury, Office of the Third Sector, July 2007. Available at www.hm-treasury.gov.uk.

Working with the third sector

6.30 Over the next ten years the Government wants to put the third sector at the heart of work to build strong, active and connected communities, with local government acting as the most important driver in building this relationship. Budget 2006 therefore announced that the 2007 CSR would be informed by a review into the future role of the third sector in social and economic regeneration. Following the largest ever consultation with the sector, the final report of the review was published in July 2007,[7] setting out a new strategy for building the Government's relationship with the third sector. The review's recommendations are summarised in Box 6.5.

Box 6.5: The future role of the third sector in social and economic regeneration

Key announcements in the new strategy for building the Government's relationship with third sector, published in July 2007 and led by the Office of the Third Sector, include:

- a greater focus on enabling the third sector's role in campaigning and representation, including investment in innovative consultation approaches and better use of the Compact agreement with government to protect the right of organisations to campaign;

- a new £50 million local endowment match fund enabling local independent foundations to develop community endowments to provide sustainability in future grant making, building on the £80 million small grants programme for community action announced in Budget 2007;

- at least £10 million of new investment in community anchor organisations and community asset and enterprise development, in addition to the £30 million Community Assets Fund announced in the 2006 Pre-Budget Report;

- £117 million of new resources for youth volunteering, building on the work of **v**, the charity established by the Government in 2004 to develop a new framework for youth volunteering;

- building the capacity of third sector organisations to improve public services, investing up to £65 million Futurebuilders Fund and better training for commissioners of public services;

- additional investment to raise awareness of the social enterprise business model and support for departments to investigate its potential to support service delivery; and

- over £85 million of new investment for third sector infrastructure development through Capacitybuilders, with new programmes on voice and campaigning, social enterprise and a focus on reaching down to the smallest community groups.

Supporting public services **6.31** The Government's new performance framework also recognises the valuable contribution that a thriving third sector can make to the transformation of public services and the engagement of the public in the design and delivery of services. To support this, the third sector will be a key delivery partner across the full set of Public Service Agreements, particularly in the areas of youth services, access to employment, waste and recycling, and community transport; as well as specifically contributing to the PSA to build more cohesive, empowered and active communities through increased volunteering and growth in social enterprise.

---

[7] *The future role of the third sector in social and economic regeneration*, HM Treasury and Cabint Office, July 2007. Available at www.hm-treasury.gov.uk.

Reforming third sector funding **6.32**   Creating a stable funding system for third sector organisations is essential to secure the long-term strength and success of the sector. The Government is therefore setting a new expectation across government that three year funding plans for third sector organisations will become the norm rather than the exception over the CSR07 period. This will ensure that third sector organisations are able to make medium and long-term commitments to serve their beneficiaries, as well as recruit, retain and invest in skilled and well-motivated staff.

Unclaimed assets **6.33**   The 2005 Pre-Budget Report set out the Government's proposals to allow unclaimed assets to be reinvested in society. The bank and building society sector has been instrumental in taking these plans forward, enabling proposals for legislation to be included in *The Governance of Britain: The Government's Draft Legislative Programme*. The Government has also released two consultation documents this year on the scheme's operation and distribution of assets, which it will respond to shortly.

Promoting sports and culture

6.34   Over the last decade the Government has delivered record levels of investment in cultural and sporting activities, recognising their value in raising people's quality of life and bringing communities together. Funding for museums and galleries has increased by around 30 per cent, which by enabling free access for all has helped increase visitor numbers by 60 per cent. The Government will build on this investment in the CSR07 period to encourage more people to lead an active lifestyle and to ensure the UK's reputation for creativity and cultural excellence continues, including by:

- maintaining funding in real terms for the arts, museums and galleries, ensuring the continuation of free access to national museums and contributing to the staging of the Cultural Olympiad; and

- delivering an improved offer of 5 of hours school sports a week for all children aged 6 to 19.

Delivering the Olympics **6.35**   Over the next three years the Government will also drive forward preparations for the 2012 Olympic and Paralympic Games, including developing the Olympic Park and delivering a lasting cultural and sporting legacy for the nation, with benefits for tourism, skills and employment across the country. To galvanise the cross-government collaboration needed to deliver this complex programme, the Government is setting a PSA to deliver a successful Olympic and Paralympic Games with a sustainable legacy, including encouraging more children and young people to take part in high quality physical education and sport.

6.36   In March 2007, the Government announced a total budget of £9.325 billion for the 2012 Olympic Games and Paralympic Games, funded through central government (£5.975 billion), the National Lottery (£2.175 billion) and the Mayor of London (£1.175 billion). As the first part of this funding package, the 2007 CSR makes full budgetary provision for central government's contribution of £3.623 billion that falls due over the next three years, which alongside contributions from the National Lottery and London, put preparations for 2012 on a sound financial footing far earlier than any previous host city.

SAFE AND SECURE NEIGHBOURHOODS

A fair and effective criminal justice system

6.37 Reducing levels of crime is an essential step to creating an environment in which strong communities can flourish. The Government has therefore increased spending on public order and safety by over 50 per cent in real terms since 1997, which together with reforms across the criminal justice system have helped to deliver significant improvements. The number of offences brought to justice has increased by 40 per cent in the last five years, overall crime has fallen by around a third in the last ten years, the fear of crime has reduced and re-offending rates fell by 6.9 per cent between 1997 and 2004.

6.38 The priority now is to respond to the needs of a changing, more mobile and diverse society, driving up public confidence in the system and improving the experience of victims and witnesses. More needs to be done to tackle the root causes of crime and disorder, and to ensure that lower level offending and anti-social behaviour are dealt with swiftly and efficiently so that a greater focus can be given to tackling more serious offences. To provide the cross-departmental focus needed to deliver these goals, **the Government is setting three new PSAs to:**

- **make communities safer** – which will focus on reducing serious violent and acquisitive crimes, establishing a framework to deliver local priorities to cut crime and anti-social behaviour and reduce re-offending;

- **deliver a more effective, transparent and responsive Criminal Justice System for victims and the public** – bringing offenders to justice through simple and efficient processes and strengthening public confidence in the fairness of the system; and

- **reduce the harm caused by alcohol and drugs** – improving treatment for drug users, and for the first time extending this focus to alcohol misuse, thereby reducing the harm to communities as a result of associated crime, disorder and anti-social behaviour.

6.39 **To help deliver these goals total resources for the Home Office, Ministry of Justice and Law Officers' Departments will increase by £1.3 billion by 2010-11, which combined with value for money savings of £2.5 billion will enable the Government to:**

- implement the recommendations of its new crime strategy,[8] which sets out the priority areas for action and a new, more tailored approach to combating different types of crime, together with steps to tackle the most intractable problems relating to offending such as mental health problems and alcohol and drug related offending;

- deliver 9,500 new prison places, with firm plans already in place to deliver 8,500 by 2012. This builds on the 20,000 increase in prison capacity since 1997 and the strengthening of the probation service with 7,000 extra staff. The Government will continue to invest in reducing reoffending, building on the reductions already achieved through the development of offender management and much closer partnership working at national, regional and local levels;

- complete the roll-out of Neighbourhood Policing Teams in every neighbourhood across England and Wales by 2008, enabling the police to understand and address local concerns and priorities, build trusting

---

[8] *Cutting Crime, a new partnership 2008-11*, Home Office, July 2007. Availiable at www.homeoffice.gov.uk.

relationships with communities to facilitate better flows of information, and work more effectively with other local delivery agencies. This community focused approach will be complemented by the extension of the community justice model developed in Liverpool and Salford to a further ten areas, with a longer-term aim of rolling it out across the country;

- developing and consulting on a new drugs strategy, to build on the current 10 year strategy which ends in 2008. This will be accompanied by the updated alcohol strategy,[9] which focuses on the minority of drinkers who cause or experience the most harm to themselves, their communities and their families; and

- complete the implementation of the 'simple, speedy, summary' reforms in all 360 magistrates' courts in England and Wales, enabling district judges, defence, prosecutors, police, courts and probation service to work more effectively together to reduce delays and improve efficiency. In the four test areas most simple cases were completed within six weeks from charge to disposal, down from a current average of 21 weeks.

Controlling the UK's borders **6.40** Increased globalisation brings significant economic and cultural gains to the UK, but also increases the importance of delivering a secure and efficient system of border control. The Government has already begun delivering the e-Borders programme which will enable the electronic screening of all passengers as they check in to travel to the UK. This will allow journeys to be recorded and individuals to be counted into and out of the country. The pilot to this scheme has already issued over 15,000 alerts on those crossing the UK's borders, which have resulted in over 1,200 arrests. This programme will be rolled out over the CSR07 period, covering 95 per cent of all passenger movements across UK borders by 2010-11. In addition a new Unified Border Force will strengthen the powers and surveillance capability of the agencies that work to control immigration, tackle crime and facilitate travel and trade. This will integrate the work of the Border and Immigration Agency, HM Revenue and Customs, and UK Visas.

Countering the threat from international terrorism

6.41 While the UK has faced terrorist threats in the past, the reach, capability and sophistication of international terrorist groups places the current threat on a scale not previously encountered. In recent years Al Qaida and associated terrorist groups have attacked over 25 countries and killed thousands of people. The challenge facing the UK and all countries in defeating this violence will last at least a generation, demanding a determined, coherent and long-term approach.

6.42 The Government has responded to this new challenge by significantly increasing the capacity of the intelligence and security agencies and the police to detect and disrupt terrorist attack planning; undertaking work to isolate and prevent violent extremism; and improving the UK's preparedness for emergencies, including terrorist attacks. By the end of 2007-08, spending on counter-terrorism and intelligence across departments will be £2½ billion a year – more than double the amount before 9/11. **This investment will continue in the CSR07 period, with dedicated spending on counter-terrorism and intelligence rising to over £3½ billion by 2010-11. This includes an addition of over £220 million by 2010-11 for the Home Office, taking the real terms increases in its budget to 1.1 per cent a year on average over the CSR07 period.**

---

[9] *Safe. Sensible. Social. The next steps in the alcohol strategy,* DH, HO, DfES and DCMS, June 2007. Availiable at www.dh.gov.uk.

6.43   The Government recognises that additional resources alone are not enough to defeat the threat now faced by the UK. The links between terrosist networks in the UK and overseas erode distinctions between domestic and international security, and between those departments traditionally tasked with security policy and other areas of government. It demands a new approach, harnessing all the means at the Government's disposal – law enforcement, security, military, diplomatic, economic and cultural. Following a wide-ranging review of security and counter-terrorism, the Government is therefore announcing a new PSA to reduce the risk to the UK and its interests overseas from international terrorism, supported by:

- a new single security and intelligence budget which brings together all direct spend on counter-terrorism to improve visibility and accountability for investment decisions. The Ministerial Committee on National Security International Relations and Development will review the spending plans for this budget on an annual basis;

- action to combat money laundering and the financing of international crime and terrorism, implementing the conclusions of the strategy published in February 2007[10] to strengthen the financial system's response to these threats, including through the establishment of a new unit in the Charity Commission to work with the charitable sector to protect it from terrorist exploitation; and

- a more co-ordinated approach to reducing violent Islamist extremism. An additional £100 million has been allocated over the next three years to fund activities aimed at supporting communities to reject and condemn violent extremism and specifically supporting those individuals most at risk of becoming involved in violent extremism. This will be complemented by the work of the BBC World Service and British Council to break down cultural barriers and misunderstanding between communities at home and abroad, as set out in more detail in Chapter 7.

---

[10] *The financial challenge to crime and terrorism*, HMT, February 2007, available at www.hm-treasury.gov.uk.

7   A MORE SECURE, FAIR AND ENVIRONMENTALLY SUSTAINABLE WORLD

The Government is committed to ensuring that the UK plays a leading role in responding to the global challenges of climate change, meeting the Millennium Development Goals including tackling poverty, and promoting peace and stability. The 2007 Pre-Budget Report and Comprehensive Spending Review set out the next stage in the Government's strategy to meet these challenges.

Tackling climate change, including:

- **increasing the Department for Environment, Food and Rural Affairs' budget by an average of 1.4 per cent a year in real terms, from £3,508 million in 2007-08 to £3,960 million in 2010-11.** This includes increasing funding for flood and coastal erosion risk management from £600 million in 2007-08 to £800 million in 2010-11;

- **creating an Environmental Transformation Fund of £1.2 billion over the CSR07 period,** to support the demonstration and deployment of new energy and efficiency technologies in the UK and to advance poverty reduction through environmental protection in developing countries;

- **publishing the interim report of the King Review** on vehicle and fuel technologies which over the next 25 years could help 'decarbonise' road transport; and

- **replacing air passenger duty with a duty payable per plane rather than per passenger, from 1 November 2009.**

Tackling global poverty through:

- **increases to the Department for International Development's (DfID) budget by 11 per cent per year in real terms over the CSR07 period, from £5.4 billion in 2007-08 to £7.9 billion in 2010-11;** and

- an overall CSR07 settlement **that puts the UK on track to spend 0.56 per cent of Gross National Income (GNI) on Official Development Assistance (ODA) by 2010-11,** meeting the EU's collective commitment, and on course to reach 0.7 per cent of GNI by 2013;

Securing international peace and stability, through:

- **a new Stabilisation Aid Fund jointly managed by DfID, the Foreign and Commonwealth Office (FCO) and the Ministry of Defence (MoD) worth over £260 million** during the CSR07 period, for conflict stabilisation activity in volatile or hostile areas;

- **an increase for the MoD budget of 1.5 per cent a year in real terms over the CSR07 period,** enhancing capability including funding for two new aircraft carriers, new protected vehicles for the Army, further Air Transport capability, while providing the resources necessary to sustain the UK's nuclear deterrent; and

- **a CSR07 settlement for the FCO,** which enhances security across the overseas diplomatic network, funds a new embassy in Kabul, and provides an additional £21 million by 2010-11 for a Farsi TV service and for a 24/7 Arabic TV service.

7.1   Advances in transport and communication technology mean the links between different nations are more immediate than ever before. However, along with the opportunities that these advances bring, there are also challenges, with social, economic, environmental and security risks no longer easily contained within one country. In responding to these challenges, the Government firmly believes the UK must continue to be an outward-facing country, taking a lead in developing global solutions.

7.2 The major global challenges of climate change, tackling global poverty and securing international peace and stability are all closely related. Without action to tackle climate change, efforts to promote economic development and poverty reduction will be undermined, particularly in the poorest countries. Poverty and environmental degradation contribute to fierce competition for resources, which can lead to violence and instability. Conflict impedes efforts to reduce poverty and generates greater human distress and insecurity and environmental damage by displacing populations. This chapter sets out the Government's response to these interdependent challenges.

Climate change **7.3** The most serious and pressing global environmental challenge is tackling climate change. A year ago, the review by Sir Nicholas Stern[1] concluded that the costs of stabilising the climate are significant but manageable, whereas delay will be costly and dangerous. The Review found that climate change would affect the basic elements of life for people around the world – access to water, food production, health and the environment. The Review estimated that temperature increases associated with current business as usual emissions could lead to damage equivalent to as much as 5-20 per cent of global GDP. But if the world takes action now, and with the right policies in place, stabilisation of greenhouse gas concentrations at a level that avoids the most dangerous impacts of climate change could cost around 1 per cent of global GDP. This is significant, but is clearly less than the costs of not taking action.

Global poverty **7.4** Significant progress has been made on tackling global poverty. In 1990 more than 28 per cent of the world's population lived in extreme poverty, but by 2002 this had decreased to 19 per cent and is projected to fall to 12 per cent in 2015. However, despite progress, nearly 1 billion people remain in extreme poverty, and as the 2015 deadline for achieving the Millennium Development Goals draws closer, the international community faces a much more demanding development agenda.

International peace and stability **7.5** The UK's security and prosperity depends more than ever on international peace and stability. While the UK does not currently face a significant direct threat of attack from other states, conflict and instability elsewhere has the potential to increase risks to the UK, as well as the threat from global terrorism, as highlighted in Chapter 6. The UK must therefore continue to be active on the international stage in shaping global developments, for the benefit of its citizens, and to ensure a safer, more just and prosperous world.

TACKLING CLIMATE CHANGE AND PROTECTING THE ENVIRONMENT

Response to climate change **7.6** Since 1990, the Kyoto baseline year, UK greenhouse gas emissions have fallen by 19 per cent, including reductions through the EU Emissions Trading Scheme. However, as the Stern Review makes clear, there is still much more to do to. Since its publication, the Review has had a significant impact in making the case for early and cost effective action to tackle climate change around the world. The Review, and the most recent reports of the Intergovernmental Panel on Climate Change, have highlighted that human activities are causing concentrations of greenhouse gases to reach unprecedented and dangerous levels.

---

[1] *The Stern Review on the Economics of Climate Change*, commissioned by the Chancellor of the Exchequer in July 2005, was set up to understand more comprehensively the nature of the economic challenges of climate change and how they can be met, both in the UK and globally. It was published on 30 October 2006, and employed economic methods to assess both the human and environmental impacts of, and responses to, climate change.

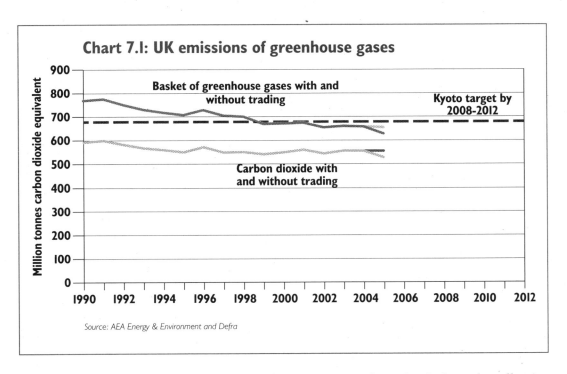

Chart 7.1: UK emissions of greenhouse gases

Source: AEA Energy & Environment and Defra

International response

7.7 Climate change is a global problem that must be solved through collective international action. The UK can help prevent climate change by showing the international community that a strong low-carbon economy is possible and affordable, while building a consensus to drive forward the necessary multilateral action. The G8 summit in June was key in taking forward resolute international action in order to reduce global greenhouse gas emissions. In particular, leaders agreed on the need for a global emissions goal and the central role of the United Nations Framework Convention on Climate Change in international negotiations.

7.8 However, the international community also needs to build on the existing international framework to take forward global action proportionate to the scale and urgency of the threat, particularly to the world's most vulnerable countries and communities. By strengthening this framework it will be possible to provide the global policy certainty needed to drive greater investment in low-carbon technology and financial flows to developing countries, as well as encouraging countries to adapt to the unavoidable impacts. The global community must therefore collectively agree and deliver a plan to reduce greenhouse gas emissions to a level that avoids dangerous climate change.

EU response

7.9 The Spring European Council agreed an ambitious package of climate change and energy measures. The EU committed to reduce greenhouse gas emissions by 20 per cent by 2020, compared with 1990 levels, or by 30 per cent as part of a wider international agreement, and reaffirmed the central role that emissions trading must play in achieving these long-term goals. The European Council also agreed a target of 20 per cent renewable energy in overall EU consumption by 2020. The UK Government is working with the Commission and other Member States to ensure that policies are effective in achieving the EU's greenhouse gas objectives, and that they provide a credible path to cost-effective delivery, in line with the Stern Review's recommendations.

Implementing the Stern Review

7.10 The Government is today publishing *Moving to a global low-carbon economy: implementing the Stern Review* alongside the 2007 Pre-Budget Report and Comprehensive Spending Review, setting out how the Government is taking forward the Stern Review and incorporating its findings within government policies.

7.II As part of the 2007 Pre-Budget Report and Comprehensive Spending Review, the Government announces a new PSA to lead the global effort to avoid dangerous climate change. This PSA aims to secure effective and robust global commitments for the period after 2012, adopt and promote cost-effective policies which reduce UK net greenhouse gas emissions, and adapt to unavoidable climate change.

7.I2 Furthermore, the Government announces an increase for the Department for Environment, Food and Rural Affairs (Defra) of 1.4 per cent per year in real terms over the CSR07 period to help meet the long-term challenges on climate change and natural resource protection.

Legislative **7.I3** The Government has set out its intended legislative framework to tackle climate **framework** change through the draft Climate Change Bill, published for consultation in March 2007, enshrining the Government's long-term targets to reduce UK emissions through domestic and international action by at least 60 per cent by 2050 and 26-32 per cent by 2020, both compared with 1990 levels. The draft Bill proposes to move towards these targets by setting five-year 'carbon budgets' which will create binding limits on these emissions.

7.I4 In May 2007, the Government published the Energy White Paper *Meeting the energy challenge.* The White Paper's ambitious package of measures, together with the impact of the EU Emissions Trading Scheme, is estimated to put the UK on course to meet the emissions targets through improved energy efficiency, bringing forward new low-carbon technologies, and ensuring secure reliable energy supplies. The Energy Bill will take forward the legislative measures necessary to support investment in more low-carbon sources of energy. Taken together with the Planning Bill reforms for major infrastructure projects set out in Chapter 4, these Bills form a package of action to accelerate the UK's transition to becoming a low-carbon economy.

Implementing the Stern framework

7.I5 The Stern Review identified the need for a shared international vision of long-term goals and the key pillars for an international framework to help each country to play its part in meeting these common goals. This Pre-Budget Report and Comprehensive Spending Review, together with *Moving to a global low-carbon economy: implementing the Stern Review*, sets out how the Government is responding under each of these pillars:

- carbon pricing – creating a common price for carbon through trading, tax or regulations;

- technology policy – shifting to new or improved technology in key sectors to bring forward low-carbon alternatives and increase efficiency; and

- behavioural change – through tax, regulation, information or financing of energy efficiency improvements.

7.I6 The Government maintains its principled approach to developing environmental policy as detailed in the 2005 Pre-Budget Report, using the most effective instrument to achieve its aims. Intervention can be through a number of different instruments including taxation, trading schemes, regulation and spending programmes. Where tax is used, it will aim to shift the burden of tax from 'goods' to 'bads'. In meeting its environmental aims, the Government takes into account the impact of action on wider economic and social objectives. While the policy framework continues to develop and evolve over time, the Government is committed to looking strategically at the overall regulatory burden and developing a policy framework that delivers emissions reductions with minimum regulatory requirements.

Carbon pricing

EU Emissions **7.17** The EU Emissions Trading Scheme (EU ETS) is the UK's principal carbon pricing
Trading Scheme instrument, covering half of the UK's emissions. It is designed to keep emissions within fixed
limits while allowing emissions to be reduced at least cost. In October 2006 the Government
published its vision for the long-term future of international emissions trading, with the aim
of developing the EU ETS as the basis of a global carbon market. The UK's key proposals are:

- to foster a deeper, more liquid market by considering expansion of the EU ETS
to cover more sectors and gases;

- to move towards more auctioning of allowances in future phases; and

- to extend the scheme beyond Europe by enabling similar schemes in other
countries to trade with the EU ETS and to guarantee that credits from Clean
Development Mechanism projects in developing countries will be valid for
compliance in EU ETS beyond 2012.

7.18 The European Commission is expected to publish its proposals on the future of the
EU ETS post-2012 in December 2007. The Government is pressing for the setting of caps that
ensures a well-functioning market with scarcity of allowances. **It also intends to make greater
use of auctioning in the UK for Phase III with, in particular, a significant increase in
auctioning to distribute allowances in the large electricity producers' sector.**

7.19 The Government will auction 7 per cent of allowances in Phase II (2008-12), plus any
from closures or surplus from the New Entrants Reserve. It is the Government's intention to
appoint the Debt Management Office to run the auctions of allowances for Phase II.

Engaging with **7.20** The Government is committed to strengthening the EU ETS to build investor
business confidence in the existence of a multilateral long-term carbon price signal. The Government
is providing better market information and analysis, such as in the forthcoming *Energy
Markets Outlook* publication, and in the context of this work, is engaging with business to
understand the impact of climate change policy, as one of many factors, on their investment
decisions.

Combined heat **7.21** Combined heat and power (CHP) is the simultaneous generation of usable heat and
and power power (usually electricity) in a single process. CHP is a more efficient way to use both fossil
and renewable fuels and can be employed over a wide range of sizes, applications, fuels and
technologies. The Government will aim to ensure that arrangements for future phases of the
EU ETS continue to recognise the carbon savings that CHP delivers.

Carbon markets **7.22** Budget 2007 announced a proposal to host an international conference on carbon
conference markets. This will take place in London in November 2007. It will bring together international
finance officials and market participants to discuss how to develop and operate effective
international carbon markets. Ensuring such a market is deep, liquid, and efficient is central
to tackling climate change while protecting economic growth and development.

Technology policy

7.23 In addition to carbon pricing, technology policies can accelerate the shift to a low-
carbon economy in key sectors such as power generation and transport.

Domestic ETF **7.24**   The domestic element of the Environmental Transformation Fund (ETF), led by Defra and the Department for Business, Enterprise and Regulatory Reform (BERR), is a dedicated fund that brings together the Government's existing and new funding commitments within the UK to support the demonstration and deployment of new energy and energy efficiency technologies. **Over the CSR07 period, Defra will spend £170 million and BERR will spend £200 million, creating a domestic fund of at least £370 million.** The international element of the ETF (paragraph 7.78) will support development and poverty reduction through environmental protection and help developing countries to tackle environmental challenges.

7.25   The ETF is a critical part of the Government's response to the technology challenge, along with the Energy Technology Institute and the Technology Strategy Board (discussed in Chapter 4). The Government is developing a new low-carbon energy technology strategy, to be published in 2008. This will focus on applying the principles from the Stern Review to the Government's funding for innovation across the full chain from initial research and development to demonstration, deployment and diffusion, in order to maximise the cost-effective potential for cutting emissions in the UK and internationally.

Energy **7.26**   Budget 2006 announced the Government's intention to establish a new Energy
Technology Technologies Institute (ETI), expected to be fully operational in 2008, as a 50:50 partnership
Institute with industry. The ETI brings together some of the world's biggest companies, including BP, Caterpillar, EDF Energy, E.ON UK, Rolls-Royce and Shell, with the aim of raising up to £1.1 billion over a ten-year period for low-carbon energy technologies.

Carbon capture **7.27**   The Stern Review highlighted carbon capture and storage (CCS) as a key technology
and storage for tackling global carbon emissions. CCS has the potential to reduce carbon emissions from fossil fuel power stations by 90 per cent and in Budget 2007 the Government announced that it would launch a competition to design and build a full-scale demonstration of the full capture, transport and storage chain.

7.28   The Secretary of State for BERR is today announcing details of the competition and launching a short period of discussion with industry prior to the formal start of the competition in November 2007. This competition will ensure the UK is a world leader in bringing forward this globally important technology for tackling climate change, which is important not only to the UK, but also to achieve the EU's aspiration to have 10 to 12 demonstration projects by 2015, and encourage the transition to a low-carbon economy in China and India.

Microgeneration **7.29**   The Government provides support for microgeneration through: the Low Carbon Buildings Programme; reduced VAT on installations; access to Renewable Obligation Certificates; and tax exemptions for revenues earned from domestically generated electricity exported to the grid. The installation of microgeneration equipment in business premises can trigger an increased liability for business rates. Subject to state aid clearance, **the Government will therefore not include microgeneration investments in ad hoc re-assessments of business rates liability from 2008.** Such investments will now only be taken into account at the five-year re-valuation of business rates, providing up to five years worth of benefit to rate payers.

Biofuels **7.30**   The Renewable Transport Fuel Obligation (RTFO) will become the principal mechanism for encouraging the development of biofuels, leading to a significant reduction in emissions of greenhouse gases from the transport sector, by increasing the use of biofuels. The total net carbon savings associated were initially estimated to be in the region of 3.6 $MtCO_2$ per year by 2010. Estimating the precise carbon savings from biofuels is an emerging area of work and in order to reflect more accurately the marginal impact that biofuels may have on the fuel efficiency of vehicles, the Government has revised its estimates downwards to 2.6-3 $MtCO_2$ per year by 2010.

Renewable Transport Fuel Obligation   **7.31**   In June this year, the Government announced that from 2010 the RTFO would reward biofuels according to the carbon that they save. In addition, from 2011, the RTFO will also reward only biofuels that meet appropriate sustainability standards. These aims will enhance the environmental focus of the RTFO, directly benefiting those who produce and sell the most sustainable biofuels. With its additional environmental focus, the Government continues to believe that the RTFO will be the most effective mechanism for encouraging the use of biofuels. The Government has today laid in Parliament the draft RTFO Order to prepare for the introduction of the RTFO in April 2008.

ECA for the cleanest biofuels plant   **7.32**   The RTFO will provide all biofuel producers with a valuable incentive to produce the cleanest sustainable biofuels. The Government has been pursuing state aid clearance for an enhanced capital allowance (ECA) for the cleanest biofuel plant. However, it has become clear that in order to make it compliant, it would offer little value to the limited number of businesses who would be eligible whilst introducing considerable administrative complexity and uncertainty. As such, **the Government has decided to focus on ensuring that the RTFO encourages the production of the cleanest and most sustainable biofuels, and will therefore not pursue state aid clearance for the proposed ECA.** Biofuels producers can still seek financial assistance to ensure cleaner fuel production through investing in good quality CHP installations, which are eligible under the existing ECA scheme.

Extending the duty incentive   **7.33**   In addition, building on the package of measures announced in Budget 2007, **the Government will extend the current duty incentive for biofuels to biobutanol on a pilot basis, with the aim of assessing its environmental benefits and performance as a transport fuel.**

Behavioural change

7.34   The third essential element in the policy framework identified by the Stern Review is overcoming barriers and encouraging long-term behavioural change. Energy efficiency is particularly important. Making more effective use of energy can provide a significant contribution towards climate change mitigation, making it easier to achieve EU ETS caps at low or even negative cost; however, for a variety of reasons many opportunities are not taken up. The Government has therefore sought to complement EU ETS with a range of measures to improve business energy efficiency.

Climate change levy   **7.35**   The climate change levy (CCL) was introduced in 2001 to encourage business to reduce energy demand. Independent analysis by Cambridge Econometrics[2] estimated that the levy delivered cumulative savings of 60 $MtCO_2$ to 2005. By 2010, it is estimated that the levy will have reduced energy demand in the commercial and public sector by around 15 per cent a year compared with the levy package not being in place. The full impact of the levy package was set out in a report published alongside Budget 2006.

7.36   Improving energy efficiency helps businesses to reduce their energy costs and makes them less vulnerable to energy market volatility. Therefore, targeting energy efficiency effectively continues to be the right focus for CCL. As announced in Budget 2007, the Government confirms that CCL rates will increase in line with inflation from 1 April 2008 to maintain the levy's environmental impact. The Government will continue to explore how energy efficiency objectives can be further improved in the future.

---

[2] *Modelling the Initial Effects of the Climate Change Levy,* Cambridge Econometrics, March 2005. www.hmrc.gov.uk

Climate change agreements

7.37   Over 50 energy intensive sectors are now able to benefit from an 80 per cent discount in CCL in return for signing climate change agreements (CCAs) under which firms agree to improve energy efficiency and/or reduce emissions. By 2010, it is estimated that CCAs will deliver savings of around 10.2 $MtCO_2$ per year. Regular reviews of existing CCAs by Defra continue to ensure the energy efficiency improvements and emissions reductions delivered by the agreements are maximised. To consolidate the success of CCAs, the Government announces that the scheme will continue until 2017, subject to state aid approval, and will discuss with business the most effective way of taking this forward.

Household energy efficiency

7.38   Households account for over a quarter of UK energy consumption and carbon emissions. The main mechanism introduced by the Government to encourage the take up of energy efficiency measures in homes is the Energy Efficiency Commitment (EEC), soon to be replaced by the Carbon Emissions Reduction Target (CERT). Alongside the EEC, the Warm Front and Decent Homes programmes provide insulation and other energy efficiency options free to low-income households and to the social housing sector.

7.39   There is also a range of tax measures in place to encourage household energy efficiency including: a reduced rate of VAT that applies to professionally-installed energy-saving materials; the Landlords Energy Saving Allowance; and a stamp duty land tax (SDLT) exemption on the first acquisition of a new home meeting the zero carbon standard costing up to £500,000. Zero carbon homes costing in excess of £500,000 will receive a reduction of £15,000 to the SDLT bill. The tax relief will apply to acquisitions of zero carbon homes from 1 October 2007. Regulations bringing the relief into effect will be laid before Parliament later this month. The Government published earlier this month revised guidance setting out the zero carbon home standard under the Code for Sustainable Homes which will help the construction industry respond to the challenge of meeting the Government's zero carbon homes target.

More efficient home and office products

7.40   Improving the energy efficiency of the products used in homes and offices provides one of the most cost-effective ways to meet the Government's climate change and energy goals, with savings of 3.5-10 $MtCO_2$ by 2020. Priorities are consumer electronics, lighting, office equipment (ICT), pumps and motors, heating and air conditioning, white goods and standby. Because action in this area is best taken at EU level, the Chancellor and the Secretaries of State for BERR and Defra have today written to other Member States and the Commission, calling on the EU to:

- make clear its priorities, targets and future plans for efficiency standards, and transparently and regularly update them;

- improve product information and compliance to help consumers make better choices and drive fair competition;

- work with international partners to make policy more effective;

- urgently accelerate delivery of mandatory, cost-effective energy efficiency standards for priority products; and

- allow the introduction of a reduced VAT rate for the most energy-efficient products (the Chancellor and French Finance Minister have together written to EU Finance Ministers and the European Commission to recommend that this reduced rate be introduced as soon as possible).

7.41 In addition, the Government is seeking voluntary action by retailers, manufacturers and service providers to phase out the least efficient products and to raise their own standards. Following a commitment in Budget 2007, the Government announced on 27 September 2007 that major retailers, with the support of manufacturers and energy companies, have agreed an ambition to phase out inefficient incandescent light bulbs by 2011. The Government will be consulting on standards and targets for other products shortly.

King Review of **7.42** Alternative fuel and vehicle technologies have the potential to deliver significant
low-carbon cars environmental benefits. Budget 2007 announced a review, led by Professor Julia King, Vice Chancellor of Aston University and former Director of Advanced Engineering at Rolls-Royce plc, working with Sir Nicholas Stern, to examine the vehicle and fuel technologies which over the next 25 years could help to 'decarbonise' road transport, particularly cars. The Government welcomes the Review's interim report, published today. The Review's final report, including policy recommendations, will be published in time to inform Budget 2008.

Box 7.1: King Review of low-carbon cars

Key points from the interim report include:

- in the long term, decarbonisation of road transport is achievable but will require clean power sources and major breakthroughs in vehicle technology;

- meanwhile, there is great potential for reducing emissions, immediately and at low cost;

- vehicle technology exists that can deliver CO_2 reductions of 30 per cent compared with today's equivalent models and these could be standard within 5-10 years, if manufacturers see a market for them;

- consumers play an important role, and low carbon choices can be made now, for example, by choosing the most efficient vehicle in the preferred class. A typical driver can reduce their CO_2 emissions (and fuel bill) by 25 per cent; and

- fuels must be considered on the basis of their life-cycle CO_2 emissions. Biofuels offer potential for CO_2 savings but care must be taken not to expand demand too quickly before crop breakthroughs and robust environmental safeguards are in place.

Fuel efficiency **7.43** In February 2007, the European Commission published its proposals for the
of vehicles successor regime to voluntary agreements for new cars which are due to expire in 2008-09. They have proposed that car manufacturers achieve a mandatory target to reduce average new car emissions to 130g/km of CO_2 by 2012. Discussions on this are ongoing, and the Commission is expected to publish its full legislative proposal by the end of 2007.

Vehicle excise **7.44** Vehicle excise duty (VED) for cars was reformed in 2001 and is now based on
duty graduated carbon dioxide bands, giving a clear signal to motorists to choose more fuel-efficient vehicles. Fuel efficiency labels matching the graduated VED structure were introduced into car showrooms in 2005, raising consumer awareness of the potential fuel savings that can be achieved.

7.45 Budget 2007 set out car VED rates for the next three years to further sharpen the environmental signals to motorists and to continue to support the development of the low-carbon market.

7.46   The Government today announces inflation-only increases on motorcycle VED rates in 2008-09, while VED rates for special types vehicles, combined transport vehicles and all vehicle categories that are linked to the basic goods rate will be frozen. It also announced on 1 October 2007 that heavy goods vehicles (HGV) VED rates would be frozen in 2008-09. All changes take effect from licences commencing 1 April 2008.

Taxation of business travel   **7.47**   The Government recognises there are interactions between rates of company car tax (CCT), employee car ownership schemes (ECOS), tax-free mileage allowances (AMAPs), and tax relief on business cars, that work together to determine car purchase and usage choices. The Government wants to ensure that the tax system properly reflects and supports business activity, in addition to promoting fairness and environmentally friendly travel.

7.48   Company car tax was reformed in 2002 and is now based on carbon emissions, encouraging the take up of more fuel-efficient cars in company fleets. These changes are forecast to deliver significant savings of between 1.5-3.3 $MtCO_2$ per year by 2020. Budget 2008 will set out the company car tax thresholds for 2010-11.

Company car fuel benefit change   **7.49**   The company car fuel benefit charge – paid by employees who drive company cars and receive free fuel for private use – was reformed in 2003 to align it with the environmental principles of the company car tax system. **The Government today announces that from 6 April 2008 the fixed figure on which the company car fuel benefit charge is based will be increased, from £14,400 to £16,900, in line with the change in the retail prices index since April 2003, to enhance the environmental incentives to drive fewer miles.**

7.50   Following HM Revenue and Customs' review of the taxation of ECOS, the Government has decided not to impose a benefit in kind charge. Budget 2007 also announced that HMRC would undertake discussions with business to review AMAPs. In advance of the Budget, the Government will continue to consider the representations received from industry.

7.51   In March 2007 the Government published an update of its consultation on the tax relief for business expenditure on cars. **A summary of the responses to the consultation is published today.**

7.52   The Government appreciates the importance of considering the framework of taxation of cars used for business travel as a whole, and will make announcements on future policy in this area in Budget 2008.

Vehicle emissions standards   **7.53**   The EU has reached agreement on the Euro V and VI emission standards for cars and small vans. Euro V and VI will become mandatory from 1 January 2011 and 1 September 2015 respectively. As announced in Budget 2007, the Government is considering the case for incentivising the early uptake of Euro V and subsequently Euro VI technology. Any incentive for Euro VI take-up cannot be provided until Euro V is mandatory.

Air passenger duty   **7.54**   Aviation accounts for 6.3 per cent of the UK's CO_2 emissions and this is projected to rise to as much as 15 per cent by 2030. Aircraft also contribute to climate change through high-altitude emissions of nitrogen oxides, contrails and the formation of cirrus clouds. The Government's policy, as set out in the 2003 Air Transport White Paper, is that aviation should pay the costs it imposes on society at large. The Government's priority has been to work to include aviation in the EU Emissions Trading Scheme, which will help to ensure that the aviation sector plays its part in delivering real carbon reductions across Europe. The Government continues to make good progress on securing this goal.

7.55   The Government believes that domestic air passenger duty (APD) is playing a valuable role in encouraging behavioural change, reducing emissions from aviation and ensuring that air travel makes a fair contribution towards the Government's spending priorities, including public transport and the environment. The changes to APD rates announced in the 2006 Pre-Budget Report will deliver reductions equivalent to 2.75 $MtCO_2$ a year by 2010. Following an earlier consultation, with effect from 1 November 2008, the Government will correct an anomaly to ensure passengers on 'business class only' flights are liable for the standard rate of APD.

7.56 The Government now intends to reform the taxation of aviation to send better environmental signals and ensure aviation makes a greater contribution to covering its environmental costs. **Therefore from 1 November 2009, the Government proposes to replace APD with a duty payable per plane rather than per passenger, and will begin a consultation** shortly. The consultation will consider ways to make aviation duty better correlated to distance travelled and encourage more planes to fly at full capacity. In introducing this duty, the Government will also take into account the impact on freight and transit and transfer passengers, consistent with its wider economic and social objectives. In advance of the introduction of a per plane duty, **APD rates will be frozen at their current level for 2008-09.**

Adaptation

7.57 The Stern Review also emphasises the importance of adaptation, as some impacts of climate change are no longer avoidable.

Domestic **7.58** The Stern Review and the *2004 Foresight Future Flooding* report both highlighted that
adaptation: flood climate change in the UK is likely to increase the severity and frequency of flooding events. In
risk management line with this, **total Government expenditure on flood and coastal erosion risk management will rise from £600 million in 2007-08 to £800 million in 2010-11. The Government will also introduce an adaptation toolkit of £10 million per year, to assist communities in adapting to change where constructing defences is not the most appropriate means of managing flood and coastal erosion risk.**

Help for flood **7.59** On 25 July 2007 the Chancellor of the Exchequer announced a package of measures
victims for individuals and businesses affected by severe flooding. As part of that package, the Government will bring forward legislation in next year's Finance Bill to allow the Commissioners of HMRC to waive interest and surcharges on tax paid late due to the floods.

Protecting the UK's environment

Sustainable **7.60** While tackling climate change at home and abroad is the most pressing issue for
development ensuring growth in the global economy is environmentally sustainable, the Government, in accordance with the principles of sustainable development, recognises the importance of protecting and enhancing our natural environment so that domestic growth is more environmentally sustainable.

Long-term **7.61** Despite the progress made in recent years, challenges remain in some areas and in
challenges some cases will intensify under the influence of factors such as growing and changing population patterns, economic growth and climate change. These pressures on the natural environment, as identified in *Long-term opportunities and challenges for the UK,* are:

- improving water quality and maintaining stable and sustainable supply;

- dealing with waste, especially from households, in a way that reduces its environmental impact;

- reversing the historic decline in biodiversity; and

- maximising the benefit people derive from a healthy and attractive natural environment.

7.62   The Government therefore announces a new PSA to secure a healthy natural environment for today and in the future. This demonstrates the Government's commitment to ensuring a healthy natural environment for everyone, monitoring key components such as water quality, air quality, the marine environment, biodiversity and the impacts of farming on the natural environment, as well as recognising the significant role that farmers and land managers play in protecting and enhancing the natural environment. Delivery arrangements for this PSA emphasise the positive impact that improvements in these measures can have on people's well-being, health and prosperity.

Water Strategy **7.63**   Defra will publish a Water Strategy early next year, which will take a long-term look at challenges in the water sector and outline the Government's priorities. The aim is to improve standards of service and quality, while balancing environmental impacts (including diffuse water pollution), water quality, supply and demand, and social and economic effects.

Waste Strategy **7.64**   The 2007 Waste Strategy set out the good progress made in England, with household recycling rates up from 7.5 per cent in 1996-97 to 26.7 per cent in 2005-06. The 2007 Comprehensive Spending Review provides for significant investment in more sustainable waste management options, which will allow continued reduction of the amount of waste that ends up in landfill. Funding through the Private Finance Initiative will total £2 billion over the CSR07 period, rising from £280 million in 2007-08 to £700 million by 2010-11.

Landfill tax **7.65**   Landfill tax increases the costs of waste disposal by landfill, encouraging more environmentally sustainable ways of dealing with waste. Budget 2007 announced that from 1 April 2008 and until at least 2010-11, the standard rate of landfill tax will increase by £8 per tonne each year. The lower rate applying to inactive waste will also increase from £2 to £2.50 per tonne from 1 April 2008. The Government plans to make an announcement on the future of the exemption from landfill tax for waste arising from contaminated land at Budget 2008.

Landfill tax dredging exemption **7.66**   The Government recognises that dredging inland waterways can prevent floods. However, the EU Landfill Directive being phased in necessitates the treatment of dredged waste so that it doesn't contain free-draining liquids. Therefore, from 30 October 2007, the landfill tax exemption will be extended to include treated waste from dredging.

Air quality **7.67**   The Government is committed to delivering cleaner air to protect people's health and the environment. The Government's revised Air Quality Strategy was published in July 2007, and sets out a way forward for work and planning on air quality issues. The strategy also sets out details of the objectives to be achieved and introduces a new policy framework for tackling fine particles, similar to the approach being proposed in the new European Air Quality Directive, which is currently under negotiation.

TACKLING GLOBAL POVERTY

7.68   The Government believes that, as one of the richest countries in the world, the UK has a moral obligation to contribute to international efforts to reduce global poverty. At the 2005 Gleneagles G8 summit, the Government led the world's richest nations to promise faster progress towards this goal. In today's interdependent world, eradicating extreme poverty also serves the UK national interest. Many of the most serious threats to the UK's prosperity and security are global, and are caused or exacerbated by poverty in developing countries, such as conflict, climate change, international organised crime and the spread of diseases like HIV/AIDS.

7.69   The UK has played a leading role in international efforts to tackle global poverty and achieve the internationally agreed Millennium Development Goals. Over the past decade, the Department for International Development's (DfID) budget has more than doubled in real terms between 1997-98 and 2007-08. DfID estimates that each year it helps to reduce permanently the number of people living in poverty by 3 million. However, significant challenges remain:

- just under a billion people – one in six of the world's population – still live in extreme poverty, that is on less than US$1 a day;

- every day 30,000 children die because of preventable diseases, and average life expectancy in Africa is 47 years; and

- by 2015, nine out of ten of the world's poorest people will live in Africa and South Asia, around half in countries without effective governments.

Millennium **7.70**   International development therefore remains a key priority for the Government. This
Development is reaffirmed by its **new PSA to reduce poverty in poorer countries through quicker progress**
Goals **towards the Millennium Development Goals.** This PSA sets out the Government's commitment to build a global partnership on development that stretches beyond traditional aid programmes – working with and through international partners, focusing UK action where it is most needed in Africa and South Asia. The clear and resounding message of the Make Poverty History campaign – actively supported by more than 1 in 4 people in the UK – has demonstrated that this commitment is strongly supported by the public. Success on this goal demands a cross-government approach to development, and requires that DfID help to reform the international development system to ensure that it is equipped to respond to new challenges, and to disburse increased aid flows effectively.

Financing development

7.71   The sustained and substantial increases to DfID's budget over the last decade are at the centre of the Government's efforts to tackle global poverty. To accelerate progress, **the 2007 Comprehensive Spending Review will increase DfID's budget by 11 per cent a year in real terms from £5.4 billion in 2007-08 to £7.9 billion in 2010-11.** These resources will be concentrated where they will have the maximum impact on poverty reduction: countries with the largest numbers of poor people and fragile states, especially those vulnerable to conflict.

Official **7.72**   Under the UK's presidencies of the G8 and EU in 2005, the Government achieved
Development international agreement to provide a historic level of debt relief to Nigeria. As a result, the
Assistance UK's cumulative spending on Official Development Assistance (ODA) during the 2004
Spending Review period was £17.8 billion, significantly higher than the £16.9 billion forecast.
ODA, which was projected to be 0.42 per cent of GNI in 2006-07, actually reached 0.51 per
cent in 2006, and this early delivery means that ODA is forecast to be lower than projected –
0.37 per cent – in 2007-08. **The 2007 Comprehensive Spending Review puts the UK on track
to spend 0.56 per cent of GNI on ODA by 2010-11, meeting the EU's collective commitment,
and on course to reach 0.7 per cent of GNI, the UN's recommended level, by 2013,[3] two years
ahead of the EU target.**

Financing the **7.73**   In allocating these resources, the Government will help partner countries promote
MDGs economic growth, good governance and delivery of basic services, to get children into school,
improve healthcare and increase access to clean water and sanitation. The UK is leading
action in a number of these areas, for example as the only major international donor to make
a ten-year education funding commitment of £8.5 billion. The Government is also driving
forward efforts to approach poverty reduction in new ways, by developing innovative
financing mechanisms like Advance Market Commitments and the International Finance
Facility for Immunisation (IFFIm), which address market failures and help to provide a more
stable and predictable flow of donor resources to developing countries. The UK is the leading
donor to IFFIm, which will help to save over 5 million children's lives by 2015.

Debt relief **7.74**   The UK remains committed to full implementation and financing of the Heavily
Indebted Poor Countries (HIPC) initiative and Multilateral Debt Relief Initiative (MDRI),
which together have already reduced the debt burden of the world's poorest countries by over
US$100 billion. In addition, the UK has renounced debt payments from the world's poorest
countries, exceeding commitments under the HIPC initiative, and offering debt relief
unilaterally for qualifying, non-HIPC poor countries that can use the savings for poverty
reduction, through the UK MDRI. The Government will continue to encourage other donors
to follow. The savings from debt relief provide long-term and predictable resources to fund
country-owned strategies for poverty reduction and improve the conditions for economic
growth. In countries receiving debt relief, debt service has been cut by two-thirds and annual
spending on anti-poverty programmes has increased from US$4 billion to US$11 billion since
1999.

Development beyond aid

Sustainable **7.75**   There is clear evidence that growth reduces poverty: a recent report[4] found that,
economic averaged over the countries studied, an increase of 1 per cent in GDP per head reduced
growth poverty by 1.7 per cent in the 1990s. Growth that is sustained and inclusive will have the
greatest impact on poverty reduction. Recognising the importance of growth, DfID, working
with partners across Government including HM Treasury, will assist developing countries in
identifying and overcoming the constraints to growth, increasing access to financial services,
improving transparency, strengthening public financial management systems and addressing
poor infrastructure. Overcoming these constraints will ensure that poor people can access the
economic opportunities that they need to benefit from growth.

[3] 2013 refers to calendar year 2013, which is the basis on which ODA is accounted for by the Organisation for Economic
Co-operation and Development, Development Assistance Committee.
[4] *Pro-poor growth in the 1990's; Lessons and insights from 14 countries*, Operationalising Pro-Poor Growth Research
Programme, June 2005, page 18.

Trade 7.76   Economic openness and trade reform can, under the right circumstances, play a significant role in increasing economic growth and reducing poverty. In an increasingly integrated world economy, it is crucial that developing countries be supported in participating in the world trading system. The UK continues to work hard with World Trade Organisation (WTO) partners to deliver an ambitious and pro-development outcome to the Doha round of world trade talks. Bold and concerted political leadership is needed to take forward negotiations on the basis of the Texts produced by the Negotiating Group chairs. Building on these Texts, the negotiations could achieve significant increases in market access, an end to export subsidies, a substantial reduction of all trade distorting agricultural domestic support, and provide effective special and differential treatment to enable developing countries to capture the gains from trade.

Aid for trade 7.77   Trade reform alone is not sufficient: investment is needed to support developing countries in overcoming supply-side constraints, such as inefficient customs systems or poor transport. UK support for aid for trade is expected to increase by 50 per cent to £409 million per year in 2010. The Government welcomes the successful outcome of the 25 September 2007 high-level pledging conference for the Enhanced Integrated Framework (EIF), which is a multilateral aid for trade fund for the 50 Least Developed Countries. The overall fund could be as much as US$400 million over 5 years, to which the UK contribution will be £15.5 million for the first 2 years and thereafter 20 per cent of overall commitments, up to a total maximum of £38 million.

International ETF 7.78   Climate change, alongside natural resource depletion, poses the most serious long-term threat to economic growth. The primary challenge for DfID is to ensure that economic growth is environmentally sustainable and that developing countries acquire the capacity to adapt to climate change. Developing country interests must also be taken into account in international policies to reduce climate change. **The 2007 Comprehensive Spending Review therefore establishes an Environmental Transformation Fund (ETF), with an interational element that provides £800 million over the CSR07 period, to advance poverty reduction through environmental protection. The ETF will be managed by DfID and Defra, and will work to support adaptation to climate change, provide access to clean energy, and help tackle unsustainable deforestation.**

Governance 7.79   Effective, stable and well-governed countries are more likely to attract investment and generate long-term economic growth which will reduce poverty. As such, improving governance in developing countries will remain a priority for DfID during the CSR07 period. DfID, in conjunction with the Foreign and Commonwealth Office, will increase its focus on supporting fragile states with weak governance, institutions and capacity. Fragile states comprise 9 per cent of the developing world's population but over a quarter of the extreme poor, and so a failure to make an impact on these states will jeopardise achieving the MDGs and pose risks that can cross borders, through civil conflicts, public health emergencies and humanitarian crises.

Conflict prevention and stabilisation 7.80   Violence and conflict keep people poor: of the 34 countries furthest from reaching the MDGs, 22 are in, or just emerging from, conflict. Accordingly, DfID, working closely with the MoD and the FCO, will continue to work to prevent conflict and manage its after-effects. The UK has been a leader in this area, and as outlined below, the Government will undertake a series of reforms to strengthen its approach during the CSR07 period.

STRENGTHENING INTERNATIONAL PEACE AND STABILITY

7.81 In an increasingly integrated world, the UK's security and prosperity depends on international peace and stability. While the UK does not currently face a significant direct threat of attack from other states, conflict and instability elsewhere has the potential to increase the risks to the UK. The challenge from global terrorism is serious and complex. In the period ahead changes in the geopolitical balance, climate change and resource pressures may also increase the risk of conflict between states, and the incidence and complexity of internal conflict.

Integrated **7.82** In facing these interrelated threats and challenges, an integrated response is
response essential: military, diplomatic and development interventions all have a part to play. The 2007 Comprehensive Spending Review strengthens the UK's ability to play its part in this response with and alongside the multilateral institutions and the wider international community.

7.83 Within a transformed geopolitical environment, the FCO has reviewed its international network in order to position the department at the forefront of the UK's efforts to counter global challenges, among them the growing terrorist threat. The MoD is renewing Britain's nuclear deterrent while ensuring that this does not come at the expense of the conventional capability the Armed forces need.

Resources and **7.84** The settlements for the MoD and FCO announced in this 2007 Comprehensive
investment Spending Review continue this progress. Alongside the increase to DFID's budget, this CSR07 delivers:

- **1.5 per cent annual average real growth over the CSR07 period for the MoD**, enhancing conventional capability across the armed services, including two new aircraft carriers, new protected vehicles for the Army, and further Air Transport capability. The settlement also funds the additional activity necessary over this CSR07 period to sustain the UK's nuclear deterrent;

- **a sustained increase in spending on counter-terrorism and intelligence through the new single security and intelligence budget, rising to more than three times pre 9/11 levels by 2010-11.** The new single security and intelligence budget will rise from £2½ billion in 2007-08 to £3½ billion by 2010-11, boosting the counter-terrorism effort in the UK and overseas;

- an additional £123 million by 2010-11 for the FCO, enabling the department to step up its engagement with critical areas of the globe, while improving its efficiency and reducing back-office costs. Among other improvements to the network, this settlement funds a new embassy in Kabul; and

- an increase in resources for the BBC World Service and British Council which will enable them to continue their vital public diplomacy work providing trusted news and information to millions around the globe and supporting efforts to build trust and break down cultural barriers. With £21 million in additional funding by 2010-11, the BBC World Service will launch Farsi TV and 24/7 Arabic TV services from 2008-09. The British Council will take forward its Reconnect programme with an additional £3 million per year by 2010-11, building understanding with Muslim societies particularly among alienated younger populations.

7.85   Alongside these spending commitments, the Government announces today a new PSA to reduce the impact of conflict through enhanced UK and international efforts. This embeds a strategic and comprehensive approach to reducing conflict and its impact, creating the conditions required for effective state building and economic development, monitoring progress to strengthen international institutions and building the UK's capability to plan, co-ordinate and deploy civilian and military resources. As part of the delivery arrangements for this PSA, the 2007 Comprehensive Spending Review announces a number of reforms to the way conflict prevention and stabilisation activity is co-ordinated and managed within Government.

Conflict **7.86**   The Government intends to merge the existing Global and Africa Conflict Prevention
stabilisation and Pools to reduce bureaucracy, focus effort where it can deliver best returns, and ensure that the
prevention new single Pool remains an effective instrument for long-term conflict prevention.

7.87   Conflict prevention is most effective where the immediate effects of conflict have been addressed through stabilisation activities. Responsibility for these activities in 'hot' conflict zones will become the responsibility of a new £269 Stabilisation Aid Fund established in the 2007 Comprehensive Spending Review. The Fund, for which DfID, FCO and MoD will be keyholders, will fund civil conflict stabilisation activities in volatile or hostile areas where the security situation does not yet permit the roll-out of programmes that the Pools have traditionally funded. This Fund will take on responsibilities currently handled by the Global Conflict Prevention Pool for civil effect in the operational theatres of Iraq and Afghanistan, allowing the new single Conflict Prevention Pool to refocus on prevention activity in other parts of the world.

7.88   The Government will continue to develop the role and capability of the cross-departmental Post Conflict Resolution Unit – to be renamed the Stabilisation Unit in recognition of its role in management of the new Stabilisation Aid Fund on behalf of DfID, FCO, and MoD. The Unit will be responsible for providing the civilian teams to support the design and delivery of UK civilian activities, including quick impact projects, in insecure environments often alongside UK military forces, and filling critical capability gaps in UK and international operations such as the rule of law, governance and policing advisers. The Stabilisation Unit will also facilitate cross-government assessment and planning to stabilise countries emerging from conflict, and will identify and integrate lessons from UK interventions into future stabilisation activities.

Special Reserve **7.89** International peace support operations play a vital role in strengthening global stability, and the UK's continued engagement in these operations is an important component in achieving our foreign, defence and development policy objectives. In Budget 2007, the Government announced £400 million of provision for the special reserve in 2007-08, to be reviewed at the time of the Pre-Budget Report, to help meet continuing international commitments in Iraq, Afghanistan and elsewhere. **The CSR07 allocates a further £400 million for the special reserve in 2007-08 to support ongoing operations.**

Table 7.1: The environmental impacts of Budget measures

Budget measure	Environmental impact
Climate Change and Air Quality	
Climate change levy (CCL) package	Climate change levy is estimated to deliver annual emissions savings of over 12.8 million tonnes of carbon ($MtCO_2$) by 2010[1].
	Climate change agreements are estimated to deliver annual emissions savings of 10.3 $MtCO_2$ a year by 2010.
	Total CCL package, including Carbon Trust, is estimated to deliver annual emissions savings of over 27.5 $MtCO_2$ a year by 2010.
Carbon capture and storage	Carbon capture and storage demonstration is expected to deliver savings of around 0.7 $MtCO_2$ per year by 2020.
Fuel duty	Fuel duty increases announced for 2007 to 2010 are expected to result in carbon savings of 0.7 $MtCO_2$ a year by 2010-11.
Support for biofuels	The RTFO is estimated to deliver savings of between 2.6 and 3 $MtCO_2$ a year by 2010. (see paragraph 7.30.)
Rebated fuels	Maintaining the differential with main road fuels will reduce levels of fraud, and will deliver small CO_2 and local air pollution benefits through increased use of less polluting fuels and less use of rebated fuels, which are more polluting.
Vehicle excise duty (VED)	The environmental signals provided by VED will help deliver reductions in CO_2 emissions. The number of vehicles in the 3 lowest CO_2 emission graduated VED bands is forecast to grow significantly in the longer term in part due to VED reform.
Company car tax (CCT)	CO_2 emissions savings of reformed CCT system estimated to be 0.7 to 1.8 $MtCO_2$, in 2005, forecast to rise to between 1.5 and 3.3 $MtCO_2$ per year in the long run[2].
Company car fuel benefit charge (FBC)	The number of company car drivers getting free fuel for private use has fallen by around 600,000 since 1997, partly as a result of changes to the company car tax system in April 2002 and changes to the fuel benefit rules in April 2003, helping to reduce levels of CO_2 emissions, local air pollutants and congestion[3]. Increasing the FBC in line with the changes in the retail prices index in 2008-09 will deliver a small additional reduction in CO_2 emissions.
Landlord's Energy Saving Allowance (LESA)	Small reduction of carbon emissions.
Reduced rate of VAT on professionally-installed energy saving materials and microgeneration (from 17.5 per cent to 5 per cent)	Small reduction of carbon emissions.
Reduced rate of VAT on domestic fuel and power (from 8 per cent to 5 per cent)	Estimated to increase carbon emissions by 0.7 $MtCO_2$ by 2010[4].
Improving Waste Management	
Landfill tax	Between 1997/98 and 2006/07 the total quantity of waste disposed to landfill sites registered for landfill tax fell by 26 per cent, while the amount of active waste disposed to landfill fell by 19 per cent[5].
Landfill communities fund	Landfill tax credits scheme (now the landfill communities fund) has provided almost £780 million for projects since its introduction.
Protecting the UK's countryside and natural resources	
Aggregates levy and aggregates levy sustainability fund	An 8 per cent reduction in sales of aggregates in Great Britain between 2001 and 2005. Reductions in noise and vibration, dust and other emissions to air, visual intrusion, loss of amenity and damage to wildlife habitats.

[1] Modeling the initial Effects of the Climate Change Levy, Cambridge Econometrics, available at www.hmrc.gov.uk.
[2] HMRC modeling.
[3] HMRC modeling.
[4] HMRC modeling.
[5] Data at www.uktradeinfo.com, in calendar years.

A THE ECONOMY

In 2007, the UK economy has continued to perform strongly, and has now expanded in 60 consecutive quarters. GDP growth in the first half of the year reached $3\frac{1}{4}$ per cent on a year earlier, towards the upper end of the Budget 2007 forecast range. External forecasters expect the UK to grow more strongly in 2007 than any other G7 economy. The world economy is expected to remain robust in 2007, growing by 5 per cent, with emerging markets continuing to expand rapidly.

As forecast at Budget 2007, UK inflation has returned close to target in the second half of this year, falling to 1.8 per cent in August. Employment has reached a new record high, above 29 million, and unemployment has fallen, with the claimant count lower in 11 consecutive months and down by more than 100,000 since September 2006.

Evidence from the cyclical indicators monitored by the Treasury, and latest National Accounts data, imply the economy may have moved up through trend towards the end of 2006. However, it is too soon to assess whether or not the economic cycle has ended.

The disruption in global financial markets has meant economic prospects have become more uncertain, and events need to unfold further before the impact on the economy can be rigorously quantified. For the purposes of the economic forecast, it has been assumed that there will be some feed-through to tighter credit conditions and to household and company spending in the short term.

Reflecting the combination of momentum in the economy, but higher interest rates than markets expected at the time of Budget 2007, the 2007 Pre-Budget Report economic forecast is for:

- GDP growth of 3 per cent in 2007, slowing to 2 to $2\frac{1}{2}$ per cent in 2008, before returning to its trend rate of $2\frac{1}{2}$ to 3 per cent in 2009 and 2010; and

- CPI inflation to remain close to target throughout the forecast horizon.

Financial market disruption presents clear risks to the economic forecast, though these are judged to be broadly balanced. Considerable uncertainty surrounds the timing and extent to which the disruption might affect the wider economy, and the longer it persists, the greater the risk of it detracting from growth. However, the UK economy has proved resilient to a number of shocks over the past decade, demonstrating the pay-off to the Government's macroeconomic framework and promotion of open and flexible labour, product and capital markets. As such, growth could also slow by less than expected.

INTRODUCTION[1,2]

A.1 This chapter discusses recent economic developments and provides updated forecasts for the UK and world economies in the period to 2010. It begins with an overview of developments and prospects in the world economy, which set the global context for recent developments and prospects in the UK. It then outlines the UK economic forecast, before concluding with a more detailed discussion of sectoral issues, the components of growth, and the risks and uncertainties surrounding the forecast.

---

[1] The UK forecast is consistent with National Accounts and balance of payments statistics to the second quarter of 2007 released by the Office for National Statistics on 26 September 2007. A detailed set of charts and tables relating to the economic forecast is available on the Treasury's internet site (http://www.hm-treasury.gov.uk). Copies can be obtained on request from the Treasury's Public Enquiry Unit (020 7270 4558).

[2] The forecast is based on the assumption that the exchange rate moves in line with an uncovered interest parity condition, consistent with the interest rates underlying the economic forecast.

THE WORLD ECONOMY

Overview

A.2   The world economy grew by $5\frac{1}{4}$ per cent in 2006, the fastest rate since 1990. This reflected strong growth in advanced economies and particularly in the emerging markets, which accounted for more than half of total world growth. This was the third consecutive year of global growth above $4\frac{1}{2}$ per cent. It is expected to ease slightly in 2007, though to remain high by historical standards at 5 per cent.

A.3   Although global growth is expected to remain healthly, prospects have moderated in recent months reflecting the effects of financial market disruption. In 2007, G7 growth is expected to slow to 2 per cent, due in particular to the ongoing slowdown in the US, and to remain moderate in 2008. Growth in some emerging markets is expected to ease somewhat from the very high rates of recent years, but to remain strong. Emerging markets are expected to continue to account for the majority of world growth. Against this background, world trade is forecast to grow at $7\frac{3}{4}$ per cent in 2007, feeding through to UK export markets growth of 7 per cent.

Table A1: The world economy

	Percentage change on a year earlier, unless otherwise stated				
			Forecast		
	2006	**2007**	**2008**	**2009**	**2010**
World GDP	$5\frac{1}{4}$	5	5	$4\frac{3}{4}$	$4\frac{3}{4}$
Major 7 countries[1]					
Real GDP	$2\frac{3}{4}$	2	2	$2\frac{1}{2}$	$2\frac{1}{2}$
Consumer price inflation[2]	$1\frac{3}{4}$	$2\frac{1}{2}$	$2\frac{1}{2}$	$2\frac{1}{2}$	$2\frac{1}{2}$
Euro area GDP	3	$2\frac{1}{2}$	2	2	2
World trade in goods and services	10	$7\frac{3}{4}$	$7\frac{3}{4}$	$7\frac{3}{4}$	$7\frac{3}{4}$
UK export markets[3]	9	7	$6\frac{1}{2}$	$6\frac{3}{4}$	$6\frac{3}{4}$

[1] G7: US, Japan, Germany, France, UK, Italy and Canada.

[2] Per cent, Q4.

[3] Other countries' imports of goods and services weighted according to the importance of imports from the UK in those countries' total imports.

A.4   Recent falls in headline inflation rates in the G7 have mainly reflected developments in energy prices, with core inflation remaining low and stable by historical standards. Since Budget 2007, central banks in most advanced economies have tightened monetary policy, although the Federal Reserve in the US cut interest rates by $\frac{1}{2}$ a percentage point in September, in response to recent financial market disruption. This was the first cut since 2003.

Global financial markets

A.5   Since July 2007, there has been considerable financial market disruption around the world. Underlying these developments has been an ongoing re-pricing of risk, and further deterioration of the US sub-prime mortgage market, where a combination of higher interest rates, slower house price growth, and looser lending standards has caused the number of borrowers defaulting on their loans to rise. In recent years, many types of loan, including these higher-risk mortgages, have been combined and repackaged into securities that accrue an income stream from future interest payments. In some cases, these asset-backed securities were further repackaged into different tranches offering varying degrees of risk and rates of return, and sold to global investors and held in investment vehicles. A number of hedge funds and major banks have suffered significant losses due to their exposure to some asset-backed securities and related derivatives, triggering a widening in spreads in money and credit markets, described in Box A1.

A.6   The timing and extent to which these developments might affect the wider economy is not yet clear. Events need to unfold further before the economic impact can be properly quantified. As such, the global and UK economic prospects discussed in this chapter have become more uncertain. The risks associated with financial market disruption are discussed in more detail from paragraph A.78.

G7 activity and inflation

United States **A.7**   Revisions to US National Accounts data released in July 2007 showed that US GDP growth slowed marginally in 2006, and was slightly lower than previously estimated. Below-trend growth has continued in the first half of 2007, as the correction in the housing market has persisted. Against a background of weaker home sales and falling property prices, the inventory of unsold houses has increased sharply compared with early 2007. So far, other components of demand have partly compensated for negative growth in residential investment.

A.8   US GDP growth is set to continue at below-trend rates in 2007 and early 2008, and to recover more gradually through 2008. This reflects a more protracted contraction in residential investment than expected at the time of Budget 2007, and the effects of recent financial market disruption. The latest estimates of consumption growth suggest that it has started to moderate, as a result of tighter financing conditions, weakness in the housing market and softer employment growth. Against this, the outlook for net exports remains positive, which should support the recent improvement in the US current account position.

Euro area **A.9**   Stronger euro area growth in 2006 has been carried through into the first half of 2007, with growth this year driven by strong domestic demand, particularly business investment. The labour market has continued to improve: employment growth across the region has been strong, particularly in Germany, and the unemployment rate has this year fallen below 7 per cent for the first time since 1993. Survey readings of euro area and country-specific business and consumer confidence have fallen during the recent period of financial market disruption, potentially signalling a slower expansion in the quarters to come, although they remain above historical averages.

A.10   Solid growth is forecast to continue during the rest of 2007, largely due to the momentum implied by stronger than expected outturn data in the first half of the year. Growth is expected to moderate to around its trend rate in 2008.

Box A1: Developments in global financial markets

Recent financial market developments have been associated with changes in the pricing of risk. The period of disruption since July was triggered by renewed concerns about the US sub-prime mortgage market, following earlier periods of stress in February and March. The impact soon spread to a range of markets for asset-backed securities and related commercial paper (chart a). Uncertainty over which institutions were exposed to potential losses, the size of any exposures, and the extent to which banks might have to bring many of these assets back onto their balance sheets, caused money market liquidity to contract and inter-bank lending rates to rise sharply in all major financial centres (chart b). As investors' appetite for risk diminished, the value of a range of higher-risk assets fell, including lower-rated corporate bonds, emerging market bonds and equities (chart c), and even high-yielding currencies like the Australian and New Zealand dollars. By contrast, the price of US Treasury bills, often seen as a safe haven in times of volatility, increased sharply causing the yield, which moves inversely with the price, to fall well below the US policy rate (chart d).

Central banks have offered more liquidity at slightly longer maturities, including in the three-month money market, and, in some cases, against a broader range of collateral than usual. The spread of three-month inter-bank lending rates over expected policy rates has since fallen, while stock, bond and currency markets have stabilised somewhat. However, while the disruption has eased, inter-bank spreads remain high, while more specialised credit markets remain illiquid.

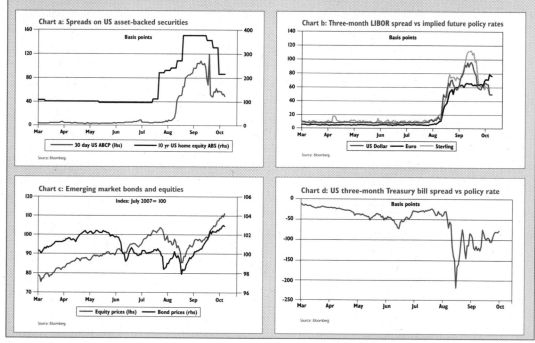

Japan **A.11** In Japan, recorded GDP growth in the first half of 2007 has been volatile: a very strong first quarter was followed by contraction in the second quarter. Some modest underlying strength is expected to continue, reflecting a positive contribution to growth from business investment and net exports, with private consumption growth remaining sluggish. The Japanese economy is expected to grow at slightly above-trend rates in 2007, before slowing in 2008.

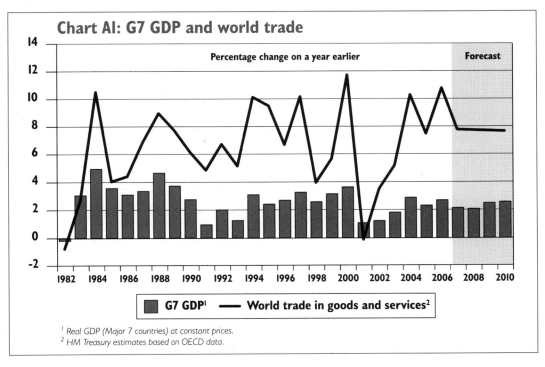

Chart AI: G7 GDP and world trade

Percentage change on a year earlier

Forecast

■ G7 GDP¹ —— World trade in goods and services²

¹ Real GDP (Major 7 countries) at constant prices.
² HM Treasury estimates based on OECD data.

G7 inflation prospects

A.12 Recent falls in headline inflation rates among the G7 economies have mainly reflected developments in energy prices. Core inflation has remained broadly stable, and low by historical standards. G7 inflation is expected to remain at moderate rates throughout the forecast horizon.

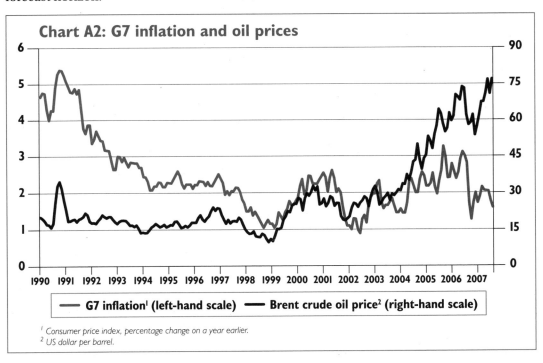

Chart A2: G7 inflation and oil prices

—— G7 inflation¹ (left-hand scale)   —— Brent crude oil price² (right-hand scale)

¹ Consumer price index, percentage change on a year earlier.
² US dollar per barrel.

Emerging markets and developing economies

Emerging Asia

A.13 Emerging Asia is expected to continue growing strongly this year and next, continuing the pattern of recent years. The Chinese economy grew by more than 11 per cent in 2006, and the growth rate picked up further in the first half of 2007. Rapid export growth has been an important driver, as reflected in the expanding trade surplus. Inflation has picked up sharply as a result of higher food prices, while asset prices have risen rapidly. Policy tightening is expected to cause a small moderation of growth from 2008. The recent performance of the Indian economy has also been impressive, with growth of more than 9 per cent in 2006. This year, GDP growth is expected to moderate slightly, as a result of higher interest rates and appreciation of the Indian rupee. These factors have also helped to reduce inflation.

Emerging Europe **A.14**   In Russia, output in 2007 is expected to grow by more than 6 per cent for the fifth consecutive year. In the wider region, momentum in domestic demand since 2006 is expected to carry through to this year, with growth expected to moderate to more sustainable rates from 2008. Some countries have experienced a pick-up in inflation on the back of rapid demand growth and tighter labour markets.

Latin America **A.15**   Following strong GDP growth in 2006, the expansion in Latin America is expected to ease through 2007 and 2008, reflecting the impact of slower US growth on the region's net exports. Higher food prices have resulted in a pick-up in inflation in several countries in the region, which in turn has led to concern about overheating and, in some cases, prompted tighter monetary policy.

World trade and UK export markets

A.16   As forecast at the time of Budget 2007, world trade growth slowed in the first half of 2007, to $7^3/_4$ per cent on a year earlier, reflecting a broad-based slowdown across all regions. From 2008 onwards, world trade is expected to grow at rates slightly above the historical average. Recent momentum in world trade has largely reflected strength across emerging markets: in 2007, Asia excluding Japan and emerging Europe are expected to account for around half of total world trade growth.

A.17   Slower-growing mature economies make up a larger proportion of UK export markets than of overall world trade. As a result, consistent with the expected moderate growth in the G7 economies, and particularly the US, growth in UK export markets is forecast to be slightly below that of world trade.

Oil and commodity prices

A.18   Since 2002, the price of a barrel of Brent crude oil, the European standard, has more than trebled. It has averaged around $68 so far in 2007, close to the $66 average in 2006, but considerably above the $20 a barrel average over the decade to 2002.

A.19   Since Budget 2007, oil prices have risen above consensus forecasts, reaching new nominal highs over the past month. Various factors, including resilient demand, weak supply growth, unexpected difficulties in the US refining sector, and real and perceived risks to supply, have put upward pressure on prices. The average of independent forecasts is for the price of Brent crude to ease slightly in 2008. The outlook for oil prices remains sensitive to geo-political, regulatory and weather-related risks in the major producer and consumer nations.

A.20   Non-fuel commodity prices remain high. The price of metals has continued to rise strongly in 2007, although most prices have moderated more recently in response to financial market developments. Some agricultural commodities have experienced significant and more widespread price increases in 2007, notably the price of wheat, which reached an 11-year peak in nominal terms over the past month due to the poor crop in a number of major producing countries, and rising demand for bio-fuels.

THE UK ECONOMIC FORECAST

The Treasury's approach to economic forecasting

A.21 The Treasury's approach to forecasting macroeconomic developments, set out in detail in Budget 2007,[3] accords with the growth cycle approach favoured by many policymakers. The essential building blocks of this approach are the estimate of the 'trend' level and rate of growth of output, and analysis of cyclical movements around that trend, the 'output gap'. The trend growth projection provides the medium-term anchor for the forecast. The current output gap estimate, and an assessment of the economy's momentum based on analysis of the individual output, income and expenditure components of activity, informs judgement on the short-term path of the economy back to trend.

A.22 Once the effects of known shocks are forecast to have dissipated and the economy is judged to have returned to trend, growth is generally held at its trend rate and the output gap at zero. That is not to suggest that the growth rate will actually be constant in later periods of the forecast, but rather that future shocks to the economy are as likely to be positive as negative so that, on average, the best forecast of growth once present shocks have worked through will be the trend rate.

A.23 The Treasury assesses trend output growth on the basis of non-oil gross value added (GVA) rather than overall GDP because, while the oil and gas sector affects output, it has little direct impact on capacity pressures in the rest of the economy, and hence the sustainable level of non-oil activity or employment.

Overview of recent developments

A.24 The UK's macroeconomic performance continues to be strong and stable. GDP in the UK has now expanded for 60 consecutive quarters, the longest expansion since quarterly National Accounts began in the mid-1950s. According to the latest Office for National Statistics (ONS) estimates, since late 2005 quarterly growth rates have been slightly above trend and have varied by no more than 0.1 percentage points.

GDP growth **A.25** Between Budget and Pre-Budget Reports, National Accounts data are typically subject to significant revisions during the annual Blue Book process, at which time the ONS takes on information from new and more comprehensive data sources, as well as making improvements to statistical methodologies. As a result of resource reprioritisation necessary to deliver modernised National Accounts in 2008, the 2007 Blue Book process was limited in scope.[4] The revisions to GDP growth contained in Blue Book 2007 were therefore smaller than those in recent Blue Books: no more than 0.1 percentage points in any year. In consequence, there could be larger than normal revisions in Blue Book 2008.

A.26 As reported in Budget 2007, the UK economy grew by $2^3/_4$ per cent in 2006. Data released since Budget time show that GDP grew by 0.8 per cent in each of the first and second quarters of 2007, bringing output growth in the first half of the year to $3^1/_4$ per cent on a year earlier, towards the upper end of the Budget 2007 forecast range for the year as a whole. Non-oil GVA growth in the year to the second quarter of 2007 was above trend at $3^1/_4$ per cent, slightly stronger than expected at the time of Budget 2007.

---

[3] See paragraphs B.30 to B.35, Budget 2007.

[4] Blue Book 2007 included improvements to the measurement of own-account software investment, but delayed until 2008 improvements to the treatment of banking sector output, known as FISIM (financial intermediation services indirectly measured), and the normally annual process of benchmarking and balancing the accounts. For more detail see *Modernising the UK's National Accounts*, Economic & Labour Market Review, ONS, April 2007.

A.27   The process of rebalancing between the domestic components of demand that began in 2005 has continued. In 2006 as a whole, private consumption grew by 2 per cent, below the 2³/₄ per cent rate of the whole economy, while business investment grew by 7¹/₂ per cent. In the first half of 2007, consumption was up 3 per cent on a year earlier, compared with 3¹/₄ per cent for whole economy GDP, and business investment was 8³/₄ per cent higher. In terms of the rebalancing between domestic and external demand, net exports continued to subtract from growth in 2006, but appear to have been more neutral in the first half of 2007, though trade data are subject to possible measurement difficulties discussed in paragraph A.62. On the output side, while the service sector remained the main source of growth, manufacturing has also contributed positively to growth over the past year and a half, while oil production picked up during the first half of 2007 after an extended period of negative growth.

Inflation **A.28**   Having risen during 2006, consumer price inflation continued to rise during the first quarter of 2007, peaking at 3.1 per cent in March. The rise in headline inflation was initially driven by energy price developments, caused by high oil and wholesale gas prices. On top of that, food price inflation was pushed higher by the effects of the unusually hot UK summer in 2006 and, thereafter, global supply and demand pressures. RPI inflation increased by more than CPI inflation, peaking at 4.8 per cent in March, mainly reflecting the impact of tighter monetary policy on mortgage interest payments.

A.29   CPI inflation has fallen back sharply from its peak in March to stand at 1.8 per cent in August, mainly due to the ongoing effect of utility price cuts, and some supermarket-led reductions in food prices. RPI inflation has also eased, to 4.1 per cent by August. Volatile movements in the price of furniture and furnishings, with monthly changes more than twice as large during 2007 than on average over the preceding decade, have made short-term forecasting of inflation more difficult. Nevertheless headline inflation has eased as expected.

A.30   Despite record employment levels and high oil prices, inflation expectations have remained anchored to target, and there has been little sign of any significant upward pressure on wages. The Government has demonstrated its commitment to ensuring that wage pressures remain consistent with the 2 per cent CPI inflation target by delivering overall headline awards for Pay Review Body groups in 2007-08 that average 1.9 per cent.

Monetary and **A.31**   The Bank of England has continued to tighten monetary policy since Budget 2007,
fiscal policy raising Bank Rate by a ¹/₄ percentage point in May and again in July, taking the cumulative tightening to 1¹/₄ percentage points since August 2006. Market-derived interest rate expectations at the end of July implied a further tightening of monetary policy, but since then market expectations have shifted significantly and now point to some easing over coming months. At 5³/₄ per cent, Bank Rate remains significantly below the 9¹/₂ per cent average of the first half of the 1990s, and further still below the 11³/₄ per cent average of the 1980s. During the period of above-trend growth in 2006-07, monetary policy was supported by a fiscal tightening.

Financial markets **A.32**   The global financial market disruption described in Box A1 has had an impact on UK financial markets, in common with other major financial centres. Most notable has been the rise in short-term interest rates on lending between financial institutions, where the spread between Bank Rate and the three-month sterling LIBOR[5] interest rate, normally around 20

---

[5] The 'London inter-bank offered rate', LIBOR, is the rate at which banks are willing to lend to one another on an unsecured basis.

basis points, rose to more than 100 basis points in the first half of September before easing in recent weeks. At the current rate of around 6¹/₄ per cent, three-month interest rates remain low compared with the 9¹/₂ per cent average of the early 1990s and the 12 per cent average of the 1980s.

Money growth and credit conditions **A.33** Beyond any direct impact of financial market disruption on incomes and profits in the financial sector, recent developments could affect the wider economy through their impact on credit conditions for households and companies. Growth rates of the broad money supply and lending to the private sector remained strong during the year to August 2007, though they have eased slightly from the historically high rates seen during the second half of 2006. The Bank of England's new *Credit Conditions Survey*, published for the first time on 26 September, suggested that recent financial market disruption had yet to impact on credit conditions facing households, although there was evidence that it was to some extent affecting the price and availability of credit to the corporate sector. Bank of England data on effective interest rates on deposits and lending for August 2007 presented a similar picture, with more muted increases in borrowing rates for households than for companies.

Assessment of the output gap

Evidence from the cyclical indicators **A.34** Since Budget 2007, upward revisions to estimates of non-oil GVA growth in 2006, combined with estimates of 0.8 per cent growth in each of the first two quarters of 2007, show the UK economy to have been growing at slightly above-trend rates for seven consecutive quarters through to mid-2007. Evidence from the broad range of cyclical indicators monitored by the Treasury,[6] set out in the following paragraphs, suggests the economy may currently be operating slightly above trend and that output may have moved up through trend towards the end of 2006.

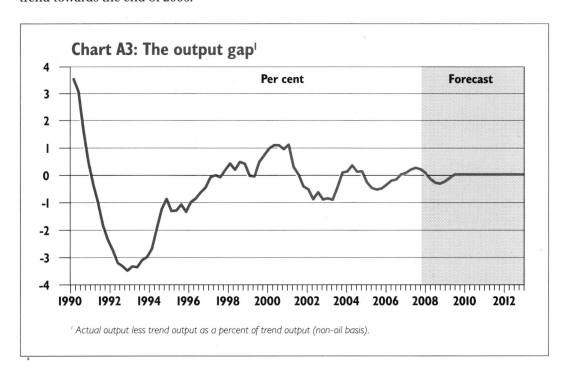

Chart A3: The output gap[1]

[1] Actual output less trend output as a percent of trend output (non-oil basis).

---

[6] Details of these indicators can be found in the *Technical note on cyclical indicators*, HM Treasury, December 2005.

A.35   Private sector business surveys suggest that capacity utilisation in the manufacturing and service sectors had moved to levels consistent with the economy being marginally above trend by the second quarter of 2007. These indicators have generally risen since Budget 2007.

A.36   Indicators of recruitment difficulties, which at the time of Budget 2007 signalled spare capacity remaining in the labour market, have also picked up, providing evidence of diminishing slack. The Bank of England Regional Agents' score for recruitment difficulties has risen progressively since January 2007, and by August had moved fractionally above its long-run average. Other indicators provide further evidence of diminishing slack and strong demand for labour. For example, claimant count unemployment has fallen for 11 consecutive months, and by more than 100,000 since September 2006. The Labour Force Survey unemployment rate has edged down, although it remains above its lows in 2005. The number of vacancies has risen to a six-year high. Labour market developments typically lag changes in output, so signs of the labour market tightening through 2007 would be consistent with the economy moving upwards through trend towards the end of 2006.

A.37   Average earnings growth has so far remained subdued, with whole economy measures including and excluding bonuses standing at just $3\frac{1}{2}$ per cent on a year earlier in the second quarter of 2007. More generally though, indicators of domestically-generated inflation appear consistent with the economy operating close to trend, with recent fluctuations in headline CPI inflation not driven by domestic cyclical factors.

A.38   The trend growth arithmetic,[7] based on the latest National Accounts data and the Treasury's trend output assumptions, implies output passed through trend in the final quarter of 2006 and that a small positive output gap, of around a $\frac{1}{4}$ per cent, has opened up. However, with output assessed still to be close to trend, National Accounts data more than usually subject to revision, and growth forecast to slow in 2008, it is too soon to assess whether or not the economic cycle has ended.

Assessment of trend growth

A.39   The Treasury's neutral estimate of the economy's trend rate of output growth for the 2007 Pre-Budget Report remains at $2\frac{3}{4}$ per cent a year to the end of the projection period, the same assumption that underpinned the previous two economic forecasts.[8]

A.40   Table A2 presents estimates of trend output growth and its decomposition to the end of 2006, and the Treasury's projection thereafter.

Summary of   **A.41**   The latest National Accounts data show that the average rate of growth of non-oil GVA
outturns from   between the 2001 on-trend point and the final quarter of 2006 was 2.77 per cent, in line with
2001 to 2006   the Treasury's trend output projection for that period, which has been consistently maintained since it was introduced at Budget 2002.[9] In terms of the composition of trend growth, the latest data suggest that average annual productivity growth over the period was slightly higher than the projections set out in Budget 2007, while the average annual growth rates of the working-age employment rate and average hours were slightly lower.

---

[7] See paragraph B.34 of Budget 2007 for a fuller explanation of the trend growth arithmetic.

[8] For a full discussion of the most recent review of the Treasury's trend growth projections, see *Trend growth: new evidence and prospects*, HM Treasury, December 2006.

[9] See *Trend growth: recent developments and prospects*, HM Treasury, April 2002.

A.42 Despite the data underlying these calculations remaining subject to revision, the evidence suggests that, for the time being, small technical adjustments should be made to the projected growth rates of the components of trend growth for the period from 2007 onwards, to align these component projections with latest data. As such, the projection for trend productivity growth on an unadjusted basis has been increased from 2.15 to 2.30 per cent, and projections for the annual trend rate of growth of the employment rate and average hours worked have been changed from 0.2 to 0.1 per cent and -0.2 to -0.25 per cent respectively. These adjustments offset each other within the unchanged overall projection for trend output growth, which remains at $2^3/_4$ per cent a year.

Table A2: Contributions to trend output growth[1]

	Estimated trend rates of growth, per cent per annum					
	Trend output per hour worked[2,3]		Trend average hours worked[3]	Trend employment rate[3]	Population of working age[4]	**Trend output**
	Underlying	Unadjusted				
	(1)	(2)	(3)	(4)	(5)	(6)
1986Q2 to 1997H1						
Latest data	2.13	1.95	−0.11	0.36	0.25	**2.46**
Over the recent past						
1997H1 to 2001Q3						
Latest data	2.89	2.70	−0.46	0.38	0.53	**3.17**
2001Q3 to 2006Q4						
Budget 2002[5]	2.10	2.00	−0.1	0.2	0.6	**$2^3/_4$**
PBR 2006 and Budget 2007	2.25	2.15	−0.2	0.2	0.7	**$2^3/_4$**
Latest data[6,7]	2.35	2.32	−0.27	0.06	0.65	**2.77**
Projection[8]						
2006Q4 onwards						
PBR 2006 and Budget 2007	2.25	2.15	−0.2	0.2	0.6	**$2^3/_4$**
PBR 2007[9]	2.35	2.30	−0.25	0.1	0.6	**$2^3/_4$**

[1]Treasury analysis based on judgement that 1986Q2, 1997H1 and 2001Q3 were on-trend points of the output cycle. Figures independently rounded. Trend output growth is estimated as growth of non-oil gross value added between on-trend points for the past, and by projecting components going forward.
Columns (2) + (3) + (4) + (5) = (6).
Full data definitions and sources are set out in Annex A of 'Trend growth: new evidence and prospects', HM Treasury, December 2006.
[2] The underlying trend rate is the unadjusted trend rate adjusted for changes in the employment rate, i.e. assuming the employment rate had remained constant.
Column (1) = column (2) + (1-a).column (4), where a is the ratio of new to average worker productivity levels. The figuring is consistent with this ratio being of the order of 50 per cent, informed by econometric evidence and LFS data on relative entry wages.
[3] The decomposition makes allowances for employment and hours worked lagging output. Employment is assumed to lag output by around three quarters, so that on-trend points for employment come three quarters after on-trend points for output, an assumption which can be supported by econometric evidence. Hours are easier to adjust than employment, and the decomposition assumes that average hours worked lag output by just one quarter, though this lag is harder to support by econometric evidence. Hours worked and the employment rate are measured on a working-age basis.
[4] UK resident household basis.
[5] Interim projections between Budget 2002 and PBR 2006 are provided in an expanded table in '2007 Pre-Budget Report: the economy and public finances – supplementary charts and tables', HM Treasury, October 2007.
[6] Estimates based on the assumption that the economy passed up through trend in the final quarter of 2006.
[7] Estimates have been adjusted in line with the mid-year population estimates published in August 2007. Labour market statistics consistent with the latest population estimates will be published by the ONS in due course.
[8] Neutral case assumptions for trend from 2006Q4.
[9] Underlying trend assumptions around which the mid-points of the GDP forecast growth ranges from 2006Q4 are anchored.

Labour market developments **A.43** Employment grew by around 275,000 in the year to the fourth quarter of 2006, with roughly 30 per cent of that increase accounted for by workers of above the State Pension age. As a result, while the working-age employment rate was broadly stable through the year at around 74$\frac{1}{2}$ per cent, the employment rate for older workers increased from 10$\frac{1}{2}$ to 11 per cent. Despite that increase, the employment rate among all adults has remained broadly stable at around 60 per cent. Employment rose by 84,000 in the three months to July and stands at a record high above 29 million. Private sector employment growth has been solid, up around 175,000 on year earlier in the second quarter, while public sector employment has fallen by more than 40,000 over the same period. Employment rates among the working-age and older workers have remained stable in 2007.

A.44 At the time of the 2006 Pre-Budget Report, the Treasury revised up its estimate of the economy's trend rate of output growth from 2007 onwards based on analysis of evidence that pointed to the contribution of net migration being a $\frac{1}{4}$ percentage point a year higher than previously assumed. The ONS's latest population estimates published in August 2007, and the long-term net migration assumption for UK population projections published in September, were consistent with the assumption underpinning the 2$\frac{3}{4}$ per cent trend growth estimate. Evidence relating to short-term migrants from the new EU Member States suggests the flow in the year to the second quarter of 2007 continued at a similar rate to that in 2006.

GDP and inflation forecasts

Table A3: Summary of forecast[1]

	2006	Forecast			
		2007	2008	2009	2010
GDP growth (per cent)	2$\frac{3}{4}$	3	2 to 2$\frac{1}{2}$	2$\frac{1}{2}$ to 3	2$\frac{1}{2}$ to 3
CPI inflation (per cent, Q4)	2$\frac{3}{4}$	2	2	2	2

[1] See footnote to Table A9 for explanation of forecast ranges.

GDP and the output gap **A.45** GDP growth in the first half of 2007 was towards the upper end of the Budget 2007 forecast range for the year as a whole, itself unchanged since the 2005 Pre-Budget Report, at 3$\frac{1}{4}$ per cent on a year earlier. With recent growth in non-oil GVA having been slightly stronger than expected at the time of Budget 2007, the output gap in mid-2007 is estimated to be slightly positive, compared with zero in the Budget forecast. On unchanged trend output growth assumptions, this implies a little less scope for growth over the year ahead if the inflation target is to be met.

A.46 Private sector business surveys, most notably those published by the Chartered Institute of Purchasing and Supply, and the Bank of England's Regional Agents' scores, suggest the economy carried significant momentum into the second half of 2007. In light of such evidence, the 2007 Pre-Budget Report forecast is for GDP growth of 3 per cent in the year as a whole, in line with the Budget 2007 forecast. Growth of non-oil GVA is forecast to be slightly stronger than it was in Budget 2007.

A.47 The MPC has raised Bank Rate by more than financial markets expected at Budget time, which can be expected to impact on growth in 2008. In addition, disruption in financial markets has meant economic prospects have become more uncertain, and events need to unfold further before the impact on the economy can be rigorously quantified. For the purposes of the economic forecast, it has been assumed that there will be some feed-through to tighter credit conditions and to household and company spending in the short term. Market expectations of future Bank Rate have moved lower since July 2007, and now point to some easing over coming months. The UK economy has proved resilient to a number of shocks over the past decade, demonstrating the pay-off to the Government's macroeconomic framework and promotion of open and flexible labour, product and capital markets, but it would be unreasonable to assume the effects of an unexpected shock could be absorbed immediately.

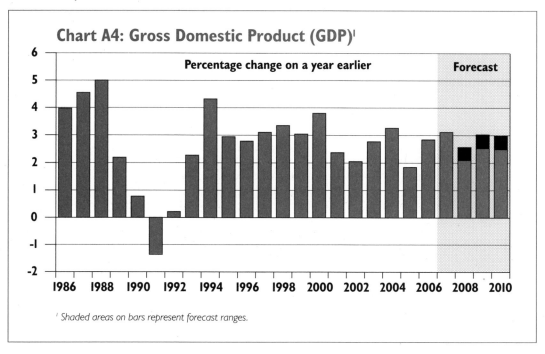

Chart A4: Gross Domestic Product (GDP)¹

Percentage change on a year earlier

Forecast

¹ Shaded areas on bars represent forecast ranges.

A.48 Against this backdrop, GDP growth in 2008 is forecast to slow to 2 to 2¹/₂ per cent, below its trend rate, consistent with keeping inflationary pressures in check. The economy is forecast to return to trend in 2009, with growth forecast to be in the range of 2¹/₂ to 3 per cent from then onwards.

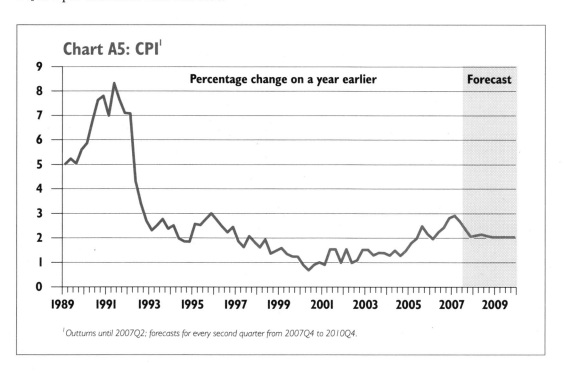

Chart A5: CPI¹

Percentage change on a year earlier

Forecast

¹ Outturns until 2007Q2; forecasts for every second quarter from 2007Q4 to 2010Q4.

Inflation A.49 CPI inflation is forecast to remain close to the 2 per cent inflation target throughout the forecast horizon reflecting the offsetting effects of a number of factors. These include upward cost pressures from food and oil prices, and downward pressures from the ongoing effect of monetary policy tightening over the past year and below-trend growth in 2008.

UK DEMAND AND OUTPUT IN DETAIL

A.50 During the early years of this decade, the strength of private consumption growth relative to the other components of demand caused its share of the economy to rise to historic highs. The process of rebalancing between the sources of growth, described in paragraph A.27 above, is forecast to continue. Private consumption is forecast to grow at rates slightly below that of the whole economy, while business investment growth is forecast to be slightly stronger and the contribution of net trade to return to broad neutrality.

Table A4: Contributions to GDP growth[1,2]

| | Percentage points, unless otherwise stated | | | | | | |
| | Average | | | Forecast | | | |
	2000 to 2004	2005	2006	2007	2008	2009	2010
GDP growth, per cent	$2\frac{3}{4}$	$1\frac{3}{4}$	$2\frac{3}{4}$	3	2 to $2\frac{1}{2}$	$2\frac{1}{2}$ to 3	$2\frac{1}{2}$ to 3
Main contributions							
Private consumption	$2\frac{1}{4}$	1	$1\frac{1}{4}$	2	$1\frac{1}{4}$	$1\frac{1}{2}$	$1\frac{1}{2}$
Business investment[3]	$\frac{1}{4}$	$\frac{1}{4}$	$\frac{3}{4}$	$\frac{3}{4}$	$\frac{1}{2}$	$\frac{1}{2}$	$\frac{1}{2}$
Government[3,4]	$\frac{3}{4}$	$\frac{1}{2}$	$\frac{1}{2}$	$\frac{3}{4}$	$\frac{3}{4}$	$\frac{1}{2}$	$\frac{1}{2}$
Change in inventories	0	0	$-\frac{1}{4}$	0	0	0	0
Net trade	$-\frac{1}{2}$	0	$-\frac{1}{4}$	$-\frac{1}{4}$	0	0	0

[1] Components may not sum to total due to rounding and omission of private residential investment, transfer costs of land and existing buildings and the statistical discrepancy.

[2] Based on central case. For the purpose of projecting the public finances, forecasts are based on the bottom of the GDP forecast range.

[3] Excludes exceptional transfer of BNFL nuclear reactors to central government in 2005Q2.

[4] The sum of government consumption and government investment.

Households and consumption[10]

A.51 Private consumption is the largest expenditure component of demand, accounting for around 63 per cent of nominal GDP. In line with the recent rebalancing of the economy, that ratio has come down from a peak of 66 per cent in mid-2001.

Table A5: Household sector[1] expenditure and income

| | Percentage change on a year earlier, unless otherwise stated | | | | |
| | | Forecast | | | |
	2006	2007	2008	2009	2010
Household consumption[2]	2	3	$1\frac{3}{4}$ to $2\frac{1}{4}$	$2\frac{1}{4}$ to $2\frac{3}{4}$	$2\frac{1}{4}$ to $2\frac{3}{4}$
Real household disposable income	$1\frac{1}{4}$	$1\frac{1}{2}$	$1\frac{3}{4}$ to $2\frac{1}{4}$	$2\frac{1}{4}$ to $2\frac{3}{4}$	$2\frac{1}{4}$ to $2\frac{3}{4}$
Saving ratio[3] (level, per cent)	5	$3\frac{1}{2}$	$3\frac{3}{4}$	4	$4\frac{1}{4}$

[1] Including non-profit institutions serving households.

[2] Chained volume measures.

[3] Total household resources less consumption expenditure as a per cent of total resources, where total resources comprise households' disposable income plus the increase in their net equity in pension funds.

[10] In the National Accounts, private consumption is comprised of final consumption expenditure by households and non-profit institutions serving households (NPISH). Throughout this section, the terms 'household consumption' and 'private consumption' always refer to total final consumption expenditure by households and NPISH.

Disposable **A.52** Real household disposable incomes grew by 1¼ per cent in 2006, with growth having
income moderated from 2005. Growth of wages and salaries remained solid, with the slowdown primarily explained by growth in net property income, the difference between interest and dividends received and paid by households, which fell from 20 per cent in 2005 to 1 per cent in 2006. Growth of real incomes is expected to firm from 2007.

Box A2: Developments in private sector balance sheets

Developments in private sector balance sheets are a key element of the macroeconomic backdrop against which to analyse the potential impact of higher market and policy interest rates on demand. Over the past decade, the success of the Government's macroeconomic policy framework in delivering stability with low interest rates has given households and companies the confidence to borrow and invest. The size of household and corporate sector financial balance sheets relative to GDP has expanded on both the asset and liability sides.

In aggregate, household sector net worth, the value of all financial and non-financial assets less financial liabilities, is almost £7 trillion. Households now have almost £4 trillion of financial assets, up from £2.2 trillion at the beginning of 1997, outweighing around £1.3 trillion of outstanding debt. Within their financial assets, households have more than £1 trillion worth of cash and bank deposits, and while the ratio of these liquid assets to GDP has continued to rise over the past three years, households' unsecured borrowing has stabilised. The household sector's net financial assets are more or less matched by the corporate sector's net financial liabilities, since it is through companies' investment of those funds that returns are generated for investors and savers.

In both the household and corporate sectors, interest-bearing financial assets and liabilities, deposits and loans, have been growing more strongly than other components of the financial balance sheet. As such, changes in effective interest rates on the stock of assets or liabilities will lead to larger changes in total interest receipts and payments than in the past. The net effect of these larger flows will tend to be broadly offsetting at the macroeconomic level, although it will depend on the extent to which interest rates on saving and borrowing move in step.

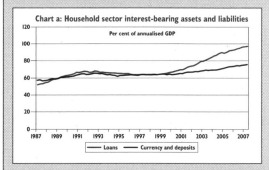

Chart a: Household sector interest-bearing assets and liabilities

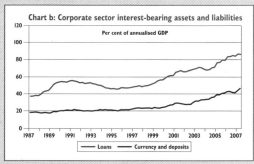

Chart b: Corporate sector interest-bearing assets and liabilities

While these macroeconomic balance sheet measures are key to understanding the potential effect of changes in interest rates on activity, developments will not have been uniform within sectors. So, while the household sector in aggregate has accumulated financial assets and liabilities, there will be disparities across households. The Government recognises that for a small minority of households, excessive personal debt can become a problem, leading potentially to financial difficulties. Actions to address these issues are set out in Chapter 5.

Household spending

A.53 Private consumption grew by 2 per cent in 2006, and by 3 per cent on a year earlier in the first half of 2007, somewhat stronger than expected at Budget time. It is expected to grow by 3 per cent in 2007, slightly above the Budget 2007 forecast range. Retail sales volumes in July and August were up by $1\frac{1}{2}$ per cent on the second quarter. This suggests that consumption may continue to grow at rates close to that of the whole economy in 2007, although retail sales account for only around a third of total consumer spending.

A.54 With Bank Rate currently somewhat higher than financial markets expected at the time of Budget 2007, consumption growth is forecast to slow, with growth of $1\frac{3}{4}$ to $2\frac{1}{4}$ per cent in 2008, lower than forecast at Budget time, before returning to rates of growth just below that of the whole economy from 2009. So far there appears to have been little evidence of financial market disruption feeding through to credit conditions for households, and the September GfK consumer confidence survey suggested households remained relatively upbeat about the prospects for their own finances over the coming 12 months.

Saving ratio

A.55 The household saving ratio is estimated to have fallen from 5 per cent in 2006 to $2\frac{1}{2}$ per cent in the first half of 2007, though early estimates can be subject to substantial revision. For example, initial estimates of 3 per cent for the saving ratio in mid-2000 have been subsequently revised up to almost 5 per cent. The saving ratio is forecast to rise over the forecast horizon, with disposable income growing slightly faster than consumer spending.

House prices

A.56 The latest releases from the main mortgage lenders report house price inflation of around 9 per cent on a year earlier. There is, though, evidence that house price inflation is easing, with monthly increases averaging 0.4 per cent since May 2007, compared with 1.0 per cent during the first four months of the year. House price inflation is expected to continue to ease over the coming year.

A.57 Investment in dwellings increased by $8\frac{1}{2}$ per cent in 2006, contributing around $1\frac{1}{2}$ percentage points to the $8\frac{1}{4}$ per cent growth of whole economy investment, and is forecast to grow by $4\frac{1}{4}$ per cent in 2007. Growth in later years of the forecast is expected to be slightly above that of whole economy GDP, supported by the Government's target for house building set out in the Green Paper *Homes for the future: more affordable, more sustainable*.[11]

Companies and investment

A.58 As currently measured, business investment accounts for slightly more than 10 per cent of nominal GDP, but its importance to the economy extends beyond that through its role in increasing the capital intensity of the UK economy, a key driver of labour productivity growth. Indeed, as discussed in Box A3 and the Treasury Economic Working Paper published alongside the Pre-Budget Report, its role in the economy may be greater than suggested by conventional measures of investment, given the growing importance of investment in intangible assets in the UK's increasingly knowledge-intensive economy. A rising share of investment in intangible assets would help to resolve some of the apparent puzzle concerning past business investment growth.

---

[11] *Homes for the future: more affordable, more sustainable*, Communities and Local Government, July 2007.

Company finances **A.59**   Profit growth and profitability remained strong in the first half of 2007. The gross operating surplus of the private non-financial corporate sector, a measure of nominal profits, rose by $11\frac{1}{2}$ per cent on a year earlier, and the sector's financial surplus reached 3 per cent of GDP. The net rate of return on capital, a measure of profitability, reached new record highs in the second quarter, at $15\frac{3}{4}$ per cent across all private non-financial companies and $21\frac{1}{2}$ per cent in the service sector.

A.60   External financing conditions have become somewhat less supportive over recent months, particularly in the credit markets. Spreads on corporate bonds have widened, most notably for companies with lower credit ratings. Growth in bank lending to the corporate sector remained strong in the year to August 2007, although the Bank of England's *Credit Conditions Survey*, released on 26 September, suggested that financial market disruption was to some extent affecting the price and availability of credit to non-financial companies. However, non-financial company equity prices have firmed over the past month, and are up around 6 per cent since Budget 2007.

Table A6: Gross fixed capital formation

| | Percentage change on a year earlier | | | | |
| | | | Forecast | | |
	2006	**2007**	**2008**	**2009**	**2010**
Whole economy[1]	$8\frac{1}{4}$	$5\frac{3}{4}$	$3\frac{1}{4}$ to $3\frac{3}{4}$	$3\frac{1}{4}$ to $3\frac{3}{4}$	$3\frac{1}{4}$ to $3\frac{3}{4}$
of which:					
Business[2,3,4]	$7\frac{1}{2}$	6	$3\frac{1}{4}$ to $3\frac{3}{4}$	$3\frac{3}{4}$ to $4\frac{1}{4}$	$3\frac{3}{4}$ to $4\frac{1}{4}$
Private dwellings[3]	$8\frac{1}{2}$	$4\frac{1}{4}$	$2\frac{1}{4}$ to $2\frac{3}{4}$	$2\frac{3}{4}$ to $3\frac{1}{4}$	$2\frac{3}{4}$ to $3\frac{1}{4}$
General government[3,4]	6	$10\frac{1}{2}$	$7\frac{1}{2}$	3	5

[1] Includes costs associated with the transfer of ownership of land and existing buildings.

[2] Private sector and public corporations' non-residential investment. Includes investment under the Private Finance Initiative.

[3] Excludes purchases less sales of land and existing buildings.

[4] Excludes exceptional transfer of BNFL nuclear reactors to central government in 2005Q2.

Business investment **A.61**   Business investment growth picked up from 3 per cent in 2005 to $7\frac{1}{2}$ per cent in 2006, the fastest rate since 1998. Although quarterly growth rates slowed in the first half of 2007, the level of investment remained high, up $8\frac{3}{4}$ per cent on a year earlier, and business investment is forecast to grow by 6 per cent in the year as a whole. Strong profitability, combined with survey evidence of positive investment intentions and capacity constraints beginning to bind, point to ongoing business investment growth. However, with evidence that the cost of capital has risen since Budget time, business investment growth is forecast to slow in 2008, to $3\frac{1}{4}$ to $3\frac{3}{4}$ per cent.

Box A3: Intangible investment and Britain's productivity

Rapid technological change and the emergence of newly industrialised economies are intensifying competition in the global economy, with knowledge and other intangible assets of growing importance in maintaining competitiveness. A Treasury Economic Working Paper published alongside the Pre-Budget Report investigates the consequences for a range of macroeconomic variables, including productivity, of treating spending on knowledge as investment.[a]

The knowledge assets considered are scientific R&D, software, design, non-scientific R&D and spending by firms on reputation, human and organisational capital. By assembling investment data on these knowledge assets and adjusting National Accounts macroeconomic variables in the appropriate way, the research finds that treating spending on knowledge as investment would have the following impact:

- business investment in 2004 would have been about double the conventional measure. Investment in intangibles was £123 billion, compared with tangible investment of £96 billion;

- the value of measured market sector output would have been higher by about 6 per cent in 1970 and 13 per cent in 2004;

- instead of the ratio of nominal business investment to market sector output falling since 1970, it would have been rising;

- growth in labour productivity and capital deepening would have been higher than previously estimated;

- total factor productivity growth would not have slowed down since 1990, as it appears on current measures, but would have been picking up; and

- comparing the results with the US suggests that the share of intangible investment in market sector output is similar in both countries.

These results suggest that conventional measures of investment may not be capturing the dynamic changes that are taking place as knowledge-intensive industries increase in importance. The Government has identified investment and innovation as two of the key drivers for raising productivity growth, and has implemented major reform programmes under each (discussed further in Chapter 4). The results in the working paper highlight the importance of these two drivers, and of focusing on more than just conventional measures of tangible capital.

---

[a] Giorgio Marrano, M. , Haskel, J. and Wallis, G. (2007), *Intangible investment and Britain's productivity,* Treasury Economic Working Paper No.1 (new series), available on the Treasury website: www.hm-treasury.gov.uk

Trade and the balance of payments

A.62   As set out in Budget 2007, annual growth in recorded exports and imports of goods and services has been distorted by activity related to missing trader intra-community fraud (MTIC), which significantly inflated the value of measured goods trade in the first half of 2006. Since the second half of 2006, Government measures to tackle MTIC fraud have led to a sharp fall in estimated MTIC-related activity, to a low level. In view of inevitable measurement difficulties involved in estimating MTIC-related activity, the ONS advises that comparisons of trade volumes and prices "should be treated with a great deal of caution".[12] The forecast abstracts from MTIC effects by assuming that beyond the latest quarter of data, export and import volumes grow in line with underlying trade, excluding MTIC-related activity. The forecast is therefore based on the neutral assumption that the level of MTIC-related activity remains constant throughout the forecast at the latest quarterly estimate. Table A7 presents export and import growth forecasts excluding the effect of MTIC-related activity.

---

[12] *First release: UK trade, July 2007*, ONS, September 2007.

Exports of goods and services

A.63 Growth in the volume of exports of goods and services excluding MTIC-related activity is estimated to have moderated progressively over the past year and a half, from $11\frac{1}{2}$ per cent on a year earlier in the first half of 2006 to 3 per cent in the second half and minus 1 per cent in the first half of 2007. Growth in services export volumes picked up from $4\frac{1}{2}$ per cent in 2006 to $8\frac{3}{4}$ per cent in the first half of 2007, so all of the slowdown was explained by lower, then negative, growth in goods export volumes. The slowdown in measured goods trade volumes this year has been at odds with evidence from a broad range of private sector business surveys, which are consistent with growth having picked up. The latest monthly estimates of export growth point to a stronger third quarter of 2007.

A.64 Given the pattern of measured export growth so far in 2007, the volume of exports excluding MTIC-related activity is forecast to grow by $3\frac{1}{4}$ per cent in 2007, below the Budget 2007 forecast range. Growth is expected to pick up to rates of around $4\frac{1}{2}$ to $5\frac{1}{4}$ per cent from 2008. One channel through which global financial market disruption could affect the UK economy is its impact on the financial sectors of key trading partners. For example, exports of financial services to the US made up around $7\frac{1}{2}$ per cent of total UK exports in 2006.

Imports of goods and services

A.65 Estimates of imports of goods and services excluding MTIC-related activity have followed a very similar pattern to exports, with annual growth slowing from $9\frac{1}{4}$ to $4\frac{1}{2}$ to $1\frac{1}{4}$ per cent over successive half-year periods. Again, the volume of services imports picked up in the first half of 2007, from $3\frac{1}{2}$ per cent on a year earlier in 2006 to $7\frac{1}{4}$ per cent, so the slowdown has been entirely accounted for by the volume of goods imports. Together these developments suggest that some of the recent moderation in the growth of goods trade volumes could be related to the measurement difficulties outlined above. Since the estimated slowdown has been of a similar magnitude for imports and exports, estimates of net trade should be broadly unaffected.

A.66 As with exports, import growth excluding MTIC-related activity in 2007 is expected to slow from 2006, to $3\frac{3}{4}$ per cent on a year earlier. With UK consumption and investment growth forecast to ease in 2008, import growth is forecast to pick up slightly less than export growth, to around $3\frac{3}{4}$ to $4\frac{1}{2}$ per cent. As a result, having subtracted a $\frac{1}{4}$ percentage point from growth in 2006 and 2007, the contribution of net trade to growth is forecast to return to neutrality from 2008.

Table A7: Trade in goods and services

	Percentage change on a year earlier					£ billion
	Volumes (excluding MTIC)[1]		Prices[2]			Goods and
					Terms of	services
	Exports	Imports	Exports	Imports	trade[3]	balance
2006	7	$6\frac{3}{4}$	$2\frac{1}{2}$	$2\frac{1}{2}$	0	$-48\frac{1}{4}$
Forecast						
2007	$3\frac{1}{4}$	$3\frac{3}{4}$	$1\frac{1}{2}$	0	$1\frac{1}{2}$	$-45\frac{3}{4}$
2008	$4\frac{1}{2}$ to 5	$3\frac{3}{4}$ to $4\frac{1}{4}$	$\frac{1}{2}$	$\frac{1}{2}$	0	$-45\frac{1}{4}$
2009	$4\frac{3}{4}$ to $5\frac{1}{4}$	4 to $4\frac{1}{2}$	$1\frac{1}{4}$	$1\frac{1}{2}$	0	$-45\frac{3}{4}$
2010	$4\frac{3}{4}$ to $5\frac{1}{4}$	4 to $4\frac{1}{2}$	2	$2\frac{1}{4}$	0	$-46\frac{3}{4}$

[1] Table A9 contains figures including the effects of MTIC-related activity.

[2] Average value indices.

[3] Ratio of export to import prices.

Current account balance **A.67** The UK's deficit on trade in goods and services narrowed to 3$\frac{1}{2}$ per cent of GDP in the first half of 2007 from 3$\frac{3}{4}$ per cent in 2006, reflecting a slightly larger surplus on trade in services and a broadly stable deficit on trade in goods. On the goods side, the UK's balance of trade in crude oil returned to surplus in the first half of 2007 from a small deficit in 2006. The UK's surplus on investment income was 1$\frac{1}{2}$ per cent of GDP in the first half of 2007, unchanged from 2006. Within that, the surplus on FDI-related earnings picked up from 3$\frac{1}{4}$ to 3$\frac{3}{4}$ per cent of GDP, as UK companies continued to earn significantly higher returns on their investments overseas than are earned by foreign companies on their assets in the UK.

A.68 The UK's current account deficit narrowed from 3$\frac{1}{4}$ per cent of GDP in 2006 to 3 per cent of GDP in the first half of 2007. It is expected to continue to narrow in 2008 and to stabilise at around 2$\frac{3}{4}$ per cent of GDP.

Foreign direct investment **A.69** The UK continues to attract large amounts of inward FDI. Foreign companies invested a further £46$\frac{1}{2}$ billion in the UK in the first half of 2007, having invested £77 billion in 2006 and a record £108 billion in 2005. UK companies also continue to invest overseas, with the flow of outward FDI reaching £32$\frac{1}{4}$ billion in the first half of 2007, on top of almost £70 billion in 2006.

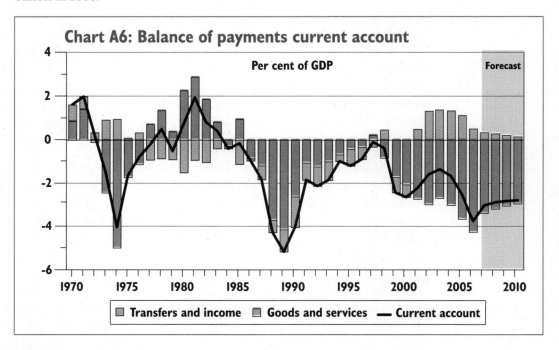

Chart A6: Balance of payments current account

Service sector output

A.70 The share of UK output accounted for by the service sector has risen steadily in recent years to reach 75 per cent. That is higher than in most developed economies, and its share has risen more quickly in the UK than in other G7 economies. The service sector also plays a larger role in UK exports than it does for other G7 economies, its share having risen from less than a quarter to more than a third in just 10 years.

A.71 Service sector output growth rose from 3 per cent in 2005 to 3$\frac{3}{4}$ per cent in 2006 and the first half of 2007. Within that, the finance and business services sector has been notably strong, accounting for around half of measured whole economy output growth. The financial sector alone has seen annual growth rates pick up from 5$\frac{3}{4}$ per cent in 2005 to 8$\frac{1}{2}$ per cent in 2006 and 10$\frac{1}{2}$ per cent in the first half of 2007. That momentum seems likely to diminish in the short term in light of recent financial market developments, though it is notable that the UK's innovative financial sector was relatively quick to recover following periods of financial market disruption in 1998 and 2001.

Manufacturing and North Sea output

Manufacturing **A.72** Manufacturing accounts for around 14 per cent of the UK economy. In 2006, boosted by the pick-up in export growth in the first half of the year, and the strength of business investment growth throughout the year, manufacturing output grew by $1\frac{1}{4}$ per cent on a year earlier. Consistent with investment as the key driver, growth was strongest in the capital goods sector, at $3\frac{3}{4}$ per cent. Manufacturing output was up 1 per cent on a year earlier in the first eight months of 2007, somewhat below the rate consistent with evidence from a range of private sector business surveys. The sector is forecast to grow 1 per cent in 2007 as a whole, picking up to $1\frac{1}{2}$ to 2 per cent in 2008.

North Sea **A.73** In the period to the end of 2006, a succession of temporary factors exacerbated the underlying decline in output from the North Sea to the extent that total output from the oil and gas sector had fallen by 30 per cent over three years. In the first half of 2007, helped by the Buzzard oil fields commencing output, oil production rose by around $5\frac{1}{2}$ per cent on the second half of 2006, though gas production fell by a similar amount. In addition to Buzzard, a number of smaller start-ups in 2007 and 2008 should temporarily boost oil production.

Independent forecasts

A.74 Since the 2006 Pre-Budget Report, the average of independent forecasts for GDP growth in 2007 has increased from 2.4 to 2.9 per cent, rising to within the Treasury's forecast range maintained since the 2005 Pre-Budget Report. The increase mainly reflects upward revisions to the average forecast for fixed investment growth, from 3.4 to 5.3 per cent, and for private consumption growth, from 2.3 to 2.8 per cent.

A.75 In its September 2007 interim assessment, the OECD revised up its forecast of UK growth in 2007 from 2.7 to 3.1 per cent.[13] According to the September survey by Consensus Economics,[14] growth in the UK in 2007 is currently projected to exceed that of all other G7 economies and to outperform the euro area.

A.76 The average independent GDP growth forecast for 2008 stands at the lower end of the 2007 Pre-Budget Report forecast range, at 2.0 per cent. Since Budget 2007, the average independent forecast for 2008 has been revised down by around a $\frac{1}{4}$ percentage point. The average of independent forecasts for inflation is for it to remain at target this year and next.

A.77 Treasury forecasts for GDP growth since 1997 have, on average, outperformed the independent consensus. They continue to compare well against a sample of forecasters that includes leading international organisations (IMF, OECD, EC), research institutes (Oxford Economics, NIESR) and private sector forecasters (Goldman Sachs, HSBC, JP Morgan).

---

[13] *What is the outlook for OECD countries? An interim assessment*, Organisation for Economic Cooperation and Development, September 2007.

[14] *Consensus forecasts*, Consensus Economics Inc., September 2007.

Table A8: Pre-Budget Report and independent[1] forecasts

	Percentage change on a year earlier, unless otherwise stated					
	2007			2008		
	October	Independent		October	Independent	
	PBR	Average	Range	PBR	Average	Range
GDP growth	3	2.9	2.5 to 3.1	2 to 2½	2.0	−0.3 to 2.8
CPI (Q4)	2	2.0	1.7 to 2.4	2	2.0	1.5 to 2.5
Current account (£ billion)	−41	−43.5	−53.2 to −35.0	−41	−45.9	−59.3 to −32.0

[1] 'Forecasts for the UK economy: A comparison of independent forecasts', October 2007.

FORECAST ISSUES AND RISKS

Global financial markets **A.78** The economic outlook has recently become more uncertain. Since Budget 2007, developments in global credit markets have led to higher market interest rates across almost all developed and emerging economies. Considerable uncertainty exists over the timing and extent to which these developments might affect the wider economic outlook. Among the developed economies, the longer the recent financial disruption persists, the greater the risk of it feeding through to tighter credit conditions for households and companies, and detracting from growth. Were this to happen, the effects could spill over to the rest of the global economy through financial, trade and confidence channels.

Global economy **A.79** Among the major economies, growth in the US could slow further if the effects of the weaker housing market were to spread to the wider economy. Potentially, weaker US demand for imports could pose a risk to a number of developed and emerging economies where recent growth has been driven by net exports. However, macroeconomic fundamentals in many emerging markets have improved, which, coupled with sustained momentum, could result in output growth that exceeds current expectations. The euro area economy could prove more resilient to the US slowdown than forecast, while the monetary policy response in the US could reduce the extent of that slowdown.

A.80 Growing inflationary pressures, noted at the time of Budget 2007, remain a risk. Inflation rates have moderated in most developed countries, but have yet to recede in many emerging markets, most notably China. Energy and food prices pose an ongoing risk to inflation in developed and emerging economies alike.

A.81 The US current account deficit has narrowed from almost 7 per cent of GDP in late 2005 to 5½ per cent by mid-2007, the lowest since 2004. While this represents a positive development, the risk of a disorderly unwinding of global imbalances remains.

UK economy **A.82** Financial market disruption could affect the UK economy through a number of channels. In relative terms, the UK has a larger financial sector than in most advanced economies. If the recent disruption were to persist, the direct impact of slower growth in the financial sector could be larger than assumed. However, if the UK's innovative financial sector, and flexible economy in general, were to absorb the shock more quickly than has been assumed, growth could be stronger than forecast.

A.83 It is too soon to quantify rigorously the effect of higher market interest rates feeding through to tighter credit conditions and to household and company spending. Indeed, the spread between market interest rates and Bank Rate has fallen significantly since mid-September, and if the spread continues to fall and rapidly reverts to historically normal levels, the economy could slow by less than expected. However, if the effective interest rates received and paid by households and companies were to rise, the impact on disposable incomes could be larger than would have been the case in the past due to the growth of private sector balance sheets described in Box A2.

Table A9: Summary of economic prospects[1]

| | Percentage change on a year earlier, unless otherwise stated | | | | | Average errors from past forecasts[5] |
| | | Forecast[2,3,4] | | | | |
	2006	2007	2008	2009	2010	2008
Output at constant market prices						
Gross domestic product (GDP)	2¾	3	2 to 2½	2½ to 3	2½ to 3	¾
Manufacturing output	1¼	1	1½ to 2	1¾ to 2¼	1¾ to 2¼	1½
Expenditure components of GDP at constant market prices[6]						
Domestic demand	3	3¼	2 to 2½	2½ to 3	2¼ to 2¾	¼
Household consumption[7]	2	3	1¾ to 2¼	2¼ to 2¾	2¼ to 2¾	1
General government consumption	2	2½	2½	2	2	1
Fixed investment	8¼	5¾	3¼ to 3¾	3¼ to 3¾	3¼ to 3¾	2¾
Change in inventories[8]	–¼	0	–¼ to 0	0 to ¼	0	¼
Exports of goods and services[9]	10¼	–3¼	4½ to 5	4¾ to 5¼	4¾ to 5¼	2¼
Imports of goods and services[9]	9¾	–2	3¾ to 4¼	4 to 4½	4 to 4½	3
Exports of goods and services (excluding MTIC)	7	3¼	4½ to 5	4¾ to 5¼	4¾ to 5¼	–
Imports of goods and services (excluding MTIC)	6¾	3¾	3¾ to 4¼	4 to 4½	4 to 4½	–
Balance of payments current account						
£ billion	–42	–41	–41	–42½	–44¼	10¾
Per cent of GDP	–3¼	–3	–2¾	–2¾	–2¾	¾
Inflation						
CPI (Q4)	2¾	2	2	2	2	–
Producer output prices (Q4)[10]	2	3	2	2	2	1
GDP deflator at market prices	2½	3¼	2¾	2¾	2¾	½
Money GDP at market prices						
£ billion	1302	1386	1453 to 1461	1530 to 1546	1609 to 1634	11
Percentage change	5½	6½	5 to 5½	5¼ to 5¾	5¼ to 5¾	¾

[1] The forecast is consistent with National Accounts data for the second quarter of 2007, released by the Office for National Statistics on 26 September 2007. See footnote 1 on the first page of this annex.

[2] All growth rates in tables throughout this annex are rounded to the nearest ¼ percentage point.

[3] As in previous Budget and Pre-Budget Reports, the economic forecast is presented in terms of forecast ranges, based on alternative assumptions about the supply-side performance of the economy. The mid-points of the forecast ranges are anchored around the neutral assumption for the trend rate of output growth of 2¾ per cent. The figures at the lower end of the ranges are consistent with the deliberately cautious assumption of trend growth used as the basis for projecting the public finances, which is a ¼ percentage point below the neutral assumption.

[4] The size of the growth ranges for GDP components may differ from those for total GDP growth because of rounding and the assumed invariance of the levels of public spending within the forecast ranges.

[5] Average absolute errors for year-ahead projections made in autumn forecasts over the past 10 years. The average errors for the current account are calculated as a percent of GDP, with £ billion figures calculated by scaling the errors by forecast money GDP in 2008.

[6] Further detail on the expenditure components of GDP is given in Table A10.

[7] Includes households and non-profit institutions serving households.

[8] Contribution to GDP growth, percentage points.

[9] Figures up to and including 2007 are distorted by estimates of MTIC-related activity.

[10] Excluding excise duties.

Table A10: Gross domestic product and its components

		£ billion chained volume measures at market prices, seasonally adjusted									
		Household consumption[1]	General government consumption	Fixed investment	Change in inventories	Domestic demand[2]	Exports of goods and services	Total final expenditure	*Less* imports of goods and services[3]	*Plus* statistical discrepancy[3]	GDP at market prices
2006		776.2	251.7	217.1	1.2	1246.3	357.1	1603.5	394.9	0.8	1209.4
2007		798.9	257.7	229.4	0.5	1287.1	345.8	1632.9	386.7	0.8	1246.9
2008		812.2 to 816.7	264.5	237.0 to 238.3	–1.7 to –0.2	1312.0 to 1319.2	361.1 to 363.1	1673.1 to 1682.3	401.3 to 403.5	0.8	1272.6 to 1279.6
2009		829.6 to 838.2	270.1	244.6 to 247.1	–0.9 to 1.9	1343.4 to 1357.4	378.0 to 382.0	1721.4 to 1739.4	417.5 to 421.9	0.8	1304.7 to 1318.3
2010		848.3 to 861.3	275.8	252.8 to 256.7	–1.8 to 2.4	1375.1 to 1396.2	396.0 to 402.0	1771.0 to 1798.2	434.6 to 441.3	0.8	1337.3 to 1357.8
2006	1st half	385.4	125.5	105.8	0.2	617.0	189.7	806.6	206.8	0.4	600.2
	2nd half	390.8	126.3	111.3	1.0	629.4	167.4	796.8	188.0	0.4	609.2
2007	1st half	397.0	127.5	113.8	1.1	639.8	168.1	808.0	189.3	0.4	619.0
	2nd half	401.9	130.3	115.6	–0.6	647.2	177.7	824.9	197.4	0.4	627.9
2008	1st half	404.5 to 406.2	131.8	117.3 to 117.8	–0.9 to –0.3	652.7 to 655.5	180.2 to 181.0	832.9 to 836.4	200.0 to 200.8	0.4	633.3 to 636.0
	2nd half	407.7 to 410.5	132.7	119.7 to 120.5	–0.8 to 0.1	659.3 to 663.8	180.9 to 182.1	840.2 to 845.9	201.4 to 202.7	0.4	639.3 to 643.6
2009	1st half	412.4 to 416.2	134.3	121.5 to 122.7	–0.6 to 0.6	667.6 to 673.8	186.1 to 187.8	853.8 to 861.6	206.3 to 208.2	0.4	647.8 to 653.8
	2nd half	417.2 to 422.1	135.8	123.1 to 124.5	–0.3 to 1.3	675.8 to 683.6	191.9 to 194.2	867.7 to 877.8	211.2 to 213.7	0.4	656.9 to 664.5
2010	1st half	421.8 to 427.8	137.1	125.2 to 127.0	–0.7 to 1.3	683.5 to 693.2	196.1 to 198.8	879.6 to 892.0	215.3 to 218.3	0.4	664.7 to 674.1
	2nd half	426.4 to 433.5	138.6	127.6 to 129.7	–1.2 to 1.1	691.5 to 703.0	199.9 to 203.2	891.4 to 906.2	219.3 to 222.9	0.4	672.6 to 683.7
		Percentage change on a year earlier[4,5]									
2006		2	2	8 1/4	-1/4	3	10 1/4	4 1/2	9 3/4	0	2 3/4
2007		3	2 1/2	5 3/4	0	3 1/4	–3 1/4	1 3/4	–2	0	3
2008		1 3/4 to 2 1/4	2 1/2	3 1/4 to 3 3/4	0	2 to 2 1/2	4 1/2 to 5	2 1/2 to 3	3 3/4 to 4 1/4	0	2 to 2 1/2
2009		2 1/4 to 2 3/4	2	3 1/4 to 3 3/4	0	2 1/2 to 3	4 3/4 to 5 1/4	3 to 3 1/2	4 to 4 1/2	0	2 1/2 to 3
2010		2 1/4 to 2 3/4	2	3 1/4 to 3 3/4	0	2 1/4 to 2 3/4	4 3/4 to 5 1/4	3 to 3 1/2	4 to 4 1/2	0	2 1/2 to 3

[1] *Includes households and non-profit institutions serving households.*

[2] *Also includes acquisitions less disposals of valuables.*

[3] *Expenditure adjustment.*

[4] *For change in inventories and the statistical discrepancy, changes are expressed as a percent of GDP.*

[5] *Growth ranges for GDP components do not necessarily sum to the 1/2 percentage point ranges for GDP growth because of rounding and the assumed invariance of the levels of public spending within the forecast ranges.*

B THE PUBLIC FINANCES

The interim projections for the public finances published in this Pre-Budget Report and Comprehensive Spending Review show that the Government is meeting its strict fiscal rules over the economic cycle:

- the current budget since the start of the economic cycle in 1997-98 shows an annual average surplus throughout the projection period, ensuring that the Government is meeting the golden rule on the basis of cautious assumptions. By 2009-10, the current budget moves clearly into surplus; and

- public sector net debt is projected to remain low and stable over the forecast period, stabilising below 39 per cent of GDP, and so meeting the sustainable investment rule.

The 2007 *End of year fiscal report* is published alongside this Pre-Budget Report, underlining the Government's commitment to transparency in fiscal policy by providing detailed information on the public finances in 2005-06 and 2006-07.

INTRODUCTION

B.1   Chapter 2 describes the Government's fiscal policy framework and shows how the projections of the public finances presented in this Pre-Budget Report are consistent with meeting the fiscal rules. This chapter explains the latest outturns and the fiscal projections in more detail.[1] It includes:

- five-year projections of the current budget and public sector net debt, the key aggregates for assessing performance against the golden rule and the sustainable investment rule respectively;

- projections of public sector net borrowing, the fiscal aggregate relevant to assessing the impact of fiscal policy on the economy;

- projections of the cyclically-adjusted fiscal balances;

- detailed analyses of the outlook for government receipts and expenditure; and

- a discussion of long-term fiscal sustainability given the long-term socio-economic challenges that will be faced in coming decades.

B.2   The fiscal projections continue to be based on deliberately cautious key assumptions audited by the National Audit Office (NAO).

B.3   This Pre-Budget Report updates the projections of the public finances contained in Budget 2007, to take account of subsequent developments in both the public finances and the world and UK economies.

B.4   As described in Chapter 2, the 2007 *End of year fiscal report* is published alongside this Pre-Budget Report. The report underlines the Government's commitment to transparency in fiscal policy by providing detailed retrospective information on the state of the public finances in 2005-06 and 2006-07, including their performance against the fiscal rules and published forecasts and plans. The information set out in the 2007 *End of year fiscal report* supplements the historical and provisional outturn data published in this Annex.

---

[1] For further detail see 2007 *Pre-Budget Report and Comprehensive Spending Review: the economy and public finances – supplementary charts and tables*. This includes charts and tables on public expenditure, sub-sector and economic category analyses, and historical series data.

MEETING THE FISCAL RULES

B.5   Table B1 shows five-year projections for the current budget and public sector net debt, the key aggregates for assessing performance against the golden rule and the sustainable investment rule respectively. Outturns and projections of other important measures of the public finances, including net borrowing and cyclically-adjusted fiscal balances, are also shown.

B.6   As explained in Chapter 2, the Government's judgment is that 1997-98 represented the beginning of a new economic cycle. The latest National Accounts data and the Treasury's trend output assumptions imply that output passed through trend towards the end of 2006. However, it is too soon to assess whether or not the economic cycle has ended.

Table B1: Summary of public sector finances

	Per cent of GDP							
	Outturn		Estimate	Projections				
	2005-06	2006-07	2007-08	2008-09	2009-10	2010-11	2011-12	2012-13
Fairness and prudence								
Surplus on current budget	-1.1	-0.4	-0.6	-0.3	0.2	0.6	0.8	1.1
Average surplus since 1997-1998	0.2	0.1	0.1	0.0	0.1	0.1	0.1	0.2
Cyclically-adjusted surplus on current budget	-0.9	-0.2	-0.7	-0.2	0.3	0.6	0.8	1.1
Long-term sustainability								
Public sector net debt[1]	36.1	36.7	37.6	38.4	38.8	38.9	38.8	38.6
Core debt[1]	35.3	35.8	36.9	37.6	38.0	38.1	38.1	37.9
Net worth[2]	27.7	26.0	25.3	24.1	23.4	22.8	22.5	22.4
Primary balance	-1.4	-0.7	-1.0	-0.9	-0.4	-0.1	0.2	0.3
Economic impact								
Net investment	1.9	2.0	2.1	2.2	2.2	2.3	2.3	2.3
Public sector net borrowing (PSNB)	3.0	2.3	2.7	2.5	2.0	1.7	1.5	1.3
Cyclically-adjusted PSNB	2.8	2.2	2.8	2.4	1.9	1.7	1.5	1.3
Financing								
Central government net cash requirement	3.3	2.8	2.7	2.6	2.4	2.0	2.0	1.6
Public sector net cash requirement	3.2	2.7	2.4	2.4	2.3	1.8	1.8	1.5
European commitments								
Treaty deficit[3]	3.0	2.6	2.9	2.8	2.4	2.1	1.8	1.6
Cyclically-adjusted Treaty deficit[3]	2.8	2.4	3.0	2.7	2.3	2.1	1.8	1.6
Treaty debt ratio[4]	42.5	43.4	43.9	44.8	45.1	45.3	45.2	44.9
Memo: Output gap	-0.5	-0.1	0.2	-0.3	0.0	0.0	0.0	0.0

[1] Debt at end March; GDP centred on end March.
[2] Estimate at end December; GDP centred on end December.
[3] General government net borrowing on a Maastricht basis.
[4] General government gross debt measures on a Maastricht basis.

The golden rule   **B.7**   The economy appears to have passed through trend in the final quarter of 2006. On this basis, and on the basis of cautious assumptions, the Government would have met the golden rule with a margin of £18 billion, higher than estimated at Budget 2007.

B.8   The Pre-Budget Report projections show that the current budget moves into surplus in 2009-10, with the surplus rising to 1.1 per cent of GDP by 2012-13. At this early stage, and based on cautious assumptions, the Government is therefore on course to meet the golden rule in the next economic cycle. The cyclically-adjusted surplus, which allows a clearer view of underlying or structural trends in the public finances by removing the estimated effects of the economic cycle, also shows a rising surplus from 2009-10.

The sustainable   **B.9**   The Government's primary objective for fiscal policy is to ensure sound public
investment rule   finances in the medium term. This means maintaining public sector net debt at a low and sustainable level. Public sector net debt remains below 39 per cent of GDP throughout the projection period, and starts to decline by 2012-13, reaching 38.6 per cent of GDP. Therefore, the Government meets its sustainable investment rule while continuing to fund increased long-term capital investment in the public services. The projections for core debt, which exclude the estimated impact of the economic cycle, rise to a maximum of 38.1 per cent of GDP. This is consistent with the fiscal rules, and with the key objective of intergenerational fairness that underpins the fiscal framework.

Net worth   **B.10**   Net worth is the approximate stock counterpart of the current budget. Modest falls in net worth are expected for the remainder of the projection period from the high level of 26 per cent of GDP in 2006-07. At present, net worth is not used as a key indicator of the public finances, mainly due to difficulties involved in accurately measuring many government assets and liabilities.

Net investment   **B.11**   Public sector net investment has increased rapidly in recent years from $1\frac{1}{4}$ per cent of GDP in 2003-04 to 2 per cent of GDP in 2006-07. As a result of decisions taken in the 2004 Spending Review and in this Comprehensive Spending Review, net investment will increase further, and then remain at around $2\frac{1}{4}$ per cent of GDP from 2008-09 onwards.

Net borrowing   **B.12**   Public sector net borrowing fell sharply from 3.0 per cent of GDP in 2005-06 to 2.3 per cent in 2006-07. It is expected to rise in 2007-08 but then fall in every year of the forecast period from 2.7 per cent of GDP in 2007-08 to 2.5 per cent in 2008-09, and then to 1.3 per cent of GDP by 2012-13.

Financing   **B.13**   The central government net cash requirement was 2.8 per cent of GDP in 2006-07. It is projected to be around 2.7 per cent in 2007-08, and to fall to 1.6 per cent of GDP by 2012-13, mirroring the profile of net borrowing.

European   **B.14**   Table B1 shows the Treaty measures of debt and deficit used for the purposes of the
commitments   Excessive Deficit Procedure – Article 104 of the Treaty. These Pre-Budget Report projections meet the EU Treaty reference value for general government gross debt (60 per cent of GDP) by a considerable margin. The treaty deficit in 2006-07 was 2.6 per cent of GDP. The deficit rises to 2.9 per cent of GDP in 2007-08 and then falls in each year of the forecast. The projections are therefore consistent with the Government's prudent interpretation of the Stability and Growth Pact.

CHANGES TO THE FISCAL BALANCES

B.15 Table B2 compares the latest estimates for the main fiscal balances with those in Budget 2007.

Table B2: Fiscal balances compared with Budget 2007

	Outturn[1]	Estimate[2]	Projections			
	2006-07	2007-08	2008-09	2009-10	2010-11	2011-12
Surplus on current budget (£ billion)						
Budget 2007	-9.5	-4.3	3	6	9	13
Effect of revisions and forecasting changes	4.7	-3.6	-6 1/2	-4	-1 1/2	-1
Effect of discretionary changes	0.0	-0.4	- 1/2	1	1 1/2	1 1/2
2007 Pre-Budget Report	**-4.7**	**-8.3**	**-4**	**3**	**9**	**14**
Net borrowing (£ billion)						
Budget 2007	35.0	33.7	30	28	26	24
Changes to current budget	-4.7	4.0	7	2 1/2	0	-1
Changes to net investment	0.8	0.4	0	0	2	2
2007 Pre-Budget Report	**31.0**	**38.0**	**36**	**31**	**28**	**25**
Cyclically-adjusted surplus on current budget (per cent of GDP)						
Budget 2007	-0.5	-0.3	0.2	0.4	0.6	0.8
2007 Pre-Budget Report	**-0.2**	**-0.7**	**-0.2**	**0.3**	**0.6**	**0.8**
Cyclically-adjusted net borrowing (per cent of GDP)						
Budget 2007	2.5	2.4	2.0	1.8	1.6	1.4
2007 Pre-Budget Report	**2.2**	**2.8**	**2.4**	**1.9**	**1.7**	**1.5**
Net debt (per cent of GDP)						
Budget 2007	37.2	38.2	38.5	38.8	38.8	38.6
2007 Pre-Budget Report	**36.7**	**37.6**	**38.4**	**38.8**	**38.9**	**38.8**

[1] The 2006-07 figures were estimates in Budget 2007.
[2] The 2007-08 figures were projections in Budget 2007.

2006-07 outturn **B.16** The outturn for the current budget in 2006-07 shows a deficit of £4.7 billion, £4.7 billion lower than expected at Budget 2007 and an improvement of £9.3 billion relative to the deficit in 2005-06. The changes since Budget 2007 reflect higher central government receipts, largely VAT, lower central government current expenditure, and a lower-than-forecast deficit across the rest of the public sector. The 2006-07 outturn for net borrowing is £3.9 billion lower than the Budget 2007 estimate, slightly less than the fall in the current deficit, due to slightly higher-than-expected net investment.

2007-08 estimate **B.17** The downward revisions to the public sector current budget in this Pre-Budget Report from 2007-08 onwards are largely due to falls in receipts, driven in part by the expected impact of recent financial market disruption on receipts and changes to the economic forecast in 2008. Further details of these changes are given in the receipts section of this Annex.

FORECAST DIFFERENCES AND RISKS

B.18 The fiscal balances represent the difference between two large aggregates of expenditure and receipts, and forecasts are inevitably subject to wide margins of uncertainty. Over the past ten years, the average absolute difference between year-ahead forecasts of net borrowing and subsequent outturns has been around 1 per cent of GDP. This difference tends to grow as the forecast horizon lengthens and uncertainties increase accordingly. A full account of differences between the projections made in Budget 2005 and Budget 2006, and the subsequent outturns is provided in the 2007 *End of year fiscal report*, published alongside this 2007 Pre-Budget Report.

B.19 As explained in Annex A, UK GDP is expected to grow by 3 per cent in 2007, in line with the Budget 2007 forecast. Recent disruption in financial markets has meant economic prospects have become more uncertain. Reflecting higher interest rates than markets expected at the time of Budget 2007, and some assumed feed-through from financial market disruption to tighter credit conditions and to household and company spending in the short term, growth is forecast to slow to 2 to $2\frac{1}{2}$ per cent in 2008, below trend, before returning to trend rates from 2009.

B.20 The use of cautious assumptions audited by the National Audit Office (NAO) builds a margin into the public finance projections to guard against unexpected events. One of the key audited assumptions is that for the trend rate of GDP growth, which is assumed to be $\frac{1}{4}$ per cent below the neutral view. This means that the rate of economic growth used to forecast the public finances is the bottom end of the projection range. For example, in this Pre-Budget Report, the forecast for economic growth used in the public finances projections over the period 2007-08 to 2012-13 averages $2\frac{1}{2}$ per cent, $\frac{1}{4}$ per cent below the central case.

B.21 A further important source of potential error results from misjudging the position of the economy in relation to trend output. To minimise this risk, the robustness of the projections is tested against an alternative scenario in which the level of trend output is assumed to be one percentage point lower than in the central case.

B.22 The Government adopts the cautious case and uses NAO-audited assumptions to build a margin in the public finances against unexpected events. Combined with the decision to consolidate the public finances when the economy was above trend, this has resulted in lower debt. As a result, this has allowed the Government to increase investment in priority public services, allow the automatic stabilisers to work fully during a period of global economic uncertainty, and meet in full the UK's international commitments, while continuing to meet the fiscal rules.

ASSUMPTIONS

B.23 The fiscal projections are based on the following assumptions:

- the economy follows the path described in Annex A. The fiscal projections assume that trend growth will be $2\frac{1}{2}$ per cent to 2012-13. In the interests of caution, these projections continue to be based on the assumption that trend output growth will be $\frac{1}{4}$ percentage point lower than the Government's neutral view;

- rates, thresholds and limits, including for 2008-09, increase in line with projected indexation or announced policy. The 2008-09 rates and allowances for income tax, national insurance contributions, the Working and Child Tax Credits and Child Benefit/Guardian's Allowance will be published after the September RPI becomes available;

- there are no tax or spending policy changes beyond those announced in or before this Pre-Budget Report, and all rates and allowances remain constant in real terms;

- firm Departmental Expenditure Limits (DEL) for 2007-08 are as set out in the 2004 Spending Review, adjusted for the impact of policy decisions and reclassifications;

- total Annually Managed Expenditure (AME) programmes for 2007-08 have been reviewed, and the total has been adjusted for reclassifications and for the cost of spending measures in this Pre-Budget Report;

- DELs from 2008-09 to 2010-11 are as fixed in this Comprehensive Spending Review. AME expenditure from 2008-09 to 2010-11 has been forecast consistent with the economic assumptions and policy decisions included in this report. Total Managed Expenditure (TME) increases by an average of 2.1 per cent a year in real terms over the Comprehensive Spending Review period;

- public sector current expenditure in 2011-12 and 2012-13 is assumed to grow at 2.0 per cent in real terms; and

- net investment is assumed to remain at $2\frac{1}{4}$ per cent of GDP in 2011-12 and 2012-13, meaning that in real terms, TME will increase by $2\frac{1}{2}$ per cent a year on average over the forecast period.

Table B3: Economic assumptions for the public finance projections

| | Percentage changes on previous year | | | | | | |
| | Outturn | Estimate | | Projections | | | |
	2006-07	2007-08	2008-09	2009-10	2010-11	2011-12	2012-13
Output (GDP)	3	3	2	2 3/4	2 1/2	2 1/2	2 1/2
Prices							
CPI	2 1/2	2 1/4	2	2	2	2	2
GDP deflator	2 3/4	3 1/4	2 3/4	2 3/4	2 3/4	2 3/4	2 3/4
RPI[1] (September)	3 1/2	4	2 3/4	2 3/4	2 3/4	2 3/4	2 3/4
Rossi[2] (September)	3	2 1/4	2 1/2	2 1/4	2 1/4	2 1/4	2 1/4
Money GDP[3] (£ billion)	1,323	1,404	1,471	1,550	1,630	1,714	1,802

[1] Used for revalorising excise duties in current year and uprating income tax allowances and bands and certain social security benefits in the following year.

[2] RPI excluding housing costs, used for uprating certain social security benefits.

[3] Not seasonally adjusted.

B.24 The projections for 2007-08 are based on all available data within the Treasury and other government departments involved in producing tax and spending forecasts.

B.25   The key assumptions underlying the fiscal projections are audited by the National Audit Office (NAO) under the three-year rolling review process. Details of the audited assumptions are given in Box B1. None of these assumptions were due for review in this Pre-Budget Report.

Box B1: Key assumptions audited by the NAO[a]

Trend GDP growth[f]	2¹/₂ per cent a year to 2012.
Dating of the cycle[c]	The end date of the previous economic cycle was in the first half of 1997.
Composition of GDP[f]	Shares of labour income and profits in national income are broadly constant in the medium term.
Consistency of price indices[e]	Projections of price indices used to project the public finances are consistent with the CPI.
Oil prices[c]	$68 a barrel in 2008, the average of independent forecasts, and then constant in real terms.
Equity prices[e]	FTSE All-share index rises from 3366 (close 4 October) in line with money GDP.
VAT[f]	The underlying VAT gap will rise by 0.5 per cent per year from the estimated outturn for the current year.
Tobacco[f]	The underlying level of duty paid on consumption of cigarettes will be set at least three per cent per year lower than the estimated outturn for the current year.
UK claimant unemployment[b, g]	Rising slowly from recent average levels of 0.86 million to 0.92 million at the end of 2009, and then staying constant at this level.
Interest rates[d]	3-month market rates change in line with market expectations (as of 28 September).
Funding[f]	Funding assumptions used to project debt interest are consistent with the forecast level of government borrowing and with financing policy.
Privatisation proceeds[f]	Credit is taken only for proceeds from sales that have been announced.

[a] For details of all NAO audits before Budget 2005, see the 2004 *Pre-Budget Report*, 2 December 2004 (Cm 6408).
[b] *Audit of Assumptions for Budget 2005*, 16 March 2005 (HC 452).
[c] *Audit of Assumptions for the 2005 Pre-Budget Report*, 5 December 2006 (HC 707).
[d] *Audit of Assumptions for Budget 2006*, 22 March 2006 (HC 937).
[e] *Audit of Assumptions for the 2006 Pre-Budget Report*, 6 December 2006 (HC 125).
[f] *Audit of Assumptions for Budget 2007*, 21 March 2007 (HC 393).
[g] This is a cautious assumption based on the average of external forecasts and is not the Treasury's central economic forecast.

PRE-BUDGET REPORT POLICY DECISIONS

B.26 Consistent with the requirements of the *Code for fiscal stability*, the updated projections take into account the fiscal effects of all firm decisions announced in this 2007 Pre-Budget Report or since Budget 2007. The fiscal impact of these measures are set out in Table B4.

B.27 Expenditure measures affecting AME and DEL in 2007-08 have been added to total AME and total DEL, respectively. Expenditure measures in the Comprehensive Spending Review period, including announcements with costs in AME, are contained within the spending envelope announced in this report.

B.28 Consistent with the *Code for fiscal stability*, the projections do not take account of decisions where the impact cannot yet be quantified or of measures proposed in this Pre-Budget Report, or where final decisions have yet to be taken. These include:

- further extensions to maternity and paternity leave; and
- further reforms to incapacity benefit.

Table B4: Estimated costs for Pre-Budget Report policy decisions and others announced since Budget 2007[1]

	£ million			
	2007-08	2008-09	2009-10	2010-11
Sustainable growth and prosperity				
Tax simplification: increase income tax self assessment payment on account threshold	0	0	-90	0
Fairness and opportunity for all				
Increase in housing benefit disregard[2]	-5	-	-	-
Implementing state second pension White Paper reforms	0	0	+290	+440
Modernisation of residence and domicile taxation	0	0	+800	+500
Increase child element of CTC by £25 in April 2008 and a further £25 in April 2010[3]	0	-30	-30	-60
Transferable inheritance tax allowances for married couples and civil partners	-100	-1,000	-1,200	-1,400
Capital gains tax reform: 18% single rate	0	+350	+750	+900
Protecting revenues				
Removal of national insurance contributions exemption	+100	+200	+200	+200
Tackling income shifting	0	+25	+260	+200
Life insurance companies avoidance	0	+35	+45	+45
Countering interest relief exploitation by individuals	+25	+10	0	.0
Vehicle excise duty enforcement	0	+10	+20	+25
Protecting the environment				
Aviation duty[4]	0	-55	+100	+520
Non-car vehicle excise duty rates for 2008-09	0	-5	-5	-10
Fuel benefit charge: revalorisation since 2003	0	+65	+40	+25
Extending the exemption for oils used in electricity generation	-5	-5	-5	-5
Enhanced capital allowances for biofuel plants	0	+30	+20	+35
Other policy decisions				
Addition to the special reserve	-400	0	0	0
TOTAL POLICY DECISIONS	-385	-370	+1,195	+1,415
Additional investment in public services	0	0	0	-2,000

[1] *Costings shown relative to an indexed base.*

[2] *From 2008-09 onwards, included within the Comprehensive Spending Review settlement.*

[3] *Negative tax costs. AME spending consequences are included within the Comprehensive Spending Review settlement.*

[4] *Intention to replace air passenger duty by per plane duty from November 2009.*

FISCAL AGGREGATES

B.29   Tables B5 and B6 provide more detail on the projections for the current and capital budgets.

Table B5: Current and capital budgets

	£ billion						
	Outturn	Estimate	Projections				
	2006-07	2007-08	2008-09	2009-10	2010-11	2011-12	2012-13
Current budget							
Current receipts	519.1	551	581	616	651	686	724
Current expenditure	506.6	541	566	593	620	650	681
Depreciation	17.2	18	19	20	21	22	24
Surplus on current budget	**-4.7**	**-8**	**-4**	**3**	**9**	**14**	**20**
Capital budget							
Gross investment[1]	43.5	48	51	54	58	61	66
Less depreciation	-17.2	-18	-19	-20	-21	-22	-24
Net investment	26.3	30	32	34	37	39	42
Net borrowing	**31.0**	**38**	**36**	**31**	**28**	**25**	**23**
Public sector net debt - end year	**500.2**	**541**	**580**	**617**	**651**	**682**	**713**
Memos:							
Treaty deficit[2]	34.0	41	41	37	34	31	29
Treaty debt[3]	574.4	616	658	699	738	774	810

[1] Net of asset sales; for a breakdown see Table 16 in Pre-Budget Report and Comprehensive Spending Review 2007: the economy and public finances - supplementary charts and tables.

[2] General government net borrowing on a Maastricht basis.

[3] General government gross debt on a Maastricht basis.

Table B6: Current and capital budgets

	Per cent of GDP						
	Outturn	Estimate	Projections				
	2006-07	2007-08	2008-09	2009-10	2010-11	2011-12	2012-13
Current budget							
Current receipts	39.2	39.2	39.5	39.7	39.9	40.0	40.2
Current expenditure	38.3	38.5	38.5	38.2	38.1	37.9	37.8
Depreciation	1.3	1.3	1.3	1.3	1.3	1.3	1.3
Surplus on current budget	**-0.4**	**-0.6**	**-0.3**	**0.2**	**0.6**	**0.8**	**1.1**
Capital budget							
Gross investment[1]	3.3	3.4	3.5	3.5	3.6	3.6	3.7
Less depreciation	-1.3	-1.3	-1.3	-1.3	-1.3	-1.3	-1.3
Net investment	2.0	2.1	2.2	2.2	2.3	2.3	2.3
Net borrowing	**2.3**	**2.7**	**2.5**	**2.0**	**1.7**	**1.5**	**1.3**
Public sector net debt - end year	**36.7**	**37.6**	**38.4**	**38.8**	**38.9**	**38.8**	**38.6**
Memos:							
Treaty deficit[2]	2.6	2.9	2.8	2.4	2.1	1.8	1.6
Treaty debt ratio[3]	43.4	43.9	44.8	45.1	45.3	45.2	44.9

[1] Net of asset sales; for a breakdown see Table 16 in Pre-Budget Report and Comprehensive Spending Review 2007: the economy and public finances - supplementary charts and tables.

[2] General government net borrowing on a Maastricht basis.

[3] General government gross debt on a Maastricht basis.

B.30   Following a deficit of 3 per cent of GDP in 1996-97, current budget surpluses of more than 2 per cent were recorded in 1999-2000 and 2000-01. These surpluses allowed the Government to use fiscal policy to support monetary policy during the economic slowdown in 2001 and 2002, and as a result the current budget moved into deficit. The current budget is expected to remain in deficit in 2007-08 and 2008-09 and then move back into surplus in 2009-10, with increasingly larger surpluses in later years, reaching 1.1 per cent in 2012-13.

B.31   The current budget surplus is equal to public sector current receipts less public sector current expenditure and depreciation. The reasons for changes in receipts and current expenditure are explained in later sections.

B.32   Table B5 also shows that net investment is projected to increase from 2 per cent of GDP in 2006-07 to $2^1/_4$ per cent of GDP from 2008-09 to 2012-13 as the Government seeks to rectify past underinvestment in public infrastructure. These increases are sustainable within the fiscal rules, with debt falling to 38.6 per cent of GDP by the end of the forecast period.

RECEIPTS

B.33   This section analyses the projections for public sector tax receipts in detail. It begins by looking at the main determinants of changes in the overall projections since Budget 2007, before examining changes in the projections of individual tax receipts. Finally, it provides updated forecasts for the tax-GDP ratio.

Changes in total receipts since Budget 2007

B.34   Receipts in all years are affected by a fiscally-neutral reclassification. In June 2007, the ONS changed its treatment of local authorities' Housing Revenue Accounts. In the National Accounts, these are regarded as 'quasi-corporations' and are included in the public corporations sub-sector. The effect of the change was to increase current expenditure of local authorities and receipts of public corporations by equal amounts in each year. The additional receipts increase the gross operating surplus component of the 'other receipts' category and amounted to £1.6 billion in 2006-07, rising thereafter.

B.35   After allowing for the effects of this classification change, overall receipts in 2006-07 were the same as forecast in Budget 2007, with higher central government receipts offset by lower receipts in the rest of the public sector. Central government receipts measured on an accruals basis were £1.2 billion higher, largely because of higher cash VAT receipts at the end of 2006-07 and early in 2007-08, which were scored to 2006-07 accruals. Although the overall current balance of local authorities has improved considerably since Budget 2007, this reflects much lower-than-forecast expenditure, partially offset by lower receipts. Very little outturn information is available on the individual components of local authority receipts and expenditure until five months after the end of the financial year.

B.36   The downward revisions to receipts for 2007-08 onwards are driven in part by the expected impact of recent financial market disruption. Other factors which reduce receipts compared to Budget 2007 are a fall in North Sea revenues, as a result of lower-than-expected oil and gas production, offset by higher oil prices, and changes to the economic forecast in 2008, especially lower wages and salaries growth. Receipts in 2007-08 also reflect lower North Sea gas prices than expected in Budget 2007 and a series of one-off corporation tax repayments.

Tax by tax analysis

B.37   Table B7 shows outturns for cash receipts in the first five months of 2007-08 and estimated receipts for the remainder of the year, along with percentage changes over the corresponding period in 2006-07. These growth rates can vary considerably across the year, partly because of the rules governing payment of each tax and the various time lags. Table B8 contains updated projections for the main components of public sector receipts for 2006-07, 2007-08 and 2008-09, as well as the changes to the projections of individual taxes since Budget 2007.

Table B7: 2007-08 Net taxes and national insurance contributions

	£ billion			Percentage change on 2006-07		
	Outturn[1]	Estimates		Outturn[1]	Estimates	
	Apr-Aug	Sep-Mar	Full year	Apr-Aug	Sep-Mar	Full year
HM Revenue & Customs						
Income tax, NICs and capital gains tax[2]	100.1	150.8	250.9	7.0	7.1	7.0
Value added tax	35.1	46.3	81.4	8.4	2.9	5.2
Corporation tax[2]	18.4	27.8	46.3	-3.1	10.1	4.4
Petroleum revenue tax	0.4	1.1	1.5	-33.7	-27.8	-29.5
Fuel duties	10.2	14.6	24.9	3.6	6.8	5.5
Inheritance tax	1.7	2.2	3.9	12.3	8.1	9.8
Stamp duties	6.6	8.5	15.1	22.6	6.2	12.8
Tobacco duties	3.4	4.7	8.1	-0.9	-0.2	-0.5
Alcohol duties	3.4	4.8	8.2	2.9	3.9	3.5
Other Customs duties and levies	4.6	5.6	10.1	14.4	14.9	14.7
Total HMRC	**184.0**	**266.5**	**450.4**	**6.3**	**6.3**	**6.3**
Vehicle excise duties	2.4	3.1	5.5	11.2	3.2	6.6
Business rates	11.2	10.7	21.9	4.1	4.8	4.5
Council tax	11.2	12.5	23.7	5.3	8.0	6.7
Other taxes and royalties	5.6	9.6	15.3	-1.2	17.9	10.1
Net taxes and NICs	**214.4**	**302.4**	**516.8**	**6.0**	**6.7**	**6.4**

[1] Provisional.

[2] Net of tax credits scored as negative tax in net taxes and national insurance contributions.

Table B8: Current receipts

	£ billion			Changes since Budget 2007 £ billion		
	Outturn 2006-07	Estimate 2007-08	Projection 2008-09	Outturn 2006-07	Estimate 2007-08	Projection 2008-09
HM Revenue and Customs						
Income tax (gross of tax credits)	147.8	154.1	161.8	0.8	-2.8	-4.2
Income tax credits	-4.4	-4.5	-4.9	0.2	-0.1	0.0
National insurance contributions	87.3	96.5	101.0	-0.7	1.4	0.2
Value added tax	77.4	81.4	85.8	0.0	1.4	0.4
Corporation tax[1]	44.8	46.8	51.5	-0.1	-3.3	-3.0
Corporation tax credits[2]	-0.5	-0.5	-0.6	0.0	0.0	0.0
Petroleum revenue tax	2.2	1.5	1.5	0.0	-0.1	-0.2
Fuel duties	23.6	24.9	26.2	-0.1	-0.2	-0.8
Capital gains tax	3.8	4.8	5.4	-0.1	0.2	0.7
Inheritance tax	3.6	3.9	3.3	0.0	-0.1	-0.9
Stamp duties	13.4	15.1	15.8	0.0	0.8	0.6
Tobacco duties	8.1	8.1	7.8	0.0	0.0	0.0
Spirits duties	2.3	2.3	2.3	0.0	0.0	0.0
Wine duties	2.4	2.6	2.8	0.0	0.1	0.1
Beer and cider duties	3.3	3.3	3.4	0.0	-0.1	-0.1
Betting and gaming duties	1.4	1.4	1.4	0.0	0.0	0.0
Air passenger duty	1.0	2.0	2.1	0.0	-0.1	-0.1
Insurance premium tax	2.3	2.4	2.5	0.0	-0.1	0.0
Landfill tax	0.8	0.9	1.1	0.0	0.0	0.0
Climate change levy	0.7	0.7	0.7	0.0	0.0	0.0
Aggregates levy	0.3	0.3	0.4	0.0	0.0	0.0
Customs duties and levies	2.3	2.4	2.3	0.0	0.0	-0.1
Total HMRC	**423.7**	**450.4**	**473.7**	**0.1**	**-3.0**	**-7.6**
Vehicle excise duties	5.1	5.5	5.9	0.0	-0.1	-0.1
Business rates	21.0	21.9	24.1	-0.3	-0.2	0.2
Council tax[3]	22.2	23.7	24.9	-0.2	0.2	0.2
Other taxes and royalties[4]	13.9	15.3	16.0	0.5	0.7	0.5
Net taxes and NICs[5]	**485.9**	**516.8**	**544.5**	**0.1**	**-2.4**	**-6.8**
Accruals adjustments on taxes	4.7	1.5	2.4	1.3	-1.0	0.1
Less own resources contribution to EC budget	-4.6	-4.7	-4.8	0.1	-0.6	-0.3
Less PC corporation tax payments	-0.3	-0.2	-0.2	-0.1	0.0	0.0
Tax credits adjustment[6]	0.5	0.5	0.6	0.0	0.0	0.0
Interest and dividends	6.3	7.6	7.5	0.3	0.5	0.3
Other receipts[7]	26.6	29.7	31.0	0.1	1.7	1.8
Current receipts	**519.1**	**551.2**	**581.0**	**1.8**	**-1.8**	**-4.9**
Memo:						
North Sea revenues[8]	9.0	7.5	9.0	0.0	-0.6	-0.3

[1] National Accounts measure: gross of enhanced and payable tax credits.

[2] Includes enhanced company tax credits.

[3] Council tax increases are determined annually by local authorities, not by the Government. As in previous years, council tax figures are projections based on stylised assumptions and are not Government forecasts.

[4] Includes VAT refunds and money paid into the National Lottery Distribution Fund.

[5] Includes VAT and 'traditional own resources' contributions to EC budget.

[6] Tax credits which are scored as negative tax in the calculation of NTNIC but expenditure in the National Accounts.

[7] Includes gross operating surplus, rent and business rate payments by local authorities.

[8] Consists of North Sea corporation tax and petroleum revenue tax.

Income tax and national insurance contributions

B.38 Cash receipts of income tax and national insurance contributions (NICs) in 2007-08 are expected to be £1.4 billion below their Budget 2007 projection, from a combinaton of the impact of the recent financial market disruption and higher than expected income tax repayments. In the first five months of 2007-08, Pay As You Earn (PAYE) and NIC receipts remained robust despite lower average earnings growth. This reflected strong growth in receipts from both the financial and business services sectors. These sectors were the fastest growing sectors of the economy in the first half of 2007 with a year-on-year growth rate of 5 per cent, as well as having a larger proportion of higher rate taxpayers than other parts of the economy.

B.39 The 2007 Pre-Budget Report forecast allows for lower receipts from bonuses in 2007-08 and 2008-09. With average earnings growth more modest than expected in recent months, the economic forecast assumes slower earnings growth than previously assumed in the Budget for 2008-09. This affects income tax and NICs receipts.

Non-North Sea corporation tax

B.40 Non-North Sea corporation tax has been lower-than-expected in the first five months of 2007-08. However, much of this change is due to much higher-than-expected repayments relating to previous years accounting periods. Net repayments are expected to be £1.3 billion higher in 2007-08 than in 2006-07, but this rise is expected to be mainly a one-off, in part reflecting HMRC efforts to finalise tax liabilities relating to historic accounting periods. The first instalment payments of corporation tax on 2007 profits made by many firms in July were consistent with continued sustained profit growth in the industrial and commercial sector and strong profit growth in the financial sector in the first half of 2007.

B.41 Over the remainder of 2007-08, the forecast assumes that corporation tax receipts from the industrial and commercial sector continue to benefit from the current momentum in the economy. However, financial market disruption is likely to have an impact on receipts from the sector. Although the extent of the impact on receipts is highly uncertain, the forecast for 2007-08 and 2008-09 takes this impact into account.

B.42 Thereafter, the forecast assumes that the financial sector recovers, consistent with the sector maintaining its international competitiveness and capacity for innovation.

North Sea revenues

B.43 Dollar oil prices during 2007 are likely to average around $68 a barrel in 2007, some $10 a barrel higher than assumed in the Budget 2007 forecast. However, North Sea revenues in 2007-08 have been revised down by around £0.6 billion in light of weaker-than-expected receipts from petroleum revenue tax and the first corporation tax instalment payments by North Sea firms on their 2007 profits. The impact from higher dollar oil prices has been offset by a variety of factors. In the first half of 2007, increased imports and a mild winter lowered gas prices and led some companies to rein back on production. There were also offsetting effects from continued cost pressures on the operating and capital expenditure of North Sea firms and the continued appreciation of sterling against the dollar.

B.44 With oil and gas prices now much higher than earlier in the year, North Sea revenues are expected to improve during the remainder of 2007-08. This is in contrast with 2006-07 when they deteriorated in the latter part of the year as prices fell. The differing pattern helps explain why the forecast for overall corporation tax assumes a stronger year-on-year growth rate for the remainder of 2007-08. The projections for North Sea revenues use the NAO-audited assumption on oil prices. In line with the average of independent forecasts, oil prices are expected to be $68 a barrel in 2008, just under $10 a barrel higher than in the Budget 2007 projection. However, there are likely to be a variety of offsetting effects from the strength of sterling against the dollar, higher costs and production levels that are expected to be lower going forward than assumed in Budget 2007.

Capital gains tax **B.45** Capital gains tax is due in the final quarter of the financial year following the year in which the gains were realised. The forecast assumes a further year of robust growth in receipts in 2007-08 reflecting the rise in equity and housing markets in 2006-07. Thereafter, receipts will be affected by the reforms announced in this Pre-Budget Report and slower asset price growth than in recent years going forward. The path of equity prices over the forecast period is expected to be close to the Budget 2007 projection.

Stamp duties **B.46** Both stamp tax on land and property and stamp duty on shares have shown robust year-on-year growth in the first five months of 2007-08. Stamp tax on land and property has been boosted by continued growth in house prices and property transactions. Stamp duty on shares has benefited from the year-on-year rises in both equity prices and volumes. However, growth in stamp duty receipts is expected to slow in the final months of 2007-08 and into 2008-09, as the drivers of recent growth lose some momentum.

VAT receipts **B.47** Cash receipts of VAT in 2007-08 are expected to be £1.4 billion above the Budget 2007 forecast, helped by the continuing success of the government's strategy for tackling Missing Trader Intra-Community (MTIC) fraud and a stronger-than-expected rise in nominal consumer spending in the first half of 2007. Consumer spending accounts for around two-thirds of the VAT base and the stronger growth reflected both higher inflation and real spending growth, above the Budget 2007 forecast range.

B.48 After 8.4 per cent year-on-year growth in cash receipts of VAT in the first five months of 2007-08, annual growth is expected to slow over the remainder of the year. This in part reflects the fact that the annual comparison will be against a period in which MTIC fraud had fallen to a low level. In addition, more VAT is likely to be repaid over the remainder of 2007-08 and into 2008-09 than in the first five months of the financial year. This follows last year's judicial rulings relating to the 3-year cap for making claims of previously overpaid or underclaimed VAT. The Government is appealing these decisions and, if successful, taxpayers would subsequently be required to repay these claims. No allowance is made in the forecast for any such recoveries.

B.49 Growth in VAT receipts in 2008-09 will be affected by a slowdown in nominal consumer spending growth. Inflation has already fallen back sharply from its March peak and is expected to remain close to target going forwards, while real consumer spending is expected to grow below the growth of the economy as a whole in 2008.

Excise duties **B.50** Fuel duties are expected to be £0.2 billion lower in 2007-08 than forecast in Budget 2007. This reflects the impact of increased pump prices, due to higher oil prices, on the demand for fuel. In a full year, the higher oil prices are expected to take around £0.3 billion off receipts. The stronger year-on-year growth in fuel duties expected in the second half of 2007-08 reflects the Budget 2007 measure to raise main fuel duties by 2 pence per litre from 1 October.

B.51 The forecast for tobacco receipts is close to the Budget 2007 projection. As in Budget 2007, the forecast allows for the impact of the smoking ban in enclosed workplaces. Tobacco receipts in 2007-08 are likely to be marginally down from 2006-07, despite the revalorisation of duties in Budget 2007. Alcohol receipts are also expected to be close to their Budget 2007 forecast.

Council tax **B.52** Council tax increases are determined annually by local authorities, not by the government. The council tax projections are based on stylised assumptions and are not govenment forecasts. The council tax figures for 2008-09 onwards are based on the arithmetic average of council tax increases over the past three years. Since changes to council tax are broadly balanced by changes to locally financed expenditure, they have little material impact on the current balance or on net borrowing.

Tax-GDP ratio

B.53 Table B9 shows projections of receipts from major taxes as a per cent of GDP. Table B10 sets out projections of the overall tax-GDP ratio, based on net tax and national insurance contributions. The tax-GDP ratio is expected to be lower throughout the forecast than in Budget 2007 projections. A key factor is higher money GDP, reflecting 2007 Blue Book revisions and higher-than-expected GDP deflator inflation in the first half of 2007.

Table B9: Current receipts as a proportion of GDP

	Per cent of GDP						
	Outturn	Estimate	Projections				
	2006-07	2007-08	2008-09	2009-10	2010-11	2011-12	2012-13
Income tax (gross of tax credits)	11.2	11.0	11.0	11.1	11.3	11.4	11.6
National insurance contributions	6.6	6.9	6.9	6.9	6.9	7.0	7.0
Non-North Sea corporation tax[1]	2.9	2.9	3.0	3.1	3.2	3.3	3.3
Tax credits[2]	-0.4	-0.4	-0.4	-0.4	-0.4	-0.3	-0.3
North Sea revenues[3]	0.7	0.5	0.6	0.6	0.6	0.6	0.5
Value added tax	5.8	5.8	5.8	5.8	5.8	5.8	5.7
Excise duties[4]	3.0	2.9	2.9	2.8	2.8	2.7	2.7
Other taxes and royalties[5]	6.9	7.1	7.2	7.2	7.2	7.2	7.1
Net taxes and NICs[6]	**36.7**	**36.8**	**37.0**	**37.3**	**37.4**	**37.5**	**37.6**
Accruals adjustments on taxes	0.4	0.1	0.2	0.2	0.2	0.2	0.3
Less EU transfers	-0.3	-0.3	-0.3	-0.3	-0.3	-0.3	-0.3
Other receipts[7]	2.5	2.7	2.6	2.6	2.6	2.6	2.6
Current receipts	**39.2**	**39.2**	**39.5**	**39.7**	**39.9**	**40.0**	**40.2**

[1] National Accounts measure, gross of enhanced and payable tax credits.

[2] Tax credits scored as negative tax in net taxes and national insurance contributions.

[3] Includes petroleum revenue tax and North Sea corporation tax.

[4] Fuel, alcohol and tobacco duties.

[5] Includes council tax and money paid into the National Lottery Distribution Fund, as well as other central government taxes.

[6] Includes VAT and 'own resources' contributions to EC budget. Cash basis.

[7] Mainly gross operating surplus and rent

Table B10: Net taxes and national insurance contributions[1]

	Per cent of GDP						
	Outturn[2]	Estimate[3]	Projections				
	2006-07	2007-08	2008-09	2009-10	2010-11	2011-12	2012-13
Budget 2007	37.2	37.7	38.0	38.1	38.1	38.1	
2007 Pre-Budget Report	**36.7**	**36.8**	**37.0**	**37.3**	**37.4**	**37.5**	**37.6**

[1] Cash basis. Uses OECD definition of tax credits scored as negative tax.

[2] The 2006-07 figures were estimates in Budget 2007.

[3] The 2007-08 figures were projections in Budget 2007.

PUBLIC EXPENDITURE

B.54 This section looks in detail at the projections for public expenditure consistent with the Comprehensive Spending Review. It includes provisional outturns for 2006-07, the latest estimates for 2007-08 and, for the first time, public expenditure plans for 2008-09 to 2010-11. The spending projections cover the whole of the public sector, using the National Accounts aggregate Total Managed Expenditure (TME).

B.55 For fiscal aggregates purposes, TME is split into National Accounts components covering public sector current expenditure, public sector net investment and depreciation. For budgeting and other purposes, TME is split into DEL (firm three-year limits for departments' programme expenditure) and AME (expenditure that is not easily subject to firm multi-year limits). Departments have separate resource budgets for current expenditure and capital budgets for investment.

B.56 Table B11 sets out projected spending on DEL and the main components of AME to the end of the 2007 Comprehensive Spending Review period in 2010-11. Table B12 shows changes since Budget 2007.

Changes in TME since Budget 2007

B.57 TME in all years is higher than at Budget 2007 because of a fiscally-neutral classification change introduced by the ONS in June 2007. This change added £1.6 billion to both receipts and expenditure in 2006-07 and is described in more detail in paragraph B.34.

B.58 After taking account of this reclassification change, the provisional outturn for TME in 2006-07 was lower than estimated in Budget 2007. Current expenditure was lower by £4.0 billion, mainly because of lower local authority spending net of current grants from central government, and net investment was higher by £0.8 billion. Aside from the classification change, there are no forecasting changes to TME in 2007-08 since Budget 2007. Forecasts for individual AME components have been revised but all changes have been absorbed within the AME margin.

B.59 Discretionary changes to TME since the Budget 2007 forecast reflect the addition of £0.4 billion to the special reserve in 2007-08 and the £2 billion addition to public investment in 2010-11, as set out in Table B4.

Table B11: Total Managed Expenditure 2006-07 to 2010-11

	£ billion				
	Outturn	Estimate	Projections		
	2006-07	2007-08	2008-09	2009-10	2010-11
CURRENT EXPENDITURE					
Resource Departmental Expenditure Limits	291.2	310.8	324.3	338.8	354.6
of which:					
Near-cash Departmental Expenditure Limits	272.3	290.0	303.4	316.5	330.6
Non-cash	18.9	20.8	20.9	22.3	24.0
Resource Annually Managed Expenditure	215.4	230.4	241.7	253.7	265.7
of which:					
Social security benefits[1]	131.8	139.0	145.9	152.3	158.2
Tax credits[1]	16.3	16.7	18.2	18.8	19.3
Net public service pensions[2]	1.2	2.2	2.7	2.9	3.5
National Lottery	0.8	0.8	0.7	0.6	0.7
BBC domestic services	3.2	3.3	3.4	3.6	3.7
Other departmental expenditure	3.2	2.9	1.7	1.3	1.1
Net expenditure transfers to EC institutions[3]	4.7	5.6	5.5	5.7	6.6
Locally-financed expenditure[4]	25.5	25.3	26.2	27.4	29.1
Central government gross debt interest	27.6	30.0	29.1	31.2	32.9
AME margin	0.0	0.1	0.9	1.8	2.7
Accounting adjustments	1.2	4.5	7.4	8.1	7.9
Public sector current expenditure	**506.6**	**541.2**	**566.0**	**592.5**	**620.3**
CAPITAL EXPENDITURE					
Capital Departmental Expenditure Limits	39.1	44.7	48.1	50.7	55.3
Capital Annually Managed Expenditure	4.4	3.3	3.4	3.4	2.7
of which:					
National Lottery	0.8	0.9	0.8	1.0	0.9
Locally-financed expenditure[4]	5.1	3.6	4.0	3.9	2.9
Public corporations' own-financed capital expenditure	5.7	4.9	5.0	5.1	5.2
Other capital expenditure	-0.5	-0.4	0.4	0.6	0.8
AME margin	0.0	0.9	0.1	0.2	0.3
Accounting adjustments	-6.8	-6.5	-6.9	-7.4	-7.4
Public sector gross investment	**43.5**	**48.0**	**51.4**	**54.1**	**58.0**
less public sector depreciation	-17.2	-18.3	-19.1	-20.2	-21.2
Public sector net investment	**26.3**	**29.7**	**32.3**	**33.9**	**36.7**
TOTAL MANAGED EXPENDITURE[5]	**550.1**	**589.2**	**617.4**	**646.6**	**678.3**
of which:					
Departmental Expenditure Limits	320.4	344.6	361.1	377.5	396.9
Annually Managed Expenditure	229.7	244.6	256.4	269.2	281.4

[1] For 2006-07 to 2008-09, child allowances in Income Support and Jobseekers' Allowance have been included in the tax credits line and excluded from the social security benefits line.

[2] Net public service pensions expenditure is reported on a National Accounts basis.

[3] AME spending component only. Total net payments to EU institutions also include receipts scored in DEL, VAT based contributions which score as negative receipts and some payments which have no effect on the UK public sector in the National Accounts. Latest estimates for total net payments, which exclude the UK's contribution to the cost of EU aid to non-Member States (which is attributed to the aid programme), and the UK's net contribution to the EC Budget, which includes this aid, are (in £ billion):

	2006-07	2007-08	2008-09	2009-10	2010-11
Net payments to EC institutions	2.9	4.3	3.3	4.8	5.7
Net contribution to EC Budget	3.5	5.0	4.1	5.7	6.5

[4] This expenditure is mainly financed by council tax revenues. See footnote to table B8 for an explanation of how the council tax projections are derived.

[5] Total Managed Expenditure is equal to the sum of public sector current expenditure, public sector net investment, and public sector depreciation

Table B12: Changes to Total Managed Expenditure since Budget 2007

	£ billion	
	Outturn 2006-07	Estimate 2007-08
CURRENT EXPENDITURE		
Resource Departmental Expenditure Limits	**-2.2**	**0.8**
of which:		
Near-cash Departmental Expenditure Limits	-2.1	0.7
Non-cash	-0.1	0.1
Resource Annually Managed Expenditure	**-0.1**	**1.8**
of which:		
Social security benefits	-0.2	-0.2
Tax credits	0.1	0.1
Net public service pensions	0.1	0.5
National Lottery	0.1	0.0
BBC domestic services	0.0	0.1
Other departmental expenditure	-0.1	0.1
Net expenditure transfers to EC institutions	0.0	0.6
Locally-financed expenditure	1.6	-0.6
Central government gross debt interest	0.1	0.9
AME margin	0.0	-0.8
Accounting adjustments	-1.9	1.0
Public sector current expenditure	**-2.4**	**2.5**
CAPITAL EXPENDITURE		
Capital Departmental Expenditure Limits	**0.3**	**0.4**
Capital Annually Managed Expenditure	**0.0**	**-0.4**
of which:		
National Lottery	-0.1	0.1
Locally-financed expenditure	3.0	1.7
Public corporations' own-financed capital expenditure	1.5	0.3
Other capital expenditure	-0.8	-0.9
AME margin	0.0	0.8
Accounting adjustments	-3.6	-2.3
Public sector gross investment	**0.3**	**0.0**
less public sector depreciation	0.5	0.4
Public sector net investment	**0.8**	**0.4**
TOTAL MANAGED EXPENDITURE	**-2.1**	**2.5**
of which:		
Departmental Expenditure Limits	-1.3	0.9
Annually Managed Expenditure	-0.8	1.6

Central government spending in 2007-08

B.60 In-year monthly spending information is only available for central government. Provisional outturn for current expenditure in the first five months of 2007-08 is 7.4 per cent higher than in the corresponding period of 2006-07. Growth is higher in the year to date than the Pre-Budget Report estimate for the year as a whole, as a result of factors which affect the pattern of debt interest spending across the year.

B.61 Debt interest payments for the year to date are 19 per cent higher than the same period last year, largely because of the impact of higher RPI inflation on the accruing uplift of index-linked gilts payments. Although debt interest payments are expected to grow more strongly than in the Budget 2007 forecast, this growth is not expected to continue because the pattern of RPI increases as they affect the uplift in 2007-08 differs from that which affected 2006-07.

B.62 Provisional outturn data for all other current expenditure for the first five months of 2007-08 show growth of 5.7 per cent over the same period in 2006-07, lower than the 6.2 per cent increase forecast for the year as a whole.

DEL and AME analysis

B.63 The detailed allocation of resource and capital DEL is shown in Table B13, including the final CSR07 DEL allocations. The departmental groupings have been updated to reflect the machinery of government changes announced in June 2007, and outturn years restated on the basis of current departmental responsibilities. A full list of the individual departments within each group is given at the end of this document. Further details of departmental DEL settlements are given in Annex C.

B.64 The latest figures include a number of classification and budgetary changes, which have no impact on National Accounts definitions or TME. The main changes are:

- a reclassification of Nuclear Decommissioning Authority expenditure from resource to capital DEL to align with the treatment in the National Accounts;

- a movement from capital to resource DEL for the Ministry of Defence in 2007-08 offset in the accounting adjustments;

- the movement of international debt write-offs from resource to capital DEL; and

- the reclassification of interest received on student loans from DEL to AME, increasing DEL and reducing AME.

Table B13: Departmental Expenditure Limits - resource and capital budgets

	£ billion				
	Outturn	Estimate		Plans	
	2006-07	2007-08	2008-09	2009-10	2010-11
Resource DEL					
Children, Schools and Families	42.1	45.0	46.9	49.2	51.9
Health	80.3	89.7	94.0	99.9	106.4
of which: NHS England	78.4	87.6	92.6	98.5	104.8
Transport	6.9	6.7	6.4	6.5	6.7
Innovation, Universities and Skills	14.4	16.1	16.9	17.6	18.7
CLG Communities	3.6	4.3	4.4	4.5	4.7
CLG Local Government	22.5	22.8	24.7	25.6	26.4
Home Office	8.3	8.6	9.0	9.3	9.6
Justice	8.4	8.9	9.3	9.4	9.4
Law Officers' Departments	0.7	0.7	0.7	0.7	0.7
Defence	33.5	33.2	33.6	35.2	36.7
Foreign and Commonwealth Office	1.8	1.8	1.6	1.6	1.6
International Development	4.2	4.6	4.9	5.5	6.4
Business, Enterprise and Regulatory Reform	2.2	2.4	2.3	2.2	2.2
Environment, Food and Rural Affairs	3.2	3.0	2.9	3.0	3.0
Culture, Media and Sport	1.5	1.6	1.6	1.7	1.8
Work and Pensions	7.6	7.8	7.6	7.4	7.1
Scotland	22.4	23.6	24.5	25.4	26.5
Wales	11.6	12.5	13.0	13.6	14.2
Northern Ireland Executive	7.1	7.6	7.9	8.2	8.5
Northern Ireland Office	1.2	1.1	1.2	1.2	1.2
Chancellor's Departments	5.0	4.9	4.8	4.6	4.5
Cabinet Office	1.7	1.9	2.1	2.3	2.5
Independent Bodies	0.7	0.8	0.8	0.9	1.0
Modernisation Funding	-	-	0.5	0.4	0.1
Reserve	-	0.6	2.5	2.8	3.0
Unallocated special reserve[1]	-	0.8	-	-	-
Total resource DEL	**291.2**	**310.8**	**324.3**	**338.8**	**354.6**
Capital DEL					
Children, Schools and Families	4.1	5.8	6.0	6.4	7.6
Health	3.3	4.3	4.7	5.5	6.2
of which: NHS England	3.2	4.2	4.6	5.4	6.1
Transport	6.5	6.6	7.3	7.6	8.1
Innovation, Universities and Skills	1.9	1.9	2.0	2.2	2.3
CLG Communities	5.4	5.9	7.0	7.3	7.5
CLG Local Government	0.2	0.1	0.1	0.1	0.1
Home Office	0.6	0.8	0.9	0.8	0.9
Justice	0.5	0.7	0.7	0.8	0.7
Law Officers' Departments	0.0	0.0	0.0	0.0	0.0
Defence	7.1	7.1	7.9	8.2	8.9
Foreign and Commonwealth Office	0.2	0.1	0.2	0.2	0.2
International Development	0.8	0.7	0.9	1.4	1.6
Business, Enterprise and Regulatory Reform	1.1	1.2	1.2	1.2	1.2
Environment, Food and Rural Affairs	0.9	0.9	1.0	1.1	1.2
Culture, Media and Sport	0.3	0.4	1.0	0.4	0.6
Work and Pensions	0.2	0.1	0.1	0.1	0.1
Scotland	3.0	3.1	3.1	3.3	3.6
Wales	1.3	1.6	1.6	1.7	1.8
Northern Ireland Executive	0.8	1.0	1.0	1.1	1.2
Northern Ireland Office	0.1	0.1	0.1	0.1	0.1
Chancellor's Departments	0.3	0.3	0.3	0.3	0.3
Cabinet Office	0.3	0.3	0.4	0.4	0.4
Independent Bodies	0.1	0.1	0.0	0.0	0.0
Reserve	-	1.5	0.7	0.7	0.8
Total capital DEL	**39.1**	**44.7**	**48.1**	**50.7**	**55.3**
Depreciation	**9.9**	**10.8**	**11.3**	**12.1**	**13.0**
Total Departmental Expenditure Limits	**320.4**	**344.6**	**361.1**	**377.5**	**396.9**
Total Education spending	70.5	77.7	81.8	86.1	92.0

[1] This represents provisions for the costs of military operations in Iraq and Afghanistan, as well as the UK's other international obligations.

B.65 Resource budgets are divided into near-cash and non-cash elements. Near-cash is expenditure that impacts directly on the surplus on the current budget, and includes pay, procurement, and current grants. The near-cash control totals set for each department in the 2007 Comprehensive Spending Review are shown in Table B14.

B.66 Table B15 shows administration budgets by departmental group. Administration budgets are a control total in resource DEL and help drive economy and efficiency in the running of government itself by limiting expenditure on civil service pay, procurement of goods and services including professional services and consultancy, and the resource costs of assets used by civil servants. Administration budgets were reviewed and adjusted in the 2004 Spending Review to better reflect the boundary between frontline and administrative costs and ensure increased resources were focused on frontline public service, as recommended in Sir Peter Gershon's review of public sector efficiency. As part of the 2007 Comprehensive Spending Review some further spending on activities directly supporting frontline delivery has been reclassified into programme expenditure and the outturn years have been restated on the current basis to provide a consistent series. The figures here also reflect the outcome of work announced in the 2006 Pre-Budget Report to ensure departmental spending on consultancy is properly captured by the administration costs regime.

B.67 The Ministry of Defence is set an administration control total for the first time in the 2007 Comprehensive Spending Review, meaning all central government departments are now within the administration control regime.

Table B14: Near-cash in resource DEL

	£ billion				
	Outturn	Estimate		Plans	
	2006-07	2007-08	2008-09	2009-10	2010-11
Near-cash in resource DEL					
Children, Schools and Families	42.1	45.0	46.9	49.3	51.9
Health	77.7	85.8	90.8	96.5	102.7
of which: NHS England	75.7	83.7	89.5	95.1	101.2
Transport	6.4	6.2	6.2	6.2	6.1
Innovation, Universities and Skills	13.3	14.5	15.0	15.6	16.5
CLG Communities	3.5	4.1	4.2	4.3	4.4
CLG Local Government	22.5	22.8	24.7	25.6	26.4
Home Office	8.2	8.4	8.8	9.1	9.4
Justice	8.0	8.5	8.7	8.7	8.7
Law Officers' Departments	0.7	0.7	0.7	0.7	0.7
Defence	23.5	22.8	22.9	23.7	24.5
Foreign and Commonwealth Office	1.7	1.7	1.4	1.5	1.5
International Development	4.1	4.5	4.8	5.4	6.3
Business, Enterprise and Regulatory Reform	2.1	2.3	2.2	2.1	2.1
Environment, Food and Rural Affairs	2.6	2.7	2.6	2.6	2.6
Culture, Media and Sport	1.4	1.4	1.4	1.4	1.5
Work and Pensions	7.3	7.6	7.4	7.2	6.9
Scotland	21.4	22.7	23.5	24.4	25.5
Wales	11.3	12.0	12.5	13.0	13.6
Northern Ireland Executive	6.8	7.3	7.6	7.9	8.2
Northern Ireland Office	1.0	0.9	0.9	0.9	0.9
Chancellor's Departments	4.7	4.5	4.4	4.3	4.2
Cabinet Office	1.5	1.6	1.8	1.9	2.1
Independent Bodies	0.6	0.6	0.7	0.7	0.9
Modernisation Funding	-	-	0.5	0.4	0.1
Reserve	-	0.6	2.5	2.8	3.0
Unallocated Special Reserve[1]	-	0.8	-	-	-
Total near-cash in resource DEL	272.3	290.0	303.4	316.5	330.6

[1] This represents provisions for the costs of military operations in Iraq and Afghanistan, as well as the UK's other international obligations.

Table B15: Administration budgets

	£ million				
	Outturn	Estimate	Plans		
	2006-07	2007-08	2008-09	2009-10	2010-11
Administration budgets					
Children, Schools and Families	223	220	218	212	207
Health	277	277	270	264	257
Transport	295	290	282	275	269
Innovation, Universities and Skills	67	72	70	68	67
CLG Communities	294	287	281	274	267
Home Office	399	434	429	419	409
Justice	418	459	448	438	426
Law Officers' Departments[1]	60	72	74	72	72
Defence[2]	2,357	2,317	2,261	2,206	2,152
Foreign and Commonwealth Office	351	396	386	377	368
International Development	197	168	163	159	155
Business, Enterprise and Regulatory Reform	401	400	382	373	364
Environment, Food and Rural Affairs	399	437	356	347	339
Culture, Media and Sport	51	50	49	48	47
Work and Pensions	5,867	5,802	5,661	5,524	5,389
Northern Ireland Office	79	79	77	75	73
Chancellor's Departments	4,827	4,702	4,595	4,481	4,369
Cabinet Office	260	347	332	324	316
of which: Security and Intelligence Agencies2	88	89	87	85	83
Total administration budgets	**16,823**	**16,808**	**16,335**	**15,935**	**15,545**
Administration budgets as a percentage of					
Total Managed Expenditure	**3.1**	**2.9**	**2.6**	**2.5**	**2.3**

[1] Plans includes additional funding of £3.6m / £3.8m / £4.9m (2008-09 to 2010-11) on top of core adminsitration budgets for the implementation of the Fraud Review.

[2] The historical data for the MoD and the SIA are estimates. These series will be reviewed for Public Expenditure Statistical Analyses 2008.

AME **B.68** The AME forecast for the Comprehensive Spending Review period is set out here for the first time. The main assumptions underpinning the AME projections are set out in Box B1 and Table B3.

B.69 Projections for social security expenditure in 2007-08 are slightly less than at Budget 2007. Downward movements in the NAO-audited unemployment assumption have more than offset other small increases.

B.70 The 2007-08 forecast for expenditure on the Child and Working Tax Credits has increased slightly since Budget 2007. The revised projection incorporates revisions to expected average earnings growth in the population receiving tax credits, and stronger-than-expected growth in childcare costs. The increase in profile between 2007-08 and 2008-09 reflects the effects of the Budget 2007 personal tax package.

B.71 Net public service pensions expenditure is measured on a National Accounts basis, and reports benefits paid less contributions received by central government unfunded public service pension schemes. Forecast expenditure from 2007-08 reflects actuarial advice on the rate and level at which benefits are expected to come into payment, and has been updated in the light of newly available information relating to scheme demographics. The change in forecast in 2007-08 since Budget 2007 is largely due to outturn data on the level of offsetting employer and employee contributions in 2006-07 being lower than expectd. The increasing level of net expenditure across the period is largely a feature of payments to pensioners: in addition to the demographic profile, the forecast includes an increase reflecting the amount of pension commuted into lump sum by those retiring, corresponding with the higher level permitted in the simplified tax regime for pensions introduced in April 2006, as scheme rules are introduced which allow for this from 2007 onwards. This increase in spending in the near-term will be balanced by lower expenditure in the longer-term.

B.72 National Lottery figures reflect the latest view on timing of drawdown by the distributing bodies. The 2007-08 estimate is broadly unchanged from Budget 2007. The forecasts for 2008-09 to 2010-11 are consistent with projections of revenue from ticket sales.

B.73 The decreasing profile of other departmental expenditure across the CSR period largely reflects the downward trend of net expenditure from the coal health liabilities scheme. The scheme is expected to wind down from 2008-09 as the majority of claims have been processed.

B.74 Net expenditure transfers to EC Institutions, which consist of the Gross National Income (GNI) based contribution less the UK abatement, are higher than forecast at Budget 2007 for 2007-08. The main driver is the use of later information provided by the Commission on the 2008 EC Budget. The increase in 2010-11 compared with 2009-10 is due to changes in the calculation of the UK abatement from 2009, budgeted from 2010. Under these arrangements, expenditure on economic development in the new Member States will gradually be disapplied from the abatement calculation.

B.75 Locally financed expenditure mainly consists of local authority self-financed expenditure (LASFE) and Scottish spending financed by local taxation. LASFE is the difference between total local authority expenditure, net of capital receipts, and central government support to local authorities.

B.76 Outturn and forecasts for LASFE have been revised in the light of a definitional change that takes effect from this Pre-Budget Report. This change has removed adjustments that are applied to the local authorities' own data within the National Accounts, and included these adjustments instead within the accounting adjustments line. This means that the LASFE component now only reflects data returned by local authorities to the Department for Communities and Local Government and the Devolved Administrations, and there is a clear distinction between local authorities' own data and the adjustments applied to those data within the National Accounts.

B.77 Movements in forecasts for 2007-08 for LASFE since Budget 2007 reflect minor adjustments in respect of the level of reserves used, capital expenditure financed from the revenue account, and revised forecasts of council tax benefit payments. The main determinant of the LASFE forecast going forward is council tax. Council tax increases are determined by local authorities, not by government, and since changes to LASFE are broadly balanced by changes to council tax, they will have little material impact on the fiscal aggregates. The capital forecast reflects forecasts based on historical information and departmental returns on the use of capital receipts, capital expenditure financed from revenue, prudential borrowing plans, and forecast asset sales. The capital LASFE forecast also includes forecast borrowing by the Greater London Authority (GLA) to part-finance the Crossrail project.

B.78 Forecasts for central government gross debt interest payments have been revised in light of the latest economic determinant assumptions. The 2007-08 projection has increased, largely because of higher RPI inflation affecting the uplift on index-linked gilts and National Savings and Investments savings certificates. Market expectations of interest rates have also risen since Budget 2007, and these have affected the forecast for interest paid on short-term financing instruments. The fall in the level of forecast payments between 2007-08 and 2008-09 is partly the result of lower assumptions for economic determinants, and partly because of redemptions of high-coupon gilts.

B.79 Public corporations' own-financed capital expenditure (PCOFCE) is the amount of capital expenditure by public corporations that is not financed by central government. The profile for PCOFCE falls in 2007-08, largely because of scheduled net increases in government financing already included in departments' budgets.

B.80 The AME margin has been set at £1 billion, £2 billion and £3 billion for the years 2008-09 to 2010-11 respectively.

B.81 The accounting adjustments reconcile the budgeting aggregates DEL and AME with the National Accounts definition of TME, removing items that score in DEL or AME but not in TME, and adding in items included in TME but not in DEL or AME. The forecasts include a new National Accounts adjustment, which the ONS introduced in June 2007 for local authorities' imputed subsidies for the injection of equity into Housing Revenue Accounts (HRAs). This increases TME but is offset by additional HRA gross operating surplus within current receipts, and is therefore neutral across the public finances as a whole. The spending envelope for the CSR07 period has been adjusted to allow for this change, and for changes to forecast depreciation that reduce TME and reduce the public sector's gross operating surplus. The receipts offset is set out in more detail in paragraph B.34. Other changes to accounting adjustments since Budget 2007 include offsets to reflect classification and budgetary change to DELs described in paragraph B.64.

FINANCING REQUIREMENT

B.82 Table B16 presents projections of the net cash requirement by sub-sector, giving details of financial transactions that do not affect net borrowing (the change in the sub-sector's net financial indebtedness) but do affect its financing requirement.

Table B16: Public sector net cash requirement

	£ billion							
	2007-08				**2008-09**			
	General government				**General government**			
	Central government	Local authorities	Public corporations	Public sector	Central government	Local authorities	Public corporations	Public sector
Net borrowing	**38.6**	**2.7**	**-3.3**	**38.0**	**37.5**	**3.6**	**-4.7**	**36.4**
Financial transactions								
Net lending to private sector and abroad	3.1	0.1	-0.3	2.9	0.1	0.1	-0.3	-0.1
Cash expenditure on company securities	-1.9	-2.1	2.1	-1.9	-0.2	-1.8	2.1	0.0
Accounts receivable/payable	-0.1	0.2	0.3	0.4	2.6	0.2	0.3	3.1
Adjustment for interest on gilts	-4.6	0.0	0.0	-4.6	-3.8	0.0	0.0	-3.8
Miscellaneous financial transactions	-0.2	0.0	-0.6	-0.8	-0.2	0.0	0.0	-0.2
Own account net cash requirement	35.0	1.0	-1.9	34.0	36.0	2.1	-2.6	35.5
Net lending within the public sector	2.3	-1.6	-0.7	0.0	1.7	-1.2	-0.5	0.0
Net cash requirement[1]	**37.3**	**-0.6**	**-2.6**	**34.0**	**37.6**	**0.9**	**-3.1**	**35.5**

[1] *Market and overseas borrowing for local government and public corporation sectors.*

B.83 In line with the updated fiscal forecasts, the revised financing arithmetic for 2007-08 is shown in Table B17. The central government net cash requirement (CGNCR) for 2007-08 is now forecast to be £37.3 billion, a decrease of £0.3 billion from the Budget 2007 forecast. In addition, the impact of other factors set out below result in a reduction in the net financing requirement (NFR) for 2007-08 of £1.6 billion from Budget 2007, so that the NFR is now forecast to be £58.3 billion.

B.84 In order to meet the decrease in the NFR, the Debt Management Office's (DMO's) remit has been revised. The stock of Treasury bills will be marginally reduced by £0.1 billion instead of the increase of £1.5 billion forecast at Budget 2007. Gilt issuance is unchanged.

B.85 The latest financing arithmetic set out in Table B17 also takes account of the following changes since Budget 2007:

- an increase in the forecast net contribution to financing of £1.4 billion in 2007-08 from National Savings & Investments (NS&I);

- buy-backs of illiquid gilts in the secondary market by the DMO of £0.1 billion; and

- a reduction of £0.1 billion in the planned short-term financing adjustment for 2007-08.

B.86 Details of changes to the financing arithmetic and a revised financing table for 2007-08 together with information on the progress of gilts sales so far this year against the DMO financing remit can be found on the DMO's website at www.dmo.gov.uk

Table B17: Financing requirement forecast

	£ billion		
	2007-08		
	Original Remit Budget 2007	Revised Remit April 2007[1]	2007 Pre-Budget Report
Central government net cash requirement	37.6	37.6	37.3
Gilt redemptions	29.2	29.2	29.2
Financing for the Official Reserves	0.0	0.0	0.0
Buy-backs[2]	0.0	0.0	0.1
Planned short-term financing adjustment[3]	-4.2	-4.1	-4.1
Gross financing requirement	62.6	62.7	62.5
less			
Assumed net contribution from National Savings and Investments	2.8	2.8	4.2
Net financing requirement	59.8	59.9	58.3
Financed by:			
1. Debt issuance by the Debt Management Office			
(a) Treasury bills	1.4	1.5	-0.1
(b) Gilts	58.4	58.4	58.4
2. Other planned changes in short-term debt[4]			
Change in Ways & Means	0.0	0.0	0.0
3. Unanticipated changes in short-term cash position[5]	0.0	0.0	0.0
Total financing	59.8	59.9	58.3
Short-term debt levels at end of financial year			
Treasury bill stock in market hands	17.0	17.1	15.5
Ways & Means	13.4	13.4	13.4
DMO net cash position	0.5	0.5	0.5

[1] The financing arithmetic in Budget 2007 was revised on 24 April 2007 to reflect outturn data for 2006-07.

[2] Purchases of "rump" gilts which are older, small gilts, declared as such by the DMO and in which Gilt-edged Market Makers (GEMMs) are not required to make two-way markets. The Government will not sell further amounts of such gilts to the market but the DMO is prepared, when asked by a GEMM, to make a price to purchase such gilts.

[3] To accommodate changes to the current year's financing requirement resulting from: (i) publication of the previous year's outturn CGNCR; (ii) an increase in the DMO's cash position at the Bank of England; and / or (iii) carry over of unanticipated changes to the cash position from the previous year.

[4] Total planned changes to short-term debt are the sum of: (i) the planned short-term financing adjustment; (ii) Treasury bill sales; and (iii) changes to the level of the Ways & Means advance.

[5] A negative (positive) number indicates an addition to (reduction in) the financing requirement for the following financial year.

B.87 In April 2007, the Government announced that it would undertake a feasibility study into the benefits and costs of issuing a wholesale sterling Islamic financial instrument. An update on the progress of the feasibility study is provided in Box B2.

Box B2: Government sukuk issuance

In April 2007, the then Economic Secretary announced a feasibility study, to be undertaken by HM Treasury and the Debt Management Office, on the benefits and costs of the case for the Government to become a sovereign issuer of wholesale sterling Islamic financial instruments and the practical and legal implications of doing so.

The objectives of potential sukuk issuance were set out by the then Economic Secretary in a speech on 23 April 2007[a]. He said that 'We are determined to do everything we can to deliver greater opportunities for British Muslims – and also to entrench London as a leading centre for Islamic finance in the world'.

NS&I is examining separately the feasibility of the Government becoming an issuer of retail Islamic financial products and will report in Spring 2008.

The feasibility study has also considered the implications of any sukuk issuance by the Government for the Government's existing gilt and Treasury bill issuance programmes that are undertaken consistently with the debt management policy objective of minimising long-term cost, taking into account risk.

The Government has identified a number of potential benefits of sukuk issuance flowing to the City of London and to the wider community. London is already growing as a leading global gateway for Islamic financial activity, and Government sukuk issuance could further spur the development of the City as a centre for Islamic finance, boosting its ability to attract further sukuk structuring activity. In addition, it could potentially facilitate the development of a greater range of shariah-compliant retail financial products. These products would be available to all retail customers but would be of particular benefit to those British Muslims who would be otherwise unable to access routine financial services because of their faith.

The Government has also identified a number of potential costs, including the costs of structuring and launching sukuk issuance, and other costs that are dependent on the size and nature of the issuance.

The Government is urgently examining the risks associated with sukuk issuance, particularly the risks relating to price and demand. In this context, the Government is examining the feasibility of issuing sukuk that would have similar characteristics to gilts or Treasury bills. The Government is considering the features that a sukuk would need in order to be issued at the same price as a gilt or Treasury bill.

The feasibility study has identified several important structural issues that need to be resolved prior to any sukuk issuance. These issues include:

- the need for - and content of - any primary legislation to facilitate sukuk issuance;
- the identification of an asset(s) to be transferred to a special purpose vehicle (on the assumption of an ijarah structure) to facilitate sukuk issuance; and
- the tax treatment of assets upon transfer to and from a special purpose vehicle and any other taxation or regulatory issues.

The Government remains of the view that there is real potential, not only for the City of London, but also for addressing wider issues of financial inclusion, in continuing to develop policy in this area. To that end, it will hold further detailed and specific consultation. HM Treasury and the Debt Management Office will publish a consultation document later in the Autumn. Following the consultation, the Government will announce its decision and next steps including the timetable for any primary legislation.

[a] Speech by Ed Balls MP to the FSA's Principles-based Regulation Conference, 23 April 2007

PREPARING FOR LONG-TERM FISCAL CHALLENGES

B.88   The 2007 Comprehensive Spending Review identifies five areas of change that the Government will have to confront in the decade ahead, including the challenges of demographic and socio-economic change. An assessment of the long-term sustainability of the public finances should take into account not only the key challenges of the next ten years, but also look over a still longer time horizon.

B.89   The Government believes that sustainable public finances are a prerequisite to achieving high and stable rates of long-term economic growth, which are shared by all, and to ensuring that spending and taxation impact fairly between generations.

B.90   Since 2002, the Government has published the Long-term public finance report on an annual basis,[2] with the intention of providing a comprehensive analysis of long-term socio-economic and demographic developments, and their likely impact on the public finances. The focus of the report is on long-term demographic trends such as the ageing of the population or changes to the overall population size over the coming decades and as such it relies on the latest available population projections for its analysis.

New population projections   **B.91**   Up to 2005, the Government Actuary's Department (GAD) was the producer of the official population projections for the UK. This responsibility moved to the Office for National Statistics (ONS) in January 2006. The ONS will publish a new set of population projections on 23 October 2007. These projections will be based on the mid-year population estimate for 2006, which the ONS published on 22 August 2007, and on a new set of assumptions regarding the key three vital statistics: fertility, net migration and longevity. Given that ONS will publish its 2006-based population projections on 23 October 2007, the next Long-term public finance report will be published at a later date to ensure it incorporates the most up-to-date data. Updated estimates of the unfunded public service pension liability will be published alongside the next Long-term public finance report.

Long-term socio-economic and other trends   **B.92**   The Government is committed to updating and regularly reporting on its assessment of long-term fiscal sustainability, based on the most up to date information, so that the Government can make the right strategic policy decisions to address the long-term socio-economic challenges that it will face in the coming decades. For example, the structure of the UK population is projected to change dramatically over the coming decades, with only a fraction of these changes taking place over the next decade. This is illustrated by Chart B1: while the number of people aged 85 years and over is projected to quadruple over the next 50 years using the latest available population projections (GAD's 2004-based projections), the projected increase over the next decade will be much more modest. Similarly, the UK's total population is projected to increase from around 60 million at present, to 63½ million by 2017, but to near 70 million by mid-century. The projected increase over the long term is likely to create its own opportunities and challenges, which the UK will have to deal with in the decades ahead.

---

[2] See, for example, the 2006 *Long-term public finance report: an analysis of fiscal sustainability*, HM Treasury, December 2006.

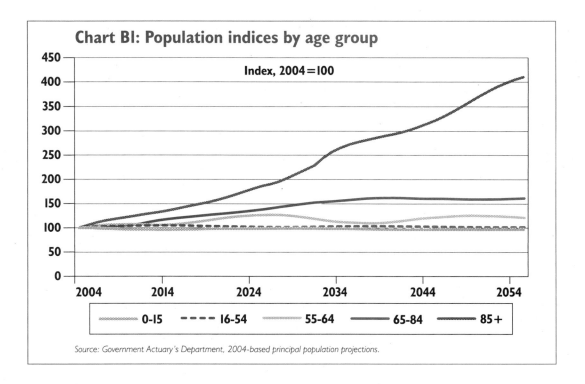

Chart BI: Population indices by age group

Index, 2004=100

0-15 · 16-54 · 55-64 · 65-84 · 85+

Source: Government Actuary's Department, 2004-based principal population projections.

B.93   Chart B2 shows the age distribution of the UK's population in 2001 and 2006. The two most prominent features of the 2001 distribution are the spike around the 55-year age group and the much larger hump around the 35-year groups. The former represents the immediate post-war baby boom, the latter the more sustained and pronounced second baby boom of the 1960s. By 2006, the large cohorts of the two baby booms had aged by five years, as represented by the shift to the right of the profile over these years. Females of the immediate post-war baby boom are now leaving the labour force and entering state pension age, with males following within the next few years. The cohorts of the second baby boom are currently at their prime in the labour market but will reach state pension age in the late 2020s to the early 2030s.

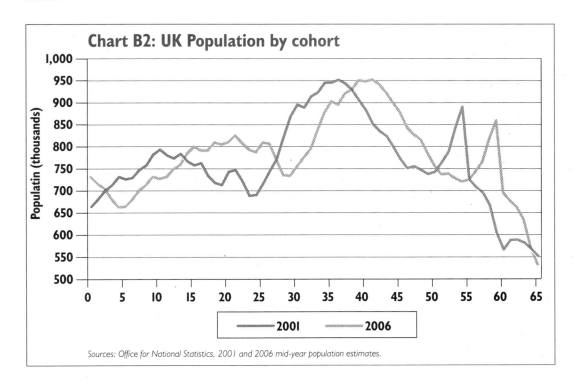

Chart B2: UK Population by cohort

Populatin (thousands)

2001 · 2006

Sources: Office for National Statistics, 2001 and 2006 mid-year population estimates.

B.94 The 2006 *Long-term public finance report* provided a detailed analysis on how employment might evolve over the coming decades. Using the cohort method of projecting employment trends and GAD's 2004-based principal population projections, the 2006 *Long-term public finance report* projected that periods of employment increases were balanced by periods of employment declines.[3] As a result of this, employment changes are projected to have a neutral effect on long-term trend growth, with productivity growth the main source of real GDP growth.

B.95 The 2006 *Long-term public finance report* showed that public spending, as a share of GDP, should increase slightly over the coming decades. A projected increase in total age-related spending explains most of this slight increase. Together, health and long-term care spending were projected to increase the most in absolute terms as a result of an ageing population. Spending on state pensions was projected to grow and public service pension spending was also projected to grow, but by a small amount, driven in part by long-term longevity. The 2006 report also projected that demographic change should lead to an increase in revenue, as a share of GDP, partially offsetting the projected increase in spending.

B.96 The Long-term public finance report uses a range of well-established techniques to assess the sustainability of the public finances. The analysis shows that the public finances are long-term sustainable in the light of demographic change, which puts the Government in a strong position to deal with the potential financial impacts arising from other long-term trends, such as climate change. The 2006 *Long-term public finance report* concluded that the public finances are sustainable in the long term and that the UK is well placed relative to many other developed countries to deal with the fiscal challenges arising from ageing populations in the future.

Table B18: Assumptions for the 2004- and 2006-based principal population projections

	Assumptions	
	2004-based	2006-based
Fertility rate[1]	1.74	1.84
Life expectancy at birth (years) in 2031		
Males	81.4	82.7
Females	85.0	86.2
Long-term annual net migration	145,000	190,000

[1] *Long-term average number of children per woman.*

Source: GAD, 2004-based principal population projections and ONS, 2006-based principal population projections.

Updated fertility, migration and longevity assumptions

B.97 On 27 September 2007, the ONS published the assumptions it will use for the 2006-based principal population projections. As Table B18 shows, the assumptions are markedly different to those used for the 2004-based population projections. The fertility rate assumption has increased, net migration has also increased from an annual 145,000 to 190,000 and assumed life expectancy at birth is now marginally higher than previously. These changes will be incorporated in the 2006-based population projections, which will be published on 23 October 2007. The next long-term public finance projections will be based on the 2006-based population projections.

---

[3] See 2006 *Long-term public finance report: an analysis of fiscal sustainability*, HM Treasury, December 2006, pages 23 to 27 for a more detailed discussion of the employment trends projected using the cohort method.

C

PUBLIC SERVICE AGREEMENTS

INTRODUCTION

C.1   Each Public Service Agreement (PSA) priority outcome is underpinned by a single Delivery Agreement shared across all contributing departments and developed in consultation with delivery partners and frontline workers. Delivery Agreements are published today and set out plans for delivery and the role of key delivery partners.[1] They also describe the small basket of national outcome-focused performance indicators that will be used to measure progress towards each PSA outcome.

C.2   The PSAs and indicators, with the Government's overarching goals, are summarised below. A subset of indicators also have specific national targets or minimum standards attached, where this is the case the indicator is highlighted with an asterisk[*] and details are set out in the relevant Delivery Agreement. All other national indicators are expected to improve against baseline trends over the course of the 2007 Comprehensive Spending Review (CSR) period.

C.3   PSAs will typically be delivered across many departments. However, in order to ensure robust accountability, one Secretary of State will be in the lead. The new Cabinet Committees announced in July[2] will drive performance by regularly monitoring progress, holding departments and programmes to account and resolving inter-departmental issues where they arise. Each PSA will also have a Senior Responsible Officer, who will chair a senior official PSA delivery board comprising all lead and supporting departments and reports to the relevant Cabinet Committee/s.

C.4   Details of the Government's Service Transformation Agreement, which will support effective delivery across the PSA set, are also set out below.

SUSTAINABLE GROWTH AND PROSPERITY

PSA 1: Raise the productivity of the UK economy[3]

- Labour productivity (output per hour worked) over the economic cycle

- International comparisons of labour productivity (per worker, per hour worked)

PSA 2: Improve the skills of the population, on the way to ensuring a world-class skills base by 2020[4]

- Proportion of people of working age achieving functional literacy and numeracy skills*

- Proportion of working age adults qualified to at least full Level 2*

- Proportion of working age adults qualified to at least full Level 3*

---

[1] Available from the HM Treasury website: http://www.hm-treasury.gov.uk/pbr_csr/pbr_csr07_index.cfm

[2] http://www.cabinetoffice.gov.uk/secretariats/downloads/committees_list.pdf

[3] Lead department: Department for Business, Enterprise and Regulatory Reform (BERR).

[4] Lead department: Department for Innovation, Universities and Skills (DIUS).

- Proportion of apprentices who complete the full apprentice framework*

- Proportion of working age adults qualified to Level 4 and above*

- Higher education initial participation rate*

PSA 3: Ensure controlled, fair migration that protects the public and contributes to economic growth[5]

- Deliver robust identity management systems at the UK border*

- Reduce the time to conclusion for asylum applications*

- Number of removals year-on-year

- Number of 'harm' cases removed as a proportion of total cases removed

- By effective management of migration, reduce the vacancy rate in shortage occupations

PSA 4: Promote world-class science and innovation in the UK[6]

- UK percentage share of citations in the leading scientific journals*

- Income generated by UK Higher Education Institutions and Public Sector Research Establishments through research consultancy and licensing of Intellectual Property*

- Percentage of UK business with 10 or more employees "innovation active"*

- Number of UK PhD completers in STEM subjects at UK Higher Education Institutions*

- Number of young people taking A-levels in Mathematics, Physics, Chemistry and Biological sciences

- UK R&D intensity in the 6 most R&D intensive industries relative to other G7 economies*

PSA 5: Deliver reliable and efficient transport networks that support economic growth[7]

- Journey time on main roads into urban areas*

- Reliability on the strategic road network

- Capacity and crowding on the rail network*

- Expected benefits of approved investments

---

[5] Lead department: Home Office (HO).

[6] Lead department: DIUS.

[7] Lead department: Department for Transport (DfT).

PSA 6: Deliver the conditions for business success in the UK[8]

- International comparisons of UK competition regime with world's best*

- International comparisons of UK corporate governance regime with world's best*

- Assessment of UK labour market flexibility

- International comparisons of UK industrial gas and electricity retail prices*

- Total cost/benefit ratio of new regulations

- Percentage by which administrative burdens are reduced across Government*

PSA 7: Improve the economic performance of all English regions and reduce the gap in economic growth rates between regions[9]

- Regional Gross Value Added (GVA) per head growth rates

- Regional GDP per head levels indexed to the EU15 average

- Regional productivity as measured by GVA per hour worked indices

- Regional employment rates

FAIRNESS AND OPPORTUNITY FOR ALL

PSA 8: Maximise employment opportunity for all[10]

- Overall employment rate taking account of the economic cycle

- Narrow the gap between the employment rates of the following disadvantaged groups and the overall rate: disabled people; lone parents; ethnic minorities; people aged 50 and over; those with no qualifications; and those living in the most deprived Local Authority wards

- Number of people on working age out-of-work benefits

- Amount of time people spend on out-of-work benefits

---

[8] Lead department: BERR.

[9] Lead department: BERR.

[10] Lead department: Department for Work and Pensions (DWP).

PSA 9: Halve the number of children in poverty by 2010-11, on the way to eradicating child poverty by 2020[11]

- Number of children in absolute low-income households

- Number of children in relative low-income households*

- Number of children in relative low-income households and in material deprivation

PSA 10: Raise the educational achievement of all children and young people[12]

- Attainment at early years foundation stage*

- Proportion achieving Level 4 in both English and Mathematics at Key Stage 2*

- Proportion achieving Level 5 in both English and Mathematics at Key Stage 3*

- Proportion achieving five A*-C GCSEs (or equivalent) at Key Stage 4 including English and Mathematics*

- Proportion of young people achieving Level 2 at age 19*

- Proportion of young people achieving Level 3 at age 19*

PSA 11: Narrow the gap in educational achievement between children from low income and disadvantaged backgrounds and their peers[13]

- Gap in attainment at early years foundation stage*

- Achievement gap between pupils eligible for Free School Meals and their peers at Key Stages 2 and 4

- Proportion of pupils progressing by 2 Levels in English and Mathematics at each of Key Stages 2, 3 and 4*

- Proportion of children in care at Key Stage 2 achieving Level 4 in English and Level 4 in Mathematics at Key Stage 2*

- Proportion of children in care achieving five A*-C GCSEs (or equivalent) at Key Stage 4*

- Proportion of young people from low-income backgrounds progressing to higher education

---

[11] Lead department: HM Treasury.

[12] Lead department: Department for Children, Schools and Families (DCSF).

[13] Lead department: DCSF.

PSA 12: Improve the health and well-being of children and young people[14]

- Breastfeeding at six to eight weeks

- Take up of school lunches

- Childhood obesity*

- Child emotional health and well-being

- Services for disabled children

PSA 13: Improve children and young people's safety[15]

- Children and young people who have experienced bullying

- Initial assessments for children's social care carried out within 7 days of referral

- Hospital admissions caused by unintentional and deliberate injuries to children and young people

- Preventable child deaths as recorded through child death review panel processes

PSA 14: Increase the number of children and young people on the path to success[16]

- 16 and 17 year olds not in education, employment or training*

- Young people participating in positive activities

- Young people frequently using drugs, alcohol or volatile substances

- Under-18 conception rate*

- First-time entrants to the Criminal Justice System aged 10-17

PSA 15: Address the disadvantage that individuals experience because of their gender, race, disability, age, sexual orientation, religion or belief[17]

- Gender gap in hourly pay

- Level of choice, control and flexibility to enable independent living

- Participation in public life by women, ethnic minorities, disabled people and young people

- Discrimination in employment

---

[14] Lead department: DCSF.
[15] Lead department: DCSF.
[16] Lead department: DCSF.
[17] Lead department: Government Equalities Office.

- Fairness of treatment by services

PSA 16: Increase the proportion of socially excluded adults in settled accommodation and employment, education or training[18]

- Care leavers at 19 in suitable accommodation

- Offenders under probation supervision and in settled and suitable accommodation

- Adults in contact with secondary mental health services in settled accommodation

- Adults with learning disabilities in settled accommodation

- Care-leavers at 19 in education, training and employment

- Offenders under probation supervision in employment

- Adults in contact with secondary mental health services in employment

- Adults with learning disabilities in employment

PSA 17: Tackle poverty and promote greater independence and well-being in later life[19]

- Employment rate age 50-69: percentage difference between this and overall employment rate

- Pensioner poverty

- Healthy life-expectancy at age 65

- Over 65s satisfied with home and neighbourhood

- Over 65s supported to live independently

STRONGER COMMUNITIES AND A BETTER QUALITY OF LIFE

PSA 18: Promote better health and well-being for all[20]

- All age, all cause (AAACM) mortality rate*

- Gap in AAACM mortality rate in disadvantaged areas*

- Smoking prevalence*

- Proportion of people supported to live independently

- Access to psychological therapies

---

[18] Lead department: Cabinet Office.
[19] Lead department: DWP.
[20] Lead department: Department of Health (DH).

PSA 19: Ensure better care for all[21]

- Patient/user experience

- Referral-to-treatment times:

  i. admitted patients*

  ii. non-admitted patients*

- Percentage of women seeing a midwife by 12 weeks

- People with long-term conditions supported to be independent and in control of their condition

- Patient-reported experience of GP access

- Healthcare acquired infection rates:

  i. MRSA*

  ii. Clostridium Difficile*

PSA 20: Increase long-term housing supply and affordability[22]

- Net additional homes provided*

- Trends in affordability

- Affordable homes delivered*

- Households in temporary accommodation*

- Efficiency rating of new homes

- Adoption of development plan documents*

PSA 21: Build more cohesive, empowered and active communities[23]

- Percentage of people who believe people from different backgrounds get on well together in their local area

- Percentage of people who have meaningful interactions with people from different backgrounds

- Percentage of people who feel they can influence decisions in their locality

- Percentage of people who feel that they belong to their neighbourhood

- Thriving third sector

- Percentage of people who participate in culture or in sport

---

[21] Lead department: DH.

[22] Lead department: Department for Communities and Local Government (CLG).

[23] Lead department: CLG.

PSA 22: Deliver a successful Olympic Games and Paralympic Games with a sustainable legacy and get more children and young people taking part in high quality PE and sport[24]

- Meet critical milestones for the venue and infrastructure*

- Maximising the physical, economic and social legacy of the Games

- Delivery of the Olympic Delivery Authority sustainability strategy

- Numbers of people taking part in programmes associated with the Games

- Children and young people's participation in sport

PSA 23: Make communities safer[25]

- Level of most serious violent crimes

- Level of serious acquisitive crimes

- Public confidence in local agencies involved in tackling crime and anti-social behaviour

- Percentage of people perceiving anti-social behaviour as a problem

- Level of proven re-offending by young and adult offenders

- Level of serious re-offending

PSA 24: Deliver a more effective, transparent and responsive Criminal Justice System for victims and the public[26]

- Effectiveness and efficiency of the Criminal Justice System (CJS) in bringing offences to justice

- Public confidence in the fairness and effectiveness of the CJS

- Victim and witness satisfaction with the CJS and the police

- Understanding and addressing race disproportionality at key stages in the CJS

- Recovery of criminal assets*

---

[24] Lead department: Department for Culture, Media and Sport.
[25] Lead department: HO.
[26] Lead department: Ministry of Justice.

PSA 25: Reduce the harm caused by alcohol and drugs[27]

- Percentage change in the number of drug users recorded as being in effective treatment

- Rate of hospital admissions per 100,000 for alcohol related harm

- Rate of drug related offending

- Percentage of the public who perceive drug use or dealing to be a problem in their area

- Percentage of the public who perceive drunk and rowdy behaviour to be a problem in their area

PSA 26: Reduce the risk to the UK and its interests overseas from international terrorism[28]

- Indicators are classified.

A MORE SECURE, FAIR AND ENVIRONMENTALLY SUSTAINABLE WORLD

PSA 27: Lead the global effort to avoid dangerous climate change[29]

- Global CO_2 emissions to 2050

- Proportion of areas with sustainable abstraction of water

- Size of the global carbon market

- Total UK greenhouse gas and CO_2 emissions*

- Greenhouse gas and CO_2 intensity of the UK economy

- Proportion of emission reductions from new policies below the Shadow Price of Carbon

---

[27] Lead department: HO.

[28] Lead department: HO.

[29] Lead department: Department for Environment and Rural Affairs (DEFRA).

PSA 28: Secure a healthy natural environment for today and the future[30]

- Water quality

- Biodiversity

- Air quality

- Marine health

- Land management: positive and negative impact of farming

PSA 29: Reduce poverty in poorer countries through quicker progress towards the Millennium Development Goals[31]

- Proportion of population below US$1 (PPP) per day

- Net enrolment ratio in primary education

- Ratio of girls to boys in primary, secondary and tertiary education

- Under-five mortality rate

- Maternal mortality ratio

- HIV prevalence among 15-49 year-old people

- Proportion of population with sustainable access to an improved water source

- The value (in nominal terms), and proportion admitted free of duties, of developed country imports (excluding arms and oil) from low income countries

PSA 30: Reduce the impact of conflict through enhanced UK and international efforts[32]

- Number of conflicts globally, in particular in sub-Saharan Africa, Europe, Central and South Asia, and the Middle East and North Africa

- Impact of conflict in specific countries and regions (Afghanistan, Iraq, Balkans, Middle East, Sierra Leone, DRC and the Great Lakes region, Horn of Africa, Nigeria and Sudan)

- More effective international institutions, better able to prevent, manage and resolve conflict and build peace

- More effective UK capability to prevent, manage and resolve conflict and build peace

---

[30] Lead department: DEFRA.

[31] Lead department: Department for International Development.

[32] Lead department: Foreign and Commonwealth Office.

SERVICE TRANSFORMATION AGREEMENT

C.5 A government-wide commitment to build services around the needs of citizens and businesses will be integral to the achievement of each of the PSA outcomes set out above. The Government has today published a Service Transformation Agreement, which underpins delivery of the whole of the new PSA framework, setting out Government's vision for building services around the citizen and specific actions for each department in taking forward this challenging agenda. The Minister for the Cabinet Office and the Chief Secretary to the Treasury will hold departments to account for delivery of these commitments as part of the overall performance management framework.

D 2007 COMPREHENSIVE SPENDING REVIEW SETTLEMENTS

Annex D sets out the 2007 Comprehensive Spending Review (2007 CSR) settlements for the main government departments including:

- Departmental Expenditure Limits (DEL) for the years 2008-09, 2009-10 and 2010-11;

- Departmental Strategic Objectives and priorities for investment and reform; and

- key elements of the departments' plans for delivering better value for money over the CSR07 period.

In addition, it provides information on:

- the overall funding provided by the 2007 CSR for devolved public services and economic development in Scotland, Wales and Northern Ireland;

- funding for the Regional Development Agencies, including plans to refocus their powers, responsibilities and accountabilities; and

- the funding provided in the 2007 CSR for local government as well as on the steps the Government is taking to provide greater flexibility for Local Authorities.

DI DEPARTMENT FOR CHILDREN, SCHOOLS AND FAMILIES

The Department for Children, Schools and Families (DCSF) was created in June 2007, to lead work across all departments to ensure that every child, regardless of circumstances, gets the best possible start in life. Budget 2007 announced an early 2007 CSR settlement for education. The 2007 Comprehensive Spending Review (2007 CSR) announces:

- **an additional £250 million in total over the CSR07 period to help ensure that all children at school are ready to learn and able to benefit from truly personalised services and support;** and

- **an additional £200 million of capital investment to accelerate the primary capital programme and newly build or entirely refurbish an additional 75 schools by 2010-11. Together with further funding of £550 million available within the existing DCSF CSR07 settlement, this will allow at least one school to be newly built in every authority by 2010-11.**

These investments, together with the settlement for the Department for Innovation, Universities and Skills, sees:

- **education spending in England rising on average by 2.8 per cent a year in real terms;**

- **UK education spending as a proportion of GDP projected to increase from 4.7 per cent in 1996-97 to 5.6 per cent by 2010-11;** and

- **per-pupil funding in maintained schools rising by almost 20 per cent in cash terms** (10 per cent in real terms) from £5,550 in 2007-08 to over £6,600 by 2010-11.

This additional investment will be accompanied by value for money reforms, realising annual net cash-releasing savings of £4.5 billion by 2010-11. Together these will provide for:

- **3500 Sure Start Children's Centres,** one in every community, by 2010;

- **extending the weekly entitlement for three and four year-olds to free early years education from 12.5 to 15 hours by 2010;** and

- **additional support for the Government's vision for personalised education,** including one-to-one teacher led tuition for over 300,000 under-attaining pupils a year in English by 2010-11, and over 300,000 pupils a year in Maths.

Achievements so far

DI.1 Improving the life-chances of children and young people, and enhancing services and support for families, has been a priority for increased investment over the last decade. Sustained investment, matched with reform, has focussed on raising standards for all, with greater support for the most disadvantaged. This has resulted in almost all three and four year-olds benefiting from free early years education, the proportion of pupils achieving five GCSEs at grades A* to C rising from 45.1 per cent in 1997 to 58.5 per cent today, and a significant increase in the number of young people continuing in education or training post-16.

Responding to challenges ahead

DI.2 A strong start in life for all children and young people is crucial in enabling them to make the transition to adulthood ready to thrive in a global economy and a 21st century society. Too many children and young people are failing to meet expected levels, with those from disadvantaged backgrounds disproportionately underperforming – only one-third of 15 year-olds on free school meals (FSM) achieve five A* to C compared to just under two-thirds of non-FSM pupils. Alongside parents and families, Government has a key role in supporting all children and young people to get the best possible start in life. DCSF aims to deliver a step change in education provision and integrated support to all children and their families and to support Government's long-term ambitions to eradicate child poverty by 2020.

Delivery of these priorities will be driven by Departmental Strategic Objectives to:

- secure the well-being and health of children and young people;
- safeguard the young and vulnerable;
- achieve world-class standards in education;
- close the gap in educational achievement for children from disadvantaged backgrounds;
- ensure young people are participating and achieving their potential to 18 and beyond; and
- keep children and young people on the path to success.

DI.3   DCSF will lead delivery of the cross-governmental Public Service Agreements (PSAs) to improve the health and well-being of children and young people, improve children and young people's safety, narrow the gap in educational achievement between children from low income and disadvantaged backgrounds and their peers, raise the educational achievement of all children and young people and increase the number of children and young people on the path to success.

RESOURCES AND REFORM

DI.4   Recognising the importance of sustained investment to ensuring all children can reach their potential, **education spending in England will rise by an average of 2.8 per cent a year in real terms** (5.5 per cent a year in nominal terms) **between 2007-08 and 2010-11.**[1] **Total spending on education in the UK will grow by £14.3 billion over the CSR07 period from £77.7 billion in 2007-08 to £92.0 billion in 2010-11, with UK education spending as a proportion of GDP projected to increase from 4.7 per cent in 1996-97 to 5.6 per cent by 2010-11.** DCSF's total budget will increase by £2.8 billion in 2008-09, £5.4 billion in 2009-10 and £9.4 billion in 2010-11.

DI.5   This additional investment will be accompanied by value for money reforms realising annual net cash-releasing savings of £4.5 billion by 2010-11. These reforms will be delivered across the full range of DCSF spending and include estimated savings of:

- over £500 million per year by 2010-11 from continuing the rollout of schools capital initiatives, including the Building Schools for the Future Programme;
- over £500 million per year by 2010-11, building on work in the 2004 Spending Review period to improve the use of resources in schools.

DELIVERING WORLD CLASS EDUCATION AND SERVICES

Children's Plan **DI.6**   The 2007 CSR announces, an additional £250 million in total over the CSR07 period to help ensure that all children at school are ready to learn and able to benefit from truly personalised services and support. Specific allocations and the detail of individual programmes will be announced by the Secretary of State for Children, Schools and Families in the Children's Plan later this year.

---

[1] Total education spending in England is made up of spending on education by DCSF, DIUS and Local Authorities.

Childcare and Early Years

DI.7 Building on the commitments set out in *Choice for parents, the best start for children: a ten-year strategy for childcare*, and supporting the Government's goal of halving child poverty by 2010, the 2007 CSR allows the Government to deliver a **nationwide network of 3,500 Sure Start Children's Centres, one in every community, by 2010**. Additional funding will also support two outreach workers in every centre serving the most disadvantaged areas, further support for fathers, and delivery of evidence based parenting programmes to 30,000 parents from 2010-11. Building on progress over the last decade to provide children the best start in life, the 2007 CSR also extends **the weekly entitlement for three and four year-olds to free early years education to 15 hours by 2010** and allows significant progress towards the Government's commitment to have a graduate level Early Years Professional in every full daycare setting by 2015, with two graduates in those settings in the most disadvantaged areas.

Disabled Children

DI.8 Disabled children are less likely to achieve as much in a range of areas than their non-disabled peers. Underpinned by £340 million of investment, the 2007 CSR provides support to empower disabled children and their families, and deliver a step change in the provision of responsive, high quality services and timely support. This includes **£35 million in total to improve access to childcare for families with disabled children and £280 million in total to deliver a significant increase in the provision of short breaks for severely disabled children over the CSR07 period.**

Personalised Learning

DI.9 The 2007 CSR will allow schools to take the next steps in raising attainment for all and narrowing the persistent attainment gaps that exist across the system. The 2007 CSR provides an additional £400 million a year by 2010-11 to enable a step change in teacher-led one-to-one support for pupils who are falling behind in English and Maths. This includes rolling out the Every Child a Reader programme – which provides higher intensity one-to-one support for five and six year-olds who are further behind in literacy – to benefit over 30,000 children a year by 2010-11; and providing a similar level of support for young children who are significantly behind in numeracy. The settlement also provides for an average of ten hours of one-to-one teacher-led tuition for over 300,000 under-attaining pupils a year in English by 2010-11 and 300,000 under-attaining pupils a year in Maths.

Extended Services

DI.10 To support the delivery of the Government's commitment that all schools should provide extended hours services by 2010, the 2007 CSR provides additional funding which, together with significant existing levels of resource across the system, will be sufficient to support extended service co-ordinators in secondary schools and clusters of primary schools. **To ensure that all pupils, regardless of income, are able to benefit from participation in a full range of extended activities, the DCSF settlement includes £217 million a year by 2010-11 to support access to two hours a week of free extended activities for pupils eligible for Free School Meals, with two weeks of free part-time provision during the holidays.**

Teachers

DI.11 Teachers are central to raising standards. Over the last decade there has been a significant increase in teacher numbers, rising to almost 435,000 in January 2007, and a substantial increase in numbers of teaching assistants and other education support staff. Building on good recruitment and retention and restored professional status, the Government will continue to invest in improving the overall quality of teaching and embedding a strong culture of ongoing professional development.

Schools Estate

DI.12 The 2007 CSR settlement sees schools capital investment rise to £8.2 billion in 2010-11, allowing the Government to continue to make good progress in transforming the school estate. The primary capital programme aims to deliver 21st century learning facilities, including high quality environments that support personalised learning and allow schools to offer a full range of extended services at the heart of their communities. The 2007 CSR announces £200 million of new investment to accelerate the programme and newly build or entirely refurbish an additional 75 schools by 2010. Together with further funding of

£550 million available within the existing DCSF CSR07 settlement, this will allow a further 275 primary schools to be built or entirely refurbished – with at least one in every local authority – by 2010-11, on top of the 400 schools covered by previously announced primary capital plans. By the end of the CSR07 period, the Government also expects 1,000 secondary schools to be benefiting from investment through the Building Schools for the Future programme. With over 200 academies open or in the pipeline by 2010-11, the Government will take the next steps in pursuing its long-term ambition for 400 academies, serving some of the most deprived areas of the country.

Young People   **DI.I3**   The 2007 CSR allows the Government to make further progress in increasing the number of young people participating in positive activities and continuing in education and training post-16 – helping to improve skills and life chances. **Money from dormant bank accounts, along with £60 million of Government investment in total over the CSR07 period, will be used to improve youth facilities, with a new or improved places for young people to go in every constituency by 2018.** Further investment will allow the Government to expand programmes of activities with personal support for disadvantaged young people, and put them in the lead in influencing and delivering activities at a local level. The 2007 CSR will also allow the Government to make further progress towards ensuring all young people can learn in ways that motivate and engage them, including **from 2008, introducing new diplomas for 14 to 19 year-olds.**

Table DI: Children, Schools and Families baseline and additions

	£ million			
	Baseline	**Additions**		
	2007-08	**2008-09**	**2009-10**	**2010-11**
Resource DEL	44,501	2,410	4,718	7,403
of which near-cash	*44,512*	*2,426*	*4,741*	*7,414*
of which administration	*195*	*−5*	*−10*	*−14*
Capital DEL	5,648	363	728	1,983
Total DEL[1]	**50,135**	**2,775**	**5,449**	**9,389**

	£ billion			
	Estimate	**Projections**		
	2007-08	**2008-09**	**2009-10**	**2010-11**
Total education (England)[2]	63.9	67.0	70.4	75.0

[1] *Full resource budgeting basis, net of depreciation.*

[2] *Total education (England) comprises spending on education by DCSF, DIUS and local authorities, and is measured consistently with international definitions from the UN classifications of the functions of government (COFOG). Actual outcomes are subject to spending decisions by local authorities.*

Table D2: UK education[1] spending

	£ billion			
	Estimate	**Projections**		
	2007-08	**2008-09**	**2009-10**	**2010-11**
Total UK education	77.7	81.8	86.1	92.0
UK education as a proportion of GDP (per cent)	5.5	5.6	5.6	5.6

[1] *UK education measured consistently with intenational definitions from the UN classifications of the functions of government (COFOG). Actual outcomes are subject to spending decisions by local authorities and devolved administrations. These figures reflect HM Treasury's latest indicative assumptions on the expenditure of local authorities and devolved administrations.*

D2 DEPARTMENT OF HEALTH

The 2007 Comprehensive Spending Review (2007 CSR) will **increase spending on the NHS by 4 per cent per year in real terms, taking its budget from £90 billion in 2007-08 to £110 billion by 2010-11. Together with value for money savings of at least £8.2 billion, and following the interim Darzi Review, this investment will enable the delivery of the Government's vision of an NHS that is fair, personalised, effective, safe, and locally accountable.** This includes:

- **improved access to GP services,** with additional resources for over 100 new GP practices in the 25 per cent of Primary Care Trusts (PCTs) with the poorest provision, and 150 new health centres open seven days a week;

- **cleaner hospitals**, with the introduction of MRSA screening for all elective patients next year, and for all emergency admissions as soon as practicable within the next three years, deep cleaning of hospitals and increased powers for matrons and ward sisters to report concerns; and

- **a more innovative NHS**, with a new Health Innovation Council to drive innovation, and fully funding the Cooksey Review recommendations, increasing Department of Health Research and Development spending to over £1 billion by 2010-11, taking the single fund for health research to £1.7 billion.

The Government remains committed to investment in adult social care. Building on the record investment over the last decade, **resources for local authorities, which provide adult social services, will be £2.6 billion higher by 2010-11 than in 2007-08, representing an annual average growth of 1 per cent in real terms.** As part of its plans to enhance services, the Government will:

- **increase direct funding for social care by £190 million** to £1.5 billion by 2010-11, including funding to enable greater personalisation of services, and more support for carers;

- **provide a personalisation, choice and control package for social care** including individual budgets, preventative projects for older people, advocacy and information services, and investment in the social care workforce; and

- **consult on reform of the public support and care system** focusing particularly on older people, to ensure a sustainable system that targets resources effectively, is affordable and promotes independence, well-being and control for those in need.

Achievements so far

D2.1 The Wanless Review of 2002 demonstrated that while the NHS of 1997 had the right system of funding, it lacked the investment and capacity needed to deliver the standards of healthcare achieved in other leading countries. Over the last decade, the Government has almost doubled real NHS funding, the largest sustained increase in NHS history. This investment has brought more staff and modernised infrastructure. In addition, overall local government funding has increased by almost 40 per cent in real terms, increasing resources for adult social care. Investment has been accompanied by reforms to ensure services respond to changing demands placed upon them. The balance of power in the NHS has fundamentally shifted towards the local level.

D2.2 Investment and reform have meant major improvements. People are living longer, healthier lives, with greater choice over how to access the services they need. In 1997, over 280,000 people were waiting more than six months for an operation; in 2007 virtually no-one waits six months, and the average wait is under six weeks. Improvements in public health, along with better treatment for cancer and heart disease, had already helped to increase life expectancy by 2.1 years for men and 1.4 years for women by 2004. Having responded to the need for more capacity, the NHS is increasingly addressing the productivity challenge – for example average length of stay in hospital has fallen to 5.5 days from 8.8 days in 1997. Social care standards have also risen. The target set for improving quality of life for older people by ensuring 30 per cent of those with intensive needs received care in their own homes was met two years early.

Responding to challenges ahead

D2.3 Substantial challenges remain for health and social care services. Public expectations rightly continue to rise. People want care that is closer to home and tailored to their specific needs. Individuals need to be supported to take control of their own care, while services need to be provided where and when they are most convenient. In the long term, increasing life expectancy and lifestyle changes pose additional challenges. Future technological developments need to be grasped to further improve the quality of life people are able to enjoy. After a decade focused on expansion and reform, the levers are now in place to lock in sustained productivity improvements to ensure further advances are delivered with value for money to the taxpayer. **Delivery of these priorities will be driven by the Departmental Strategic Objectives to:**

- **ensure better health and well-being for all: helping you stay healthy and well, empowering you to live independently and tackling health inequalities;**

- **ensure better care for all: the best possible health and social care when and where you need help giving you choice and control; and**

- **provide better value for all.**

D2.4 The Department of Health will lead on two cross-governmental Public Service Agreements (PSAs) to promote better health and well-being for all, and to ensure better care for all.

RESOURCES AND REFORM

D2.5 Building on the progress of the last ten years, and recognising the future challenges, the 2007 CSR secures the investment made by this Government and **increases spending on the NHS by 4 per cent per year in real terms, taking its total budget from £90 billion in 2007-08 to £110 billion by 2010-11.**

D2.6 This additional investment will be accompanied by value for money reforms realising annual net cash-releasing savings of at least £8.2 billion by 2010-11. It will be for individual NHS bodies to decide the best measures for their local circumstances, but an initial assessment of the more significant areas of opportunity are:

- a series of measures to change the way health services are delivered, for example improving community-based services to help those with long-term conditions avoid traumatic and expensive emergency admissions, realising net cash-releasing savings of around £500 million per year by 2010-11;

- reducing variations in productivity across the NHS by spreading new technologies and best practice across the NHS. Reducing such unnecessary variation could potentially generate net-cash-releasing savings of £1.5 billion per year by 2010-11; and

- improving procurement practices, which could realise net cash-releasing savings of up to £1bn per year by 2011.

DELIVERING BETTER HEALTH

D2.7   Value for money reforms, together with the sustained investment set out above, will deliver the resources required to achieve the Government's vision for the NHS. As set out in Lord Darzi's *Our NHS, Our Future* interim report, this is an NHS that is fair, personalised, effective, safe, and locally accountable.

A fair NHS   **D2.8**   The NHS was founded upon the values of universality and fairness. These values are as relevant today as when they were set out almost 60 years ago. Over the CSR07 period, the Government will develop a new comprehensive strategy to reduce health inequalities to ensure the NHS continues to benefit all regardless of circumstances.

A personalised NHS   **D2.9**   It is increasingly necessary for the NHS to respond to the needs and wants of each individual. This settlement allows further progress to be made on making the health service fit around patients, rather than patients having to fit around the service. Access to GP services will be improved with the development of greater flexibility in opening hours. and additional resources for over 100 new GP practices in the 25 per cent of PCTs with the poorest provision and 150 GP-run health centres, open seven days a week, 8am to 8pm.

D2.10   Access to services is to be further improved with the delivery of a maximum 18 week wait from GP referral to hospital treatment by the end of 2008, virtually ending long waits. In addition, better support is to be provided for those with long term conditions to live independently and control their own condition, including by moving towards a care plan for every person with a life limiting illness.

An effective NHS   **D2.11**   The 2007 CSR will also enable the NHS to deliver outcomes for patients that are among the best in the world – saving more lives and improving the quality of life. To achieve this, a new Health Innovation Council is to be set up to increase innovation across the NHS. The 2007 CSR also announces full funding of the Cooksey Review recommendations to maximise translation of research excellence into health and economic benefit. This will take Department of Health Research and Development spending to over £1 billion by 2010-11 and taken with the £682 million from the Medical Research Council, will help to take the single fund for health research to £1.7 billion.

A safe NHS   **D2.12**   It is fundamental that the NHS of the future is as safe as it can possibly be, giving patients and the public full confidence in the care they receive. The 2007 CSR will deliver this with funding for visibly cleaner hospitals, increased powers for matron to target on MRSA and the introduction of MRSA screening for all elective patients next year, and for all emergency admissions as soon as practicable within the next three years.

A locally accountable NHS   **D2.13**   Healthcare will continue to evolve at a rapid pace, and the NHS will have to change over the coming years to keep up. However, where change is necessary, the Government wants to empower staff locally to lead change and innovate, engaging early and effectively with the public and ensuring that change is based on best clinical evidence and meets local needs.

Adult social care **D2.14** Adult social care continues to play a central role in protecting and promoting independence and well-being amongst the elderly and some of the most vulnerable groups in society. Investment in Local Authorities, which provide adult social services, will be £2.6 billion higher by 2010-11 than in 2007-08. Growth in the Department's social care funding which directly supports new policy initiatives will increase by £190m taking it to £1.5 billion by 2010-11. This funding will enable social services to build on progress already made in developing personalised services that give service users and their carers greater choice and control over the way in which their needs are met. In particular this investment will enable:

- further expansion of care tailored to the individual, including individual budgets, subject to a thorough evaluation to be completed in 2008. This will build on progress made so far in enabling people to stay as independent and in control of their lives as possible;

- continued investment in prevention, enabling service users to retain their independence and improve their quality of life. This includes expanding the Partnership for Older People's Projects; and

- NHS residential accommodation for those with learning disabilities to be phased out, with individuals being supported to live independently in their own homes in communities.

D2.15 The Government also plans to consult on reform of the public support and care system focusing on older people, to ensure a sustainable system that targets resources effectively, is affordable and promotes independence, well-being and control for those in need.

Table D3: NHS England baseline and additions

	£ million			
	Baseline	**Additions**		
	2007-08	**2008-09**	**2009-10**	**2010-11**
Resource DEL	86,848	5,793	11,651	17,985
of which near-cash	*83,796*	*5,680*	*11,266*	*17,354*
Capital DEL	4,177	412	1,175	1,909
Total DEL[1]	**90,352**	**6,078**	**12,545**	**19,454**

[1] *Full resource budgeting basis, net of depreciation.*

Table D4: Adult social care baseline and additions

	£ million			
	Baseline	**Additions**		
	2007-08	**2008-09**	**2009-10**	**2010-11**
Resource DEL	1,205	32	88	190
of which near-cash	*1,191*	*32*	*88*	*190*
Capital DEL	121	0	0	0
Total DEL[1]	**1,314**	**32**	**88**	**190**

[1] *Full resource budgeting basis, net of depreciation.*

Table D5: Food Standards Agency baseline and additions

	£ million			
	Baseline	**Additions**		
	2007-08	**2008-09**	**2009-10**	**2010-11**
Resource DEL	144	–4	–7	–10
of which near-cash	*141*	*–3*	*–7*	*–10*
Capital DEL	1	0	0	0
Total DEL[1]	**143**	**–3**	**–7**	**–10**

[1] *Full resource budgeting basis, net of depreciation.*

Table D6: Department of Health[1] and Food Standards Agency baseline and additions

	£ million			
	Baseline	**Additions**		
	2007-08	**2008-09**	**2009-10**	**2010-11**
Resource DEL	88,198	5,822	11,732	18,165
of which near-cash	*85,129*	*5,709*	*11,347*	*17,534*
of which administration	*277*	*–7*	*–13*	*–20*
Capital DEL	4,299	412	1,175	1,909
Total DEL[2]	**91,809**	**6,107**	**12,626**	**19,634**
	£ billion			
	Estimate	**Projections**		
	2007-08	**2008-09**	**2009-10**	**2010-11**
Total UK public sector health spending[3]	104.8	111.1	118.6	126.7

[1] *Department of Health comprises NHS England and adult social care.*

[2] *Full resource budgeting basis, net of depreciation.*

[3] *UK public sector health spending measured consistently with international definitions from the UN classifications of the functions of government (COFOG). Actual outcomes are subject to spending decisions by devolved administrations.*

D3 DEPARTMENT FOR TRANSPORT

> The 2007 Comprehensive Spending Review (2007 CSR) **confirms the 2¹/₄ per cent annual real increase in the Department for Transport's (DfT) programme budget set out in the overall Long Term Funding Guideline for transport announced in the 2004 Spending Review.**[1] This increase in funding over the CSR07 period will be accompanied by value for money reforms delivering annual net cash-releasing savings of £1.8 billion by 2010-11, releasing funds from within the department's budget to invest in transport priorities. **The 2007 CSR also extends the 2¹/₄ per cent real growth in the Long Term Funding Guideline to 2018-19, meaning that over the 20 years from 1997 UK spending on transport will have more than doubled in real terms.** Together these resources will allow DfT to:
>
> - **commence main construction of Crossrail,** as part of an agreement with Transport for London (TfL), with grants from DfT of over £5 billion and the first services expected to run from 2017;
> - **provide £15 billion of Government funding in the rail network over five years** to enhance capacity, including longer trains in and around major cities, the Thameslink upgrade in London, and removal of pinch points on key inter-urban lines;
> - **take forward road pricing,** including support for local schemes and work to establish whether large scale distance-based charging is technically feasible while safeguarding privacy; and
> - introduce **free off-peak bus travel to all residents in England over the age of 60 and eligible disabled people** from 1 April 2008.

Achievements so far

D3.1 The Department for Transport's objective is to deliver reliable and efficient transport networks that support economic growth and improved productivity. Over the last decade a 70 per cent real increase in transport spending, coupled with reforms to delivery, has ensured significant improvements to the performance of the transport network. DfT has completed more than 100 road schemes which has helped alleviate congestion. More people are travelling further by rail than at any time since the 1940s, and bus use is increasing year on year for the first time in decades. DfT has also made safety one of its key priorities, resulting in a reduction in the number of adults and children killed or seriously injured in road accidents by a third and a half respectively since 1998.

Responding to challenges ahead

D3.2 The Eddington Transport Study[2] set out the UK's long-term transport needs and a far-reaching programme of reform for the Department to implement to ensure transport investment meets the challenges of sustaining the UK's economic productivity, growth and stability, within the context of the Government's commitment to sustainable development. This settlement will allow DfT to respond to increasing demands on the transport system over the coming decades, with the Department working better to understand, plan for, and influence how transport systems and usage may develop. The Government's aim is transport that works for everyone – this means a transport system which balances the needs of the economy, the environment and society. DfT aim to address these challenges by identifying sustainable solutions as efficiently as possible. In this context, DfT has set itself the following Departmental Strategic Objectives over the CSR07 period:

---

[1] Average annual real growth for the Department as a whole will be 2.1 per cent rather than 2.25 per cent due to savings in DfT's administration budget.

[2] *The Eddington Transport Study, Main Report: Transport's role in sustaining the UK's productivity and competitiveness*, Sir Rod Eddington, December 2006.

- to sustain economic growth and improved productivity through reliable and efficient transport networks;

- to improve the environmental performance of transport;

- to strengthen the safety and security of transport; and

- to enhance access to jobs, services and social networks, including for the most disadvantaged.

D3.3 DfT will also lead delivery of the cross-governmental Public Service Agreement (PSA) to deliver reliable and efficient transport networks that support economic growth.

RESOURCES AND REFORM

D3.4 Building on the 6.1 per cent annual average real increase in transport spending in the last decade, the 2007 CSR confirms the $2\frac{1}{4}$ per cent per year real increase in DfT's programme expenditure set out in the Long Term Funding Guideline for transport at the time of the 2004 Spending Review. Furthermore, the settlement confirms that growth in the Long Term Funding Guideline will be extended to 2018-19 at $2\frac{1}{4}$ per cent per year in real terms, to enable the Department to continue to plan future transport spending over a ten year horizon. Meeting the Long-Term Funding Guideline will mean that, over the two decades to 2018-19, UK public spending on transport will have more than doubled in real terms.

D3.5 To focus these increased resources on the highest priority areas, this increase in funding will be accompanied by value for money reforms generating net cash-releasing savings of £1.8 billion per year by 2010-11. The programme includes:

- securing rail savings through further efficiency improvements in Network Rail's management processes and cost control together with robust and effective franchise agreements realising net cash-releasing savings of £1,238 million per year by 2010-11. For example, Network Rail will be given further cost efficiency targets for the period 2009-14 on top of the 31 per cent saving target that Network Rail is required to achieve by 2009; and

- standardising and tightening major maintenance contracts which will contribute to annual net cash-releasing savings by the Highways Agency of £144 million by 2010-11.

DELIVERING RELIABLE AND EFFICIENT TRANSPORT NETWORKS

D3.6 This combination of sustained increases in funding and continued efficiency gains will allow DfT to pursue its ambitions across the full range of programmes and meet the challenges set out in the Eddington Study. In taking forward its investment programme, the Department will prioritise growing and congested urban areas and their catchments; key inter-urban corridors and major international gateways. It will do this by putting in place a policy and decision-making framework incorporating Sir Rod Eddington's strategic recommendations into its Departmental Strategics Objectives. DfT will publish further details shortly.

Crossrail **D3.7** The 2007 CSR makes provision for Crossrail (see box 4.3), a significant addition to the capital's transport infrastructure which support London's growth and the future prosperity of the UK. Crossrail will be taken forward by Cross London Rail Links, which will become a wholly owned subsidiary of Transport for London, subject to certain rights retained by DfT to reflect the Department's contribution to the project. DfT will contribute around one third of the total estimated cost of up to £16 billion, with the remainder being contributed through Crossrail fare up to payers (used to service debt) and the private sector. Subject to Royal Assent, main construction will be underway in 2010, with the first services commencing in 2017.

Rail services **D3.8** The High Level Output Specification for the passenger railway[3] was published by DfT in July alongside the Statement of Funds Available, which set out that £15.3 billion of government support was available over five years for the railways in England and Wales. This will enable new capacity on the railway while improving safety, reliability and reducing rail's carbon footprint. Subject to the Office of Rail Regulation's determinations, the Department aims to deliver significant improvements in rail services for 2009-14 including new capacity through the Thameslink programme, provision of new inter-city trains, a programme of station improvements and raising the level of punctuality to at least 92 per cent.

Roads and road pricing **D3.9** The 2007 CSR provides for significant investment in roads, consistent with the conclusions of the *Eddington Transport Study*, to support the needs of a growing economy. It allows provision for increasing capacity on a number of the nation's most congested roads. Furthermore, the 2007 CSR confirms the Government's commitment to use resources from the Transport Innovation Fund to tackle congestion through supporting local road pricing schemes, subject to appropriate proposals coming forward. The Government will be looking in detail at proposals received, including for accompanying public transport.

Concessionary bus travel **D3.10** Buses remain a key means of making facilities accessible to older and disabled people in particular. DfT will provide over £200 million a year to allow for the introduction of an enhanced national bus concession entitling residents of England aged 60 and over, and eligible disabled people, to free off-peak local bus travel anywhere in England from 1 April 2008.

Table D7: Department for Transport baseline and additions

	£ million			
	Baseline	Additions		
	2007-08	2008-09	2009-10	2010-11
Resource DEL	6,274	169	219	399
of which near-cash	5,678	479	472	380
of which administration	290	-8	-15	-21
Capital DEL	6,660	633	954	1,452
Total DEL[1]	**12,556**	**842**	**1,219**	**1,909**

	£ billion			
	Estimate	Projections		
	2007-08	2008-09	2009-10	2010-11
Total UK transport[2]	20.0	21.9	22.5	23.7

[1] *Full resource budgeting basis, net of depreciation.*

[2] *UK transport measured consistently with international definitions from the UN classifications of the functions of government (COFOG). Actual outcomes are subject to spending decisions by local authorities and devolved administrations. These figures reflect HM Treasury's latest indicative assumptions on the expenditure of local authorities and devolved administrations.*

[3] *Delivering a Sustainable Railway – White Paper CM 7176. www.dft.gov.uk*

D4 DEPARTMENT FOR INNOVATION, UNIVERSITIES AND SKILLS

The Department for Innovation, Universities and Skills (DIUS) was created by the Prime Minister in June 2007 to drive forward delivery of the Government's long-term vision to make Britain one of the best places in the world for science, research and innovation, and to deliver the ambition of a world-class skills base. The 2007 Comprehensive Spending Review (2007 CSR) **provides DIUS with a total budget of £18.7 billion in 2008-09, £19.7 billion in 2009-10 and £20.8 billion in 2010-11, equivalent to 2.2 per cent annual average real growth.** This includes:

- **increasing investment in the UK's public science base, which will rise by an annual average rate of 2.5 per cent in real terms over the CSR07 period,** meeting the commitment in the ten-year framework; and

- spending **on Higher Education and Skills[1] rising by 2.0 per cent in real terms over the CSR07 period.**

This additional investment will be **accompanied by value for money reforms generating annual net cash-releasing savings of £1,543 million by 2010-11.** Together these provide for the delivery of:

- **£5.3 billion a year by 2010-11 to increase adult skills and apprenticeships** and make progress against the Leitch ambitions for world-class skills;

- **total public funding for business innovation led by the Technology Strategy Board of over £1 billion over the CSR07 period**; including co-funding of at least £120 million committed by the Research Councils, and co-funding of £180 million committed by the Regional Development Agencies;

- **more than £1 billion in additional funding for Higher Education** over the CSR07 period to increase participation, maintain the per student funding level and provide more generous student support for 250,000 students;

- **£682 million for the Medical Research Council (MRC) contribution to the £1.7 billion fund to implement the recommendations of the Cooksey Review** of health research; and

- **implementation of the Sainsbury Review** to further improve the UK science and innovation system.

Achievements so far

D4.1 Over the last decade the Government has made real progress in delivering against its objectives of an excellent science base and world-class skills levels. The UK remains second only to the US in global scientific excellence despite increased global competition and there are continuing positive trends in knowledge transfer activities. The UK skills base also compares well with other OECD countries in terms of higher-level skills.[2] The number of home and overseas students has increased by over 400,000 in the last ten years while completion rates have been maintained at a high level by international standards. At the lower skill levels, over 1.7 million adults have improved their basic skills since 2001. Since 1997 the proportion of adults qualified to at least level 2 (five or more GCSEs Grade A* to C) has increased by over 9 percentage points to 73.9 per cent.

---

[1] Includes spending on science Higher Education.
[2] Equates to university degree level and above.

Responding to challenges

D4.2 The global economy is changing at an unprecedented rate and in all countries businesses are under pressure to move up the value chain. While globalisation brings new opportunities both for employers and individuals, it also brings the challenge of succeeding against highly skilled, lower wage competitors. The Treasury commissioned two independent reviews to inform the Government's response to these challenges: the Sainsbury Review of Science and Innovation; and the Leitch Review of the UK's long-term skills needs. Implementing the conclusions of these reviews are a key priority for DIUS going forward and delivery will be driven by the Departmental Strategic Objectives to:

- accelerate the commercial exploitation of creativity and knowledge, through innovation and research, to create wealth, grow the economy, build successful businesses and improve quality of life;

- improve the skills of the population throughout their working lives to create a workforce capable of sustaining economic competitiveness, and enable individuals to thrive in the global economy;

- build social and community cohesion through improving social justice, civic participation, and economic opportunity by raising aspirations, and broadening participation, progression and achievement in learning and skills;

- pursue global excellence in research and knowledge, promote the benefits of science in society, and deliver science, technology, engineering and mathematics skills in line with employer demand;

- strengthen the capacity, quality and reputation of the Further and Higher Education systems and institutions to support national economic and social needs; and

- encourage better use of science in Government, foster public service innovation, and support other Government objectives which depend on the DIUS expertise and remit.

D4.3 DIUS will also lead delivery of the cross-governmental Public Service Agreements (PSAs) to promote world-class science and innovation in the UK; and improve the skills of the population, on the way to ensuring a world-class skills base by 2020.

RESOURCES AND REFORM

D4.4 To ensure the UK maintains its position as one of the best locations in the world for science, research and innovation, and has the skilled workforce it needs to compete in the global economy, the total DIUS 2007 CSR settlement provides 2.2 per cent annual average real growth in expenditure over the CSR07 period, from £18 billion in 2007-08 to £20.8 billion in 2010-11. This will ensure that:

- total public investment in the science base will rise by 2.5 per cent from £5.4 billion to £6.3 billion by 2010-11 meeting the commitment in the ten-year framework to increase investment in the public science base at least in line with the trend growth rate of the economy; and

- total spending on Higher Education (HE) and Adult Skills[3] will rise by 2.0 per cent from £14.2 billion in 2007-08 to £16.4 billion by 2010-11.

---

[3] This includes DIUS funding for research and knowledge transfer in English Universities as in Table D8.

D4.5 This additional investment will be accompanied by value for money reforms generating annual net cash-releasing savings of £1,543 million by 2010-11. The programme consists of a number of initiatives including:

- a continuation of the Research Council's value for money programme which will reduce the costs of Research Council institutes, raise the level of co-funding, and support the reprioritisation of research programmes, generating annual net cash releasing savings of £243 million by 2010-11;.

- the reprioritisation of funding for innovation within the ring-fenced Technology Programme generating annual net cash releasing savings of £9 million by 2010-11 to be channelled towards the activities of the Technology Strategy Board; and

- by 2010-11 reprioritising about £100 million a year of HE funding to increase and widen participation, by focusing public funding mainly on students participating in the system for the first time.

WORLD-CLASS INNOVATION, UNIVERSITIES AND SKILLS

Science and innovation **D4.6** Over the CSR07 period the Government will continue to meet the commitment to increase investment in the public science base by an annual average rate of 2.5 per cent in real terms. The CSR07 settlement will allow the Government to continue to deliver against its ambitions of sustaining and improving the UK's excellent science base, and facilitate the translation of research into business innovation and economic growth. Further detail can be found in Chapter 4; key points include:

- **funding for the Medical Research Council budget of £682 million** by 2010-11 to support excellence in medical research and help deliver a range of new priorities, including increased support for translational research and clinical trials to implement the recommendations of the Cooksey Review. This will form part of the single health research fund to be managed by the new Office for the Strategic Coordination of Health Research (OSCHR);

- **Research Councils ensuring that their activities support a broad range of interdisciplinary research challenges**, including a major contribution to a £1 billion programme on "Living with Environmental Change", and increased investment in key areas of national importance such as energy research and stem cells; and

- **a boost to funding for knowledge transfer programmes**, including the Higher Education Innovation Fund (HEIF) which will receive £150 million a year by 2010-11 to strengthen links between academia and business and help take research to the market. HEIF will also be more clearly focused on business facing universities.

Technology Strategy Board **D4.7** The business-led Technology Strategy Board (TSB) has a key role in supporting business R&D and innovation by identifying investment priorities in areas of technology which have the potential to drive future economic growth. Building on the emerging recommendations of the Sainsbury Review, Budget 2007 set out an enhanced remit for the TSB, with greater independence from Government to deliver a national, business-focused innovation strategy across all areas of the economy. To support this vision, the TSB became an executive Non-Departmental Public Body (NDPB) of DIUS on 1 July 2007, and the TSB budget will rise from £197 million in 2007-08 to £267 million by 2010-11. Together with co-funding of at least £120 million over the CSR period committed by the Research Councils, and co-funding of £180 million committed by the Regional Development Agencies, total public support for business innovation in support of the Technology Strategy will amount to over £1 billion over the CSR period.

The Sainsbury Review **D4.8**   The Sainsbury Review reported in October 2007 and made recommendations to further improve the science and innovation system in the UK. Taking these recommendations forward will be a priority for DIUS over the CSR07 period. Further details on the conclusions of the Sainsbury Review can be found in Chapter 4.

Skills **D4.9**   The DIUS 2007 CSR settlement will allow total funding for adult skills and apprenticeships to rise to around £5.3 billion a year by 2010-11, delivering 3.7 million adult qualifications over the CSR07 period. In July 2007 the Government published *World Class Skills: Implementing the Leitch Review of Skills in England*, which set out how it is taking forward the Leitch Review's recommendations with the additional resources made available in the CSR. The document set out the progress the Government provisionally expected to be able to make in improving skill levels in England. These trajectories form the basis for the new skills PSA.

D4.10   Underpinning the new, greater ambitions for improving the skills of the workforce, the Government will deliver a programme of reform to improve quality, enhance responsiveness to individual and employer demand and to focus the skills system on training that has clear economic value. The proportion of public funding for adult skills that is demand led will be increased and **expenditure on the employer demand-led Train to Gain service is expected to rise from £460 million in 2007-08 to over £900 million in 2010-11.** More detail on the Government's plans for implementing the Leitch Review can be found in Chapter 4.

Higher Education **D4.11**   The additional resources for education announced in the 2007 CSR will enable continued progress towards the Government's ambitions to increase participation in higher education, including exploring new ways of delivering higher-level skills in the workplace and helping to deliver the higher level skills business needs to innovate and compete. The Government will also maintain per student spending levels in real terms over the CSR07 period. This, together with the introduction of variable tuition fees, and continued capital investment, will enable higher education institutions to become more independent and better resourced. Alongside this, the Government will increase the generosity of student maintenance grants, provide more choice around the repayment of loans and greater certainty at an earlier age about what financial support potential students can expect. This will help raise participation in higher education, particularly amongst students from poorer backgrounds, opening up the benefits of higher education to a wider number of people.

Table D8: Innovation, Universities and Skills baseline and additions

	£ million			
	Baseline	Additions		
	2007-08	2008-09	2009-10	2010-11
Resource DEL	16,039	849	1,610	2,654
of which near-cash	*14,471*	*545*	*1,135*	*2,067*
of which administration	*72*	*-2*	*-3*	*-5*
Capital DEL	2,057	-67	148	203
Total DEL[1]	**17,986**	**747**	**1,706**	**2,792**
	£ million			
	Estimate	Projections		
	2007-08	2008-09	2009-10	2010-11
Total UK science spending[2]	5,397	5,608	5,903	6,287
of which:				
DIUS science budget	*3,383*	*3,525*	*3,746*	*3,971*
DIUS funding for research and knowledge transfer				
in English Universities	*1,655*	*1,710*	*1,775*	*1,926*
UK science spending as a proportion of GDP				
(per cent)	**0.38**	**0.38**	**0.38**	**0.39**

[1] *Full resource budgeting basis, net of depreciation.*
[2] *Actual outturns are subject to spending decisions by the devolved administrations. Excludes non-cash items.*

D5 DEPARTMENT FOR COMMUNITIES AND LOCAL GOVERNMENT

The 2007 Comprehensive Spending Review (2007 CSR) **delivers 2.9 per cent real growth per year to the Department for Communities and Local Government's (CLG's) budget over the CSR07 period taking CLG's total budget from £10.3 billion in 2007-08 to £12.1 billion in 2010-11.** This sustained increase in funding will be **accompanied by value for money reforms generating annual net cash-releasing savings of over £880 million by 2010-11.** Together, over the period, these provide for the delivery of:

- **progress towards achieving the Government's ambition of at least 240,000 net additional homes per annum in England by 2016;**

- **a 50 per cent increase in construction of new social rented houses to reach 45,000 units per year by 2010-11,** with a goal to reach 50,000 in the next spending review period;

- **£1.7 billion of targeted funding over the CSR07 period for infrastructure in Growth Areas, the Thames Gateway, New Growth Points and eco-towns, including £300 million to continue the Community Infrastructure Fund;**

- **£500 million over the CSR07 period for the new Housing and Planning Delivery Grant,** to incentivise local authorities to improve housing supply and planning for housing;

- **£2 billion for neighbourhood and local renewal programmes,** with a new strategic approach strengthening the emphasis on economic development and promoting strong communities; and

- **£50 million for places where community relations face challenges from new patterns of diversity,** to support the settled community and enable the integration of new arrivals.

Achievements so far

D5.1 CLG's aim is to create sustainable communities - places where people want to live and which promote opportunity and a better quality of life. CLG has made significant gains in these areas. Responding to the housing needs and aspirations of a growing population, housing supply is at its highest level since 1988 and there are over one million fewer social sector non-decent homes.

Responding to challenges ahead

D5.2 Population and household growth, driven by rising life expectancy, smaller household size and migration, will increase pressures on services and infrastructure such as housing in the years ahead. To meet the social and economic challenges of globalisation, CLG will work to equip communities at the regional, city and local level, putting 'place' at the heart of public policy making, through strengthened local governance and leadership. In this context, CLG has set itself the following Departmental Strategic Objectives for the CSR07 period:

- support local government that empowers individuals and communities and delivers high quality services efficiently;

- improve the supply, environmental performance and quality of housing that is more responsive to the needs of individuals, communities and the economy;

- build prosperous communities by improving the economic performance of cities, sub-regions and local areas, promoting regeneration and tackling deprivation;

- develop communities that are cohesive, active and resilient to extremism;

- provide a more efficient, effective and transparent planning system that supports and facilitates sustainable development, including the Government's objectives in relation to housing growth, infrastructure delivery, economic development and climate change; and

- ensure safer communities by providing the framework for the Fire and Rescue Service and other agencies to prevent and respond to emergencies.

D5.3 CLG will lead delivery of the cross-governmental Public Service Agreement (PSA) to build more cohesive, empowered and active communities and improve long-term housing supply and affordability.

RESOURCES AND REFORM

D5.4 CLG's predecessors received significant growth in previous Spending Reviews (with annual average growth of 5.2 per cent and 3.3 per cent in the 2002 and 2004 Spending Reviews respectively), and the 2007 CSR locks in these historical increases and raises spending in real terms by 2.9 per cent over the CSR07 period, taking CLG's total budget from £10.3 billion in 2007-08 to £12.1 billion in 2010-11.

D5.5 This enables increased investment to support housing growth, new social housing and low cost home ownership, as well as continuing investment in decent homes, housing market renewal pathfinder and neighbourhood and local renewal programmes.

D5.6 These resources will be accompanied by value for money reforms generating annual net cash-releasing savings of over £880 million by 2010-11. The programme consists of initiatives including:

- savings estimated at over £730 million from new affordable housing by 2010-11, achieved by utilising Housing Association capacity to allow for more borrowing to finance affordable housing, and the Housing Corporation refining its investment programme;

- continuing the momentum for modernisation in the Fire and Rescue Service to deliver savings of £110 million by 2010-11 through effective risk management and improved procurement methods; and

- achieving a smaller, more strategic central department with delivery functions devolved to the new Homes and Communities Agency and a more streamlined Government Office network to generate savings of £43 million by 2010-11.

DELIVERING SUSTAINABLE COMMUNITIES

D5.7 The Government is committed to creating places where people want to live and work, now and in the future. Recognising that housing growth alone does not create flourishing communities, the Government will ensure that commitments to increase housing supply are supported by the necessary investment in social, transport and environmental infrastructure to meet the diverse needs of existing and future populations.

Housing supply and infrastructure

D5.8 The Government has set a target to increase housing growth to at least 240,000 net additional homes per year by 2016. This would deliver two million homes by 2016 and a further million by 2020. The 2007 CSR provides:

- £1.7 billion of targeted funding over the three year period for infrastructure in Growth Areas, the Thames Gateway, New Growth Points and eco-towns, including £300 million to roll forward the Community Infrastructure Fund.

- £500 million of incentives over the three year period via the Housing and Planning Delivery Grant to drive improvements in housing supply and ensure that by 2011 Local Planning Authorities have the necessary development plan documents in place to support housing delivery.

Planning reform

D5.9 Building on the Barker Review of Planning[1] and taking forward the Planning White Paper[2], the 2007 CSR provides funding of over £175 million over the period to increase the efficiency and effectiveness of the planning system, including implementation of reforms to the planning regime for major infrastructure, improving the capacity of Local Planning Authorities, sector-led support and ensuring the planning system effectively contributes towards combating climate change.

Affordable homes

D5.10 Building on the 50 per cent increase in social housing supply funded in the 2004 Spending Review, the 2007 CSR will provide for another 50 per cent increase, delivering 45,000 units of social housing per year by 2010-11. Government will be investing over £6.5 billion in social housing over the next three years, supported by the realisation of savings arising from greater efficiencies and better use of housing association assets. It will also directly assist 120,000 households to enter homeownership by 2010-11.

Homes for all

D5.11 The Government will ensure all have access to decent housing, through:

- **reducing the number of households in temporary accommodation by 50 per cent by 2010-11**, compared with the end of 2004;

- **the Decent Homes programme**, which by 2010-11 will have reduced the number of non-decent social rented homes by a further 500,000; and

- **the Supporting People programme**, with continuing investment ensuring that disadvantaged and vulnerable groups receive the help and support they need, and a reformed allocation formula to better match need.

Prosperous communities

D5.12 The Review of sub-national economic development and regeneration (SNR) recommended reforms that place local government at the heart of creating prosperous communities. CLG will support Local Authorities in this role, continuing to lead on regeneration and renewal across government and setting a clear tasking framework for the new Homes and Communities Agency.

D5.13 To support the most deprived areas **the 2007 CSR provides over £2 billion for neighbourhood and local renewal.** This includes continuing the New Deal for Communities partnerships, a new programme to strengthen communities during estate transformation and a new enterprise and renewal fund to target resources more intensively according to neighbourhood deprivation. In line with the recommendations in the SNR, the new fund will have a stronger emphasis on tackling worklessness, promoting enterprise and improving skills, and will include a reward element to strengthen incentives to improve performance.

---

[1] http://www.hm-treasury.gov.uk./media/3/A/barker_finalreport051206.pdf

[2] http://www.communities.gov.uk/documents/planninganbuilding/pdf/320546

D5.14 For communities to thrive, economic prosperity needs to be accompanied by a shared sense of purpose and belonging in which communities are empowered. Increasing diversity has brought enormous economic benefits, but that change and new migration patterns have also created challenges. In light of recommendations from the Commission on Integration and Cohesion, CLG will work with local partners to help create communities in which people from different backgrounds develop a shared sense of belonging and citizenship.

D5.15 Many people do not believe they can influence decisions that affect their localities, undermining local democracy and reducing satisfaction with local services. To give people a real sense of civic power, CLG will be taking forward an ambitious community empowerment programme to reconnect citizens with local public institutions. The challenge is to spread good practice established by many Local Authorities, so that more communities can benefit and local democracy can thrive. CLG will lead work across government to increase participation in a range of services; change attitudes and perceptions; and improve local public services and quality of life.

The Fire and Rescue Service **D5.16** The 2007 CSR provides sustained investment in the Fire and Rescue Service (FRS) to improve fire safety and prevention, build on progress in reducing accidental domestic fire related deaths, and strengthen the FRS's national fire resilience capability, through delivery of the New Dimension civil resilience programme, Fire Link radio communication, and Fire Control infrastructure projects.

Table D9: CLG Communities baseline and additions

	£ million			
	Baseline	Additions		
	2007-08	2008-09	2009-10	2010-11
Resource DEL	4,224	127	293	436
of which near-cash	4,096	102	224	353
of which administration	287	-6	-13	-20
Capital DEL	6,105	870	1,232	1,419
Total DEL[1]	**10,281**	**995**	**1,523**	**1,839**

	£ billion			
	Estimate	Projections		
	2007-08	2008-09	2009-10	2010-11
Housing UK[2]	12.0	12.5	13.1	13.7
of which housing investment	8.1	8.7	9.1	9.5
Housing England	8.8	9.1	9.6	10.0
of which housing investment	6.0	6.4	6.7	7.0

[1] *Full resource budgeting basis, net of depreciation*

[2] *UK and England Housing and Community Amneties measured consistently with international definitions from the UN classification of the functions of government (COFOG). Actual outturns are subject to spending decisions by local authorities.*

D6 LOCAL GOVERNMENT

The 2007 Comprehensive Spending Review (2007 CSR) ensures that local government can better deliver high quality public services, promote sustainable economic development, and empower individuals and communities. The settlement will enable local authorities to keep council tax rises low, and the Government expects the overall increase to be well under 5 per cent in each of the next three years.

Over the last ten years, Government grants to local government have increased by 39 per cent in real terms. The 2007 CSR grows resource DEL **for local government at an average 1 per cent per year in real terms over the next three years**. In addition, provision has been made in Department for Transport budgets of over £200 million a year from 2008-09 to support delivery of a national scheme for concessionary bus fares through local government. These increases in resources will be underpinned by an ambitious **value for money programme, realising annual net cash-releasing savings of £4.9 billion by 2010-11**. An additional £150 million will support the delivery of this efficiency programme. Together this will enable local government to deliver:

- **improved, modern, and personalised public services that meet rising individual expectations**, including reforms to improve services for families in need and children in care; proposals to promote independence for old and vulnerable people; and increasing the rate of recycling and composting household waste to 40 per cent by 2010; and

- **stronger local leadership in economic development and neighbourhood renewal**, with resources for a reformed Local Authority Business Growth Incentive Scheme.

The 2007 CSR will also deliver greater flexibility for local authorities to meet local priorities and improve local areas by:

- removing ring-fencing and other controls from grants totalling over **£5 billion by 2010-11**;

- streamlining performance management through **a single set of 198 performance indicators** for all outcomes that local government delivers alone or in partnership, and **no mandatory targets** in Local Area Agreements; and

- **introducing new powers** for Local Authorities. To invest in economic development through business rate supplements, subject to clear accountability to business.

Achievements so far
D6.1 The 2006 Local Government White Paper, *Strong and Prosperous Communities*, set out the Government's vision of local government providing stronger local leadership, raising local prosperity and providing public services that meet individuals' needs. As the next step in delivering this vision and empowering local government to take up the place-shaping role set out in the Lyons Inquiry, the 2007 CSR significantly advances the Government's agenda of devolution to the local level.

D6.2 Sustained increases in funding over the last decade matched with reforms have delivered significant enhancements to the efficient provision of public services at the local level such as the extension of direct payments in social care and allowing deprived families free school transport. Councils' performance has improved such that in the Comprehensive Performance Assessment (CPA), results for single tier and county councils announced in February 2007 showed that no councils are in the bottom CPA category, and 79 per cent of councils achieved one of the top two star ratings.

Challenges ahead **D6.3** Over the next decade local authorities will face new challenges: long-term demographic changes will place rising demands on adult social care; meeting European Union environmental commitments will accelerate the need to radically reduce landfill for household waste; and local councils will play a vital and increasing role in shaping cohesive communities. Rightly, there are also rising expectations from citizens for modern and personalised public services.

Economic development and regeneration **D6.4** The changing pace of economic growth in the context of increasing globalisation also means prosperity will increasingly depend on the ability of local areas to develop and maintain competitive advantage. The *Review of sub-national economic development and regeneration (SNR)* clarified and strengthened the definition of local government's role in promoting local economic growth and set out the functions which the Government believes local authorities should undertake to fulfil this role. The SNR set out how the Government intends to strengthen incentives and powers, for example through reforms to the Local Authority Business Growth Incentive scheme (LABGI) and through bringing forward proposals for business rates supplements. These reforms will be backed up with greater devolution from Regional Development Agencies and focused support for capacity-building.

Clear incentives to promote economic growth at local and sub-regional levels

The SNR concluded there are considerable opportunities for local authorities to play a stronger role in economic development and neighbourhood renewal. The Review concluded that further reform was needed to improve the flexibilities and incentives for local authorities to work with business to identify opportunities for growth and to take the necessary steps to make their areas more attractive to business investment.

Following the SNR's recommendations, the Government is announcing detailed proposals to strengthen and simplify the incentives for local authorities to take a leading role in economic development and regeneration by publishing today:

- *Building better incentives for local economic growth,*[1] an issues paper which sets out the Government's commitment to creating **a permanent incentive for councils that encourages sustainable economic growth fully integrated with the local government finance system.** The Government will work closely with the Local Government Association and Local Authorities, so that the new approach builds on the lessons of the existing LABGI scheme. The new incentive will be phased in from 2009-10, with funding of £50 million doubling to £100 million in its second year; and

- *Business rates supplements – a White Paper,* on the introduction of **a power for Local Authorities to raise and retain supplements on the local business rate.** Further details are set out in Chapter 4.

DELIVERING VALUE FOR MONEY THROUGH LOCAL GOVERNMENT

D6.5 Over the last ten years, Government grants to local government have increased by 39 per cent in real terms. The 2007 CSR grows resource DEL for local government by 1 per cent a year on average in real terms over the CSR07 period, alongside an ambitious value-

---

[1] *Building better incentives for local economic growth,* HM Treasury and CLG, October 2007.

[2] *Business rate supplements: a White Paper,* HM Treasury and CLG, October 2007.

for-money programme that will see local government deliver savings of 3 per cent per year. This will provide the resources to enable local authorities to deliver improving services while maintaining the low council tax rises of recent years, and the Government expects the overall increases in council tax to be well under 5 per cent in each of the next three years.

Value for money reform   **D6.6**   The Value for Money Delivery Plan published alongside the 2007 CSR shows that £4.9 billion of annual net cash-releasing value for money savings will be achieved by 2010-11 through:

- business process improvements and collaboration initiatives, which could deliver up to £1.8 billion annual net cash releasing savings by 2010-11;

- smarter procurement, which could deliver up to £2.8 billion annual net cash releasing savings by 2010-11. There will be significant investment in order to support this activity; and

- better asset management which could deliver up to £300 million net cash releasing savings per annum by 2010-11.

D6.7   To support the delivery of these savings, the Government is providing an additional £150 million for efficiency support over the CSR07 period. A new Improvement and Efficiency Strategy will also be developed between local and central government and published later this year. This strategy will set out how wider improvement and efficiency resources can be best utilised through a collaborative approach to improvement, addressing underperformance that targets key priorities.

Making resources flexible   **D6.8**   *Strong and Prosperous Communities* set out a clear framework for determining the allocation of funding to increase flexibility and allow local authorities to meet local priorities more efficiently. From 2008 onwards, the presumption for all revenue funding is that it will be delivered through Revenue Support Grant. Where this is not possible for distributional reasons, funding may be distributed through a specific grant delivered through an area-based grant (previously known as a Local Area Agreement grant). Only where a programme is particularly novel, or expenditure has little or no discretionary element at the local level, would any ring-fence be appropriate. In line with this commitment, the Government is meeting its ambition, set in Budget 2007, to deliver a significant reduction in the level of funding provided through specific and ring-fenced grants such that in total over £5 billion will be provided through area-based grant or mainstreamed into Revenue Support Grant by 2010-11.

A simpler performance framework   **D6.9**   In line with the commitments made in 2004 Spending Review to reduce and rationalise the performance-monitoring burden on local authorities, on which *Strong and Prosperous Communities* built last year, the 2007 CSR announces:

- a single, balanced and coherent set of priority outcomes for local government working alone or in partnership, as set out in the relevant Public Service Agreements and Departmental Strategic Objectives;

- a single set of 198 national indicators to manage performance delivery outcomes. The Secretary of State for Communities and Local Government will announce details of these indicators which will replace all other performance indicators set by central government; and a commitment that

- any and all targets reflecting national priorities – to a maximum of 35 – will be negotiated through Local Area Agreements.[1] There will be no mandatory targets for Local Area Agreements nor any other target setting mechanism for outcomes local government is delivering alone or in partnership.

---

[1] Plus 17 statutory educational attainment and early years targets from DCSF

D6.10 To ensure that the new approach to Local Area Agreements is properly embedded with local partners working together to deliver ambitious, cross-cutting targets, the 2007 CSR also announces a third round of reward grant at a level that will maintain effective incentives whilst recognising that partnerships are now significantly stronger as a result of previous rounds of investment. The Government will set out the level of funding available in November 2007, and will then test with local stakeholders the model for distribution of reward funding with a view to finalising it in January 2008.

Asset management **D6.11** Local authorities have a key role in delivering the Government's fixed asset disposal target of £30 billion by 2010-11 in addition to financial asset sales including student loans and are forecast to achieve total asset sales of around £24 billion. To support this, the Department of Communities and Local Government have developed an asset management programme proposing improving local authority capacity, updating existing guidance and working with the Audit Commission to place greater weight on asset management in the local government performance framework.

SPENDING PLANS

Table D10: CLG Local Government baseline and additions

	£ million			
	Baseline	Additions		
	2007-08	2008-09	2009-10	2010-11
Resource DEL	23,714	986	1,888	2,695
of which LG programmes	*594*	*619*	*632*	*546*
of which Net AEF[1]	*23,120*	*24,081*	*24,920*	*25,763*
of which LABGI[2]	*–*	*–*	*50*	*100*
Capital DEL	143	–49	–29	–51
Total DEL[3]	**23,857**	**937**	**1,859**	**2,644**

[1] *Net Aggregate External Finance comprises Revenue Support Grant (RSG) and National Non-Domestic Rates (NNDR).*

[2] *Local Authority Business Growth Incentive scheme.*

[3] *Full resource budgeting basis, net of depreciation.*

THE HOME OFFICE, MINISTRY OF JUSTICE AND LAW OFFICERS' DEPARTMENTS

> The Home Office, Ministry of Justice, and Law Officers' Departments all received early 2007 Comprehensive Spending Review (CSR) settlements, which gave these departments more time to plan their long-term strategy and facilitated the transfer of responsibilities and resources associated with the creation of the Ministry of Justice on 9 May 2007.
>
> The 2007 CSR confirms the following settlements:
>
> * additional resources of £220 million a year by 2010-11 have been made available for the Home Office as part of the cross-government CSR07 settlement for counter-terrorism, increasing its budget from £9.2 billion in 2007-08 to £10.3 billion in 2010-11, equivalent to average real growth of 1.1 per cent a year;
> * the Ministry of Justice's budget will rise from £9.5 billion in 2007-08 to £9.7 billion in 2010-11, together with modernisation funding of over £100 million for the transformation of the courts and tribunals service; and
> * the Law Officers' Departments are taking forward an ambitious value for money programme which will see their budget fall by 3.2 per cent in real terms over the CSR07 period, supported by £19 million in modernisation funding.
>
> Together with value for money reforms generating annual net cash-releasing savings of over £2.5 billion by 2010-11, these settlements provide for the delivery of:
>
> * a comprehensive strategy to **reduce the risk to the UK and its interests overseas from international terrorism;**
> * a **new crime strategy** with a stronger focus on serious violence and more freedom and flexibility for local partners and the frontline;
> * the establishment of a new **National Fraud Strategic Authority, Lead Police Force** and **National Fraud Reporting Centre** to strengthen efforts in tackling fraud;
> * a **robust approach to serious and violent offenders with 9,500 new prison places,** of which 8,500 will be in place by 2012;
> * a **new alcohol strategy** focusing on the groups which cause the most harm and a **new drugs strategy to be published in April 2008 to improve prevention and treatment;**
> * **investment in neighbourhood policing** to ensure it is embedded across the country, enabling forces to better respond to local concerns, increase intelligence and build up trust; and
> * **managed migration, harnessing its benefits while further securing the UK's borders** with increased investment in a new e-Borders system to count people coming in and going out of the country, and implementation of a new points-based migration system that will ensure the UK gets the skilled migrants it needs for economic growth.

Responding to challenges ahead

D7.1 The Government is committed to building a tolerant and just society, underpinned by safer and stronger communities. Over the last decade it has delivered sustained investment coupled with reform to deliver these objectives, helping deliver a reduction in crime of around one third in the last ten years. Prison capacity has increased by 20,000 places since 1997. The Crown Prosecution Service (CPS) and police are working more closely together to ensure the charge is right first time, and over 1.4 million offences were brought to justice in the last year, an increase of 40 per cent since March 2002. The number of people in drug treatment has more than doubled. In 1998 the Government legislated to incorporate the European Convention on Human Rights so that everyone can enforce their human rights through the UK courts. And the introduction of firmer, faster and fairer immigration and asylum systems has increased border security while ensuring the UK economy continues to benefit from migration.

Responding to challenges ahead

D7.2 However, a more mobile and diverse society poses new challenges to the criminal justice system. A range of complex and interconnected trends and risks, both at home and abroad, will shape the safety and security of UK citizens over the next decade. The threat to the UK from terrorist attack remains high, requiring a co-ordinated response across departments to protect the public's saftey. The misuse of drugs and alcohol continues to be among the biggest drivers of crime, requring continued efforts to tackle both the causes and the anti-social behaviour that can result. Migration is delivering greater economic benefits to the UK than ever before, but this must be accompanied by concerted action to prevent abuse of immigration laws.

HOME OFFICE

D7.3 To strengthen the UK's capacity to deal with the real and unprecedented threat of terrorism, the Prime Minister announced in March 2007 a strengthened role for the Home Secretary, and the creation of the Office for Security and Counter-terrorism within the Home Office. The subsequent changes to the structure of the Home Office in May 2007 have focused the department more clearly on the Government's objectives for crime, counter-terrorism and immigration. Over the CSR07 period the Home Office will deliver the following Departmental Strategic Objectives to:

- help people feel secure in their homes and local communities;

- cut crime, especially violent, drug and alcohol related crime;

- lead visible, responsive and accountable policing;

- protect the public from terrorism;

- secure our borders and control migration for the benefit of our country;

- safeguard people's identity and the privileges of citizenship; and

- support the efficient and effective delivery of justice.

D7.4 The Home Office will also lead delivery of the cross-governmental Public Service Agreements (PSAs) to make communities safer; reduce the risk to the UK and its interests overseas from international terrorism; reduce the harm caused by alcohol and drugs; and ensure controlled, fair migration that protects the public and contributes to economic growth.

Resources and reform

D7.5 The early settlement for the Home Office announced at Budget 2006 locked in the historically high funding of the last decade, enabling the Home Office to retain the cash-releasing savings from its ambitious value for money programme worth an annual £1.4 billion by 2010-11. With the help of the new National Police Improvement Agency, the police service is identifying and building on the impressive results of existing pilots to drive out cash-releasing savings of over £900 million and improve performance across the service. On top of these resources and savings, the CSR07 counter-terrorism settlement provides the Home Office with an additional £220 million a year by 2010-11, delivering overall increases in the department's budget of 1.1 per cent a year in real terms over the CSR07 period.

MINISTRY OF JUSTICE

D7.6   The Ministry of Justice was created on 9 May 2007. It assumed the functions of the former Department for Constitutional Affairs (DCA), alongside responsibility for the National Offender Management Service and trilateral responsibility for the Office for Criminal Justice Reform. The Ministry of Justice has set the following Departmental Strategic Objectives:

- support a vigorous democracy in which everyone can influence decisions which affect their lives;

- support the efficient and effective delivery of justice;

- help to protect the public and reduce re-offending;

- work to create a culture of rights and responsibilities so both can be delivered effectively; and

- help to avoid and resolve civil and family disputes.

D7.7   The Ministry of Justice will also lead delivery of the cross-governmental Public Service Agreement (PSA) to deliver a more effective, transparent and responsive criminal justice system for victims and the public.

Resources and reform

D7.8   Resource for prisons and probation have increased by over 40 per cent in real terms since 1997, with resources this year 8 per cent higher than 2006-07, funding an increase in prison capacity of 20,000 places and 7,000 more probation workers. The early settlement for the Home Office and the subsequent transfer of prisons and probation to the Ministry of Justice locked in this record investment with funding transferring for the CSR07 years in line with 2007-08 levels in real terms. Over the CSR07 period, the Ministry of Justice, building on plans from the DCA, will be taking forward value for money programmes generating annual net cash-releasing savings of over £1 billion by 2010-11. This allows the Ministry to continue to deliver on its priorities in within budgets falling by 1.7 per cent a year in real terms over the CSR07 period. The value for money programme includes reforms in the Probation Service to improve processes and ensure all probation boards deliver as efficiently as the best performers. Reform of legal aid will also deliver annual net cash-releasing savings of £193 million by 2010-11.

LAW OFFICERS' DEPARTMENTS

D7.9   The Law Officers' Departments have set the following Departmental Strategic Objectives:

- Crown Prosecution Service – to bring offenders to justice, improve services to victims and witnesses and promote confidence, by applying the code for Crown Prosecutors, adopting a proportionate approach to determine which offenders should be charged and which should be diverted from court, and by ensuring the firm and fair presentation of cases in court;

- Revenue and Customs Prosecutions Office – to continue to be an effective and independent prosecuting authority which commands the confidence of the public, the judiciary and the legal profession;

- Serious Fraud Office – to investigate and prosecute cases of serious or complex fraud in England and Wales, thus contributing to deterring fraud in England and Wales, sustaining the delivery of justice and the rule of law and maintaining confidence in the UK's business and financial institutions; and

- Treasury Solicitor's Department – to provide high quality legal services to enable clients to operate effectively within the law, maximise the value of legal services, minimise legal risk and achieve best outcomes.

Resources and reform

D7.10   Over the CSR07 period, the Law Officers' Departments will be taking forward value for money programmes generating annual net cash-releasing savings of £79 million by 2010-11. Together with £19 million of modernisation funding, this programme will allow the departments to continue to deliver on their priorities with budgets falling by 3.2 per cent in real terms over the CSR. The value for money programmes include the Crown Prosecution Service generating savings of more than £34 million by 2010-11 through streamlining and improving operational processes.

DELIVERING ON PRIORITIES

Counter   **D7.11**   The creation of the Office for Security and Counter-Terrorism will enable the Home
terrorism   Office to lead more effectively the cross government effort to reduce the risk of international terrorism in the UK. The Department will continue to work closely with the Security and Intelligence Agencies, other government departments and international partners.

Crime   **D7.12**   The Government's new crime strategy, *Cutting Crime, a new partnership 2008-11*, sets out a more holistic approach to tackling crime, from prevention through to rehabilitation, with a stronger focus on tackling serious violence, and continued pressure on anti-social behaviour. It describes a more mature relationship with local partners, allowing crime reduction agencies much greater flexibility on how they respond to local priorities. Alongside this, a new £50 million fund will give the police access to modern crime fighting technology such as mobile fingerprinting devices.

Fraud **D7.13** Building on the recommendations of the Fraud Review, the Government is providing an additional £11 million by 2010-11 to establish a National Fraud Strategic Authority, Lead Police Force, and National Fraud Reporting Centre. These bodies, working with existing agencies, will enable the UK to develop for the first time a managed programme that attacks fraud through the entire pipeline of deterrence, prevention, detection, investigations, sanctions and redress, promoting a strong anti-fraud culture across government, industry and society.

Prisons **D7.14** The Government has announced that a further 9,500 prison places will be made available, and firm plans are already in place to deliver 8,500 of these by 2012. Investment in probation has allowed an expansion of tough and effective community sentences, supported by a 30 per cent increase in staff numbers. The Government will continue to invest in reducing reoffending and protecting the public. Through the development of offender management and much closer partnership working at national, regional and local levels, the Ministry of Justice will build on the reduction in reoffending already achieved, The Government has asked Lord Carter of Coles to conduct a review of the prison estate, the efficiency of HM Prison Service, and sentencing. He will report later this year.

Drugs and alcohol **D7.15** Drug misuse can perpetuate the social exclusion of users and families, and is a key driver of crime. Research shows that retention in effective treatment can reduce criminality among users by up to 50 per cent. Since 1998, there has been a 128 per cent increase in the treatment population, giving England one of the largest drug treatment programmes of any large Western country. The current 10 year strategy ends in 2008 and a new drugs strategy will be developed following a national consultation with key stakeholders and communities. The updated alcohol strategy *Safe. Sensible. Social. The next steps in the alcohol strategy*, builds on progress so far and will focus on the minority of drinkers who cause or experience the most harm to themselves, their communities and their families.

Neighbourhood Policing **D7.16** The Government is committed to rolling out Neighbourhood Policing Teams in every neighbourhood across England and Wales by 2008, supported by Police Community Support Officers. This will enable the police to better understand and address local concerns and priorities, building trusting relationships with communities to facilitate better flows of intelligence, and ensure that the police work with other local delivery agencies to ensure effective management of neighbourhoods.

Managed Migration **D7.17** Migration delivers huge economic benefits to the UK through growth, employment and tax revenues. Alongside maximising these benefits the Government must ensure the UK border is secure and that the immigration laws are respected. The Government set out its plans to deliver on these objectives in the reform document *Fair, Effective, Transparent and Trusted*, which was published by the Border and Immigration Agency in July 2006. The Government is delivering a points-based system for managed migration which will facilitate the migration of those whose skills are valuable to the UK economy, or who seek to study in the UK. It will also increase the use of technology at the border, including biometrics to ensure those who come to the UK have a right to do so. Investment of over £400 million in a new e-Borders system will allow people to be counted in and out of the country. In addition, a new Unified Border Force will strengthen the powers and surveillance capability of the agencies who work to control immigration, tackle crime and facilitate trade and travel.

Table D11: Home Office[1] baseline and additions

	£ million			
	Baseline		Additions	
	2007-08	2008-09	2009-10	2010-11
Resource DEL	8,577	468	716	1,010
of which near-cash	*8,351*	*492*	*745*	*1,048*
of which administration	*440*	*–11*	*–21*	*–31*
Capital DEL	803	50	–21	50
Total DEL[2]	**9,214**	**546**	**728**	**1,101**

[1] *Includes Assets Recovery Agency.*
[2] *Full resource budgeting basis, net of depreciation.*

Table D12: Ministry of Justice baseline and additions

	£ million			
	Baseline		Additions	
	2007-08	2008-09	2009-10	2010-11
Resource DEL	9,170	162	211	270
of which near-cash	*8,539*	*114*	*141*	*175*
of which administration	*459*	*–11*	*–21*	*–33*
Capital DEL	688	4	92	57
Total DEL[1]	**9,465**	**140**	**256**	**259**

[1] *Full resource budgeting basis, net of depreciation.*

Table D13: Law Officers' Departments baseline and additions

	£ million			
	Baseline		Additions	
	2007-08	2008-09	2009-10	2010-11
Resource DEL	728	–3	–9	–14
of which near-cash	*717*	*–3*	*–9*	*–14*
of which administration	*72*	*2*	*0*	*0*
Capital DEL	13	0	0	0
Total DEL[1]	**732**	**–3**	**–9**	**–15**

[1] *Full resource budgeting basis, net of depreciation.*

D8 MINISTRY OF DEFENCE

> The 2007 Comprehensive Spending Review (2007 CSR) continues the longest period of sustained real increases in Ministry of Defence (MoD) expenditure in almost three decades by **providing for 1.5 per cent average annual real growth over the three years to 2010-11**. This increase in funding, together with value for money reforms generating annual net cash-releasing savings of £2.7 billion by 2010-11, enables the MoD to:
>
> - **enhance conventional capability across the Armed Forces** including two new aircraft carriers for the Royal Navy, protected vehicles for the Army, and further Air Transport capability for the RAF;
>
> - **fund the renewal of Britain's nuclear deterrent** while ensuring that this does not come at the expense of the conventional capability our Armed Forces need; and
>
> - **invest £550 million in new and refurbished accommodation** for servicemen and women and their families, drawing on anticipated receipts from the sale of Chelsea barracks.
>
> In addition to the planned expenditure accounted for in this three-year settlement, the Government will continue to meet the additional costs of military operations in Iraq, Afghanistan and elsewhere from the Reserves.

Achievements so far   **D8.1**   The MoD's aim is to defend the United Kingdom and its interests and strengthen international peace and stability. The events of 11 September 2001 confirmed a shift in the global security dynamic and brought into clear perspective the strategic challenges facing the UK. The MoD and the Armed Forces continue to adapt and develop to meet these challenges. The nature of recent operations in Iraq, Afghanistan, the Balkans and Sierra Leone has borne out the underlying judgements in the Strategic Defence Review (SDR) and subsequent policy papers – that the UK needs flexible, adaptable, deployable forces with a balanced range of capabilities.

Responding to challenges   **D8.2**   In the short term, contributing to success in Afghanistan and Iraq will remain the MoD's highest priority. The existence of failed and failing states, international terrorism and the proliferation of weapons of mass destruction will also continue to pose major security challenges. The requirement for deployable, flexible, agile and capable Armed Forces will therefore remain crucial, as will the need to prepare for the longer-term.

D8.3   The MoD will also contribute over the CSR07 period to the delivery of the cross-governmental Public Service Agreements (PSAs) to reduce the impact of conflict through enhanced UK and international efforts, and reduce the risk to the UK and its interests overseas from international terrorism. These will be underpinned by Departmental Strategic Objectives to:

- achieve success in the military tasks we undertake at home and abroad;

- be ready to respond to the tasks that might arise; and

- build for the future.

RESOURCES AND REFORM

D8.4 The 2007 CSR demonstrates the Government's continued commitment to the Armed Forces, and increases planned spending on defence by an average of 1.5 per cent a year in real terms over the CSR07 period, with total planned defence spending rising from £32.6 billion in 2007-08 to a total budget of £36.9 billion by 2010-11. Taken together with the last three Spending Reviews, in 2000, 2002 and 2004, this represents a decade of sustained real growth in planned defence expenditure. Between 2001-02 and 2006-07, the Government has also provided £6.6 billion, on top of the core defence budget, to meet the costs of its international obligations in Iraq, Afghanistan and elsewhere.

D8.5 These resources will be accompanied by value for money reforms generating annual net cash-releasing savings of £2.7 billion by 2010-11, building on savings of £2.8 billion during the 2004 Spending Review period. Initiatives during the CSR07 period will include:

- a 5 per cent year-on-year reduction in the MoD's administrative overhead, including a 25 per cent saving in MoD's Head Office. This will contribute towards generating annual net cash-releasing savings in Corporate Enabling Services of £369 million by 2010-11;

- the continued simplification of single Service budgetary and headquarters structures, including the merger of Land Command and the Adjutant General's Command; and

- the merger of the Defence Logistics Organisation and the Defence Procurement Agency to form Defence Equipment and Support. This will contribute towards generating annual net cash-releasing savings of £253 million by 2010-11.

STRENGTHENING UK DEFENCE

Equipment and support   **D8.6** The MoD spends approximately £12 billion annually on buying and supporting fighting equipment. It is essential that this money is spent efficiently and effectively so that the UK's Armed Forces continue to be among the very best in the world. The Defence Industrial Strategy (DIS), announced in 2005 and to be updated shortly, provides the framework for better decision-making about equipment acquisition and support. Continued investment in military equipment includes the placing of contracts on future Aircraft Carriers for the Royal Navy, additional protected vehicles for the Army, and further Air Transport capability for the RAF.

Nuclear deterrent   **D8.7** In December 2006 the Government announced plans to sustain a credible nuclear deterrent capability into the 2020s and beyond.[1] Parliament endorsed the Government's decisions in March 2007, in particular to commence the procurement process for a new class of nuclear powered submarines to replace the current Vanguard class and to participate in a programme to extend the life of the Trident D5 missile. The Government has also made clear that it will continue the programme of investment in sustaining capabilities at the Atomic Weapons Establishment, both to ensure we can maintain our existing nuclear warhead for as long as necessary and to enable development of a replacement warhead should that be necessary. The additional resources being made available to defence will fund all the additional activity necessary over the CSR07 period to implement those decisions. The Government has committed that the renewal of the UK's nuclear deterrent will not come at the expense of the conventional capability that our Armed Forces need.

---

[1] The Future of the United Kingdom's Nuclear Deterrent, Cm 6994, December 2006.

Asset disposals and accommodation **D8.8** The MoD has disposed of over £1.5 billion of surplus assets since the 2002 Spending Review and will continue to contribute to the Government's overall target of disposal of £30 billion in surplus assets. By the end of the CSR07 period the MoD will have disposed of over £3 billion in surplus assets. Over 80 per cent of the disposal sites have been sold on for housing development, including former RAF bases and Army barracks such as Oakington and Bracknell. Investment will also continue over the CSR07 period to improve the standard of accommodation for the Armed Forces, including £550 million for single and family accommodation, drawing on anticipated receipts from the sale of Chelsea barracks. The MoD will also publish an implementation plan by May 2008 setting out its plans for the release of electromagnetic spectrum to the market. The MoD will begin the release of the bands identified in 2008 and will release a significant proportion of its spectrum holdings during 2009 and 2010.

Military operations **D8.9** The net additional cost of military operations will continue to be met from the Reserves and provision has also been made for the continued purchase of Urgent Operational Requirements. In addition, in order to target resources at short-term, quick impact development projects in 'hot' conflict zones, a Stabilisation Aid Fund of £269 million over the CSR07 period has also been created to be jointly managed by the MoD, Foreign and Commonwealth Office and Department for International Development.

Table D14: Ministry of Defence baseline and additions

	£ million			
	Baseline	Additions		
	2007-08	2008-09	2009-10	2010-11
Resource DEL	32,618	984	2,547	4,084
of which near-cash	22,007	885	1,727	2,450
of which administration	2,317	-56	-111	-165
Capital DEL	7,404	467	783	1,467
Total DEL[1]	**32,579**	**1,478**	**2,786**	**4,311**

[1] Full resource budgeting basis, net of depreciation.

D9

FOREIGN AND COMMONWEALTH OFFICE

Over the 2007 Comprehensive Spending Review (2007 CSR) period the Foreign and Commonwealth Office (FCO) will take forward an ambitious value for money reform programme, generating net cash-releasing savings of £144 million by 2010-11. This will allow the FCO to continue to deliver the Government's international priorities within a total budget rising from £1.6 billion in 2007-08 to £1.7 billion by 2010-11, including:

- a **continuing programme of modernisation**, including a rationalisation of the overseas diplomatic network, the transformation of corporate support services, and a move towards increased co-location with the Department for International Development overseas;

- a **£183 million capital investment programme over the CSR07 period**, including enhancing security across the UK's embassy network and a new embassy in Kabul;

- the launch in 2008 **of a BBC World Service Farsi television channel** and a 24/7 **Arabic TV channel**, providing a tri-media service (radio, online and TV) in the Middle East, Iran and Afghanistan; and

- contributing towards the Government's **counter-radicalisation agenda** through initiatives to address weakness in governance, education, civil society, human rights and rule of law in priority countries.

Achievements so far
D9.1   The FCO promotes the UK's interests in achieving a safe, just and prosperous world. Within a transformed geopolitical environment the FCO has been at the forefront of the UK's efforts to counter the growing terrorist threat and meet other global challenges. Working with other departments and key stakeholders, the FCO has made important contributions towards tackling the drugs trade, returning failed asylum seekers, and countering child trafficking. The BBC World Service and the British Council, the two public corporations that come under the FCO umbrella, have built on their internationally renowned reputations to further public diplomacy and break down cultural barriers and misunderstanding.

Responding to challenges ahead
D9.2   The rapidly changing global environment requires a flexible FCO, ready to address evolving and unforeseen events as well as serving the UK's international agenda. Changing patterns of globalisation, the evolving terrorist threat, and the blurring of the boundaries between the national and international arenas, mean that the FCO will work with and through others to deliver the Government's international priorities, notably in increasing the Government's engagement with and understanding of Islamic communities around the world and in the UK. With UK nationals increasingly living, working and visiting overseas, the FCO will build on and develop its current world-class consular and visa services. Delivery of these priorities will be driven by the following Departmental Strategic Objectives:

- making the world safer from global terrorism and weapons of mass destruction;

- reducing the harm to the UK from international crime, including drug trafficking, people smuggling and money laundering;

- preventing and resolving conflict through a strong international system;

- building an effective and globally competitive EU in a secure neighbourhood;

- supporting the UK economy and business through an open and expanding global economy, science and innovation and secure energy supplies;

- achieving climate security by promoting a faster transition to a sustainable, low carbon global economy;

- promoting sustainable development and poverty reduction underpinned by human rights, democracy, good governance and protection of the environment;

- managing migration and combating illegal immigration;

- delivering high quality support for British nationals abroad, in normal times and in crises; and

- ensuring the security and good governance of the UK's overseas territories.

D9.3 The Department will lead delivery of the cross governmental Public Service Agreement (PSA) to reduce the impact of conflict through enhanced UK and international efforts.

RESOURCES AND REFORM

D9.4 Over the CSR07 period the FCO has identified value for money reforms that will make annual net cash-releasing savings of £144 million by 2010-11, thereby allowing it to continue to deliver the Government's international priorities within a budget of £1.6 billion in 2007-08 rising to £1.7 billion in 2010-11. The programme will include:

- sharing services with other public bodies at home and overseas, including increased co-location with DFID, realising net cash-releasing savings of at least £22 million per year by 2010-11;

- working more flexibly and effectively in Europe, realising net cash-releasing savings of at least £9 million per year by 2010-11; and

- rationalisation of the overseas estate, enabling the disposal of £140 million of assets.

GLOBAL PROSPERITY AND SECURITY

Service transformation
D9.5 The FCO will develop its support to UK nationals, providing information packages for travellers, rolling out best practice in the approach taken by consular staff across the network, and improving efficiency in relation to passport production.

Capital investment
D9.6 This settlement provides for greater investment in security for diplomatic staff and UK nationals who work in or visit UK government buildings abroad. A new embassy in Kabul will contribute towards UK efforts in Afghanistan and the region.

Public diplomacy
D9.7 The BBC World Service and the British Council plan to build on their work in recent years to engage further with transitional countries and future opinion-makers around the world. The 2007 CSR builds on the funds made available as a result of earlier reprioritisation and the significant increase in resources they have received over the last decade, enabling them to continue to provide trusted and independent news and information, cultural and educational services to a growing and influential audience.

D9.8   As part of that effort, the BBC World Service will in 2008 begin broadcasting a Farsi television service for Iran, supported with the investment of £15 million by 2010-11. The service will offer an alternative source of opinion to upwards of eight million weekly viewers. The BBC World Service is also this year launching a 12-hour Arabic television service that, again, will build on the organisation's world-leading brand and help provide unbiased news and information in the region. The BBC World Service Arabic television will move to a 24-hour service in 2008 with the assistance of additional funds rising to £6 million a year by 2010-11.

D9.9   The British Council has ambitious plans to refocus its work on the key challenges the UK faces. It will redirect existing funding for Europe to high priority areas such as the Middle East and South Asia. In addition, its Reconnect initiative will receive an additional £3 million of funding a year by 2010-11 continue to build understanding with Muslim societies, particularly amongst alienated younger populations.

Counter- **D9.10**   The FCO will contribute towards the Government's counter-radicalisation agenda
radicalisation through funding of £37 million a year by 2010-11 for projects addressing weaknesses in governance, education, civil society, human rights and rule of law in priority countries.

Table D15: Foreign and Commonwealth Office baseline and additions

	£ million			
	Baseline	**Additions**		
	2007-08	**2008-09**	**2009-10**	**2010-11**
Resource DEL	1,551	41	57	66
of which near-cash	1,394	41	57	66
of which administration	396	-10	-19	-28
Capital DEL	148	58	68	57
Total DEL[1]	**1,581**	**99**	**125**	**123**
Of which:				
BBC World Service	193	3	8	4
British Council	246	19	26	25

[1] *Full resource budgeting basis, net of depreciation.*

DIO DEPARTMENT FOR INTERNATIONAL DEVELOPMENT

The 2007 Comprehensive Spending Review (2007 CSR) will deliver **an annual average growth rate of 11 per cent a year in real terms to the Department for International Development's (DFID) budget over the CSR07 period.** DFID's total budget will rise from £5.4 billion to £7.9 billion a year by 2010-11. This increase in funding, together with value for money reforms generating net cash-releasing savings of £492 million per year by 2010-11, will enable:

- **total UK Official Development Assistance (ODA) to reach over £9.1 billion a year by 2010-11,** which is equal to 0.56 per cent of Gross National Income (GNI), in line with the European Union's (EU) collective commitment. This puts the UK on track to spend 0.7 per cent of GNI on ODA by 2013, two years ahead of the EU target;

- **DFID to more than double its bilateral and multilateral aid to Africa between 2004 and 2010 from £1.3 billion to at least £2.6 billion;**

- **long-term commitments to support the achievement of the Millennium Development Goals,** including in education (where DFID has committed to spend £8.5 billion by 2015); and health (where DFID has committed £1 billion between 2007 and 2015 to the Global Fund for AIDS, tuberculosis and malaria); and

- **DFID to increase its contributions to cross-government efforts to tackle global development challenges,** including providing, jointly with the Department for the Environment, Food and Rural Affairs, £800 million through the international element of the Environmental Transformation Fund, and contributing to the reformed conflict stabilisation and prevention arrangements.

Achievements so far

DIO.I The Government is committed to reducing international poverty. Many developing countries have made substantial progress over the last ten years. The economies in 20 countries in Africa have grown at over 5 per cent a year for a decade. Since 1999, an additional 38 million African children have enrolled in primary school. Immunisation rates, access to protection and treatment against malaria, and the numbers of people receiving effective treatment for HIV/AIDS have all increased dramatically. The Government is at the forefront of global efforts to promote quicker progress towards the internationally agreed Millennium Development Goals (MDGs), and the UK has led the way in increasing both the volume and effectiveness of aid. DFID estimates that UK development assistance is helping to permanently reduce the number of people living in poverty by 3 million per year.

Responding to challenges ahead

DIO.2 However, having reached the midway point between the setting of the MDGs in 2000 and their delivery date of 2015, with one in six people still living in extreme poverty, an even more ambitious effort is required to meet the MDGs, as set out in the Prime Minister's Call to Action in July 2007. DFID will retain its focus on improving the effectiveness of bilateral and multilateral aid, using its influence to encourage contributions from other donors while working to reform the multilateral development system. To improve the conditions for sustainable poverty reduction in the poorest countries, DFID will work to facilitate economic growth, and strengthen its capacity beyond traditional aid programmes in areas such as managing climate change and promoting conflict prevention. Delivery of these priorities will be driven by the Departmental Strategic Objectives to:

- promote good governance, economic growth, trade and access to basic services;

- promote climate change mitigation and adaptation measures and ensure environmental sustainability;

- respond effectively to conflict and humanitarian crises and support peace in order to reduce poverty;

- develop a global partnership for development (beyond aid);

- make all bilateral and multilateral donors more effective;

- deliver high quality and effective bilateral development assistance; and

- improve the efficiency and effectiveness of the organisation.

DIO.3 Achievement of these objectives will help DFID lead delivery of the cross-government Public Service Agreement (PSA) to reduce poverty in poorer countries through quicker progress towards the Millennium Development Goals.

RESOURCES AND REFORM

UK aid budget **DIO.4** The 2007 CSR increases DFID's total budget from £5.4 million in 2007-08 to more than £7.9 billion a year by 2010-11, an average annual increase of 11 per cent in real terms over the CSR07 period. This builds on average annual real growth of 6.2, 8.1 and 9.2 per cent over the last three spending review periods.

Official development assistance **DIO.5** This strong growth in DFID's budget underpins the Government's focus on international development. UK Official Development Assistance (ODA) also includes support channelled through other departments, net investments by CDC Group and debt relief provided by the UK Government. The 2007 CSR puts the UK on track to spend 0.56 per cent of Gross National Income (GNI) on ODA in 2010-11, above a straight line to 0.7 per cent – the UN's recommended level – in 2013,[1] two years ahead of the EU's target.

Aid effectiveness **DIO.6** The UK has a development model that has been commended by aid practitioners and fellow donors,[2] and the recent DFID Capability Review[3] identified areas for DFID to further improve the high quality of UK aid. Building on these recommendations, and in the context of the rising resources delivered by the 2007 CSR, DFID will continue to take steps to increase the effectiveness of bilateral and multilateral aid, in line with the commitments in the Paris Declaration on Aid Effectiveness. This will be supported by an ambitious value for money programme, which will generate annual net cash-releasing savings of £492 million per year by 2010-11.

DIO.7 At the core of DFID's value for money programme will be £414 million savings by 2010-11 realised by targeting resources where they deliver greatest benefit. Research has shown that the poverty reduction impact of aid on a particular country is significantly influenced by the amount of aid, the level of poverty, the country's population size, and the quality of policies. During the CSR07 period DFID will ensure that aid is increasingly focused on countries where it can have the greatest impact, so that more people are lifted out of poverty for every pound spent.

---

[1] 2013 refers to calendar year 2013, which is the basis on which ODA is accounted for by the Organisation for Economic Cooperation and Development's Development Assistance Committee.

[2] Organisation for Economic Cooperation and Development's Development Assistance Committee Peer Review (2006): *Review of the Development Cooperation Policies and Programmes of the United Kingdom.*

[3] Available at www.civilservice.gov.uk.

MAXIMISING IMPACT ON DEVELOPMENT

Targeted development assistance

DI0.8   During the CSR07 period DFID will seek to maximise the impact of its bilateral aid, by enhanced targeting development assistance on those countries with the largest concentration of poor people, and on fragile states, especially those vulnerable to conflict. In particular, the Government will therefore **more than double spending to Africa through bilateral and multilateral channels between 2004 and 2010, from £1.3 billion to at least £2.6 billion.**

Growth, governance and the MDGs

DI0.9   DFID will use both bilateral and multilateral aid to support partner countries in increasing the trend rate of economic growth, for example by increasing aid for trade to £409 million a year by 2010-11; strengthen governance, including by supporting public financial management reform programmes in at least 24 countries; and delivering basic services. To provide predictable resources for achieving the MDGs, DFID will make long-term commitments to partner countries to support education, where DFID has committed to spend £8.5 billion over the period to 2015; health, where DFID has committed £1 billion between 2007 and 2015 to the Global Fund for AIDS, tuberculosis and malaria; and water and sanitation, where DFID has committed to more than doubling assistance in Africa from £95 million a year in 2007-08 to £200 million a year by 2010-11. The UK will continue to be a leader in seeking innovative financing mechanisms for development, building on its £1.4 billion commitment to the International Finance Facility for Immunisation, which will save 5 million children's lives by 2015.

Contributions to multilateral organisations

DI0.10   DFID attaches great importance to its role within the multilateral system, and this settlement provides DFID with the resources to increase substantially UK contributions to multilateral development organisations, including, at forthcoming replenishments, the International Development Association (IDA) and the African Development Bank (AfDB). The UK will use its resources and influence to encourage contributions from others, increasing overall aid flows, and to secure an intensified poverty focus for multilateral aid, so that resources delivered through these channels are increasingly effective. It is expected that, as a result, the proportion of the UK's multilateral aid flowing to the poorest countries, and in particular to Africa, will increase. Working with international partners, the UK will also seek to reform the multilateral development system, so that it minimises duplication and transaction costs, reflects the interests of developing countries and allows them to lead their own development, and holds donor and recipient countries to account for their commitments. As a signal of this intention, in September 2007 the Prime Minister launched the International Health Partnership through which the UK will work with partners to coordinate aid for health.

Sustainable economic growth

DI0.11   The lesson from the last 50 years is that inclusive economic growth is the most powerful way of lifting people out of poverty and equipping developing countries to sustain themselves in the future. DFID will continue to support developing countries to create the conditions for economic growth, for example through improved governance, increased participation in world trade and better access to financial services. DFID will increase its finance for investment in infrastructure, through the AfDB, IDA and bilateral programmes.

Research and innovation

DI0.12   The 2007 CSR provides DFID with the resources to double its research budget between 2005-06 and 2010, to over £200 million per year, strengthening the UK's leadership in this field. The Government believes that new technologies and knowledge have the power to increase significantly the impact of international efforts to tackle poverty. These additional resources will help the UK establish a strong evidence-base to maximise the effectiveness of development policies, particularly in the priority areas of sustainable agriculture, life-threatening diseases, good governance and climate change technology. Alongside this, the UK will continue to support innovative financing mechanisms such as the Advanced Market

Commitment which strengthen the incentives for the development of technologies to save lives in developing countries.

Environmental Transformation Fund

DI0.13 The 2007 CSR finances a new Environmental Transformation Fund (worth over £1.1 billion in total), with an international element which provides £800 million to advance poverty reduction through environmental protection. The international element of this fund, managed and funded jointly by DFID and Defra, will support adaptation to climate change, provide access to clean energy and help tackle unsustainable deforestation.

Debt relief

DI0.14 The UK will continue to be a leader on debt relief, which provides long-term, predictable resources for countries to spend on poverty reduction. The 2007 CSR identifies the resources for the UK's contribution to anticipated debt relief between 2008 and 2011. Through the Heavily Indebted Poor Countries (HIPC) initiative and Multilateral Debt Relief Initiative, the debt burden of the world's poorest countries is being reduced over time by some US$100 billion. Estimates suggest that debt relief is having an immediate effect on progress towards the MDGs with, on average, 65 per cent of the resources freed up by HIPC debt relief spent on health and education. In Tanzania, for example, savings from debt relief of over $6.5 billion have helped to increase the number of children in primary schools by over 50 per cent, build almost 2,500 new primary schools, and recruit 28,000 extra teachers, while Uganda has been able to remove user fees for healthcare thanks to debt relief of nearly $5.4 billion since 2000.

Table C16: International Development baseline and additions

	£ million			
	Baseline	**Additions**		
	2007-08	**2008-09**	**2009-10**	**2010-11**
Resource DEL	4,662	259	840	1,724
of which near-cash	4,594	238	813	1,694
of which administration	168	-4	-8	-12
Capital DEL	716	175	650	840
Total DEL¹	**5,354**	**436**	**1,489**	**2,563**

¹ Includes the Conflict Prevention Pool and DFID's share of the international element of the Environmental Transformation Fund.

² Full resource budgeting basis, net of depreciation.

Table D17: Official Development Assistance

	£ million			
	Estimate	**Projections**		
	2007-08	**2008-09**	**2009-10**	**2010-11**
Total UK Official Development Assistance (ODA)	5,291	6,392	7,477	9,140
ODA as a proportion of Gross National Income (per cent)	0.37	0.43	0.48	0.56

¹ ODA projections are underpinned by the increases in DFID's aid budget and include ODA spending by other government departments, CDC net investments, and debt relief provided by the UK Government. The Government is committed to reaching ODA of 0.7 per cent of GNI in 2013 and will keep the delivery of DFID's aid budget and non-DFID ODA under review.

DEPARTMENT FOR BUSINESS, ENTERPRISE AND REGULATORY REFORM

> The Department for Business, Enterprise and Regulatory Reform (BERR) was created by the Prime Minister in June 2007 to lead the Government's work to raise the rate of UK productivity through the creation of the conditions necessary for business success, and to ensure the UK responds effectively to the challenges of globalisation.
>
> The 2007 Comprehensive Spending Review (2007 CSR) **provides BERR with a total budget of £3.3 billion in 2008-09, £3.2 billion in 2009-10 and £3.2 billion in 2010-11.** This will be underpinned by an ambitious value for money reform programme, generating annual net cash-releasing savings of £307 million by 2010-11, supported by modernisation funding of up to £21 million over five years from 2006-07 to 2010-11. Together these enable BERR to deliver key priorities within a **budget fixed in nominal terms on average over the CSR07 period,** including:
>
> - **continued support for business and the promotion of enterprise,** including the allocation of a total of three rounds of Enterprise Capital Funds at £50 million per year;
> - **an ambitious better regulation programme** that reduces unnecessary regulatory burdens and works for everyone in the public, private and third sectors;
> - **additional funding for the Nuclear Decommissioning Authority** of £338 million by 2010-11 to ensure the continued safe management of nuclear waste liabilities; and
> - **funding from BERR of £200 million over the CSR07 period** for the development and deployment of new energy and energy efficiency technologies through the joint BERR/Defra **Environmental Transformation Fund.**

Achievements so far

DII.I   Through sustained increases in funding for skills, innovation and infrastructure and ambitious programmes to reform policies on enterprise and competition, the Government has continued to drive the UK's productivity and business growth over the last decade. The UK's productivity gap with France and Germany has been narrowed, supported by higher rates of business formation and small firm productivity growth.

Responding to global challenges

DII.2   Intensified cross-border economic competition and accelerated innovation and technological diffusion pose challenges to the UK's global economic position. BERR will work with other departments and stakeholders to deliver the conditions necessary for business success in the UK, including taking forward an ambitious programme of work to strengthen the links between innovation and enterprise and reducing the burdens on business from regulation. BERR will also work to ensure fair and effective employment rights that protect employees and reflect the demands of balancing work and life. In response to increased pressure on natural resources and the global climate, BERR will also promote sustainable growth in the UK and elsewhere, in particular by working with the Department for Environment, Food and Rural Affairs (Defra) to address the problem of climate change. Over the CSR07 period, delivery of these priorities will be driven by the Departmental Strategic Objectives (DSOs) to:

- promote the creation and growth of business and a strong enterprise economy across all regions;
- ensure that all departments and agencies deliver better regulation for the private, public and third sectors;
- deliver free and fair markets, with greater competition, for businesses, consumers and employees;

- ensure the reliable supply and efficient use of clean, safe and competitively priced energy;

- manage energy liabilities effectively and responsibly;

- ensure that the Government acts as an effective and intelligent shareholder, and provide a source of excellent corporate finance expertise within departments; and

- provide the professional support, capability and infrastructure to enable BERR's objectives and programmes to be successfully delivered.

DII.3   BERR will also lead delivery of the cross-governmental Public Service Agreements (PSAs) to raise the productivity of the UK economy, deliver the conditions for business success in the UK, improve the economic performance of all English regions and reduce the gap in economic growth rates between regions.

RESOURCES AND REFORM

DII.4   The 2007 CSR provides BERR with a total budget of £3.3 billion in 2008-09, £3.2 billion in 2009-10 and £3.2 billion in 2010-11. This will be supported by a far-reaching programme of value for money reforms at BERR that will generate annual net cash-releasing savings of £307 million by 2010-11. In addition, the Government will provide BERR with up to £21 million modernisation funding over five years between 2006-07 and 2010-11 to support the transitional costs of transforming the department. Together these enable BERR to deliver key priorities within a budget fixed in nominal terms over the CSR07 period, including:

- the rundown of legacy business support schemes, generating annual net cash-releasing savings of £7 million by 2010-11; and

- value for money savings by BERR's Fair Markets Group and delivery partners, realising annual net cash-releasing savings of £42 million by 2010-11.

CREATING THE CONDITIONS FOR ECONOMIC GROWTH

DII.5   As set out in Chapter 4, the UK, in common with all developed nations, is facing an increasingly competitive and globalised economic environment. Over the CSR07 period BERR will continue to address this challenge, in particular through creating an economic environment in which business can innovate, invest and prosper.

Access to finance **DII.6**   In the 2004 Spending Review the Government introduced Enterprise Capital Funds
for SMEs (ECF) to increase the availability of growth capital to small and medium-sized enterprises (SMEs) affected by the 'equity gap', so helping to alleviate what would otherwise remain a significant barrier to enterprise and productivity growth. Continuing this commitment to business growth, BERR will fund a total of three ECF rounds at £50 million per year by 2010-11.

Free and fair **DII.7**   High levels of competition in UK markets drive productivity and ensure lower prices
markets and greater choice for consumers. Value for money reforms over the CSR07 period will enable the Office of Fair Trading's budget to fall by 5 per cent a year in real terms, while also delivering measurable benefits to consumers amounting to five times its spending. Chapter 4 provides further detail on the Government's plans to improve competition within the UK and wider European Union over the CSR07 period.

Protecting employees

DII.8 The Government also believes that all employees should have core employment rights that prevent unscrupulous employers from taking advantage of vulnerable people. BERR is working with the enforcement agencies to better protect employees. It is also monitoring the implementation of the right to request flexible working to suport parents and carers in balancing their commitments at work and at home.

Nuclear Decommissioning Authority

DII.9 Over the CSR07 period, BERR will oversee the Nuclear Decommissioning Authority (NDA) to ensure that the UK's civil nuclear liabilities continue to be managed safely, securely and cost effectively. The introduction of competition and subsequent implementation of new ways of working have the potential to significantly enhance decommissioning work, and the NDA will generate annual net cash-releasing savings totalling £125 million by 2010-11. These savings, together with additional Government funding over the CSR07 period rising to £338 million by 2010-11, will allow the NDA to deliver material risk reduction at the UK's highest hazard facilities, and an appropriate strategy for the management of commercial operations at SMP (Sellafield MOX Plant) and THORP (Thermal Oxide Reprocessing Plant).

Sustainable energy

DII.10 The 2007 CSR settlement for BERR provides £200 million over the CSR07 period for the establishment of an Environmental Transformation Fund (ETF). Led by Defra and BERR, the domestic element of the ETF is a dedicated fund totalling £370 million over the CSR07 period that brings together the Government's existing and new funding commitments within England and the UK to support the demonstration and deployment of new energy and energy efficiency technologies. Chapter 7 provides further detail on the ETF.

UK Trade and Investment

DII.II The 2007 CSR will provide UK Trade and Investment (UKTI) with a programme budget of £89 million by 2010-11. In total, taking account of resources from both FCO and BERR, UKTI's budget will be £256 million by 2010-11. Over the CSR07 period, UKTI will deliver the ambitions of its new five-year strategy, focussing resources on the customers and markets with the greatest potential, and where UKTI's services add most value. UKTI's key objectives will be to deliver measurable improvement in the business performance of its international trade customers, increase the contribution of foreign direct investment, and deliver measurable improvement in the reputation of the UK in leading overseas markets as the international business partner of choice.

Tables and key figures

Table DI8: Business, Enterprise and Regulatory Reform baseline and additions

	£ million			
	Baseline	Additions		
	2007-08	2008-09	2009-10	2010-11
Resource DEL	2,130	-20	-66	-71
of which near-cash	2,033	-32	-75	-71
of which administration	325	-8	-16	-23
Capital DEL	1,136	92	93	96
Total DEL¹	**3,209**	**56**	**9**	**7**

¹ *Full resource budgeting basis, net of depreciation.*

D12 DEPARTMENT FOR ENVIRONMENT, FOOD AND RURAL AFFAIRS

> The 2007 Comprehensive Spending Review (2007 CSR) increases the budget of the Department for Environment, Food and Rural Affairs (Defra) by 1.4 per cent a year in real terms over the period, taking the Department's total budget from £3,508 million in 2007-08 to £3,960 million by 2010-11. This increase in funding will be accompanied by value for money reforms, delivering net cash-releasing savings of £379 million per year by 2010-11. Together these provide for the delivery of:
>
> - **spending for flood and coastal erosion risk management to rise from £600 million in 2007-08 to £800 million in 2010-11**, inclusive of spending through local authorities;
> - **a step-change in investment for sustainable waste management options, with funding through the Private Finance Initiative rising from £280 million in 2007-08 to £700 million in 2010-11, totalling £2 billion over the CSR07 period**; and
> - **£570 million contribution to the £1.2 billion Environmental Transformation Fund over the CSR07 period**, focusing on the development and deployment of low carbon and energy efficient technologies, and to support development and poverty reduction through environmental protection, and help developing countries respond to climate change.

Achievements so far

D12.1   Defra has brought together the interests of environmental protection, farmers and the countryside, and food production under the overall aim of sustainable development. Over the last decade the Government has worked to tackle climate change, helping reduce greenhouse gas emissions, so that in 2005 emissions were 19.1 per cent below 1990 levels (net of emissions trading). The Government has also taken over 100,000 homes out of flood risk since 2004. To protect the natural environment the Government has worked to improve air quality standards so that between 1997 and 2004 nitrous oxides emissions fell by 24 per cent, and household composting and recycling rates have increased from 8 per cent in 1997 to 27 per cent in 2006. In addition, the Government has provided 1.4 million households with measures to improve the energy efficiency and comfort of their home between June 2000 and March 2007.

Responding to challenges ahead

D12.2   The UK faces a range of pressures on natural resources and the global climate. The publication of the Stern Review in October 2006 showed that climate change could have significant global impacts, and that the costs will be manageable only if there is coordinated multilateral action, with flexibility of policy response. In England, the impacts of climate change are expected to include increases in flooding risk and drought. Defra will work to adapt to the increased risk of more severe flooding events and to address other key challenges, in particular the need to manage waste more sustainably and to secure a healthy natural environment. Delivery of these priorities will be driven by the Departmental Strategic Objectives, which are:

- climate change tackled internationally, and through domestic action to reduce greenhouse gas emissions;
- a healthy, resilient, productive and diverse natural environment;
- sustainable patterns of consumption and production;
- an economy and society resilient to environmental risk and adapted to the impacts of climate change;

- a thriving farming and food sector, with an improving net environmental impact;

- sustainable development championed across government, across the UK, and internationally;

- strong rural communities; and

- a respected Department delivering efficient and high quality services and outcomes.

D12.3   Defra will also lead delivery of the cross-governmental Public Service Agreements (PSAs) to lead the global effort to avoid dangerous climate change and secure a healthy natural environment for today and the future.

RESOURCES AND REFORM

D12.4   Over the last decade Defra's budget has risen from £2,523 million in 2002-03 to £3,508 million in 2007-08. The 2007 CSR delivers further increases in Defra's budget by an annual average real growth rate of 1.4 per cent over the period from £3,508 million to £3,960 million. These increases in funding will be accompanied by value for money reforms, delivering net cash-releasing savings of £379 million per year by 2010-11. The programme consists of a number of initiatives including:

- an increased sharing of responsibility for animal health and welfare with the industry, including further utilisation of cost sharing mechanisms. This will generate annual net cash-releasing savings of £121 million by 2010-11;

- building on the success of the 2004 Spending Review efficiency programme, where savings from procurement activities have been significantly above target, Defra will generate annual net cash-releasing procurement savings of up to £64 million by 2010-11;

- Defra will continue to implement the Renew Defra Programme. This programme is designed to further align the Defra's resources with its strategic priorities, and will involve restructuring within the Department; and

- Defra is currently planning to dispose of assets worth £52 million by 2010-11, the receipts from which will be reinvested in capital programmes.

DELIVERING A SUSTAINABLE FUTURE

Climate Change   **D12.5**   The Government will continue to take steps to tackle climate change. The UK has already made progress in reducing carbon emissions from all sectors and is on track to exceed its Kyoto target of reducing greenhouse gas emissions by 12.5 per cent by 2012. The introduction of the Climate Change Bill will, for the first time, enshrine in statute the Government's commitment to reduce CO_2 emissions by 60 per cent by 2050 as well as putting in place a system of five-year carbon budgets to move towards this target.

D12.6   In addition, the 2007 CSR allocates resources to continue the Warm Front programme, which provides heating, energy efficiency measures and benefit entitlement checks to low-income vulnerable households. The Government is also planning to substantially expand the Carbon Emissions Reduction Target (CERT) obligations on energy suppliers. Subject to final decisions, the combination of Warm Front and the focus on low-income customers through the priority group obligation in CERT mean that spending on energy efficiency and other measures in low-income households will rise in the CSR07 period compared to the previous spending period (See Chapter 7).

Flood and Coastal Erosion Risk Management **DI2.7** The Stern review,[1] and the 2004 Foresight Future Flooding report,[2] both highlighted that climate change in the UK is likely to increase the severity and frequency of flooding events. Accordingly, total government expenditure on flood and coastal erosion risk management will rise from £600 million in 2007-08 to £800 million in 2010-11. The Government will also introduce an adaptation toolkit of £10 million per year to assist communities in adapting to change where constructing defences is not the most appropriate means of managing flood and coastal erosion risk.

Environmental Transformation Fund **DI2.8** This settlement provides for the creation of an Environmental Transformation Fund. Funding from Defra over the CSR period will total £170 million towards the £370 million domestic element, jointly managed with the Department for Business, Enterprise and Regulatory Reform. It will focus on the development and deployment of low carbon and energy efficient technologies. The £800 million international element is jointly managed with the Department for International Development, with each department contributing £400 million over the three years of CSR07. This funding will support development and poverty reduction through environmental protection, and help developing countries respond to climate change.

Waste Management **DI2.9** The 2007 Waste Strategy set out the good progress made in England, with household recycling rates up from 7.5 per cent in 1996-97 to 26.7 per cent in 2005-06. The 2007 CSR provides for significant investment in more sustainable waste management options, which will allow us to continue to reduce the amount of waste sent to landfill. Funding through the Private Finance Initiative will rise from £280 million in 2007-08 to £700 million in 2010-11.

Table DI9: Environment, Food and Rural Affairs baseline and additions

| | £ million | | | |
| | Baseline | Additions | | |
	2007-08	2008-09	2009-10	2010-11
Resource DEL	2,897	38	69	76
of which near-cash	2,580	47	47	47
of which administration	365	-9	-18	-26
Capital DEL	782	218	268	418
Total DEL[1]	**3,508**	**236**	**306**	**452**

[1] Full resource budgeting basis, net of depreciation.

1 *The Stern Review on the Economics of Climate Change*, October 2006, www.hm-treasury.gov.uk/independent_reviews
2 *Future flooding*, UK Government Foresight Programme, 2004, www.foresight.gov.uk

D13 DEPARTMENT FOR CULTURE, MEDIA AND SPORT

> The 2007 Comprehensive Spending Review (2007 CSR) provides **6.6 per cent annual average real growth for the Department for Culture, Media and Sport (DCMS)** including:
>
> - an increase in resource budget from £1.6 billion in 2007-08 to £1.8 billion by 2010-11; and
>
> - capital expenditure of over £2 billion over the CSR07 period, including the Department's contribution to venues and supporting infrastructure costs of the 2012 Olympic Games.
>
> This settlement together with an ambitious value for money reform programme generating **annual net cash-releasing savings of £148 million by 2010-11** will enable DCMS to deliver key priorities in the CSR07 period, including:
>
> - **maintaining funding in real terms for the arts, museums and galleries,** within this maintaining free access to national museums and contributing to the Cultural Olympiad;
>
> - delivering **an improved offer of five hours school sports a week for all children aged 6 to 19** with the Department for Children, Schools and Families; and
>
> - effective programme management of the **2012 Olympic Games,** including a sustainable sporting legacy.

Achievements so far

D13.1 Over the last decade DCMS has worked to ensure that sports, media and culture have continued to thrive, and has successfully maintained the UK's reputation for creativity and cultural excellence. Over the last ten years, the Government has increased investment for sponsored museums in real terms by around 30 per cent, which has enabled free access to national museums and galleries and a 60 per cent increase in visits. DCMS has worked jointly with DCSF to revitalise sport in schools, as a result of which 80 per cent of pupils in school sports partnerships now participate in two hours of sport and PE a week, up from an estimated 25 per cent in 2002. DCMS has also provided the conditions within which major improvements in cultural infrastructure have been made possible, including Tate Modern, Sage, Baltic and the South Bank.

Responding to challenges ahead

D13.2 The successful delivery of the 2012 Games with a lasting, sustainable legacy for generations to come across the UK will be one of the key challenges for DCMS over the CSR07 period and beyond. In the run-up to 2012, the Department will work to ensure more people lead an active lifestyle and continue to support sport at school, community and elite levels. More widely, it will continue working to develop the contribution of culture and sport to the wider outcomes for children and young people. Delivery of these priorities will be driven by the Departmental Strategic Objectives to:

- encourage more widespread enjoyment of culture, media and sport;

- support talent and excellence in culture, media and sport;

- realise the economic benefits of the Department's sectors; and

- deliver a successful and inspirational Olympic and Paralympic Games that provides for a sustainable legacy.

DI3.3 DCMS will also lead delivery of the cross-governmental Public Service Agreement (PSA) to deliver a successful Olympic Games and Paralympic Games with a sustainable legacy and get more children and young people taking part in high-quality PE and sport. Annex D14 provides further detail on the 2012 Games.

RESOURCES AND REFORM

DI3.4 The 2007 CSR provides 6.6 per cent annual average real growth for DCMS. This includes an increase in resource budget from £1.6 billion in 2007-08 to £1.8 billion by 2010-11, as well as capital expenditure of over £2 billion over the CSR07 period, including the Department's contribution to venues and supporting infrastructure costs of the 2012 Olympic Games.

DI3.5 DCMS will take forward the recommendations for reform outlined in its 2007 Capability Review and will also implement an ambitious value for money reform programme, generating annual net cash-releasing savings of £148 million by 2010-11. The Department's value for money programme consists of a number of initiatives including:

- procurement savings, including the principal recommendations of the 2005 National Audit Office report, *Procurement in the Culture, Media and Sport sector*,[1] realising annual net cash-releasing savings of at least £15 million by 2010-11;

- completing the rationalisation of its estate; and

- a range of efficiency measures across its Non-Departmental Public Bodies which will maintain and increase the numbers taking part in culture and sport.

INVESTING IN PARTICIPATION, CREATIVITY AND INNOVATION

Support for cultural sectors **DI3.6** The cultural sectors have continued to flourish through increased Government investment over the last ten years. The 2007 CSR maintains funding for the arts and museums and galleries at least in line with inflation. This will ensure continued free access to national museums, maintaining visitor numbers, and enable an even wider range of people to benefit from these high-quality cultural experiences. The Government will also provide funding for new investments in both national and community level cultural infrastructure.

Improving the school sports offer **DI3.7** The Government is already making excellent progress in increasing sporting activity in schools. The DCMS CSR07 settlement will enable the Department to continue to deliver the manifesto commitment to provide two hours of sport in school, and will raise this to offer five hours of school sports a week for all children aged 6 to 19 to be delivered in conjunction with the Department for Children, Schools and Families.

Delivering the 2012 Games and sustainable legacy **DI3.8** As set out in Annex D14, delivery of a successful and inspirational Olympic and Paralympic Games in 2012 is a key priority for the Department and across Government over the 2007 CSR period. As such, DCMS will allocate £1,455 million in capital funding over the CSR07 period towards the Olympic venues and supporting infrastructure. This settlement also allows a contribution to a Cultural Olympiad and allocates support to the development of Olympic legacy programmes to inspire young people to take up volunteering and participate in sports and culture. This will make a significant contribution to providing positive activities for young people in line with the ten-year youth strategy.

---

[1] *Available at* www.nao.org.uk

Successful delivery of digital switchover **DI3.9** DCMS and the Department for Business, Enterprise and Regulatory Reform have joint responsibility within government for ensuring that digital switchover is implemented on-schedule, in partnership with other departments, Digital UK, Ofcom and broadcasters, as well as consumer groups and other bodies. The delivery of switchover will bring digital terrestrial TV to nearly all households for the first time, increasing choice of affordable digital TV options. It will also be more efficient for broadcasters and make the spectrum available for reuse. The Government's policy is that the spectrum released by switchover should be auctioned on a technology-neutral basis.

Table D20: Culture, Media and Sport baseline and additions

	£ million			
	Baseline	Additions		
	2007-08	2008-09	2009-10	2010-11
Resource DEL	1,562	63	124	198
of which near-cash	1,374	37	75	114
of which administration	50	-1	-2	-4
Capital DEL	227	819	179	341
Total DEL[1]	**1,688**	**870**	**292**	**523**

[1] *Full resource budgeting basis, net of depreciation.*

D14 THE 2012 OLYMPIC GAMES AND PARALYMPIC GAMES

> The Government is working with the Mayor of London, the London 2012 Organising Committee (LOCOG) and the British Olympic Association to host the Olympic Games and Paralympic Games in 2012 and leave a sustainable legacy for London and the United Kingdom.
>
> In March 2007, the Government announced a £9.325 billion budget for the 2012 Olympic Games and Paralympics Games, funded through central government (£5.975 billion), the National Lottery (£2.175 billion) and the Mayor of London (£1.175 billion). **As part of this funding package, the 2007 Comprehensive Spending Review (2007 CSR) makes full budgetary provision for central government's contribution of £3.623 billion over the next three years which, alongside contributions from the National Lottery and London, put preparations for 2012 on a sound financial footing far earlier than any previous host city.**
>
> Following the successful outcome of the bid to host the 2012 Games, work has progressed on the delivery of the Olympic Park and other venues, planning for the event itself and for the delivery of a lasting legacy. Progress on delivery will be captured in the cross-governmental Public Service Agreement to deliver a successful Olympic Games and Paralympic Games with a sustainable legacy and get more children and young people taking part in high quality PE and sport.

DELIVERING THE 2012 GAMES

D14.1 The Olympic Delivery Authority (ODA) has a challenging task to deliver the Olympic Park and venues within budget and to the absolute deadline. LOCOG is preparing for the celebration of the Games, with London becoming the focus of attention after the Beijing Games in the summer of 2008. The ODA and LOCOG have met all their key milestones to this point, including:

- securing ownership of the Olympic Park land;
- securing planning permission for the development of the Olympic Park for the Games and for its transformation to legacy uses after the Games; and
- delivering significant sponsorship deals for LOCOG.

D14.2 All the partners are determined that effective planning and budgetary discipline should be at the heart of the development of the 2012 Games.

Responding to challenges ahead   **D14.3** Over the 2007 CSR period the ODA and LOCOG – supported by the Government, the Mayor of London, the British Olympic Association, the local boroughs and many other partners – will need to deliver the foundations for successful 2012 Games. This includes:

- completion of the Olympic Park site platform in preparation for the start of venue construction in summer 2008, including decontaminating land, restoring waterways and constructing bridges and utilities networks;
- substantial progress on the five permanent venues, press and media centres, Olympic village and the temporary venues;
- delivery of the required additional transport infrastructure and finalisation of the operational plans; and
- agreement of a sustainable legacy framework for the Olympic Park and permanent venues by 2009.

D14.4 In addition, the Government will develop and implement ambitious plans to deliver a wider social, economic, health and environmental legacy for London and the UK yielding benefits for tourism, skills and employment, and British businesses. Progress on this will be captured in the cross-governmental Public Service Agreement to deliver a successful Olympic and Paralympic Games with a sustainable legacy and get more children and young people taking part in high quality PE and sport.

D14.5 Following the successful bid, the Government initiated a thorough review of the costs of construction and related elements. Building on the previous agreement, a revised £9.325 billion funding package was announced in March 2007, with additional contributions of £2.175 billion proposed from the National Lottery, £1.175 billion from the Mayor of London and £5.975 billion from central government. The funding package covers the construction, athlete preparation and security aspects of the Games.

D14.6 As part of this funding package, the 2007 CSR confirms the central government funding of £3.623 billion that falls due in the next three years. Further provision will be confirmed in subsequent Spending Reviews to fulfil the Government's full £5.975 billion funding responsibility. This investment in the construction of Olympic facilities and supporting infrastructure will be funded through a single central government Olympics budget, provided by the Department for Culture, Media and Sport, Communities and Local Government and the Department for Transport from within their budgets over the CSR07 period.

Table D21: Central government funding for the 2012 Olympics and Paralympic Games in the CSR07 period [1]

	£ million		
	2008-09	**2009-10**	**2010-11**
Culture, Media and Sport	848	222	385
Communities and Local Government	571	552	425
Transport	140	240	240
Total central government Olympic capital DEL [2]	**1,559**	**1,014**	**1,050**

[1] The £9.325 billion budget for the Olympic and Paralympic Games is funded through central government, the National Lottery and London.

[2] Central government funding is made up from ring-fenced contributions from three departments brought together in a single Olympics capital DEL. The figures presented here are also included in the settlements of these contributing departments.

DI5 DEPARTMENT FOR WORK AND PENSIONS

Over the 2007 Comprehensive Spending Review (2007 CSR) period, the Department for Work and Pensions (DWP) will take forward an **ambitious value for money reform programme generating annual net cash-releasing savings of £1.2 billion by 2010–11**. This will allow DWP to continue to deliver its priorities within a budget that falls by over 5 per cent per year on average in real terms over the CSR07 period. Together with £550 million in modernisation funding to support the transitional costs of transforming the Department, this will enable DWP to deliver:

- **increased support to help lone parents back to work**, and a new Child Maintenance and Enforcement Commission to ensure parents meet their financial responsibilities towards their children;

- **increased parental access to employment opportunities** by delivering employment advice through local children's services and incentivising Jobcentre Plus to identify the childcare needs of clients;

- **the launch of a flexible New Deal**, the national rollout of Pathways to Work for Incapacity Benefit claimants, and the introduction of the Employment and Support Allowance to replace Incapacity Benefit for new claimants; and

- **pension reforms**, including state pension reforms from 2010, and steps to introduce private pension reforms and a new low cost scheme of personal accounts from 2012.

Achievements so far **DI5.I** DWP plays a key role in delivering employment opportunity for all and tackling child and pensioner poverty. It helps individuals to achieve their potential through employment, and to provide for themselves, their children and their future retirement. There are now 2.6 million more people in work than in 1997 and the Jobseeker's Allowance (JSA) claimant count has almost halved to around 850,000. The lone parent employment rate has increased by over 12 percentage points, to 57.2 per cent, while the number of people on incapacity benefits has stabilised and begun to fall for the first time in a generation. There are 400,000 fewer children in workless households, helping lift 600,000 children out of relative poverty. The number of pensioners in absolute poverty has fallen by 2.4 million.

Responding to challenges ahead **DI5.2** Considerable challenges remain, however, to be tackled in the CSR07 period and beyond. Moving towards the Government's long-term aspiration of an employment rate equivalent to 80 per cent of the working age population will require increased employment among those facing the greatest labour market barriers. DWP must continue to improve its services in order to help meet the commitments to halve child poverty by 2010 and tackle pensioner poverty. Improving the employment prospects of people without skills or qualifications is a continuing challenge. Delivery of these priorities will be driven by the Departmental Strategic Objectives to:

- reduce the number of children living in poverty;

- maximise employment opportunity for all and reduce the numbers on out-of-work benefits;

- improve health and safety outcomes;

- promote independence and well-being in later life, continue to tackle pensioner poverty and implement pension reform;

- promote equality of opportunity for all;

- pay its customers the right benefit at the right time; and

- make DWP an exemplar of effective service delivery to individuals and employers.

DI5.3 DWP will also lead delivery of the cross-governmental Public Service Agreements (PSAs) to maximise employment opportunity for all and to tackle poverty and promote greater independence and well-being in later life.

RESOURCES AND REFORM

DI5.4 Over the 2007 CSR period DWP will deliver an ambitious value for money reform programme generating annual net cash-releasing savings of £1,225 million by 2010-11. Delivering these savings will build on progress already made in the 2004 Spending Review efficiency programme. Together with £550 million in modernisation funding, these savings will allow DWP to continue to deliver its priorities within a budget that falls by over 5 per cent a year on average in real terms. DWP's planned annual value for money savings by 2010-11 include:

- simultaneously improving customer service and reducing staff and associated costs by £455 million through continuous improvement, using lean techniques that are well established in the private sector and parts of the public sector;

- renegotiating contracts with all major suppliers to reduce the unit cost for major services and putting in place arrangements to manage down demand for procured goods and services to generate savings of £500 million; and

- working with Local Authorities to improve processes to reduce the costs to DWP of delivering housing benefits by £85 million.

OPPORTUNITY AND INDEPENDENCE FOR ALL

Children and parents

DI5.5 DWP plays a critical role in reducing child poverty by helping parents to enter and remain in employment. It will work with the Department for Children, Schools and Families to deliver employment and training advice through Sure Start Children's Centres by strengthening links between Jobcentre Plus, Childcare Partnership Managers and Local Authorities. DWP is also extending the support it gives to couple parents and is reforming the Jobcentre Plus target structure to give staff a clear focus and incentive to help parents into work.

Increasing employment opportunity

DI5.6 Chapter 5 set out the Government's approach to welfare reform and the changes proposed in the Green Paper *In work, better off* to reform support for the unemployed and lone parents. It also set out how support to help people with a health condition or disability into work will be increased through the national roll-out of Pathways to Work and the introduction of a new Employment and Support Allowance. DWP, together with the Department for Innovation, Universities and Skills (DIUS) will also ensure that employment support is focused not just on job entry, but also on retention and progression. Building on the recommendations of the Leitch Review of Skills, DWP will work with DIUS to develop a new unified employment, skills and career development service for adults.

Child Maintenance reform

DI5.7 The Child Support Agency (CSA) was established to ensure that non-resident parents met their responsibilities to provide financial support for their children. In a context of unacceptable CSA performance, the Child Maintenance and Other Payments Bill, published in June 2007, proposed introducing the Child Maintenance and Enforcement Commission to replace the CSA from 2008. In addition the Government will introduce a significantly higher maintenance disregard for parents on benefits with caring responsibilities, to ensure more money reaches the poorest children. As set out in Chapter 5, the disregard will rise from £10 to £20 per week from October 2008, and then to £40 per week in April 2010, funded in 2010-11 by savings from child maintenance reform and from elsewhere in DWP.

Pensions and older people

D15.8 DWP will promote independence and well-being in later life by continuing to tackle pensioner poverty and supporting people in making appropriate choices about work, saving, and retirement. This will be achieved by promoting take-up of benefits among older people, increasing the employment rate of men and women aged 50-69, and reforming pensions, as set out in Chapter 5. State pension reforms from 2010 will deliver fairer outcomes for women and carers and a simpler and more generous state pension. Steps to reform private pensions include introducing auto-enrolment, mandatory employer contributions and, from 2012, a new simple, low cost scheme of personal accounts, delivered at arms length from Government by the new Personal Accounts Delivery Authority.

Service transformation

D15.9 DWP has an important role to play in taking forward the recommendations of the Varney Review under the Service Transformation Agreement. This includes:

- taking responsibility for Directgov from April 2008 and its development as the Government's primary web portal for citizen focused e-services;

- leading development work on the 'Tell Us Once' change of circumstance project; and

- improving the performance of its face-to-face and telephone contact centres in line with public sector best practice benchmarks.

Table D22: Work and Pensions baseline and additions

	£ million			
	Baseline	**Additions**		
	2007-08	**2008-09**	**2009-10**	**2010-11**
Resource DEL	7,781	−199	−382	−699
of which near-cash	7,615	−195	−373	−687
of which administration	5,803	−141	−279	−414
Capital DEL	67	−2	−3	−4
Total DEL¹	**7,695**	**−197**	**−378**	**−693**

¹ *Full resource budgeting basis, net of depreciation.*

D16 THE CHANCELLOR'S DEPARTMENTS

> Over the 2007 Comprehensive Spending Review (2007 CSR) period the Chancellor's Departments will take forward an ambitious value for money programme, generating annual net cash-releasing savings of over £700 million by 2010-11. Together with £330 million in modernisation funding, this will allow the departments to deliver their key priorities within budgets that fall by 4.9 per cent per year in real terms.[1] These are:
>
> - **a customer focused HM Revenue and Customs (HMRC),** with modernised and efficient business processes that help to ensure the payment of the right amounts of tax and tax credits; and
>
> - **a smaller and more efficient HM Treasury,** with a continuing role to maintain sound public finances and ensure high and sustainable levels of economic growth, well-being and prosperity for all.

Achievements so far

D16.1 The Chancellor's Departments play an important role in delivering the Government's objectives of sound public finances, rising prosperity and a better quality of life. HMRC collects the revenue that underpins strong public finances, while HM Treasury (comprising the Treasury, the Office of Government Commerce and the Debt Management Office) develops and implements the Government's financial and economic policy.

D16.2 Over the last decade, HMRC has collected the revenue needed to fund improvements in essential public services. It has implemented major reforms to the tax system and introduced Child and Working Tax Credits. It has also modernised the service provided to its customers, reducing the administrative burden of the tax system. HM Treasury has helped foster conditions that have enabled an unprecedented period of stability, low inflation and sustained growth. Through modernising the taxation system, it has promoted fairness and opportunity for all, and a sustainable approach to economic development.

Responding to challenges ahead

D16.3 Changing patterns of economic activity and innovative technologies and financial instruments all pose challenges for the way HMRC administers the tax and credit payments system and potentially create new pressures on revenue collection. Expectations of the service HMRC should provide and the behaviour of taxpayers and claimants are also changing. To respond to these challenges HMRC is undertaking a programme of service transformation that will put customers at the heart of what it does, with new ways of interacting with its customers, modernised processes for managing information, and a more targeted, risk-based approach to its assurance work. **HMRC's Departmental Strategic Objectives for the CSR07 period are to:**

- improve the extent to which individuals and businesses pay the tax due and receive the credits and payments to which they are entitled;

- improve customers' experience of HMRC and improve the UK business environment; and

- reduce the risk of the illicit import and export of material which might harm the UK's physical and social well-being.

---

[1] 'The Chancellor's Departments' budgets now fall by 4.9 per cent per year in real terms rather than 5 per cent as announced in Budget 2006 because HMRC has taken on responsibility and funding for businesslink.gov.uk.

D16.4 Over the CSR07 period, HM Treasury will control public spending, working with other government departments to ensure value for money. The Treasury will maintain macroeconomic stability, mitigate fiscal risks while promoting economic growth, and help equip the UK to meet the global challenges of the next decade. HM Treasury's Departmental Strategic Objectives are:

- maintaining sound public finances; and

- ensuring high and sustainable levels of economic growth, well-being and prosperity for all.

D16.5 HM Treasury will also lead delivery of the cross-governmental Public Service Agreement (PSA), to which HMRC also contributes, to halve the number of children in poverty by 2010-11, on the way to eradicating child poverty by 2020.

RESOURCES AND REFORMS

D16.6 Over the CSR07 period, the Chancellor's Departments will take forward an ambitious value for money reform programme generating annual net cash-releasing savings of over £700 million by 2010-11, supported by £330 million in modernisation funding to support the transitional costs of transforming the departments. The value for money programme consists of a number of initiatives, including:

- extending the use of lean processing techniques in HMRC to make more efficient use of resources and a major consolidation and transformation of its estate releasing £280 million annual net cash-releasing savings by 2010-11;

- investing in a modern, high capacity IT infrastructure in HMRC to support higher take-up of online services, more efficient processing and communication, and better risk-based compliance checks, generating annual net cash-releasing savings of £180 million by 2010-11; and

- rationalising HM Treasury's estate and full implementation of Group Shared Services, generating annual net cash-releasing savings of £10 million by 2010-11.

Businesslink. D16.7 HMRC has also from 2007-08 taken over responsibility for businesslink.gov.uk. HMRC
gov.uk will be leading cross-government efforts to oversee the transformation of this website to enable it to become the prime online channel for government information and transactions for all businesses in the UK by 2011.

Table D23: Chancellor's Departments baseline and additions

	£ million			
	Baseline	**Additions**		
	2007-08	**2008-09**	**2009-10**	**2010-11**
Resource DEL	4,862	−106	−224	−338
of which near-cash	4,544	−99	−208	−315
of which administration	4,702	−107	−221	−332
Capital DEL	276	−7	−14	−20
Total DEL[1]	**4,941**	**−109**	**−229**	**−344**
of which:				
HM Revenue and Customs	4,547	−99	−209	−315
HM Treasury	226	−6	−12	−17
National Savings and Investment	168	−4	−8	−12
Government Actuary's Department	0.4	0	0	0

[1] *Full resource budgeting basis, net of depreciation.*

DI7 CABINET OFFICE

Over the 2007 Comprehensive Spending Review (CSR) period the Cabinet Office will be taking forward an ambitious value for money reform programme, generating annual net cash-releasing savings of £35 million by 2010-11. This will allow the Cabinet Office to continue to deliver its priorities within a budget that falls by 2.9 per cent per year in real terms over the CSR07 period. Together with £12 million modernisation funding to support the transitional costs of transforming the Department, these steps will enable the Cabinet Office to deliver:

- investment rising to nearly £150 million over the CSR07 period in third sector programmes through the Office of the Third Sector, while supporting implementation of the review on the future role of the third sector in social and economic regeneration;

- a cross-government programme of work on the new Public Service Agreement (PSA) to increase the proportion of socially excluded adults in settled accommodation and employment, education or training;

- a cross-cutting package of initiatives to make all public sector services more accessible, more personalised to the individual needs of citizens and businesses, and more efficient to deliver, as set out in the new Service Transformation Agreement; and

- further enhancement in the capabilities of the Security and Intelligence Agencies whose budget will rise from £1.5 billion in 2007-08 to £2.1 billion in 2010-11, sustaining the historic rates of growth since 9/11.

Achievements so far

DI7.I The role of the Cabinet Office is to make Government work better through:

- supporting the Prime Minister;

- supporting the Cabinet; and

- strengthening the capability of the Civil Service.

Responding to challenges ahead

DI7.2 The Cabinet Office will work with departments across government to deliver the Prime Minister's cross-cutting priorities. These include improving outcomes for the most excluded in society, building on the partnerships between the public and third sector, transforming and personalising public services and coordinating intelligence, security policy and funding across Government to respond effectively to the growing threat from international terrorism.

RESOURCES AND REFORM

DI7.3 Over the CSR07 period the Cabinet Office will be taking forward an ambitious value for money reform programme, generating annual net cash-releasing savings of £35 million by 2010-11. Supported by £12 million modernisation funding, this will allow the Cabinet Office to continue to deliver its priorities within a budget that falls by 2.9 per cent per year in real terms over the CSR07 period. The programme consists of a number of initiatives including:

- procurement savings including on travel services, IT and telecoms, realising £14.7 million annual net cash-releasing savings by 2010-11; and

- savings in administration costs realising £20.1 million net cash-releasing savings by 2010-11.

MAKING GOVERNMENT WORK BETTER

DI7.4   Over the CSR07 period the Cabinet Office will pursue the Government's ambitions across a range of programmes. These are reflected in the following Departmental Strategic Objectives the Cabinet Office has set itself for the period:

- build an effective UK intelligence community in support of UK national interests, and the capabilities to deal with disruptive challenge to the UK;

- support the Prime Minister and the Cabinet in domestic, European, overseas and defence policy making;

- drive delivery of the Prime Minister's cross-cutting priorities to improve outcomes for the most excluded adults in society and enable a thriving third sector;

- transform public services so that they are better for citizens, staff and taxpayers;

- build the capacity and capability of the Civil Service to deliver the Government's objectives; and

- ensure the highest standards of propriety and integrity in public life.

Social exclusion   **DI7.5**   Through the Social Exclusion Task Force, the Cabinet Office will continue to lead the Public Service Agreement (PSA) to increase the proportion of socially excluded adults in settled accommodation and employment, education or training across government. In addition to leading on the socially excluded adults PSA, the Cabinet Office will coordinate Government's drive to reduce social exclusion and enhance life chances, meeting the needs of the most excluded individuals and families.

Service transformation   **DI7.6**   The Cabinet Office is leading work across the public sector to transform public services. The Service Transformation Agreement published today covers a broad and diverse agenda, involving almost every part of central and local government as well as the wider public sector. The role of the Cabinet Office is to lead and coordinate: supporting cross-government structures, spreading best practice, and resolving obstacles to progress.

Security and intelligence   **DI7.7**   The settlement for the Security and Intelligence Agencies reflects the priority attached to their contribution to national security, particularly in countering international terrorism. The Cabinet Office will continue to ensure that the Government's foreign, defence and security policy decisions are usefully informed by accurate and objectively assessed intelligence, and to maintain and improve intelligence assessment standards across government.

Third sector   **DI7.8**   The 2007 CSR has included a review into the role of the third sector in society. The review was informed by the largest ever consultation with the sector, which involved over 1,000 organisations. 93 consultation events were held throughout England. This led to the publication in July 2007 of the final report on *The Future Role of the Third Sector in Social and Economic Regeneration.*

DI7.9   Taking forward the recommendations of the review, the Office of the Third Sector will continue to ensure a thriving third sector through its £515 million delivery programme. This includes overseeing the delivery of two action plans to promote the role of the sector in public service delivery and promoting social enterprise; and continuing to invest in the £215 million Futurebuilders programme, a £117 million programme for youth volunteering, £80 million in micro grants for small community organisations, and a £50 million local endowment match fund.

Civil Service reform **D17.10** Building on existing reform and improvement of leadership, skills and diversity in the Civil Service, the Cabinet Office will develop and implement further policies to ensure the Civil Service has the right staff in the right place at the right time to deliver Government priorities and excellent public services.

Policy coordination **D17.11** The Cabinet Office Secretariats will continue to carry out a proactive and effective role in the coordination of policy and advice in domestic and international affairs.

Propriety and integrity **D17.12** The Cabinet Office will continue to promote standards that ensure good governance, including adherence to the Ministerial and Civil Service Codes.

Table D24: Cabinet Office baseline and additions

	£ million			
	Baseline	**Additions**		
	2007-08	**2008-09**	**2009-10**	**2010-11**
Resource DEL	1,775	335	483	667
of which near-cash	*1,514*	*273*	*394*	*567*
of which administration	*310*	*-9*	*-16*	*-23*
Capital DEL	287	73	102	65
Total DEL[1]	**1,868**	**346**	**499**	**636**
of which:				
Cabinet Office	368	-1	-2	-3
Single Intelligence Account	1,508	347	501	639

[1] *Full resource budgeting basis, net of depreciation.*

CHARITY COMMISSION

D17.13 The Charity Commission is the regulator of the Charities sector. Over the CSR07 period it will deliver its ongoing regulatory commitments; ensure that it can implement counter terrorist financing initiatives; modernise its structure and workforce; and meet obligations under the Charities Act.

Table D25: Charity Commission baseline and additions

	£ million			
	Baseline	**Additions**		
	2007-08	**2008-09**	**2009-10**	**2010-11**
Charity Commission total DEL[1]	31.5	−0.7	−1.5	−2.2

[1] *Full resource budgeting basis, net of depreciation.*

DI8 DEVOLVED ADMINISTRATIONS AND NORTHERN IRELAND

> The 2007 Comprehensive Spending Review (2007 CSR) provides funding for devolved public services and economic development in Scotland, Wales and Northern Ireland. Resources in 2010-2011 compared to 2007-08 will be:
>
> * £3.7 billion higher in Scotland;
> * £2.2 billion higher in Wales; and
> * £1.2 billion higher in Northern Ireland.
>
> Decisions on the use of this provision will be made by the Scotland, Wales and Northern Ireland administrations.
>
> The Northern Ireland Office (NIO) aims to support stable devolved government in Northern Ireland, and, in line with the St Andrews Agreement, is making preparations to enable the devolution of policing and justice functions to occur next year. In the meantime, responsibilty for these matters rests with the NIO. Over the CSR07 period, the NIO will be taking forward an ambitious value or money reform programme, **generating annual net cash-releasing savings of £108 million by 2010-11.** This will enable the Department to deliver more effective policing and crime prevention to further reduce crime, and a modern and effective prison service, **within a total budget of £1.2 billion maintained in nominal terms over the CSR07 period.**

DEVOLVED ADMINSTRATIONS

Achievements so far
DI8.1 The Government works in partnership with the Devolved Administrations to improve economic growth and public service delivery across all the countries and regions of the UK. The Devolved Administrations are responsible for publishing their own spending plans, targets and policies. Devolution to Scotland, Wales and Northern Ireland is leading to new policies and innovation in public service delivery and economic development.

DI8.2 UK funding for the Devolved Administrations' budgets has been determined in the 2007 CSR alongside those for departments of the UK Government and in accordance with the established devolution funding arrangements. The Devolved Administrations have freedom to make their own spending decisions, within the overall totals, on functions under their control in response to local priorities. Changes to Devolved Administrations' budgets have been linked to changes in spending plans of UK Government departments by the Barnett formula. This formula gives Scotland, Wales and Northern Ireland a population-based share of planned changes in comparable spending in UK departments, as set out in the updated *Statement of Funding Policy* published by HM Treasury alongside the 2007 CSR.[1]

RESOURCES AND REFORM

DI8.3 The Devolved Administrations are carrying out their own value for money reviews. Value for money savings identified in these reviews will be retained by the Devolved Administrations and either recycled into improved front-line delivery or used to fund new priorities.

St Andrews Agreement
DI8.4 The settlement for the Northern Ireland Executive is consistent with terms of the St Andrews Agreement and with the unique financial and economic package announced by the Government on 8 May to underpin the return of devolution. In Northern Ireland the UK Government, working in cooperation with the Northern Ireland parties and the Irish

---

[1] Available at www.hm-treasury.gov.uk

Government, has announced a comprehensive peace dividend package based on a number of elements including:

- increasing investment through a unique long-term £51.5 billion public spending programme;

- increasing productivity including through the Varney review of taxation and a US investors conference in the autumn; and

- increasing employment including through new employment opportunities for the unemployed in the retail sector.

D18.5 A key feature of the package is the development of the all island economy, including an additional £400 million provided by the Irish Government to promote better road links between Northern Ireland and the Republic of Ireland.

NORTHERN IRELAND OFFICE

Achievements so far **D18.6** The aim of the NIO is to secure a lasting peace in Northern Ireland, based on the Good Friday and St Andrews Agreements, in which the rights and identities of all the people in Northern Ireland are fully respected and safeguarded; and where a safe, just and tolerant society can thrive and prosper. Sustained funding over the last decade has helped to deliver a more effective criminal justice system matched with reforms and progress with the peace process that have secured the implementation of the Good Friday and St Andrews Agreements. The Department has also achieved reform of the Police Service following the Patten Review in 1999, with a more peaceful environment and falling crime rates.

Responding to challenges ahead **D18.7** A key challenge in the short term is to complete the process of devolution to the Northern Ireland Executive by devolving policing and justice functions as envisaged in the St Andrews Agreement. Looking further ahead it will continue to be important to secure the benefits of normalisation and make further progress in tackling more serious crime including organised crime. The NIO's strategy for meeting these challenges is based on a continuing programme of reform of the police, prisons and criminal justice system. **To achieve these aims the Department has five Departmental Strategic Objectives,** which will contribute to the delivery of two PSAs in Northern Ireland (Justice for All and Safer Communities)[2]:

- **to support a stable devolved government in Northern Ireland, with responsibility for policing and justice, and a society reconciled with its past;**

- **to manage offenders securely, safely and humanely;**

- **to deliver an independent, fair and effective criminal justice system which supports and protects the community;**

- **to work in partnership with Peace Service of Northern Ireland (PSNI) and other policing partners to deliver effective and accountable policing services that can secure the confidence of the whole community; and**

- **to deliver value for money savings and to live within annual available funding.**

---

[2] NIO mirrors two PSAs, but these are adapted to circumstances in Northern Ireland: Deliver a more effective, transparent and responsive criminal justice system for victims and the public; and Make communities safer.

RESOURCES AND REFORM

DI8.8   The resources released by the value for money programme and the ongoing efficiency embedded into departmental planning, will allow the NIO to continue to deliver service improvements. The CSR07 settlement for Northern Ireland will be accompanied by value for money reforms, delivering net cash-releasing savings of £108 million a year by 2010-11 that include the following initiatives:

- the Northern Ireland Police Service has identified opportunities for adopting more efficient working practices, including the recruitment of Community Support Officers. Taken together this package of reforms is expected to deliver annual net cash-releasing savings of £74 million by 2010-11; and

- the Northern Ireland Prison Service has also reviewed its working practices, which includes exploring opportunities for recruiting support grades to release prison officers to front-line activities. Together, these changes are planned to deliver annual net cash-releasing savings of £11 million a year by 2010-11.

Police Service   **DI8.9**   For the Police Service of Northern Ireland, these reforms involve a major change in composition and investment in infrastructure, implementing of the reforms recommended in the Patten Report, including a new police college. Priority will be attached to, among other things, combating serious and organised crime.

Reforming the   **DI8.10**   Key criminal justice initiatives have included the establishment of a single, **Criminal Justice**   independent Public Prosecution Service, the creation of the Criminal Justice Inspectorate and **System**   Law Commission, and work to modernise the sentencing framework and forensic science provision. Reform of the Northern Ireland Prison Service will include implementation of a strategic review to ensure a modern, cost effective prison service, including planning for a new prison. The Department will support the effective and efficient operation of public inquiries already announced. An independent Consultative Group has been set up to review the wider question of dealing with Northern Ireland's past.

Table D26: Northern Ireland Office baseline and additions

	£ million			
	Baseline	Additions		
	2007-08	2008-09	2009-10	2010-11
Resource DEL	1,152	72	40	40
of which near-cash	929	0	0	0
of which administration	79	-2	-4	-6
Capital DEL	72	0	0	0
Total DEL'	**1,175**	**61**	**27**	**25**

' *Full resource budgeting basis, net of depreciation.*

Table D27: Scottish Executive baseline and additions

	£ million			
	Baseline	Additions		
	2007-08	2008-09	2009-10	2010-11
Resource DEL	23,443	1,012	1,971	3,058
of which near-cash	22,530	999	1,902	2,922
Capital DEL	2,974	174	368	667
Total DEL'	**26,059**	**1,185**	**2,340**	**3,725**

' *Full resource budgeting basis, net of depreciation.*

Table D28: Welsh Assembly Government

	£ million			
	Baseline	Additions		
	2007-08	2008-09	2009-10	2010-11
Resource DEL	12,392	596	1,177	1,823
of which near-cash	11,892	586	1,136	1,748
Capital DEL	1,480	88	198	362
Total DEL'	**13,588**	**684**	**1,376**	**2,184**

' *Full resource budgeting basis, net of depreciation.*

Table D29: Northern Ireland Executive baseline and additions

	£ million			
	Baseline	Additions		
	2007-08	2008-09	2009-10	2010-11
Resource DEL	7,561	311	615	956
of which near-cash	7,268	308	593	912
Capital DEL	937	57	121	219
Total DEL'	**8,421**	**368**	**736**	**1,175**

' *Full resource budgeting basis, net of depreciation.*

To inform the 2007 Comprehensive Spending Review (2007 CSR), the Government set out plans to refocus powers, responsibilities and accountabilities of the Regional Development Agencies (RDAs) in the *Review of sub-national economic development and regeneration* published in July 2007. In line with the key conclusions of this review, the 2007 CSR settlement for the RDAs:

- enhances the strategic role of the RDAs, and announces reforms to improve their capacity, efficiency and effectiveness. This enables an RDA settlement in line with the most ambitious departmental value for money programmes. **The RDAs' single programme budget will be £2.140 billion by 2010-11 from a base of £2.274 billion in 2007-08;**[1]

- **significantly simplifies the RDAs' objectives,** replacing the current tasking framework with a new outcomes framework defined by a single growth objective; and

- **enhances RDAs' responsibility for coordinating the funding and procurement of business support,** and brings together business support and skills into a single brokerage service managed by the RDAs from April 2009.

Underpinning this, the RDAs have also committed to an **ambitious value for money programme that will realise annual net cash-releasing savings of £349 million by 2010-11.**

Achievements so far **D19.1** To drive economic growth in the English regions, the Government established eight Regional Development Agencies (RDAs) in 1999 and the London Development Agency (LDA) in 2000. These have been given unprecedented autonomy to respond to the particular challenges and opportunities of their regions. The Government has also devolved significant additional resources and responsibilities to the RDAs, including for the delivery of business support, the delivery of research and development grants and support for business-university collaboration.

Responding to challenges ahead **D19.2** In Budget 2006, the Government announced a review of how to improve further the effectiveness and efficiency of sub-national governance, incentives and powers to improve regional economic performance and deliver regeneration and neighbourhood renewal. The *Review of sub-national economic development and regeneration* (SNR) was published in July 2007 and set out reforms to build on progress made since 1997 to devolve decision making to regional and local levels. The reforms are aimed at empowering Local Authorities, encouraging sub-regional collaboration, strengthening accountability, coordination and decision-making at the regional level and improving central government's interface with regions and localities. The SNR announced an enhanced strategic role for the RDAs, supported by increased freedoms and flexbilities and a simplified sponsorship framework.

RESOURCES AND REFORM

D19.3 Increasing the freedoms and flexibilities of the RDAs and developing further their strategic role, enables the RDAs to deliver significant efficiency and value for money savings. Each of the nine RDAs has developed a robust and sustainable value for money plan, which will enable them to deliver savings in line with the most ambitious departmental value for money programmes over the CSR07 period. Consistent with these value for money plans, the 2007 CSR announces that RDAs will make annual net cash-releasing savings of £349 million

---

[1] The RDA single programme budget is made up from ring-fenced contributions from six departments.

per year by 2010-11. Single Pot funding for the RDAs means that they will continue to have significant flexibility in managing their own resources to meet their regions' priorities.

DI9.4 The SNR recommended strengthening the local and regional tiers to ensure these are responsive to local economic conditions. The key recommendations for the regions include:

- introducing a single regional strategy in every region that merges the current Regional Economic Strategy and Regional Spatial Strategy;

- rationalising regional governance structures;

- better alignment of funding with strategy; and

- implementing a radically simplified sponsorship framework for performance managing the RDAs.

A single regional strategy

DI9.5 **The Government is committed to introducing a single integrated regional strategy, which will bring together the economic, social and environmental objectives for each region.** The regional strategy will set out how economic development interventions will deliver the regional growth objective and how spatial planning within each region will support delivery of the agreed increase in housing numbers. These objectives are currently set out separately in the Regional Economic Strategy and the Regional Spatial Strategy. The new single regional strategy will build the support of Local Authorities, businesses and other partners from within the region, as well as from central departments and agencies.

Reforming regional governance

DI9.6 The Government believes that regional institutions also need to be significantly reformed to ensure effective accountability and to drive more strategic decision-making at the regional level. **The Government will bring forward proposals to give the Regional Development Agencies the executive responsibility for developing the single regional strategy, including designating them as the Regional Planning Body, working closely with Local Authorities and other partners.** Regional Assemblies in their current form and function will not continue. Instead, Local Authorities in the regions will be responsible for agreeing the regional strategy with the RDAs. Local Authorities will also be responsible for effective scrutiny of RDA performance. The Government will consult further later this year on how to implement these reforms.

Regional Funding Allocations

DI9.7 Better alignment of strategy and funding is essential if the regional strategies are to be effective in prioritising resources across regions. **The Government will seek to expand the Regional Funding Allocation process further to cover a wider range of funding relevant to economic growth, potentially including the European Regional Development Fund, other aspects of transport funding, and the regeneration activities of the Homes and Communities Agency.** The Government will also explore the scope for extending Regional Funding Allocations to cover other budgets of importance to regional economic development, including with regard to skills, consistent with the Government's response to the Leitch Review.

Improving RDA value for money and effectiveness

DI9.8 **The 2007 CSR announces a package of radically simplified performance management arrangements for the RDAs.** This is aimed at building the capacity of the RDAs and improving further their value for money and effectiveness in supporting regional economic growth. The new performance management arrangements include the following key elements:

- improved clarity on the role, responsibilities and relationship between the RDAs and the Department for Business, Enterprise and Regulatory Reform;

- a significantly simplified outcomes framework, defined by a single overarching objective focused on regional economic performance;

- independent and professional assessments of each RDA, which reduce the overall audit burden on the RDAs, building on the 2006-07 Independent Performance Assessments, but enabling greater differentiation in assessment of RDA performance and value for money;

- a comprehensive, systematic and sustained evaluation of the added economic value of RDA programmes, delivered through a robust Impact Evaluation Framework; and

- reform of RDA appraisal and delegation limit procedures to enhance the value for money of RDA projects and reward good appraisal practice, particularly through increased RDA delegation limits.

INCREASING FLEXIBILITY IN THE REGIONS

D19.9   The Government will also work with the RDAs to move to a programme-based approach to management of the RDA single programme budget, rather than a project-based approach. This will require the RDAs to be clear about overall strategy and give far greater autonomy to Local Authorities and sub-regions in the allocation and management of spending. This will give greater certainty for other partners as well as improving efficiency.

Business support   **D19.10**   The RDAs will continue to have responsibility for managing Business Link and ensuring it is equipped to meet the needs of business in simplifying access to business support and providing a one-stop-shop for high quality diagnosis and brokerage services. The 2007 CSR settlement also enables the RDAs to take on responsibility for managing the response to industrial crises or natural disasters which have the potential to create substantial economic shocks and impact severely on business.

Skills   **D19.11**   The Government will work with the RDAs and the Learning and Skills Council to ensure there is no duplication and overlap in skills provision. The Government considers that a single brokerage service is the simplest way for business to access government support on skills, and will fully integrate skills brokerage with Business Link to ensure a single brokerage service managed by the RDAs by April 2009. The 2007 CSR settlement increases the Department for Innovation, Universities and Skills' contribution to the RDA Single Pot by £24 million per year to enable the RDAs to take on this responsibility, consistent with the Government's reform agenda to make the skills system more responsive to the needs of employers and to raise their demand for training. Further details are set out in Chapter 4.

Trade and investment   **D19.12**   To ensure the activities of the RDAs and UK Trade and Investment (UKTI) on overseas activity to promote inward investment are better aligned, the Government will work with the RDAs to ensure that the management and branding of overseas activity is brought together on a national basis and to improve alignment between UKTI's network of trade advisers in the regions and Business Link.

Sainsbury Review   **D19.13**   The Sainsbury Review of science and innovation sets out recommendations for improving the RDAs' role in enhancing regional innovation performance. In response to the conclusions of the Sainsbury Review, the RDAs, Technology Strategy Board (TSB) and Science and Industry Councils have committed to collaborating to support innovation priorities that deliver the national technology strategy and Regional Strategies. Utilising the Single Pot and European Funds, each RDA has committed to ear-marking investment to match fund TSB programmes on a case by case basis or as part of a regional prospectus. This will lead to a total investment from the RDA network of £180 million over the three years starting in 2008, subject to appropriate projects being identified that benefit the regions.

Northern Way D19.14 In the North of England, the three northern RDAs have come together with local, regional and private sector partners to develop the Northern Way Growth Strategy. The Northern Way is focused on those economic policy areas where a pan-regional approach is likely to be more efficient and effective, rather than adding an additional tier to decision-making. The 2007 CSR enables the three northern RDAs to provide funding of £45 million over three years to support Northern Way collaborative programmes and transformational initiatives.

Regional statistics D19.15 In response to Christopher Allsopp's review of the regional information and statistical framework needed to support the Government's regional economic performance PSA target, the Office of National Statistics (ONS) and the RDAs worked in partnership to establish a full regional statistical presence in March 2007. The 2007 CSR enables the RDAs to continue to provide funding to sustain the ONS's regional presence. The ONS has also committed to deliver real regional Gross Value Added per head estimates to enable more accurate comparison of regional growth rates by 2009.

European Structural Funds D19.16 To align European Structural Funds more effectively with domestic regional development, the Government is transferring responsibility for management of the 2007-2013 European Regional Development Fund programme from the Government Offices to the RDAs. The Government is also introducing arrangements to ensure that use of the European Social Fund is aligned to priorities set out in Regional Strategies.

Table D30: Regional Development Agencies[1] baseline and additions

| | £ million | | | |
| | Baseline | Additions | | |
	2007-08	2008-09	2009-10	2010-11
Resource DEL	1,167	−27	−29	−55
of which near-cash	1,110	−27	−29	−55
of which administration	239	−6	−11	−17
Capital DEL	1,106	−26	−53	−79
Total DEL[2]	**2,274**	**−54**	**−83**	**−134**

[1] The RDA single programme budget is made up from ring-fenced contributions from six departments. The figures presented here are also included in the settlements of the six contributing departments.

[2] Full resource budgeting basis, net of depreciation.

DEPARTMENTAL GROUPINGS

A number of tables in this publication present analyses by department. It is not possible to show figures for all individual government departments separately and so departments are grouped together in these analyses, broadly on the basis of Ministerial responsibilities. These groupings are set out below.

Title	Departments included
Children, Schools and Families	Department for Children, Schools and Families Office for Her Majesty's Chief Inspector of Schools in England (Ofsted)
Health	Department of Health Food Standards Agency
Transport	Department for Transport Office of the Rail Regulator
Innovation, Universities and Skills	Department for Innovation, Universities and Skills
CLG Communities	Department for Communities and Local Government (except Local Government)
CLG Local Government	Local Government – mainly block and transitional grants to English local authorities, the Greater London Authority, and Regional Development Agencies
Home Office	Home Office Assets Recovery Agency
Justice	Ministry of Justice The National Archives: Public Record Office and Historical Manuscripts Commission Electoral Commission Northern Ireland Court Service Land Registry Scotland Office Wales Office

Law Officers' Departments	The Crown Prosecution Service
	Serious Fraud Office
	HM Procurator General and Treasury Solicitor
	Revenue and Customs Prosecution Office
Defence	Ministry of Defence
Foreign and Commonwealth Office	Foreign and Commonwealth Office
International Development	Department for International Development
Business, Enterprise and Regulatory Reform	Department for Business, Enterprise and Regulatory Reform
	UK Trade and Investment
	Office of Fair Trading
	Office of Gas and Electricity Markets
	Office of Telecommunications
	Postal Services Commission
	Export Credits Guarantee Department
Environment Food and Rural Affairs	Department for Environment, Food and Rural Affairs
	Forestry Commission
	Office of Water Services
Culture, Media and Sport	Department for Culture, Media and Sport
Work and Pensions	Department for Work and Pensions
Scotland	Scottish Executive and its departments
Wales	Welsh Assembly Government
Northern Ireland Executive	Northern Ireland Executive and its departments
Northern Ireland Office	Northern Ireland Office

Chancellor's Departments

HM Treasury

National Savings and Investments

Government Actuary's Department

HM Revenue and Customs

National Investment and Loans Office

Royal Mint

Office of Government Commerce

Crown Estate Office

Cabinet Office

Cabinet Office

Central Office of Information

National School of Government

Single Intelligence Account

Charity Commission

Independent Bodies

House of Commons

House of Lords

National Audit Office

Statistics Board

Office of the Parliamentary Commissioner for Administration and Health Service Commissioners for England

LIST OF ABBREVIATIONS

AEF	Aggregate External Finance
AIDS	Acquired Immunodeficiency Syndrome
AME	Annually Managed Expenditure
AMLD	Amusement machine licence duty
AMS	Asset Management Strategy
APD	Air passenger duty
BCC	British Chamber of Commerce
BERR	Department for Business, Enterprise and Regulatory Reform
BHC	Before housing costs
BIA	Border and Immigration Agency
BNFL	British Nuclear Fuels Plc
BP	British Petroleum
BRC	Better Regulation Commission
BRE	Better Regulation Executive
BRTF	Better Regulation Task Force
BT	British Telecom
CAP	Common Agricultural Policy
CBI	Confederation of British Industry
CC	Competition Commission
CCAs	Climate change agreements
CCL	Climate change levy
CCPR	Climate Change Programme Review
CCS	Carbon capture and storage
CEO	Chief Executive Officer
CERT	Carbon Emissions Reduction Target
CGNCR	Central government net cash requirement
CIPFA	Chartered Institute of Public Finance and Accountancy
CJS	Criminal Justice System
CLG	Department for Communities and Local Government
CMEC	Child Maintenance and Enforcement Commission
CMPO	Centre for Market and Public Organisation
CGNCR	Central Government net cash requirement
CO2	Carbon dioxide
COMPS	Contracted out money purchase schemes
COSRS	Contracted out salary related schemes
CoVE	Centres of Vocational Excellence
CDEL	Capital Departmental Expenditure Limit
CPA	Comprehensive Performance Assessment
CPD	Continuous Professional Development
CPI	Consumer Prices Index
CPS	Crown Prosecution Service
CSA	Child Support Agency
CSR	Comprehensive Spending Review
CT	Corporation Tax
CTC	Child Tax Credit
DCSF	Department for Children, Schools and Families
DCMS	Department for Culture, Media and Sport

DCLG	Department for Communities and Local Government
DEFRA	Department for Environment, Food and Rural Affairs
DEL	Departmental Expenditure Limit
DfES	Department for Education and Skills
DFID	Department for International Development
DfT	Department for Transport
DH	Department of Health
DIUS	Department for Innovation, Universities and Skills
DIS	Defence Industrial Strategy
DMO	Debt Management Office
DPTC	Disabled Person's Tax Credit
DTI	Department of Trade and Industry
DVLA	Driver and Vehicle Licensing Agency
DWP	Department for Work and Pensions
EC	European Communities
ECA	Enhanced Capital Allowance
ECF	Enterprise Capital Fund
EEC	Energy Efficiency Commitment
EFSR	Economic and Fiscal Strategy Report
EMBI	Emerging Market Bond Index
EPC	Economic Policy Committee
ESA95	European System of Accounts 1995
ESA	Employment Support Allowance
ETF	Environmental Transformation Fund
ETS	Emission Trading Scheme
EU	European Union
EU ETS	EU Emissions Trading Scheme
FDI	Foreign direct investment
FE	Further Education
FRS	Financial Reporting Standard
FRS	Fire and Rescue Service
FSA	Financial Services Authority
FSBR	Financial Statement and Budget Report
FSCS	Financial Services Compensation Scheme
FSMA	Financial Services and Markets Act
FTI	Fast Track Initiative
FTSE	Financial Times Stock Exchange
G7	A group of seven major industrial nations (comprising: Canada, France, Germany, Italy, Japan, UK and US).
G8	The G8 is an informal group of eight countries: Canada, France, Germany, Italy, Japan, Russia, the UK and the US.
GAAP	Generally Accepted Accounting Practices
GAD	Government Actuary's Department
GCSE	General Certificate of Secondary Education
GDP	Gross Domestic Product
GGNB	General government net borrowing
GLA	Greater London Authority
GNI	Gross National Income
GOF	Global Opportunities Fund
GP	General Practitioner
GVA	Gross Value Added

HGV	Heavy Goods Vehicles
HIPC	Heavily Indebted Poor Countries
HIV	Human immunodeficiency virus
HMCS	Her Majesty's Courts Service
HMRC	Her Majesty's Revenue and Customs
HMT	Her Majesty's Treasury
IAS	International Accounting Standards
ICT	Information and Communications Technology
IDA	International Development Association
IFF	International Finance Facility
IFFIm	International Finance Facility for Immunisation
IFS	Institute for Fiscal Studies
IHT	Inheritance tax
ILO	International Labour Organisation
IMA	Investment Management Association
IMF	International Monetary Fund
IOC	International Olympic Committee
IPCC	Intergovernmental Panel on Climate Change
IS	Income support
ISA	Individual Savings Account
ISB	Invest to Save Budget
IWC	In Work Credit
JSA	Jobseeker's Allowance
LA	Local Area Agreements
LABGI	Local Authority Business Growth Incentive scheme
LASFE	Local authority self-financed expenditure
LATS	Landfill Allowance Trading Scheme
LBRO	Local Business Regulation Office
LDA	London Development Agency
LEGI	Local Enterprise Growth Initiative
LEL	Lower earnings limit
LESA	Landlords' Energy Saving Allowance
LFS	Labour Force Survey
LHA	Local Housing Allowance
LLP	Limited Liability Partnership
LOCOG	London Organising Committee for the Olympic Games
LPG	Liquefied petroleum gas
LPL	Lower profits limit
LTCS	Landfill Tax Credit Scheme
LSC	Learning and Skills Council
MDGs	Millennium Development Goals
MDRs	Marginal deduction rates
MDRI	Multilateral Debt Relief Initiative
MIG	Minimum Income Guarantee
MoD	Ministry of Defence
MOJ	Ministry of Justice
MORI	Market and Opinion Research International
MPC	Monetary Policy Committee
MRC	Medical Research Council

MtC	Million tonnes of carbon
MTIC	Missing Trader Intra-Community
NAO	National Audit Office
NAR	National Asset Register
NDA	Nuclear Decommissioning Authority
NDPB	Non Departmental Public Body
NDDP	New Deal for disabled people
NDLP	New Deal for lone parents
NDLP+	New Deal Plus for lone parents
NDP	New Deal for partners
NDYP	New Deal for young people
NEP	National Employment Panel
NEET	Not in education, employment or training
NHS	National Health Service
NI	National Insurance
NICs	National Insurance Contributions
NIESR	National Institute of Economic and Social Research
NIO	Northern Ireland Office
NMW	National Minimum Wage
NTNIC	Net taxes and national insurance contributions
NVQ	National Vocational Qualification
NWDA	North West Development Agency
ODA	Overseas Development Assistance
ODPM	Office of the Deputy Prime Minister
OECD	Organisation for Economic Cooperation and Development
OFCOM	Office of Communications
OFGEM	Office of Gas and Electricity Markets
OFT	Office of Fair Trading
OGC	Office of Government Commerce
OMO	Open Market Option
ONE	One North East
ONS	Office for National Statistics
OPEC	Organisation of Petroleum Exporting Countries
PAC	Public Accounts Committee
PAYE	Pay as you earn
PBR	Pre - Budget Report
PCSO	Police Community Support Officers
PCT	Primary Care Trust
PEP	Personal Equity Plan
PFI	Private Finance Initiative
PGS	Planning Gain Supplement
PPF	Pension Protection Fund
PPS3	Planning Policy Statement for Housing
PSA	Public Service Agreement
PSCR	Public sector current receipts
PSNB	Public sector net borrowing
PSPC	Public Sector Pay Committee
PSNI	Public sector net investment
PSPC	Public Sector Pay Committee

QC	Queen's Counsel
QR	Quality-Related
R&D	Research and Development
RAE	Research Assessment Exercise
RDA	Regional Development Agency
REITs	Real Estate Investment Trusts
RES	Regional Economic Strategy
RPC	Reduced pollution certificate
RPI	Retail Prices Index
RPIX	Retail Prices Index excluding mortgage interest payments
RTFO	Renewable Transport Fuels Obligation
S2P	State Second Pension
SBS	Small Business Service
SBRI	Small Business Research Initiative
SCS	Senior Civil Service
SDLT	Stamp Duty Land Tax
SDRT	Stamp Duty Reserve Tax
SDR	Strategic Defence Review
SEE	Small Earnings Exception
SEEDA	South East England Development Agency
SEEN	Schools Enterprise Education Network
SERPS	State Earnings Related Pension Scheme
SFLG	Small Firms Loan Guarantee
SHA	Strategic Health Authority
SI	Statutory Instrument
SIVA	Simplified import VAT accounting
SME	Small and medium-sized enterprise
SNR	Review of sub-national economic development and regeneration
SSRB	Senior Salaries Review Body
ST	Secondary threshold
STEM	Science Technology Engineering and Mathematics
TB	Tuberculosis
TFL	Transport for London
TME	Total Managed Expenditure
TMO	Tenant Management Organisations
TPAS	The Pensions Advisory Service
TSB	Technology Strategy Board
TSC	Treasury Select Committee
UKTI	UK Trade and Investment
UN	United Nations
UNCTAD	United Nations Conference on Trade and Development
VAT	Value Added Tax
VCT	Venture Capital Trust
VED	Vehicle excise duty
VI	Voluntary initiative
W&TA	Wear and Tear Allowance
WASD	Working Age Statistical Database
WCC	Women and Work Commission

WEO	World Economic Outlook
WFI	Work Focused Interview
WFTC	Working Families' Tax Credit
WTC	Working Tax Credit
WTO	World Trade Organisation

LIST OF TABLES

LIST OF CHARTS

Cover photography
JUPITERIMAGES/ Polka Dot/ Alamy
www.third-avenue.co.uk
Corbis RF/ Alamy
David Cleaves/ Alamy
Roy Peters/ reportdigital.co.uk

Printed in the UK by The Stationery Office Limited
on behalf of the Controller of Her Majesty's Stationery Office
ID5672465 10/07 379627 19585

Printed on Paper containing 75% recycled fibre content minimum.